WORLDS OF KNOWING

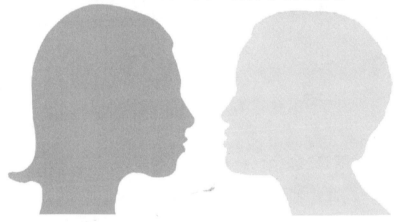

WORLDS OF KNOWING

Global Feminist Epistemologies

Jane Duran

ROUTLEDGE
New York and London

Published in 2001 by
Routledge
29 West 35th Street
New York, NY 10001

Published in Great Britain by
Routledge
11 New Fetter Lane
London EC4P 4EE

Routledge is an imprint of the Taylor & Francis Group.

Typography: Jack Donner

Library of Congress Cataloging-in-Publication Data

Duran, Jane.
    Worlds of knowing : global feminist epistemologies / Jane Duran.
      p. cm.
    Includes bibliographical references and index.
    ISBN 0-415-92739-0 — ISBN 0-415-92740-4 (pbk.)
      1. Feminist theory—Cross-cultural studies. 2. Women—Social conditions—
Cross-cultural studies. 3. Feminism—International cooperation. I. Title.

HQ1190 .D89   2001
305.42'01—dc21
                                        00-062806

Printed in the United States of America on acid-free paper
10 9 8 7 6 5 4 3 2 1

*For the Duráns, the Lópezes,
the Muñozes, and the Sánchezes*

Contents

Part 3: New World Focal Points

Preface

Contemporary work in feminist theory has been bedeviled by problems surrounding issues of essentialism, the cross-cultural, and globalism. It has seemed to many feminist theorists that it is not possible to write on core areas of inquiry with respect to gender without falling prey to such difficulties as normativizing the privileged status of white women, or ignoring cultural differences in favor of an easy—and meretricious—essentializing of things female.

Feminist epistemology might seem to be even more susceptible to such criticisms, because matters epistemic have themselves so long been associated with the more rigidly normative areas of philosophical theorizing. Contemporary American feminist epistemologists have had their hands full trying to adjudicate such disputes as those between theorists who would employ some elements of analytic theory and those who would not, or those who might favor a Marxist-oriented standpoint approach over some type of theoretical work deemed to be postmodern. An observer might well be tempted to say that it is simply too difficult a task to attempt to think in global terms with respect to feminist epistemology, or to ask questions about what multicultural approaches to feminist theories of knowledge might mean.

But surely there are theoretical versions of the notion that nothing ventured, nothing gained. If we are unwilling to ask questions about what might count as feminist epistemology in other cultures, then we also should be reluctant to inquire as to what counts for knowledge and practices of inquiry in other cultures, and yet these kinds of questions have been asked by philosophers for many years. The gender divide is a deep one, and although it may well be going too far to say that it affects all cultures, it does affect most human cultures in ways that are at least somewhat recognizable from culture to culture. With caveats in place, we can begin to work on important intercultural issues that affect the conditions of living for women globally.

Recognizing from the outset how dangerous it is to posit an Other, we must attempt to theorize in this area by investigating the relevant cultural sources and moving forward with at least some work done on knowledge-related areas in the culture itself. We cannot proceed without such a minimal framework; by the same token, we must continually bear in mind the problematized nature of the project.

The length of this work and the structure of its individual chapters reflect the parallel structure of the inquiry: those chapters actually based on a given culture are in turn in general divided into eight parts, each of which focuses on a specific issue. Although section titles vary, analogous frames of reference are employed in each chapter to help the reader along. Each such chapter opens with a general introduction to some elements of the culture that might be deemed to be philosophical (with a special emphasis, of course, on matters epistemological). This section is typically the opening section and will not employ a subheading—its contents should be obvious. Then the sections of each chapter proceed by examining different foci: the androcentric, elements of gynocentricism, historical overviews of women and the feminine, the status of contemporary women within the culture, current feminist movements, and the reconceptualization of cultural elements that so often results in what we might, for lack of a better term, describe as feminist epistemics. Then the chapter closes with a general overview.

The first and last chapters of this work provide arguments with respect to the very issues mentioned here at the outset: How can Westerners approach metaphysical, epistemological, or other such philosophical issues in another culture without importing a dangerous cultural chauvinism? Is such a thing even possible? Or is it not more likely the case that the investigator has to live with a number of paradoxes? Each major interior section of the work is structured along geographical lines. For reasons based both in scholarship and general inquiry, only two major areas are alluded to in this work, South Asia and the North American continent/Central America. It might be deemed important to have personal knowledge of an area, in addition to scholarly knowledge, particularly where feminist work is concerned. Little can substitute for lived experience within a culture, or portions of it, and no amount of reading can compensate for lack of actual acquaintance with a region. Thus this work makes little, if any reference, to substantial portions of the globe, but rather proceeds with a thorough investigation of two large geographical areas.

Much work in contemporary feminist epistemology, as done in English-speaking countries such as the United States and Great Britain, has been driven by a desire to answer the sorts of conceptual questions indicated above with respect to, for example, the importance of a certain sort of analytic theory of knowledge, or a type of position on contemporary Continental thought. But it would be a mistake to let such questions drive an inquiry into global feminist epistemologies, for these questions are, obviously, the products of their intellectual forebears, whose training reflects what might rightly be considered to be the hegemonic stance of the European and European-derived cultures.

Nevertheless, there would appear to be still another path that ought to be avoided. One could err on the side of believing that no conceptual scheme or category (such as "epistemic" or "aesthetic") could possibly be relevant to another culture, because to claim such a linkage is to beg the question or force the issue. This, of course, will have the happy outcome of preventing any work from being done, thus freeing anyone from having to write articles or books on the issue in question (or even having to think about it). As is so frequently the case, it would appear that a middle ground is the best one. It is possible, and probably even desirable, to think about issues having to do with knowledge in a global context. It may very well mean that only the roughest analogies can be employed, and in some cases these analogies may seem somewhat forced. But to fail to make the inquiry is to leave outside the arena of serious discussion any issues having to do with cultures that are significantly different from our own. This is perhaps the worst sort of colonialism, and one that can be obviated by careful planning and thought.

The structure of this work is such that, of necessity, much of the material is not overtly philosophical. Thus some readers will want to concentrate more fully on only the beginning and last three sections of each chapter dealing with a specific region—that is to say the opening section and the sections that allude, roughly, to contemporary feminism in an area, reincorporations of knowledge traditions, and summarizing views. A still greater difficulty is that, again of necessity, there is comparatively little to tie the two large sections together. Here, perhaps, is where the most profound level of analysis is needed. Although each major section—the one on South Asia and that on the New World—is woven together as a whole, little or no attempt has been made to try to force a meshing of material taken from these two disparate parts of the globe. Perhaps this is a task that the interested reader can pursue for herself or himself.

A final difficulty revolves around an area that should, at least in theory, be a familiar one to those interested in philosophy, but to which perhaps too little attention is paid today. In cultures that are neither industrially developed nor Eurocentric, much of any given worldview with deep roots within the culture will pass into thought more readily recognizable as "religious" than strictly "philosophical." But to employ such categories as firm demarcators is, of course, to make the mistake of thinking that there is a hard and fast line between such areas of inquiry, or that there have never been disputes in the history of Western thought over such uses of terminology. Thus the chapters on India, for example, contain a great deal of material that—if it is at all familiar to Westerners—is probably better known from courses in a department of religious studies than from courses in philosophy. But it is such tangles, it seems clear, that have prevented work in these areas from being done, and to this sort of concern the reply given above with respect to the concerns about employing analogies with European thought is directed again.

As indicated earlier, this work is both an outgrowth of extensive travel and, of course, substantial teaching and publication in philosophy. Contact with non-European cultures is often so confusing for the traveler that he or she scarcely knows how to begin intellectual investigation. But few investigations are more exciting. The inquiry into global feminist philosophy is one that, we can hope, will continue for a long time to come.

Acknowledgments

Worlds of Knowing, like other work that I have undertaken at the University of California, Santa Barbara, has benefited enormously from the interdisciplinary atmosphere on campus. My previous work was the outgrowth of more than one campuswide study group, many of which are supported by the Interdisciplinary Humanities Center, and this work is an offshoot of the Sociology Network Theory Discussion Group; the Science, Technology, Culture and Society Research Focus Group; and the Political Theory Reading Group. In each case discussion with group members provided valuable stimulation that helped to sharpen my general lines of argument. Especially helpful were numerous discussions on philosophy of science and science studies undertaken with Chuck Bazerman and others. Those discussions not only assisted in the writing of my book immediately previous to this one, but also helped me to focus on what might count as an epistemology cross-culturally.

Travel was, of course, the stimulus for many of the individual chapters, and those on Asian societies are especially indebted to visits to the areas in question. There is a note of poignancy here, however, since the travel took place largely in the 1970s, and might be deemed by many to be irrelevant to today's concerns. What I saw in India, Nepal, and West Bengal (while Bangladesh, in its guise as East Pakistan, was in the process of fighting for its independence) during that time period, when I was a recent graduate of the University of California at Berkeley and a participant in many political demonstrations, remained with me, and in my graduate studies in philosophy at Rutgers I often looked forward to the time when I might be able to integrate what I had learned in Asia into my scholarly work. Earlier, in the late 1960s, I had traveled to Mexico, and I owe a profound debt of gratitude to my husband's family and others I met there, particularly in the *ranchos* of Aguascalientes, for providing me with firsthand acquaintance with the Mexican culture. Later years of activism with Chicana/os helped to sharpen my awareness of Mexican-American cultures, and valuable experience in the black studies department at UCSB, where I have taught philosophically oriented courses in black American and African Diaspora thought for a number of years, made possible the work in the next to last chapter of this book.

Over the years I have done a great deal of work in feminist epistemology, philosophy of science, and related areas with the help of a number of individuals, not all of whom were directly involved with this work, but whose assistance (and indirect influence) I much appreciate. Chuck Bazerman, Jenny Cook-Gumperz, Martha Swearingen Davis, Ruth Doell, Sara Ebenreck, John Gumperz, Greg Kelly, Armen Marsoobian, Michael Osborne, Oyeronke Oyewumi, Cedric Robinson, Earl Stewart, Rosemarie Tong, Cecile Tougas, and my current editor, Gayatri Patnaik, have been of greater help than they can imagine. Such organizations as the Society for the Study of Women Philosophers, the American Society for Aesthetics, and the Society for Philosophy and Psychology have provided presentations relevant to this work, and my encounters with students of my "Race and Ethnicity in Education" seminar at the Graduate School of Education, UCSB, have also been fruitful. Sylvia Curtis of the UCSB Davidson Library has pushed me in the right direction many a time. I also owe a great deal to the staff and editors of *Hypatia*.

My interest in philosophy began when I was an undergraduate, continued as a graduate student and through some courses at Princeton, and culminated in years of teaching and research at the University of California at Santa Barbara. The visual atmosphere of our campus is stunning, and the morning view of the ocean and the Channel Islands inspirational. One cannot help but look out toward the Pacific and wonder about the lives of others. To the women of the world whose lives engage the world daily, and especially those of the Asian cultures that made such a profound impact on me decades ago, I owe the greatest gratitude of all.

Part I

Beginnings

Chapter 1

Knowledges/Foci

Much of the new work in global feminism has proceeded as if the main questions to be raised had to do with essentialism, the notion of "woman" within given cultures, and so forth. Indeed, although these questions may well be deemed to be central to feminist theory, especially insofar as it has been articulated by white/First World feminists, other sorts of questions have, for the most part, remained unasked.

If the concept of global feminist theory as an area of endeavor is to make any sense, some of the kinds of issues dealt with in much of contemporary Eurocentric feminism may well have their analogues in conceptual schemes having to do with the roles of females in other cultures. If we think of global feminist inquiry as currently being driven, at least in philosophical circles, largely by conceptual questions, then we may make inquiries about how those conceptual difficulties might be encountered in Third World and emerging cultures. Thus areas of research in feminist philosophy such as ethics, epistemology, and philosophy of religion may themselves be fruitful areas of inquiry for global feminism, even if in some cases we understand from the outset that the very terms in which the debates are cast will inevitably betray some degree of bias or privileging of the European cultures.

Feminist epistemology has been at the forefront of feminist philosophical endeavor in the academic circles of the so-called developed countries. As work in this area has kept apace of recent developments in science studies, for example, such work has inevitably been affected by our new examination of what it means to regard work in some cultures as "scientific," and thought in other nations as less than scientific.[1] But a great deal of what has been done so far in what we are calling the area of global feminism has dealt with postmodern/poststructuralist debates about the nature of categorization, the limits of theorizing, the applicability of labeling, and so forth.

What seems to be missing from current work on feminism as a global construct is work that would allow us to navigate, as it were, between areas of ethical thought in one culture, and such areas in another, or areas of epistemic inquiry, and their analogues in other cultures. This work aims at least to partially fill the gap. All human cultures have questions surrounding the use and scope of knowledge and knowledge-related constructs. Although it may well be the case that in Asian, African, and Native American societies these questions are asked in ways that may be strikingly different from the European tradition, we should be able to recognize such questions within a culture, and, more important, we should be able to recognize how these epistemic issues intersect with issues having to do with the status of women within the culture and with gender-related issues as a whole. It would seem to be a mistake to construe global feminism as one family of issues having to do with essentialism. The richness of feminist theorizing is such that many different sorts of areas of conceptual inquiry may be posed in feminist terms.

We can see some of the sorts of difficulties that we will encounter in trying to address issues in feminist epistemology, or some other area of feminist inquiry, in global fashion when we consider a smaller subset of difficulties, that having to do with women of color in the United States or other First World societies. A number of tensions arise when, for example, feminist standpoint epistemology is brought to bear on issues involving marginalized women in the United States. There seems to be a conundrum revolving around whether it makes sense to think of the standpoint(s) of the marginalized as possessing some sort of epistemic privilege not possessed by the dominant culture, or whether, indeed, it makes sense to think of epistemic privilege at all.[2] One might be entitled to inquire whether the project of pursuing standard sorts of Eurocentric philosophical questions in the context of cultures outside the dominant tradition makes sense, especially when it appears to be conceptually strained to attempt to answer some of those same sorts of questions within nonstandard areas of the dominant tradition. But there is a strong counter to this somewhat pessimistic objection: without an attempt to minimally address some of the sorts of questions that seem naturally to occur to human beings—questions about knowledge, morality, life, and death—there can be no meaningful work in global feminism. For each culture has developed ways of responding to problems surrounding the human condition, and to the status of females within that culture. In a sense, to fail to attempt to address some of these areas of inquiry is to be intellectually derelict in one's duty.

Still other problematic areas come to the fore when we strive to do conceptual analysis in epistemology or theory of knowledge (or any other traditional area) in multicultural contexts. New movements within the European philosophical tradition have cast doubt on the very nature of these enterprises, and still other movements have begun to test any such responses we might be tempted to give along the lines of colonial or postcolonial analysis. Along the first axis, we can, of course, refer to poststructuralist and/or postmodern concerns about the nature of the questions and areas of conceptual inquiry. I will return to this area shortly, but it is closely allied with the second axis, that of the nature of postcolonial theorizing in most of the areas of what we call the Third World.

Poststructuralist work casts doubt on the validity of philosophical inquiry, and on the presuppositions that drive philosophical questions. Postcolonial work seems to indicate that much of what the European-tradition theorists count as "liberatory" is so only within the framework of a tradition that is already completely set up against persons of color and non-European cultures. Thus any work in global feminist epistemology would have to begin to address these two powerful currents in contemporary thought, and again it is hard to imagine what recondite areas of theory might be in some sense safe or proof against the queries of poststructuralism/postcolonialism.

Work in global feminist epistemology has, then, some nearly insuperable tasks to complete, but contemporary conditions demand that we at least make an effort to progress in the work. Our first hurdle is to address the challenges of current poststructuralist thought.

Examining the Poststructuralist Challenge

What is meant by phrases like "poststructuralism" or the even more ubiquitous "postmodernism" has become so vague as to border on the meaningless, and yet the continued use of the terms indicates problems theoretical and otherwise for anyone who engages material that is touched by these rubrics. Lawrence Cahoone has perhaps put it most succinctly when he writes that those who employ the labels (which are frequently used almost interchangeably) "regard [them] as rejecting most of the fundamental intellectual pillars of modern Western civilization."[3] Among such pillars, according to Cahoone, is the possibility of knowledge of a real, exterior world, the unity of the human self, and so forth. To be fair, it turns out upon closer examination of many of the texts of the poststructuralist movement that it is not so much that the claims are vague as that they are grandiose—grandiose and difficult to sustain.[4] In any case, the attack on these pillars is pronounced, and has become a staple of academic discourse in recent years.

Because of the alleged difficulty in using terms "univocally," or in attaching meanings to terms on some sort of grounded basis,[5] a great deal of contemporary feminist theory has dealt with the task of destabilizing gender-related terms, or of coming to grips with what employment could be made of such terms in theoretical discourse. These shifts have made the use of categories such as "woman," "masculine," and "feminine" nearly impossible, according to some theorists. Interestingly enough, some of the early work in feminist analytic philosophy focused on such terms, but with a hearty confidence and a sense that their examination could prove liberatory.[6] No such confidence seems to infuse more recent work that makes use of these terms.

The upshot of the work of such theorists as Derrida and Foucault, however misunderstood and misemployed, has been that some parts of what might constitute global feminist inquiry are made to look naive or downright foolish. If part of the inquiry seems to assume that there is something called "woman" that survives as cross-cultural category, then the more contemporary work appears to strongly undermine such a thesis. As Victoria Barker has written in a prominent feminist journal, the "issue, especially as pursued within certain currents of recent French feminist philosophy, has sometimes been characterized as that of articulating the 'name of woman' beyond that attributed to her within the discursive order of patriarchy."[7] In any case, it is clear that, if the underground movements posed by Continental theory are taken seriously, any project that intends to examine gender constructs cross-culturally is faced with monumental problems.

Even assuming that it might be possible to make sense of the category "woman" as applying to roughly half of the human race—and here, of course, one would have to allude at least minimally to biology—an even greater difficulty for philosophical projects is the application of theoretical terms, almost all of which are of Western origin, in other cultural contexts. Thus an inquiry in global feminist epistemology must face the contention that many cultures will possess only the roughest of analogues of European knowledge-centered terms.

Nevertheless, there are surprising cultural equivalents for many concepts that might initially be deemed to be hopelessly Eurocentric. Although one contention that might bear fruit in this regard is that the conceptual apparatuses translate best from cultures that themselves possess a lengthy written, rather than oral, tradition, many Westerners are surprised to find the parallels as strong as they are (indeed, many are ignorant of the written traditions that a number of cultures do possess). The difficulty with the concept "woman" may in fact be somewhat greater than other parallels that might be drawn. For example, in the Sanskrit-derived Hindu cultures of India, a long history exists of glossing certain notions as equivalent or roughly equivalent parallels to some Western notions. Because of India's long colonial history, this process was well under way at a comparatively early time, and so well-known scholars such as Ananda Coomaraswamy have commented on structural equivalencies between Vedic thought and Platonic thought. Writing well before the poststructuralist turn that asks us to forgo belief in univocality, Coomaraswamy noted, in commenting on some of Heinrich Zimmer's work:

> *Brahman* is the life that lives in all things, [Heraclitus' "ever-living Fire," Plato's "ever-progenitive nature"]. "It is never born, nor does It ever die, nor, having once been, does It again cease to be. Unborn, eternal, permanent and primeval, It is not slain when the body is slain." (*Bhagavad Gita* 2.20) [Emphasis in original.][8]

Although there may well be genuine reason to be concerned, from an analytic standpoint, about some of the parallels in Coomaraswamy's trenchant remark, the fact that the equivalencies are there is food for thought. Part of the use of postcolonial theory has been to heighten our realization of the extent to which non-European cultures have been viewed through European lenses, frequently to the detriment of the former. But what we do find in the sort of conceptualization that we are presented with here is a point of departure for cross-cultural application of philosophical categories.

It may well be the case that we will have to do enormous work to come to grips with categories such as "woman" and "female" when trying to develop the notion of global feminist epistemologies. But it is helpful to know that there is a history of scholars' having found or created philosophical parallels, many of which will indeed turn out to be epistemic. Working with some of those epistemic parallels can provide us with a source of nutrients for further theoretical work. We may want to inquire, for example, how it is that women within a given culture have been able to reappropriate epistemic categories that are the normal province only of males within that culture. Knowing that glosses on the parallelisms already exist is helpful to us in finding a springboard from which to begin our conceptual work on these and other feminist topics.

Although many have taken the postmodern or poststructuralist crisis to indicate the futility of general attempts at the buildup of "knowledge" or "inquiry," there may well be one strand to postmodernist thought that at least allows for new areas of investigation. Because modernism is so closely tied to the rise and hegemony of industrial European culture and its global domination, any enterprise that allows us to examine the spread of knowledge categories from the Eurocentric point of view to other cultures may be said to be within the postmodern framework. Fredric Jameson, a critic whose writings on this topic are often taken as authoritative, has said, "The postmodern is, however, the force field in which very different kinds of cultural impulses . . . must make their way. If we do not achieve some general sense of a cultural dominant, then we fall back into a view of present history as sheer heterogeneity."[9]

Present history is not, of course, "sheer heterogeneity." The colonial movements and spread of European thought patterns to the rest of the world during the eighteenth and nineteenth centuries are the direct precursors of the distribution of geographic and demographic power extant today. Although feminists have sometimes been accused of failing to see the differences in the positions that "women" have in various societies, there can be little dispute about the fact that the overwhelming majority of the world's illiterate and poorly educated are women, and a disproportionately high number of infant mortalities and serious illnesses occur to females. All of these facts lend credence to our contention that the global status of females is worthy of investigation, even in this postmodern era.

Postcolonialism and Its Impact on Theorizing

Perhaps more relevant to our investigations than the current debates about poststructuralism is the theoretical stance frequently termed "postcolonial." Although this label, too, has often been applied to literary endeavors, much use can be made of the term in differing scholarly contexts. Moira Ferguson, for example, calls the writing of the black Antiguan author Jamaica Kincaid "postcolonial" because Kincaid uses the colonial condition of Antigua as a powerful metaphor for general levels of oppression.[10] Her writing may be thought of as signaling strong feminist themes, and yet it is no mistake to call the work of other, overtly feminist (and nonfictional) authors "postcolonial." Such thinkers as Chandra Mohanty and Stuart Hall have received the label, and its intersection with gender-related lines of analysis is an obvious one for any sort of theorizing that would attempt to get at the condition of women in what is usually termed the Third World.

One of the most startling initial uses of postcolonial theory for gender-driven purposes has been one that is similar to some of the work done by poststructuralism: postcolonial thought has pushed us in new directions with regard to the categories under examination here, "woman" and "female." Many thinkers have been at pains to make the case that the current use of these terms (the first, particularly) in non-Western cultures may well be so dependent upon the advent of Western thought in its original, colonial guise that it is difficult to ferret out what the terms could amount to independent of the contamination of European languages and thought.[11] Certainly, such theory has advised us, we can make no easy move from some Western construal of woman or woman-related concepts to global notions. Any such move is fraught with danger, and must be made carefully. Stating it forcefully, Mohanty herself has written:

> In my own work ... I have argued against the use of analytic categories and political positionings in feminist studies that discursively present Third World women as a homogeneous, undifferentiated group leading truncated lives, victimized by the combined weight of "their" traditions, cultures, and beliefs and "our" (Eurocentric) history.[12]

To be sure, the variety of cultures and traditions that constitute what is ordinarily taken to be the "Third World" (however odious a label, we appear to be stuck with it) is so overwhelming—combining as it does African, Asian, Latin American, Oceanic, and other broad rubrics—that any generalization is likely to be false. Mohanty is particularly concerned about such generalizations since, in one of the paradoxes that frequently occur in postcolonial scholarship, making broad claims about non-Western groups is itself an instance of Western colonialism and hegemony.

Again, the intersection of postcolonial concerns and concerns about women's knowing, feminist epistemology, or any such strand of thought is a poignant one and one that does not lend itself to easy analysis. Although almost all human cultures will have at least some terminology in the indigenous language to signal knowledge states, such terminology will depend heavily, of course, on other distinctions, such as those between orality and literacy.[13] Then again, although there will indeed be many parallels between the use of knowledge/belief terms in European languages and other languages or cultures that have a written tradition, some parallels will be closer than others. Postcolonial theory and the postcolonial stance enjoin us to exercise extreme caution in the investigation of these parallels.

Sara Mills has written that "white women were constructed as being an essential part of the ideological justification for the colonial enterprise and they played a key role in the maintenance of colonial rule."[14] Mills's point, of course, is that white women in colonial situations were seen as maintaining a sort of racial purity, and hence any other women (and, in fact, the entire culture of the colonized) were impure and polluting by comparison. Thus as Mills notes, if we can employ a term such as postcolonial feminism, it brings a feminist emphasis to postcolonial studies while at the same time investigating the status of women among the colonized and attempting to dismantle easy notions of universality. But it will also, surely, have the effect of helping us deal with the translation of Western categories of thought, since it is much of the translation of such categories that carries the potential for the harmful generalizations, with respect to women, or with respect to culture in general, about which both Mohanty and Mills are writing.

As indicated at an earlier point, it is striking to see how the work of Western investigators, or investigators familiar with their own culture but having Western training, often recapitulated European conceptualization in the writing that was done about nonWestern cultures fifty or one hundred years ago. We have already seen how Ananda Coomaraswamy, for example, in attempting to get across the notion of Brahman in the Hindu tradition, compares the concept to categories taken from Plato and Heraclitus.[15]

Such thinking will be of paramount importance in our examination of feminist epistemologies in other cultures, but the postcolonial will exhort us to not make the error of assuming either that knowledge categories in other cultures have not been affected by European categories, or of believing that parallels can hold tightly without elucidation or amelioration. Because so many of the world's indigenous cultures have been affected by the colonizing of the Europeans, it is difficult to know (with respect to the above example) how much credence to give to Coomaraswamy's assertion. Is there any way to decide whether a Hindu concept is the rough analogue of something taken from Heraclitus or Plato without begging the question? What could possibly count as a standard in such a case? The assistance rendered to us by postcolonial theory is that we now are not naive enough to think that the parallels and analogies can be constructed blindly or without further examination.

Lastly, awareness of the impact of the postcolonial will make us sensitive to the desire that many theorists—including commentators from the relevant cultures—have had to see concepts in European terms, irrespective of any relevance. It may be simpler, for example, to read a culture's history in a way that resembles some aspect of European historiography simply because this is in accord with the training of the person in question. Tsenay Serequeberhan, for example, writing of the work of Léopold Senghor on négritude, has enjoined us to see such work as a way of casting concepts of blackness in the same mold as a number of Romantic concepts of the Other.[16] Although Serequeberhan does not state this, we might take part of his thesis to be that Senghor made these moves subconsciously. They were simply the result of the strength of the French tradition in which Senghor, a top lycée student, was well schooled.

If Mills is right that much of what the colonizers left us, with respect to their commentary on the cultures of the colonized, was to place them in the light of being "negatively different,"[17] defensive maneuvers on the part of all and sundry may attempt to restructure our notions of these cultures as being "positively different," or "positively the same." In either case, since Eurocentric thought is taken as the benchmark, the conceptual situation is already fraught with difficulty. But to be fair, there seems to be little or no way around this conundrum. We are all affected by the strength of the European tradition, and it is of paramount importance, if we are to make any headway in theorizing with respect to global feminism, to at least come to grips with some of these differences. It is to our benefit to accept the caveats of postcolonial theory, even if we are not sure what to make of them. We cannot escape our intellectual heritage, but we must proceed along the lines of cautious analysis—we must be aware of our tendency to see parallels (simply because finding parallels tends to make intellectual tasks cleaner and easier), and when we do think that we have good evidence for such analogues, we must also remember that the very fact that some European concept is taken as the exemplar against which the other concept is held already prejudices the circumstances in favor of the ultimate authority of Western theory. Proceeding courageously and carefully, we can at last begin to examine epistemic concepts in other cultures and their impact and intersection with the situations of females within those cultures. When Mills reminds us that postcolonial theory focuses on the development of "particular structures of thinking and behaviour,"[18] we might be very justified in saying that she is phrasing the situation delicately and diplomatically.

Knowledge, the Epistemic, and Frames of Categorization

Human cultures around the world approach the concepts having to do with knowledge and knowledge acquisition differently, and this difference is particularly marked insofar as the more traditional aspects of some cultures are concerned. Visionary traditions that in the West have often been termed "shamanistic" or "sacred" may have a more mundane set of features in certain cultural views, not the least of which has to do with how those traditions inform the everyday lives of the persons within the culture. Many of the indigenous cultures of the Americas, for example, have strong traditions centering on the use of hallucinogenic plants. The ceremonies surrounding the use of these plants are not merely an integral part of the culture, but in some cases define it.[19] The wisdom acquired through such ceremonies may be deemed "real," while portions of daily life remain vague and shadowy by comparison.

Knowledge about trade and trading in certain West African cultures, although acquired empirically, may be the benchmark in the culture for other kinds of knowledge.[20] Portions of the Vedas in Hindu culture are invested with a sacred authority above and beyond their status as repeated or learned texts. Black American commentators often write of the strength of the oral tradition in black culture, and black American feminist thinkers such as Patricia Hill Collins have asserted that an entire epistemology can be formed on the basis of such traditional oral chaining.[21] All of the foregoing reminds us of the work that must inevitably be done if we are to make sense of global feminist epistemologies or worldviews. Because the acquisition of knowledge and one's status as "knowledgeable" are inescapably central parts of human cultures, getting at the heart of an epistemic view for a culture is crucial to understanding what drives it and how it is constructed.

Nevertheless, we can devise a set of theoretical warning devices based on our brief excursion into critical theory here. Although we can guess that most cultures will distinguish between "knowledge" and "belief," since it will become important to acquire beliefs that yield fruitful outcomes, we can also guess that this will be done so differently in many cultures that it will, in many cases, not yield strong parallels or analogues to these concepts in English-speaking societies. More important, perhaps, our notions of justification or confirmation must irretrievably be altered. Because it is clear from the examination of indigenous societies that "truths" acquired in certain states have an exalted epistemic status, nothing resembling our concept of justification can meaningfully be said to be at work here. Thus if feminists already have difficulties working within the framework of European tradition, these difficulties will be doubled or trebled for other cultures and other traditions.

The importance of the epistemic in a given culture has to do not only with its obvious relation to everyday life, but also to categories of prestige and power. In many cultures, women cannot truly be said to be "knowers." Whatever form of knowledge-gathering activity women traditionally engage in, it often fails to meet requirements of purity or rigor for the status of "knowledge" within that culture. Thus women are excluded from many of the rituals surrounding the sacred, because those rituals frequently yield a form of contact with entities or mind-sets deemed to be of exalted status. In the rare cases where women are allowed to participate, it is always made clear that the individual woman in question is an anomaly.

The importance of these conceptualization schemes cannot be overstated. The religious studies thinker Carol Christ has noted that forms of religious activity deemed to be "monotheistic" are usually held to be superior to or an advance over forms thought to be "polytheistic," and it is precisely in the polytheistic forms that women usually have more power and in which more female deities are invoked or worshiped.[22] Not only are monotheistic religions thought to be more advanced, but it is in these religions—Judaism, Christianity, and Islam—that women historically have the least say.

Because forms of knowledge acquisition revolving around the sacred are so powerful in so many cultures, women's daily knowledge—the knowledge gleaned from finding and fetching water, growing food or repairing clothing—is often denigrated, thus yielding a strong tradition across human cultures that the highest forms of knowledge are not empirically derived, or if they are so derived, they are encoded in mysteries which themselves may be expressed in nonempirical terms.[23]

That knowledge of mundane tasks has traditionally been accorded low status in most societies might seem so obvious as to not require repetition, but it is startling to follow some of the paths of such distinctions. The philosopher of education Jane Roland Martin, for example, has noted the historical track across American universities of low status attaching to any activity that is primarily undertaken by women.[24] Where there are exceptions, it is again often a case of a few men having undertaken the activity in question and temporarily altered its status. Martin and others have recommended that American schools remedy this situation by making such training available to all. If this is to happen, there clearly must be some changes in the way in which women's activities are seen.

Although notions of knowledge, belief, and justification or confirmation will appear startlingly different across cultures, many cultures will have stronger analogues to the sorts of claims that we are able to make in the Western tradition than is immediately obvious. This has to do, we can surmise, with the strength of written tradition in some cultures, and we must remember that certain of these, the Sanskrit tradition of the Indian subcontinent for example, are older than the major portion of the Western written tradition and that if anything we might be thought to be using their tradition as an exemplar. Of course, cultures that function within an oral tradition will have different analogues, and it may well be the case that some of those bear little resemblance. Nevertheless, trying to look for parallels—always bearing in mind the conceptual difficulty of doing so—is instructive and helpful.

What counts as knowledge is crucially important across human cultures precisely because what counts as the known usually helps define positions within the culture on questions central to human existence on the earth; such questions as what is constitutive of ultimate reality, or what kinds of deities exist, cannot be answered without an account of what constitutes knowledge. Thus one strand of Eurocentric thinking may in fact be relevant cross-culturally—almost all human cultures may be said to possess ontologies, and we cannot get at those ontologies without epistemologies. Seeing how women function within a culture, how their role is defined, and how women now attempt to come to grips with the historical structure of such ontologies and epistemologies is at the core of establishing a meaningful feminist theory.

The current movement within Western feminist theory that valorizes "women's ways of knowing" is simply one way of attempting to address, in a theoretical manner, the problem alluded to here earlier. What women do, how they come to acquire the daily knowledge that they have, and what they do with that knowledge have seldom been topics of investigation or interest for the hierarchy within any society. Our first attempts to create global feminist epistemologies must work from the assumption that women possess knowledge, even if the stratified power structure of a given society denies it or devalues it.

Women's Appropriation of Knowledge

In contemporary white, mainstream feminist theory, work on feminist epistemologies has proceeded along two broad fronts. One sort of endeavor, frequently employing poststructuralist theory (and its challenges) attacks what appears to be the solid foundation of Western thought and throws feminist thinking up against it, as it were, as some sort of alternative view.[25] Statistically speaking, this has probably been the more common method of attempting to do work in feminist theory of knowledge.

Another method—and here I speak broadly—attempts to take the tools and methods of standard analysis and turn them against the purposes for which they were originally devised. This is not only the case for work done within the discipline of philosophy, for example, where some feminist theorists have employed analytic categories of thought for feminist purposes (indeed, for purposes with which their originators may not be happy). Painting on a larger canvas, one can see this happening in other disciplines, and also across the culture, wherever concepts of privileged knowledge and power are in use. In religious traditions in contemporary America, for example, many women have found innovative ways to begin reappropriation of sacred categories that were once entirely closed to women. Although this does not affect academic knowledge structures directly, it is an excellent example of feminists appropriating the norms of masculinist knowledge for their own use. Within the Christian tradition, both Catholic and Protestant groups have seen women assume roles never assumed by women before, and the same has happened in the Judaic tradition, including a few challenges to established orthodoxy.

Simply to recapitulate two areas in which white Western females are currently working on feminist appropriations of masculinist knowledge paradigms, we can refer to contemporary work in the sciences and, insofar as institutional structures are concerned, political work. Work in the sciences, both theoretical—philosophy of science, history of science, science studies—and performative (doing the work of science itself) strongly involves reappropriation since the sciences were defined as exemplars of male activity.[26] Historically speaking, the growth of science involved "taking nature by force," as many early commentators would have it, and the long history of exclusion of women from science simply reaffirmed this tradition. This story has now been repeated so often as to scarcely bear another round, but it serves as a model of feminist reinvention of androcentric endeavor.

Just as the masculinist orientation of the Church is now under attack, so our political structures, which again were originally designed to exclude women, are now also being altered. Institutionally, this is one of the most important areas, for our political structures are codified, and we have written records of both the exclusion of women and of their attempts to overcome such exclusion and establish foci of strength for the development of women's issues.

In all three of these areas—the more academic arena involving the sciences, and the institutional areas of the Church and the political sphere—women have had to take tools that were originally framed for males and use them for other purposes. In some cases, this has meant simply taking the tool and putting it to new use. In other cases (such as redefining the role of the priest in the Episcopalian tradition, or the rabbi in some versions of the

Judaic tradition) it has meant a new and forceful articulation of what that tool or role could mean. The element of commonality has been, however, that in each case the role/tool was originally defined by and used by men.

In examining other cultures, then, what we will look for is current attempts by feminists working within the framework of the culture to use that culture in ways previously not available. In Hindu India, for example, this has often meant reappropriation of time-honored Vedic methods for feminist purposes. The satyagraha, Gandhi's famous method of attacking British hegemony, can, in various permutations, become a feminist tool. Goddess images are put to new use. Caste splits have meant that women in the business castes may actually have more opportunities than some others because the rise in technology has altered the way in which business is done. In Latin America a long tradition of women intellectuals working within and without the Church now culminates in a wave of feminist activity, some of it harkening back to the thought of Sor Juana Ines de la Cruz. The strong black matrilineal tradition in the United States which saw the black population through slavery and the Jim Crow era now sees a burgeoning of thinking and theorizing by black women authors.

Sadly, there is also such a phenomenon as appropriation of knowledge for uses that either perpetuate the status quo, or that are actually harmful. In strongly patriarchal societies, where so much of what a woman does and who she is is dependent on male approval, this may often take place. Elizabeth Bumiller, writing in *May You Be the Mother of a Hundred Sons*, a work on women in India, is appalled by the rapid spread of amniocentesis and like technologies—even to the poorest neighborhoods—as women attempt to find out whether they are carrying female fetuses.[27] But just as it has been difficult to prevent the rise of the misuse of this type of testing, there has been a strong growth in the activism of women social workers, many from the higher castes, who have attempted to intervene and change attitudes. Bumiller recounts a simultaneously sad and humorous story wherein such a social worker, speaking high-caste Tamil, was misinterpreted by the lower-caste mother to whom she was speaking when the social worker attempted to report the sex of a newly born infant. So devalued are females and anything having to do with the birth of a female that any such birth beyond the first is widely regarded as a tragedy.

In general, then, women's appropriation of knowledge has meant that portions of traditions that have frequently been constructed in powerfully androcentric ways may in fact be redeemed for feminist and liberatory purposes. As we have just seen, such reappropriation may take the form of simply using the knowledge in question differently, or it may take a somewhat more powerful form of altering actual interpretations of the knowledge itself. Where such knowledge is regarded as sacred or the province only of a priesthood (religious or otherwise), such reappropriation can amount to an almost revolutionary act. Training women in simple economies, or explaining to them how to counter spousal abuse, can have an overwhelming impact in a small village area.

Although we can hypothesize that a few women have always engaged in such behavior, the strength of the women's movement worldwide does indeed mean that in Bangladesh, Mexico, Guatemala, and downtown Los Angeles there are now many more women ready to engage in feminist activity than there would have been at an earlier time. It is easy to chart the spread of feminism in the so-called developed countries, and interesting to note the differences in, for example, British feminist thought and American varieties.[28] But taking note of feminist activity in the developing countries is a much more difficult endeavor. In some cases, such organizations are virtually underground. In other cases, the organizations are visible, but upon close examination they may involve only a handful of women. The fact that women most prominent and active in such movements almost always come from the better-off classes—the very classes with the greatest exposure to Western thought—complicates matters.

Work in global feminism needs and can use sustained work in global feminist epistemology. But such work must be done with some understanding of the strength of local cultural traditions and of the role that knowledge, knowers, and knowledge gathering plays in such traditions. Too often we are quick to assume, as indicated earlier, either that no parallels can be created or that it is a quick and simple matter to create strong parallels of knowledge categorization. Particularly with respect to the South Asian cultures, scholars have shown us that work in the Hindu, Buddhist, and regional Islamic traditions reveals strong traditions of knowledge categorization. It is part of our task as feminist scholars to come to grips with these traditions and to articulate how the traditions are being used by women today to make changes in their own lives.

The View from Everywhere

Global feminist epistemologies represent an exciting project, not only because of the obvious tie-in to other feminist theorizing that is currently taking place. The project also has transformational potential on many levels, including work having to do with international economic assistance and development.[29] Such projects have now proliferated to such an extent that almost every regional bank in developing areas is supporting at least some type of educational, hygienic, or cottage industry project, and many of these developmental projects are directed and run by women.

What is most remarkable about the reporting that takes place in agency newsletters and bulletins about self-help projects in developing areas is that they function on more than one level. Typically, economic assistance is only one part of the package. Frequently, an unintended by-product of such work is a change in attitude among those involved in the work, and the changes for women are often enormous.[30] Because many women in developing areas have never left their village—and in some cases virtually never been outside of the home—what appear to be small changes to an outsider can have enormous consequences.

The United Nations and other organizations have reminded us that the vast majority of the illiterate in the world are women. Because educational resources are so scarce in many Third World nations, the very few resources that are available are almost always targeted for men, unless some special effort is made to improve the lives of women. Tracking how women are able, within a traditional framework, to appropriate forms of knowledge and systems of learning can have tremendous potential for the planet's women and for the future of life on Earth.

It is also the case that global feminist epistemologies are relevant to work in the sciences. The feminist critique of science is well established, but part of the critique has often been allied with the radical critique of science, which enjoins us to take care that the results of scientific work not be exploitative of persons of color or developing countries. Tracking how women are coming to grips with their problems in other countries can assist us in articulating goals for transformative projects around the world that are sensitive to environmental needs and the needs of indigenous populations. These efforts have been difficult in the past precisely because there were so few trained scientists in developing countries and because the model of learning that they have employed has tended, of necessity, to be that of educated white Westerners. The time may be right, now, to begin to investigate how feminist work in developing nations can be attached to the feminist critique of science.

As has been argued here, cultures that contain a written heritage frequently have epistemologies that bear at least some resemblance to those of Western cultures, if only because of the extent to which modes of literacy alter cognition and conceptual patterns. We can begin to examine some of the knowledge categories of these cultures with an eye to how they have intersected with the burgeoning women's movement. We can consider the possibility that we ought to think in terms of global feminist ethics—and, of course, any such thinking brings us back into the camp of epistemologies. For if there are a number of questions surrounding reproductive rights, ecology, the dumping of products on Third World markets, and other such issues that might be construed in global terms, how women come to appropriate knowledge categories from their own cultures must be part and parcel of how we begin to address such issues.

Interestingly enough, certain types of issues—those surrounding ecofeminism seem to be among them—now seem to have emerged on a global basis. Bumiller reports that what we in the West have come to term "tree hugging" is a form of ecological protest that actually began in the 1970s in India, and not among those of the most privileged castes.[31] Women from all walks of life and from a variety of different cultural backgrounds have perhaps been quicker than many men to see the interconnectedness of lived experiences and to see how such issues have paramount importance, even when taking an interest in preservation seems to go against the concept of short-term profits. Although a naive Westerner might think that profit would always come first in a poverty-stricken area, a brief examination of some of the actual incidents constituting ecological movements seems to show otherwise.

That there are no easy answers, however, is underscored by a problem to which we have already made reference in the use of chorionic sampling or amniocentesis for sex-selective abortion. Here in most cases it is, of course, women who are making decisions to abort female fetuses. Nevertheless, it is also women who have led the fight against such gendercidal practices. And again, if, sadly enough, some women have been implicated in the rash of dowry deaths and bride burnings in the Indian subcontinent, it is also women social workers who have drawn attention to these practices.

Everywhere, women find themselves functioning on an everyday basis in a woman-unfriendly cultural environment. The laws, rules, and practices of societies are set by men. It is especially the case, as we have already noted, that sacred knowledge in almost all societies is held, in general, to be the province of males. Thus it is not surprising that many practices that involve women have consequences that are deleterious to the health and future of women, but it is encouraging to note that women are beginning to fight against these practices on almost every level. To do so involves not only physical courage, but a kind of mental strength that allows women to borrow from the culture whatever might be construed in some fashion as female friendly, and then to use it as a weapon in the overall fight. It is this particular pattern in which we have special interest, for in many cultures, finding what is female-friendly will involve reappropriation of knowledge categories or seeing these categories in a new way.

Sociology of knowledge and sociology of science can both be of some help to us here, since they emphasize the ways in which knowledge is socially constructed in the first place.[32] If it is accurate to say that what counts as knowledge in a given social situation tends to keep in place positions of prestige and power, then it is certainly obvious why it is that, in so many areas of human endeavor, women are either kept from what would count as "knowledge," or are given very little access to it. We can see this not only cross-culturally but in the hierarchies of given societies: women may be allowed access to or be allowed to participate in certain forms of knowledge acquisition at certain times, only to be excluded from the same versions of these processes that would be deemed to be more important or crucial. Since social class is also related to knowledge appropriation, it provides causal explanation for why it is that splits in women's movements also occur across predictable lines—some women are born into given social classes and thus, from the outset, have slightly or somewhat greater access to types of knowledge. Their presence may be offensive or burdensome to the very women, mainly from lower social classes, whom they try to help or assist in various ways. These splits, although all too predictable, further impede women's progress and reinforce male notions that women should not be allowed access to various forms of knowledge production.

Although our work on global feminist epistemology will, for the most part, focus on cultures not located in the geographical United States, what we know about the movement of women into heretofore male preserves in American career paths can, in some ways, serve as a model for the work we are trying to do. Work done by researchers at the University of Wyoming on women in ranching and farming recapitulates many of the kinds of social problems involved in developing feminist epistemologies cross-culturally. The researchers report that there have always been women ranch hands and "cowgirls"; they simply engaged in little self-reporting because their work was seen as a source of potential embarrassment and ridicule, and they did not want to draw attention to themselves.[33] We might think of the foregoing example as a smaller version of the problems confronting women globally. It is not that women have not managed to create access for themselves to male realms of employment, prestige, and power—but it has been dangerous to do so, and very difficult to discuss. We are now in a position where, I hope, we can begin to articulate feminist epistemologies in a cross-cultural context.

Part 2

Asian Focal Points

Chapter 2

Northern India and Its Cultures

The commentary on the philosophy of India, like so much commentary on conceptual systems and philosophical overviews on a worldwide basis, frequently seems to take as its point of departure comparison with Western thought. That this is the case is perhaps not surprising, but the comparisons implicitly or explicitly made to European philosophical systems say much not only about the hegemony of Western culture, but about various forms of category construction that we may find in other cultures. For in comparing portions of the Upanishads to Stoic or other ancient commentary, a number of structural parallels arise, not the least of which is androcentrism.

When we examine global feminist epistemologies today, we can see that the predominance of Eurocentric lines of analysis in a way is helpful to us, because it allows for a fairly facile comparison of terms that might be thought to be androcentric, or of concepts that might be masculinist. On the other hand, such comparisons can be harmful—they may import more androcentrism than is actually present in a given particular conceptual system (particularly an androcentrism of a Western type), and they may prevent us from seeing the system more clearly.[1]

In the case of India, however, and especially with respect to the classically Indian thought patterns, which tend to be associated with northern India rather than with the Dravidian cultures, the history of such associations and parallels is a long one, and cannot easily be overlooked. Many South Asian scholars themselves, trained in British or other colonial universities and long familiar with European ways, seemed to feel that they had not made an adequate attempt to valorize the thought of India or to introduce it to Westerns without explaining its strong analogues to Western (and even ancient Western) thought.

Given the richness of the Hindu conceptual system, we can focus here on only the most obvious and accessible material, but it is just this material that is used not only in presentation to others, but which now finds its way into the popular press of its nation of origin and thus becomes more accessible to all, including women. Thus our work on the reappropriation of categories by women is made somewhat easier than it would have been only a few short years ago by the accessibility of strands of thought that would not originally have been part of the popular culture.

From the standpoint of categories of knowledge, and of conceptualization that might be deemed to be epistemic or having to do with knowledge, the classical Hindu tradition is a rich one. Gavin Flood, in his monumental *An Introduction to Hinduism*, makes much of the Vedic Hindu distinction between the householder and the renouncer. If these may be seen as stages of a person's life (and the person is, of course, male) it is the renouncer tradition that yields knowledge. Here the analogue is not, of course, to what Westerners call empirical knowledge, for that is associated with the path of the everyday. But the path of renunciation and withdrawal from daily affairs is the beginning of the path toward knowledge. Again, in an effort to valorize this path, many have made the obvious parallels to Plato.[2] Flood writes, of this path to knowledge:

> From about 800 to 400 BCE Sanskrit and Prakrit texts bear witness to the new ideology of renunciation, in which knowledge (*jñana*) is given precedence over action (*karma*), and detachment from the material and social world is cultivated thorough ascetic practices (*tapas*), celibacy, poverty, and methods of mental training (*yoga*). The purpose of such training is the cultivation of altered or higher states of consciousness which will culminate in the blissful mystical experience of higher liberation.... [The traditions agree] that life is characterized by suffering and ... [liberation from] suffering is a form of spiritual knowledge or gnosis.[3]

The renouncer traditions are crucial to Hindu thought, not only in the sense that they form the basis upon which such thought is usually categorized by scholars, but because they form the basis for what is deemed to be the highest or most sacred path within the society itself. Although Hindu society is characterized much more by adherence to ritual than by any formal institutions, and although there are certainly pockets in which women's activities have, in some areas, meshed with traditional thought over the centuries, it is assumed in most of the commentary that participants in these paths are male. How this will affect contemporary women is part of our focus in this chapter.

If the renouncer traditions aim us in a direction of knowledge categorization, we need to see how such conceptualization has affected the larger culture. Speaking in terms of the development of philosophical views that might be compared, however crudely, with those of the Western tradition, we see the first development of these views in the Vedas, composed largely in the years several centuries BCE, and then a further development in the Upanishads, specific commentary on the Vedas and other doctrine, some of which may well have been composed in the early centuries AD. Because the Upanishads have been widely taken to represent Hindu thought that is overtly philosophical, examination of them can yield conceptual categories that are at least in some respect parallel to those of Western culture.

Gavin Flood, Heinrich Zimmer, and other commentators write of the "monism" that is predicated in the Upanishads, and this monism is, of course, explicable only to those whose status is high enough to allow them what we might term epistemic access.[4] The strain that is usually dubbed "mystical" in Hindu thought is directly related to these philosophical contentions: here, in a parallel that might best be made with Platonic theory, the material world is seen as being unreal, in some hierarchy of things real, and genuine reality underlies material phenomena in such a way that, through contemplation and divorce from the material, the acolyte may be able to grasp it.

Thus, as has been the case for most of the sacred traditions found in a variety of human cultures, a hierarchy of persons who might possess the epistemic virtues to enable them to come to true knowledge is established. Flood directly addresses this issue when, in characterizing the structure that underlies the most profound levels of Hinduism, he writes: "The history of Hinduism is the history of a male discourse.... [One needs to be aware that] women's self-perceptions and experience have generally been 'written out' of the tradition."[5] The combination, then, of a leisured class of priests and of those few wealthy landowners who might have time to devote to study, and the pronounced lack of women within the tradition from its point of origin, have given rise to an overwhelmingly masculinist discourse, should we choose to characterize this discourse in Eurocentric terms.

From the standpoint of philosophical categorization, then, we can see how it is that many Western commentators have not found it difficult to examine Sanskrit-derived material and to create analogues between classical Hinduism and Western thought. It is also the case that the time frame, roughly, of the origins of Hinduism as we know it now (taking into account the conquest of much of Dravidian India) corresponds roughly to the rise of Western philosophy, a fact that has been made much of in the literature. One factor that stands out in the Hindu tradition, however, is a greater univocality: unlike the debates with which we are familiar from Greek thought, wherein various monisms might compete, or wherein some thinkers would not, from the outset, be categorized as monists, Hindu thought seems to have achieved a remarkable synthesis, insofar as this material is readily available to us. Zimmer himself draws the contrast readily enough:

> In Greece this ancient stage of Aryan belief was represented in the mythology of the Homeric age.... However, with the appearance of Greek philosophical criticism in Ionian Asia Minor ... the primitive, dreamlike, anthropomorphic projections were withdrawn from the natural scene.[6]

Zimmer feels free to make the comparison because the degree of literacy of the cultures, the time frame, and the rise of somewhat parallel categories of thought all push him—as well as other commentators—in this direction.

Androcentrism and Its Manifestations

As Flood has commented, women were "written out" of Hindu thought and of the larger history of Hindu South Asia.[7] Nevertheless, attempts at global feminist epistemics must try to make clear in what precise fashion masculinist or androcentric bias makes itself felt. In contemporary mainstream feminism of the West, it has not generally been deemed sufficient merely to point to numbers or exclusionary tactics as composing the woof and warp of androcentrism. Thinkers such as Evelyn Fox Keller and Sandra Harding have given us much more detailed analyses of the degree of bias and its persistence in underlying, seldom articulated themes of philosophical thought.[8]

Despite what might at first glance appear to be areas of difficulty in creating similar analyses for Hinduism insofar as it is practiced in non-Dravidian India, there is a great deal of food for thought when the parallels that have already been created in other areas of philosophy are now applied to some of the realms we have examined here, using the conceptual apparatuses of feminism.

Part of what is being deemed to be androcentric in Western thought, particularly Western philosophy, is a desire to get at Complete Accounts. In other words, as Keller has conceptualized it, we can think of much European-derived thought, especially in the sciences, as guilty of "stylistic aggression."[9] Although Hindu thought may appear superficially to lack some of the drive of the most aggressive Western thought of the post-Renaissance era, such lack is only apparent. Indeed, part of what has made commentary on Hindu thought so ubiquitous—and according to certain Western scholars, so valuable—is that the quest for accounts of the universe parallels in recognizable ways many such European quests. So, insofar as a desire to give Complete Accounts is concerned, Hindu thought is more or less on a par with Western thinking. Hermann Kulke and Dietmar Rothermund make this explicit when they formulate the teachings of Shankara (788–820 AD) in this way:

> Shankara formulated an impressive theory of knowledge based on the philosophical thought of his age. He referred to the philosophical teachings of the Upanishads about the unity of the individual soul (*atman*) and the divine spirit (*brahman*). He taught that the individual soul as embodied in a living being (*jiva*) is tied to the cycle of rebirths (*samsara*) because it believes that this world is real although it is only illusion (*maya*).[10]

In this brief excerpt, we can plainly see that the search for an account of ultimate reality is one of the motivating factors both of Shankara's work and of Western commentary on it. Because translations from Sanskrit were fairly easily made, and because of the relationship between Sanskrit and the other Indo-European languages, it probably does not make sense to claim that Western scholars were reading too much into Hindu systems. Rather, a better explanation, based on the obvious—and apparently relatively unforced—parallels between many aspects of Hindu thought and Western philosophy is that the androcentric spirit of trying to give an account of the whole informs this realm of thought as well.

If exclusion of allusion to the female and the search for Complete Accounts can be deemed to be characteristic of androcentrism, another feature that might be thought to be a hallmark of it is also present in Hindu thought, and that is the presence of architectonic structure (which in itself exhibits some stylistic aggression), as opposed to messy particulars. A recent collection of work by feminist philosophers on the ancients (Greeks and Latin users) strives to disabuse the reader of such notions as the common assertion that "Plato [was] 'the first feminist.' "[11] Part of the argument again concerns style—Plato always looks for unifying factors, and his levels of reality exhibit architectonic simplicity. So, too, does much of what has been deemed most valuable in Hindu philosophy. The ultimate merging of *atman* and *Brahman*, referred to above, is an example of a system that has its parts fit together in neat and airtight ways. The combination of the exclusion of women from the traditional roles of householder and seeker, the stylistic aggression inherent in the quest for unifying factors and the style of architectonic wholes and structures is an overwhelming one, but it is nevertheless characteristic of Hindu thought.

It is indeed in these parallels to Western philosophy that many commentators find the ultimate value of the Hindu worldview. In trying to draw an analogy between the thought of the early ancient Greeks and that of the Hindus, Zimmer writes:

> This universal ground was understood to be identical within all things—unchanged through the changing forms. It abides supreme within the unfolding shapes of the phenomenal universe, whether in the grosser spheres of the normal human experience or in the more rarified of the empyrean. Moreover, it transcends them all, and is infinitely beyond. Gradually, with the development of this type of Brahmanical speculative thought, the complex polytheistic ritual of the earlier stages of the Vedic tradition fell into disuse, and a way of worship came into favor that was at once less elaborate, more intimate, and more profound.[12]

Here the comparison is exactly along the lines we have been making—what is valuable about Hindu thought is similar to the best of Greek thought: its search for unity, its quest for underlying factors and its refusal to accept the strands of disparate phenomena that might be encountered as having a reality of their own.

Commentator after commentator makes the parallels between Hindu philosophy and Greek, Renaissance, or later Western philosophy, and in this particular case the analogues, as has been remarked, probably are there. (What motivations remain behind the search for such parallels is another topic altogether.) But what both systems have in common, as has just been indicated, is a desire to remove ultimate accounts from the realm of day-to-day phenomena and to latch them securely to something transcendental, something that is beyond the grit of daily life. In this set of moves, then, Hinduism shows itself to exhibit much of the androcentrism that feminist thinkers have found in the exemplary portions of Western thought.

Because of the complexity of Hindu systematizing, it is difficult to provide a view of much of what transpired in the Sanskrit or Sangam-derived philosophizing of the past. Nevertheless, still more material for analysis appears when one notes the careful systems of logic, many of which mirror, at least to some extent, patterns of Western logic, in preceding thinkers. In the *Journal of Indian Philosophy*, A. K. Rai has written an article on the use of the middle term in the Nyaya system.[13] In passing, he notes that "there is a conspicuous difference between the use of the minor term in the Aristotelian syllogism and the Indian theory of inference. The reason is that the structure of the Indian theory of inference is different from the Aristotelian syllogism."[14] The fact that the author feels called upon to make this comparison not only signals to us the Eurocentrism—already mentioned here—that frequently drives comparisons of philosophical systems, but also lets us know that various Sanskrit logics exhibit the Complete Accountism that is characteristic of androcentric thought.

Hinduism has been compared to other religious systems, especially Judaism, Christianity, and Islam—especially by Westerners—for what is often regarded as its "tolerance." By this is meant the fact that Hinduism historically exhibited a tendency to absorb local deities, and in this way grafted itself onto various local systems of worship of the Dravidians. Kulke and Rothermund note that the Dancing Shiva originally began as a minor version of Shiva worship in the Chola dynasty of the South. But in an interesting word switch of near-homonyms, the place name for the dance became transcendentalized, so to speak, and the local Shiva took on cosmic aspects. The historians write: "This etymological transformation, so typical of Hinduism's evolution, then provided striking metaphysical perspectives."[15] The move toward the transcendental and cosmic provides evidence of masculinisit systematization at work.

The Strands of the Feminine

Because there is actually ample evidence, as we have seen, that links masculinist tendencies in Hinduism to both its history and the structure of much of its philosophizing, it is tempting to begin to sort out tendencies that might be deemed to be more gynocentric simply by recounting various forms of goddess worship. This is easy enough to do, because the reverence for the various manifestations of Shiva's consort (Parvati, Kali, etc.) is great and is already fully documented.

But even those who have a decided interest in goddess worship in the Hindu tradition have noted that the interesting fact about the history of women on the subcontinent is that the forms of the "powerful" or strong goddesses seem to have little to do with the lives of Indian women. Flood amply captures these difficulties when he writes:

The Goddess is a contradictory and ambivalent figure in Hinduism. On the one hand she is the source of life, the benevolent mother who is giving and overflowing, yet on the other she is a terrible malevolent force who demands offerings of blood, meat and alcohol to placate her wrath.... The Goddess, on the edges of the brahmanical world, is incorporated into orthoprax, puranic worship and her tantric worship becomes brahmanized.[16]

As Flood informs us, there is something inherently dangerous about goddess worship, especially of the "terrible" or "malevolent" goddesses. So we already see strands within the tradition that try to regularize such worship: on the one hand, the most frightful female deities are tied by spousal relationships to the male forces, and on the other hand, for daily life, women are given the model of Sita, not really a goddess at all, but the dutiful and submissive wife of Rama in the eponymous epic.

It is too simplistic, however, to deny the force of the goddess and the *shakti* energy derived from her in Hindu worship. A more complex analysis, however, might ask if there are gynocentric elements that manifest themselves in other ways. Hinduism retains an interest in ritual practice involving fire and water, and almost all villages retain local deities that provide protection without necessarily being related to the larger, transcendental orthoprax scheme. It is here—in the rituals of daily life and in their relationship to the village—that we may find the more gynocentric strands of Hinduism, strands that have been commented upon by almost all visitors because they seem absent from the Western religions to any comparable degree. The point of local worship is to establish regularity in hearth and home, and this is something at which Hinduism excels. The predominance of these beliefs signals to us the strength of various strands of female-centered influence within the culture.

A facile response to requests for information about the gynocentric within the culture might advert, as has already been mentioned, to Sita and her role as ideal wife and mother. Indeed, what has intrigued many commentators about the status of women within Hinduism has been that this emphasis seems to have predominated over all else. Such a response would by no means be an entirely naive one, since there is much in the way in which Sita is portrayed and in the general adulation of her within the culture that does indeed valorize gynocentric traits. If we think of such traits in the terms employed, for example, by Jane Roland Martin in her work on education, it is easy to see how the reverence for Sita might well be deemed to also encompass, as Martin has it, a respect for the "3 C's" of caring, concern, and connection.[17] Since such values are so overwhelmingly important for the orderly Brahmanical household, it is probably no exaggeration to say that they find themselves entrenched in Hinduism perhaps to a greater extent than in the views of some other cultures, and certainly insofar as the lives of women are concerned.

Nevertheless, this response does little to resolve the terrible tension that resides in the culture between the "toothed" and meek goddesses, or, for that matter, between the more caring aspects of the culture and those that reinforce caste divisions that so often appear to Westerners to be the epitome of callousness and noncaring. There are, however, at least two other ways in which a profound realization of the female/feminine permeates the culture and may actually be set out.

One has to do with the often misunderstood nature of tantric worship within orthoprax Hinduism. Flood, who has written extensively on this topic, makes it clear that this type of worship is fairly common among those more familiar with sacred texts, although it may well be concealed. More important, however, than its frequency is its underlying rationale, especially when seen within the framework of the stress within Hindu philosophy on ultimate monism and the strength of the *atman/Brahman* connection. As Flood writes, tantric practice actualizes the beliefs about female energy, or *shakti*, and its place within the intellectualized hierarchy of being:

> A common feature of tantric ideology is that women represent or manifest the Goddess in a ritual context. As the male worshipper becomes the male deity, especially Siva, for only a god can worship a god, so his female partner becomes the Goddess. Indeed the Goddess is manifested in all women in varying degrees.[18]

Flood also makes it clear that, in contrast to the more standard aspects of high-caste ritual, what he refers to as "left-handed" tantrism—a still more recondite school within tantrism itself—has an intriguing overview of women. While they are regarded as the "door to the divine realm" in erotic worship with their male partner, as he phrases it, "some texts make it clear that the ensuing liberation is for both partners."[19] Furthermore, in contrast to much of the rest of the entire Hindu tradition, it is within tantrism that there is a school of female renouncers, revered as teachers and dwelling at sacred sites.[20]

Tantrism then, however occult its teachings may appear both to Westerners and to some Hindus, seems to be the space within the practice of Hindu ritual that most encompasses a thoroughgoing gynocentrism in the sense that the hypothesized *shakti* of female energy is actually encompassed in practice and in a way in which women can participate. Thus a thread of aspects of the feminine runs throughout Hinduism, moving in and out of the cloth, so to speak, from the more conventional—and somewhat disabling—emphasis on Sita and householdry to the esoteric emphasis on the divine as manifest in erotic worship and also, stirringly enough, in the very fluidity of Hinduism itself with its comparative lack of written rules and regulations for conduct.

Still another aspect of the female as encompassed by the tradition is the pronounced presence of the goddess at the local or village level. Because Hinduism has so frequently proceeded historically by appropriation of more minor and localized deities, the aniconic devotion to the female in various areas is of no small import. Bushes, pots, piles of rocks, and other items may be seen by villagers as sites of the local goddess, whose power is remarkable and for whom propitiation is required.[21] Gavin Flood had opened his extensive commentary on the worship of goddesses within the Hindu tradition with a remark that serves to tie together the many different varieties of local worship, tantrism, and the other manifestations of the female. He writes:

> [T]here is ... a vital Hindu Goddess tradition and many goddesses are worshipped daily throughout South Asia. The innumerable goddesses of local tradition are generally regarded by Hindus as manifestations or aspects of a single Great Goddess or Maha Devi, whose worship may go back to prehistoric times if fifth- or sixth-millennia terracotta figurines are taken to be Goddess images.[22]

In articulating portions of Hindu belief that might be labeled gynocentric, we can do no better, then, than to advert to the continued presence of the goddess at all levels of Hindu worship and thought. The more conventional reference to feminine principles in the devotion to the ideal of Sita, the less conventional in the highly stylized Tantric practice, the tendency of metaphysical speculation to be merged into one great goddess, insofar as the feminine is alluded to—all of these arenas of belief, thought, and practice also come together at the village site. As Flood has noted, the bush, rock pile, or pond that becomes the focal point of devotion for the local goddess is simply one more manifestation of the power of the goddess.[23]

Unlike the Western religions of Judaism, Christianity, and Islam, in which it is sometimes difficult to discern strands of orthodox thought that might be manifestations of a goddess-principle, Hinduism retains such

obvious links to goddess-related origins that setting them out is not a difficult task. If any difficulty attaches to it, it has to do simply with the overwhelming nature of the material. But precisely because areas that might be
deemed to be androcentric and those that might be thought to be gynocentric are in such obvious collision and collusion with each other in Hinduism,
categorization of the two lines is made harder. If Marianist devotion in
Christianity is somehow linked to a goddess-originated line of thought, as
many believe, there is little that contends with it for that title. This is not
the case with respect to Hinduism, where the goddess suffuses virtually all
forms of worship and even some of the most sacred commentary.

An Historical View of Women

Sara Mitter, in her *Dharma's Daughters*, a rich commentary on the situation of women in India today, opens her historical chapters on the role of
women with the by now standard remarks on Aryan waves of immigration
and the status of the indigenous people.[24] But Mitter is careful to note that
what we have discussed here, the goddess and her manifestations, probably
is owed almost entirely to the indigenous groups, and has very little direct
linkage to the invaders. In developing the importance of the concept of
shakti, she ascribes the origins of the goddess to the native peoples of the
subcontinent:

> The myths and sacred rituals of these Aryan tribes, who worshiped sky gods,
> were markedly different from the religious practices of the conquered peoples
> of the Indus Valley. These latter had developed a flourishing agriculture-
> based civilization and venerated an earth goddess, a mother figure symbol-
> ized by the lotus, rather than a patriarchal deity.[25]

Here Mitter provides us with information that we can use—we can
hypothesize, based both on our knowledge of the Indus civilization and of
similar cultures in other regions, that women and women's tasks held a
higher degree of status in these cultures than they later came to hold in some
societies. Without entering into the now hoary dispute about the status of
women in hunting and gathering cultures, we can guess that women performed many of the tasks that enabled life to prosper in the pre-Aryan
cultures, and that this has much to do with the strength of the goddess figure.
Francis Watson makes similar remarks with respect to the Mohenjo-Daro
culture: "The numerous small clay figurines of an earth goddess ... point to
a popular fertility-cult."[26] He also notes that even in the early waves of

Aryan settlement there is little reference to child marriage, and that it would appear that women had a higher status than they were later granted.[27]

If there is one factor to which an analyst might point as crucial in the later declining status of women within the South Asian cultures, it probably has to do with intermarriage. The need to retain a separate, purer Aryan-based culture caused the superstructure of the *varna* system to arise (this makes reference to the ancient division of four groups, somewhat preceding the actual proliferation of castes), and fears of miscegenation probably led to a fairly quick submission of the authority of women in most areas.[28]

We can hypothesize that during the later period of the composition of the Vedas, and particularly of the Upanishads and more philosophically oriented writing (here we can speak roughly of the later centuries BCE and early centuries AD), indigenous manifestations of the power of women began to decline, and many of the trials to which women were later submitted began to increase. In any case, if these changes had not already occurred by the time of the crystallization of the Ramayana (again, dates are fluid, but much of it must have been composed during this period), they became established precisely because of its portrayal of wifely devotion, submission, and finally sacrifice. As Mitter notes, by this time conscious thought must have gone into the precept that the female was the "perpetuator of the clan, the race;"[29] because of this no amount of male abuse heaped on the female in the epics is held to be too great, and no amount of sacrifice on the part of the female, short of death itself, can possibly atone for ritual impurity or transgression of group or caste. In various versions of the *Ramayana*, Sita, after having been captured by the demon, is forced to undergo trial after trial in order to redeem herself. The fact that the capture was not her fault, and that the alleged impurity—even in the text itself—is one of ritual only has little to do with the constant fault that she must bear, a fault that in the Hindu culture will come to be captured in the notion that simply to be born female is to be at fault.

No account of the history of women in India—whether precolonial, colonial, or postcolonial (in any sense of the term)—can be adequate without reference to some of the practices involving women that have become known globally. It probably is helpful to think of the historical origin of these practices as involving mythographies similar to those of Sita, although of course in many cases we cannot know with certainty. *Sati*, or widow immolation (also sometimes spelled *suttee*) is one such practice, and because of the strength of contemporary feminist theory it has come in for comment not only in the standard sense, but also by some feminist theorists who believe that it has mistakenly been appropriated by white or

European feminists in ways that are themselves colonial. Writing of the commentary of the well-known feminist theorist Mary Daly on *sati*, Uma Narayan notes:

> Attention to the sorts of contextual variations in the practice of *sati* that Daly overlooks is important if Western feminist scholars wish to avoid what Marnia Lazreg calls "a ritual" in Western scholarship on Third-World women.[30]

By this Narayan means that failure to use appropriate historical context or sensitivity to caste or social class has too frequently resulted in a "totalizing" picture of Indian women, particularly when such a picture is created to replicate, perhaps unconsciously, the hegemonic stance of Western culture. With this well-taken caveat in mind, it is at least necessary to examine *sati*, not only because of its place in the historiography of the subcontinent, but because it also possesses an interesting place in more standard history. Unknown to many Westerners, those in opposition to *sati* in the nineteenth century within India were frequently high-caste Hindus (albeit those with some Western education). Flood notes that Ram Mohan Roy, a Bengali reformer of the period, had witnessed *sati* as a youngster, and the incident "left a deep impression on the young man."[31]

Perhaps the most important commentary that can be offered on this practice is one that is far from totalizing, but like so much having to do with Sanskrit-derived documents and texts, has to do with the mythological. That the practice existed at all—even if comparatively truncated in duration and in geographic locale—again testifies to the importance of the concept of the divine and of divine-ordered spheres of life in which women are to play certain roles. It is this aspect of the concept that has captured public attention, and so although some commentary may be wrong in details, it may not be so incorrect in its overall orientation.

The point is that as Hindu life became more severely codified, particularly for the higher castes, and after the advent of Islam during the medieval period, many rituals arose that are largely symbolic in nature. Insofar as these rituals involve women, they tend to recapitulate the status of Sita or some other consort within some tale that has been deemed to be worth repeated telling. Indeed, one might theorize that the arrival of Islam was of some import to the lower castes because it tended to pave the way for a somewhat more egalitarian view, even with respect to women in the sense that a similar ritual was not part of Islamic practice. Finally, although Narayan and others are concerned that there may be misunderstandings about the prevalence of *sati* today—it has not occurred regularly since the nineteenth century—it nevertheless is the case that there are a few contemporary incidents, apparently spurred on by the rise in fundamentalism.[32]

As British colonizing persisted after the arrival of the East India Company, some attempts were made to educate Hindu women, and, not surprisingly, some women of the higher castes did in fact achieve levels of education more marked perhaps than those of many European women. Colleges were established for women, and, as we have seen, many such educational institutions were originally constructed in and around Bengal, deriving some of their impetus, no doubt, from the strength of Bengali culture. The force of the British presence was such that colonial colleges were often called "Presidency Colleges," and in Calcutta and other areas these became formidable institutions of learning.[33]

The National Congress and other anticolonial movements of the twentieth century hastened opportunities for some women of some of the higher castes; it certainly is the case that many such women, particularly in the aristocratic circles of the various princely states that preceded independence, achieved a degree of autonomy and freedom comparable to that of many Western women. Elizabeth Bumiller, in *May You Be the Mother of a Hundred Sons*, chronicles the lives of several women artists and painters—Aparna Sen, the well-known film director, was leading a life in Calcutta in the 1940s not unlike that of many of her European counterparts. Bumiller writes:

> Aparna Sen [whose father had founded the Calcutta Film Society in 1947] grew up in a house where the Russian classic *Battleship Potemkin* was shown on the veranda wall after dinner, and where Jean Renoir, the greatest film-maker of his day and the idol of all Bengali intellectuals, came for dinner one evening and asked her, a precocious two-year-old, to sit in his lap.[34]

It should go without saying, however, that such changes among the intelligentsia and the higher castes had virtually nothing to do with the lives of most women, particularly the hundreds of millions of women in rural areas and in villages.

It has always been regarded as a paradox by many that one of India's strongest postindependence leaders has been Indira Gandhi, a woman, but she is merely, so to speak, the daughter of the king. If it is true, as Narayan has claimed, that much of what has been written about the cultures of South Asia by Western feminists is overly simplistic and homogenizing, it is also true that the lives of most women of India for thousands of years have been lives of unspeakable poverty and misery.

Women of Northern India Today

The feminist movement has begun to affect the women of urban areas in India, and even to a limited extent those of nonurban areas, but the paradoxes and tensions involved need to be articulated. Aside from the problems of totalizing theory alluded to at an earlier point, there are simple problems of logistics, and problems of the intermixture of caste and class that make it difficult for women of one group to communicate with each other. It would be no understatement to say that such difficulties are probably not extensively paralleled anywhere in the Western world. Some of the most important work has been economic—in a number of areas, collectives have been established that have enabled women who are in engaged in the cottage industries of spinning and looming to take out their own loans from banks, and to establish themselves as businesswomen, even if on a minor scale.

Because of the nature of Western influence and because of the way in which phenomena that are deemed to be American or European in origin are portrayed in the press, there has still been a tendency in the feminist movements of northern India, in particular, to receive hostile coverage in the press or coverage that still uses the (to American) ears somewhat antiquated language of "bra burners" and "women's libbers."[35] More important, however, is the tension caused by attempts to communicate to women whose caste and class boundaries may make it nearly impossible for them to welcome the well-meaning assistance of other women, be they social workers or simply concerned parties. Mitter, in her analysis of the work being done by women who have tried to forge ahead to create a nascent feminist movement despite such obstacles, provides the following brief portrait of the odds against which a young woman has had to labor:

> Bina said, "Ten years back there was some hostility. We would come to them, ask how are you and that sort of friendly question, and then start talking about their rights, and the strength that would come from alliance. They would think, 'Who is this memsahib? What can she know? Her work is to sit at a chair on a desk. What can she know about us?' "[36]

Both Mitter and Bumiller amply portray the obstacles faced by the comparatively few women who, instead of engaging in some form of socializing, actively try to better the lots of other women. Because much of the feminist movement is best thought of as having Western origins, the tensions caused that might best be analyzed along postcolonial lines are large in number and nearly intractable in nature. Yet Narayan also, in detailing

the extent to which some women have been accused of using nonindige-
nous movements (such as feminism) to promote change, notes the extent
to which technological devices, such as television, are accepted by the same
critics.[37] She also notes that she, having grown up in India, had heard
women complain about their lot throughout her childhood. These women
had not, in general, been exposed to "foreign ideas."

If postcolonial discourse can be used to interrogate categories of feminist
analysis of women, it can also be used to interrogate the status of women
themselves. Akhil Gupta, in his *Postcolonial Developments*, does a superb
job of detailing how, for most women in villages today (the vast majority of
Indian women, of course) the discourse of interrogation of gender and its
place in society has scarcely begun.[38] Thus, it seems fair to say that, outside
of larger cities, the lot of women has shown little change. Indeed, what is
remarkable is the extent to which resistance to foreign/colonial domination
is often cast in terms of how such domination prevents the local patriarchal
structure from fulfilling its original goals of protection, provision for honor,
and so on. All of these goals, of course, involve the retention of women
within the home, prohibit their public discourse, and in general are disrup-
tive of their advancement toward educational goals. In writing of a recent
contretemps over a village election in the Uttar Pradesh region, one of
northern India's largest states, Gupta notes the extent to which the participation of women in an election was crucial, but not in ways that spoke to
advantages accrued to women or to any change in their status. Gupta summarizes the situation:

> Some people claimed that Ram Singh's [a lower-caste man running for elec-
> tion] biggest mistake lay in choosing an agent who did not recognize the
> women from the village. The reason why it was harder to identify women
> was that it was customary for women, especially those from the upper castes,
> to cover their faces when talking to or passing by men, particularly older men
> and outsiders. A man who had grown up in the village could perhaps identify
> all the women by sight, but an outsider had no hope of doing so.[39]

Thus, as Gupta recounts, in this particular election the outcome was
alleged to have occurred through cheating, by use of multiple voting. The
multiple voters were supposed to have been women, who were unknown to
the voting agent because he was insufficiently familiar with the village to
be able to recognize covered women by sight.

Gupta's report on the election, which occurred within the last decade,
helps illuminate the conundrums surrounding the status of women of the

north today. Although it is a certainty that women in large urban areas have at least been exposed to a variety of notions, their lot may or may not have been improved—if, of course, we accept the fundamentally Western notion that part of what might be constitutive of improvement in their lot is in fact better education, better access to health care, and so on. All of this, of course, flies in the face of their lower status within the culture. Although critics such as Narayan and Gupta might not find themselves in agreement on many issues, it is a remarkable fact of postcolonial theorizing that it shows up tensions in a number of areas that turn out, ultimately, to be interlinked. As Narayan and Gupta would probably agree, the discourse of the preservation of Hindu culture very frequently focuses on preserving the status of women within that culture. It does this to a remarkable extent.

Gupta also notes an incident he uncovered in which, during Rajiv Gandhi's tenure as prime minister, grumbling against many of his redistribution projects and the form they took again revolved around gender. Rajiv Gandhi had hoped to institute a return to the *panchayat* system for certain local measures, a system that we can guess he felt safe in broaching since it is traditional within the Hindu culture and since it might, on some level, have signaled a recognition of tradition. But, according to Gupta, at least one critic wrote Rajiv Gandhi a letter maintaining that he, the prime minister, had no right to dictate to others, since he was without a patrilineal line (here the letter writer referred to the obvious fact that Gandhi came to power because he was his mother's son).[40] As Gupta himself notes, "Joshi's [another local village critic of contemporary India] discourse combined 'developmentalism' with patriarchy. His concern was to rescue the manly virtue that 'protects the honor of women,' rather than with the more direct issue of patriarchal violence against women themselves."[41]

All too frequently, discourses and moves designed to protect what might be deemed to be something like traditional Hindu patriarchal culture fall into a space, so to speak, where most of the protection and most of that which is deemed to be traditional has to do with gender and the subordinate status of women. That this is so contemporarily, and is commented upon by a wide variety of authors of different theoretical stripes, is indicative of both the gravity and the long-term intractability of the problem.

If it is the case that, for most of the women of India, there has been comparatively little change or growth for decades or more, it might prove enlightening to offer descriptions of physical activities in which millions of Indian women are involved on a daily basis, to some extent regardless of social origin, since poverty does have some equalizing effect. In *Dharma's Daughters*, Sara Mitter has a chapter titled "Fetchers and Carriers." The point is to underscore the nature of building construction in contemporary India, work that is often carried out (by hand) by hundreds of laborers, many of whom are women, and many of whom have small children—indeed, infants—at the construction site. Mitter writes:

> Six o'clock was quitting time for the labor crews who were constructing, lit-
> erally by hand, multistory extensions of the research institute.... The labor-
> ers were young migrant couples from parched villages in backward areas of
> Maharashtra and its neighboring states. Husbands and wives worked on the
> site, with small children keeping an eye on smaller children nearby. There
> were no hard hats, no cranes, no machinery—just bamboo scaffolding, ropes
> and pulleys, strong backs, and many, many hands.[42]

Literally and metaphorically, the plight described above is a common, everyday one for perhaps most of the women in India. If it is not labor on a construction site, it is some other type of labor, in or out of the home, under similarly arduous conditions and almost always with small children nearby. So far, unfortunately, there is little sign of change for most of India's women. If the future is to fail to resemble the past, it will most likely be because of the force of women themselves, something that the women's movement is now beginning to mobilize.

The Women's Movement in Northern India

Commentators as diverse as Mitter, Narayan, and Bumiller all agree that there is an active women's movement in India, and that it has begun to address a variety of issues, from child care on the type of construction sites just mentioned, to the fundamentalist-inspired recent *satis* and the estab-lishment of small cooperatives.[43] Nevertheless, as has already been remarked, the movement has to deal with a number of issues simultane-ously, not the least of which is the notion that it is an "imported" move-ment that has little to do with the reality of most women's lives, or, indeed, with the cultures of India.[44]

Although there are a number of foci for the movement—the three areas mentioned above are crucial, as is the current battle over amniocentesis—work on two or three may be taken as exemplary. As I will argue in the next section, in many cases women are employing aspects of the culture that are already known and used in other contexts—including aspects that might be deemed to be epistemic, metaphysical, or traditionally mythographical—to try to fight against some of the degradation inherent in the daily life of Indian women. But here the difficulties are enormous; oversimpli-fication is a great risk, and misunderstanding by Western commentators is abundant.

Offshoots of Bharatiya Janat and other similar organizations involved in the powerful Hindu fundamentalist revival of the past decade have frequently been accused of employing the rhetoric of "protecting our women" as a tool for the pursuit of many women-hostile activities. Perhaps few have received as much publicity as the most recent examples of the attempts to revive *sati*—as several commentators have noted, this practice was never as widespread as many have believed, and certainly had indeed virtually died out in the twentieth century.[45]

If *sati* is being held as an exemplary rite by fundamentalists whose intent is to gain power under the somewhat falsified rubric of "restoring the past" and by some Western feminists, it is interesting to note the extent to which Indian feminists have written on this topic. Employing in many cases postcolonial or poststructuralist theory, the intent has been to try to articu-late why *sati* has the symbolic value that it seems to possess for all con-cerned. Nevertheless, more important for our work here is some kind of overview of what, precisely, occurs when feminists attempt to draw atten-tion to the newly instantiated attempts at *sati*, particularly the two that occurred in Rajasthan in the 1980s and that were widely reported in the press.

Most intriguingly, feminists have drawn attention to the fact that the most recent cases, especially the case involving Roop Kanwar in 1988, are nonstandard by any definition. Kanwar's case involved extensive financial analysis, apparently by her late husband's family, and a detailed commen-tary on the intricacies of the financial situation is available.[46] More impor-tant, however, has been the noteworthy argument by some feminists that attempts to draw a parallel between the particulars of this case and other aspects of the lives of Indian women. Although Narayan is in general criti-cal of naive efforts by Western feminists to attempt to tackle problems of Indian women, she does note that:

[A] third feminist strategy can be described as pointing to an array of struc-tural features of the lives of women such as Roop that complicate the idea of what it might mean for Roop, or for any woman like her, to have "chosen" *sati*. As one Rajasthani woman put it, "How many women have the right to decide anything voluntarily? If a woman does not choose her husband and does not decide matters such as her own education or career, how can she choose in a matter as imperative as life or death?"[47]

Since *sati* and dowry burnings are the focus of intense postcolonial commentary by authors both feminist and nonfeminist, continued emphasis on these issues to the exclusion of others probably does a disservice to the women's movement. But at least two or three other areas, as indicated previously—the growth of collectives, the fight against the misuse of procedures such as amniocentesis, and some ecological battles—have also been the site of much feminist movement, and are worthy of extended analysis.

Bumiller notes the extent to which amniocentesis has become a controversial issue, and one that has actually led to legal provisions (although what this could possibly mean in terms of action is unclear). For a variety of reasons not unconnected to the patriarchal structures discussed here—not the least of which, of course, is the mythological status of figures such as Sita—the desire to bear a son is overwhelming in most facets of Indian society, and may very well lead to the abortion of female fetuses in the cases where prospective parents can afford to undergo the procedure. That the procedure represents "gendercide," to use an expression first employed by American feminists, is not unknown to most of the physicians involved in the practice. The use of the tests for sex-selective procedures seems to be particularly common in Maharashtra, Rajasthan, and the Punjab, and in 1988 the state legislature of Maharashtra (where Bombay is located) outlawed them.[48] Although a postcolonial analysis might well question the extent to which similar decisions regarding such procedures are made in developed nations, most analysts agree that this problem is particularly acute in northern India.[49] Bumiller tries to characterize the intersection of technology and intense patriarchy when she writes:

> In fact, Punjab's rich farmland and Maharashtra's industry made the states the two most prosperous in India, and it was a depressing irony that the "sex test" proliferated amid such plenty. Prosperity, as in the case of the *sati* in Rajasthan, had not eliminated old customs but seemed to be promoting them in alarming new ways. If nothing else, the sex-determination tests were a powerful example of what can happen when modern technology collides with the forces of a traditional society.[50]

From a critical or postcolonial standpoint, Bumiller's citation of the *sati* here is certainly not unproblematic, but nevertheless her larger point remains—the "collision" does in fact seem to be occurring in such a way that some of its effects are indeed ramifications of existing women-oppressive structures. That feminists are working on these issues is encouraging, even if in some cases misunderstood by the Western press.

The growth of collectives for women employed in the so-called cottage industries, and other industries as well, is probably one of the most hopeful of the outcomes of contemporary feminist activity. Mitter documents the long struggle of the Self-Employed Women's Association (SEWA), which started out primarily as a group of textile workers, to employ Gandhian principles and to finally break off, to some extent, from its parent organization whose origins go back to the turn of the century. Using grass-roots methods, and under the leadership of many women of lower caste, SEWA has been at the forefront of both the labor and organized women's movements.[51] Sit-ins in Ahmedabad—harkening back to Gandhi's time, and employing his tactics—have been used to negotiate directly with the city, and the establishment of cooperatives for loans and banking purposes has been crucial. Perhaps more so than most major organizations, SEWA genuinely has the support of many women who are not middle class, and this alone makes a difference in contrast to many women's organizations in India. As one young woman phrased it, "In SEWA I have met many different people. I have spoken in public, which I had never done. I was very nervous, but I did it."[52] The combination of skills left over from the colonial "quit India" movement, and genuine anger on the part of many women, some of whom have suffered spousal or familial abandonment, provides the impetus for feminist activity that is truly inspirational and replicable.

The women's movement in India has also intersected with the international environmental movement, and in ways that probably could not have been predicted. What in the United States is now termed "tree hugging" started in northern India with the work of Gaura Devi and a number of other villagers in the town of Reni in the Himalayan area.[53] Here again, as is so frequently the case, women seemed to be able to come to some valuable conclusions about what was worthwhile in their lives without the benefit of outside interference or of male explanation. As Bumiller explains,

> The Chipko Movement ... was born one morning in March 1973, in a remote hill town on the edge of the central Himalayas, when several contractors arrived, on orders from a sporting-goods store, to cut down ten of the village's precious ash trees. The villagers asked the contractors to leave the trees standing.[54]

Devi is said to have remarked early on, "This forest is our mother's home; we will protect it with all our might."[55]

The combination of movements alluded to here—those having to do with the establishment of collectives like SEWA, the awareness of the importance of the recurrence of *sati* (however exaggerated such recurrence may be), the focus on misuse of amniocentesis, and the merging of environmentalist concerns with other concerns of the women's movement—has made for a more powerful growth in the women's movement in India than some may have anticipated. Although Indian feminists have been accused of importing feminism, it is worthwhile to note the strength of indigenous and local factors, especially those of Sanskrit-derived Hindu knowledge-based traditions, in the movement. Because, as has been noted here, so much of the textual material that forms the basis for Hinduism is comparatively noncodified, simple explanations of the relationship between the material and feminist retrievals of it are more difficult to come by than they would be for comparable cases in the West. Nevertheless, the task is one that is more than worthwhile.

Feminist Retrievals of Knowledge Traditions

Despite the difficulties in drawing the distinctions, there are several areas of epistemic categorization or knowledge-related traditions to which advertence can be made in discussing contemporary feminist movements in India. These include the renouncer tradition, various versions of the story of Sita, the strength of the underlying *atman/Brahman* ontology and its epistemological ramifications, and a number of intersections with the *satyagraha* movement originally associated with Gandhi. It is important to note both that, in some cases, use of the tradition may be more metaphorical/subconscious than conscious, and also that, however straightforwardly the elements of the tradition may be employed, women's use of them almost always constitutes a reappropriation of traditional materials that were never intended to be used by women. Thus, categorizing in the terms more commonly used in the West and with which Western feminists are familiar, androcentric and transcendental facets of the tradition may be employed for gynocentric purposes.

The renouncer tradition is one stage of a lifelong process that is codified in the Vedas and that is central to most orthoprax Hindu teaching.[56] The paradigmatic Hindu is, of course, male, and his life may encompass, according to the teachings, four stages: birth and initiation into the culture; growth to maturity; maturity and the stage of "householder"; and finally (in an idealized description), "renouncer," that is, one who turns his back on the ways of the world. In the most literal sense this has always meant, of course, that the renouncer leaves society, and India is indeed today home to many—mainly males, but with a few females—who have become ascetics.

As Flood notes, "This renunciation of action could be achieved through asceticism (*tapas*) and meditation."[57] Formal renunciation does, of course, mean the leaving of the household and the withdrawal from society, but there are variations on a theme, and much of the activism that is currently taking place in Indian society involves reappropriation of this tradition of worldly renunciation for new purposes. This is not new, and to some extent reinscribes the tradition in which Gandhi himself was involved, as we shall see. But what is new is the extent to which this tradition is being used for women's aims and feminist purposes.

Ela Bhatt, the founder and originator of much of SEWA, is described by Bumiller as "an unlikely revolutionary. Small, shy and unobtrusive, she was a fifty-five-year old woman with a little girl's voice who dressed simply in handspun cotton saris."[58] Ela is not literally a renouncer, of course; rather, she is making use of the Hindu tradition of rejecting the material and the worldly to further women's aims. This is particularly remarkable given that this tradition, even when appropriated for more socially conscious purposes (and hence less purely orthodox) has most closely been identified with males.[59]

Along with the renouncer tradition comes the importance of the role of Sita as one who has learned to take the tasks of daily devotion and service to new heights. This, of course, is not a tradition that encourages the female toward the special higher knowledge that is most appropriately the analogue of nonempirical knowledge in the Western tradition. Rather, this view is the one (according to many) most responsible for traditional service by Hindu women, since it would seem to enjoin women to keep their place. However, it is intriguing to note that there is more than one version to the portions of the Ramayana that are centrally devoted to Sita, and hence more than one interpretation of her story. Although there are dangers associated with the need to read Hindu culture as still (in the present) responsible for "women going up in flames," as Narayan puts it, the fact that both the *sati* and even the dowry burnings have strong associations with the trial of Sita is probably not accidental.[60] Mitter gives this twist on Sita's story:

[There is an episode] appended to the story at a later date. It recounts how, after some time, Rama again—through personal doubts or to staunch [sic] real or imagined rumors—banishes the now pregnant Sita to a distant forest. There again she lives simply and meekly and raises her twin sons. Only after seeing the children does Rama wish to have Sita repeat the ordeal by fire, to lay all doubts incontrovertibly to rest. But here Sita draws the line: one trial by fire is enough.[61]

It might well be said that contemporary activists who are working on cases such as the Roop Kanwar episode (the late 1980s *sati* in Rajasthan) and the dowry burnings, however misunderstood these might be by Western cultures, are drawing on this part of the Sita tradition. There is a strong analogue here—Hindu women prove their devotion to their families on a daily basis. Even the sacred literature, as demonstrated above, recognizes this fact. In refusing to tolerate the new wave of Hindu fundamentalist activity that emphasizes the fire, there has been a reappropriation of the portion of the Sita story that refuses the ordeal.

Interestingly enough, some of the most forceful retrieval of elements of the culture that speak to matters both ontological and epistemic is probably related to the ecofeminist movements, many of which trace their ancestry at least partially to the Chipko movement mentioned earlier. Vandana Shiva and others have written of the retrieval of the notion that respect for matter (*prakriti*) is part of the overall respect for the ontological structure of things manifest in the *atman/Brahman* distinction.[62] When the activists at Chipko refused to let the trees be cut, they were retrieving that part of the tradition that enjoins respect for matter as still another part of the larger monistic scheme of things, in the same way that consciousness is. In the Western tradition, we might roughly liken this split to Spinoza's monism, in which he says that the divine contains an infinite number of essences, but the two with which humans are familiar are matter and consciousness. Flood asserts in his commentary on *prakriti* that there are categories "which are ontologically distinct from each other and from matter *prakriti* [but] are nevertheless related to the absolute (*brahman*) and share in its being, as sparks share in the being of a fire or a son is related to his father."[63] When Gaura Devi said, "This forest is our mother's home," she was only articulating the underlying monism that supports Hindu practice, and that can be gotten at epistemically by a respect for *prakriti* manifest in one's daily activities.[64]

The notions of retrieval from a cultural base are fascinating, and show up in unexpected and unusual places. Even a commentator like Gayatri Chakravorty Spivak—concerned as she is to provide us with literary and cultural analyses that derive from contemporary French theory—has mentioned possible analogues in her work on the subaltern studies group of Great Britain. Although Spivak is largely motivated to show how modernism might be said to coopt traditional views, she notes, in commenting on some of the work done by those in the studies group, "Gandhi's initial dynamic transaction with the discursive field of the Hindu religious Imaginary had to be travestied in order that his ethics of resistance could be displaced into the sign-system of bourgeois politics."[65] While Spivak's postmodern analysis may not be of much help in placing Gandhi within the tradition, the extent to which Bhatt and others have used similar tactics is, of course, related to their retrieval of that which Gandhi had employed—the discursive field of Hinduism.

Flood and others continually emphasize that Hinduism is largely a matter of practice, ritual, and instantiated beliefs. Unlike the so-called Western religions, Hinduism has no one body of scripture to which one can point. But in its traditions of the renouncer, the reliance on mythography such as that of Sita, its statedly monistic metaphysics and concomitant epistemology, it provides a large resource from which contemporary feminist epistemologies can begin to fashion modes of operation.

Recapitulating the Northern Indian View

A recapitulation of the material covered here with respect to feminist epistemics in the global vein and the cultures of Northern India gives us important points in a number of areas. If we have postcolonial concerns—and we must—at least the northern Indian, Sanskrit-derived cultures are probably closer analogues, in some ways, to aspects of the European cultures than other cultural constructs might be. Linguistically, the Indo-Aryan families reinforce each other, and traceable roots for many terms can be found. More saliently, it is not only the terminology that is helpful to us—key aspects of the worldview are sufficiently familiar that here we can, with alacrity, draw parallels.

Historically speaking, the philosophical views of India in general met with sympathy and something approximating understanding when the views first became translated and popularized in nineteenth-century Europe. We know, for example, that Schopenhauer was influenced by translations of the Upanishads, and as we have seen from Zimmer's commentary and from the amount of work done on the various logic systems, the ontological cuttings of the Sanskrit philosophies are not dissimilar to those of the Western world.

The problem, then, is to articulate some of the retrievals of these views that might be made by feminists without promulgating or reinforcing the colonial stance. To phrase it bluntly, this is not only difficult; it may well be impossible. As was discussed, earlier representation of another culture and attempts to draw parallels are, by necessity, already hegemonic. Perhaps the most that can be done is to raise one's awareness of the hegemony, and to be ready to address it as an issue. Chandra Mohanty is often cited in this regard, and she has phrased the problem succinctly when she writes:

In the context of the West's hegemonic position today ... Western feminist
scholarship on the third world must be seen and examined precisely in terms
of its inscriptions in these particular relations of power and struggle. There is,
it should be evident, no universal patriarchal framework which this scholarship attempts to counter and resist—unless one posits an international male
conspiracy or a monolithic, ahistorical power structure.[66]

Mohanty goes on to warn against the oversimplification and misuse of
Western feminist scholarship as it alludes to Third World issues, and she
specifically says, "Western feminist scholarship cannot avoid the challenge
of situating itself and examining its role in such a global economic and
political framework."[67] The conundrum here, of course, is that the situation
demands that one address it. That is, feminists from around the globe—
including the industrialized and European countries—can either choose to
work on issues of interest to women around the world, or they can deem
themselves unfit to work on such projects by virtue of their having been
participants in the hegemonic structure.

It would seem that some sort of considerations having to with justice and
distribution virtually demand that feminists continue to address a variety
of issues. These considerations may very well derive from the European tradition, but that is, in a sense, inescapable. Thus, as we have seen in this chapter, it is possible and certainly informative to view feminist work in a
variety of contexts as drawing, directly or indirectly, on epistemic and
metaphysical constructs within a culture and as reappropriating those constructs. Some of these appropriations may be more indirect, some more
direct, and yet, in many cases, strong linkages to the original constructs as
employed in the traditions may be shown.

Vandana Shiva, who along with several other theorists is one of the
founders of ecofeminism, has written, "Wherever women acted against ecological destruction or/and the threat of atomic annihilation, they immediately became aware of the connection between patriarchal violence against
women, other people and nature."[68] Whether we view such awareness as
stemming, in the United States and Great Britain, for example, from a tradition that goes back to Mary Astell, Damaris Masham, and beyond, or
whether we see it as a reappropriation of the monism described by most
commentators on the Hindu tradition as being fundamental to the belief
system, we are trying to draw links between the work of women in various
cultures, places, and times. On balance, given the world in which we live, it
is probably better to try to draw such links than to fail to draw them.

Finally, we can close with another examination of the extent to which the historiography of Hinduism in the West has, in many cases, been a comparison of Hindu writings and doctrine with those of the ancients, meaning, of course, the ancient Greeks and Romans. If, as was mentioned earlier in this chapter, Flood has felt free to claim that Hinduism is a "male discourse,"[69] it is also remarkable how often this male discourse has been perceived in terms of what has been deemed classical in the Western tradition.

If we can discern elements of androcentrism in the *Bhagavad Gita* (and coarse elements are easy to discern, with its warrior metaphors and constant reference to battle), then it is also an engrossing task to notice how often, in a standard translation and its introduction, reference is made to the ancients. Juan Mascaró, writing in the introduction to a standard Penguin edition often used for teaching, begins the comparison almost immediately, within the first two pages. Among other construals, he writes:

> Sanskrit literature is a great literature. We have the great songs of the Vedas.... There are, however, two great branches of literature not found in Sanskrit. There is no history and there is no tragedy; there is no Herodotus or Thucydides; and there is no Aeschylus or Sophocles or Euripides.[70]

Mascaró's introduction—similar to many, of course—gives new meaning to the term "postcolonial." The strength and force of European culture means that not only is it the case that today Sanskrit literature must be judged by this Western yardstick, but that, more important, this is the measure by which it was judged when first encountered by Europeans and first translated.

Thus it is not possible to escape the inevitable comparisons between Western thought and Sanskrit-derived Hindu thought, particularly when we remember that, in this particular case, the comparisons may well be more apt than they would be to say, Yoruba thought of the Nigeria region, because of the relationships between the languages and because of the age of the written Sanskrit culture.[71] But each comparison makes us reflect on the need for commentary—as Narayan, Mohanty, and others have argued, the work done by the Western feminist must inevitably be tainted with the preexisting hegemony, and there does not seem to be a way out of the dilemma.

If there can be no happy resolution, perhaps the brightest hope is to remember, as we have mentioned here, that in many cases women working within Third World cultures have to some extent begun the task of articulating what their reappropriation of a given doctrine amounts to. When Vandana Shiva writes of treatment of *"prakriti,"* she is drawing on beliefs that are already subsumed under this very tradition of scholarship, colonial or hegemonic, that we have examined.[72] Beliefs that are deeply embedded in the practices of a culture—and this is, of course, the case with Hinduism, since commentators are unanimous in indicating its lack of cohesiveness in a theoretical or nonpractical vein—are frequently held at the edge of consciousness and just as frequently scarcely articulated. Yet again with respect to some of these beliefs we find something amounting to unanimity of commentary, both with respect to Hindu and European writers.

We began our chapter with a reference to the monism of classical Hindu thought, and with a reference to the extent to which it might be deemed to be addressing philosophical questions in a way that is fairly strongly analogous to the manner in which they have been addressed in our inevitable standard, Western culture. Juan Mascaró notes:

> From nature outside in the Vedas, man goes in the Upanishads into his own inner nature; and from the many he goes to the ONE. We find in the Upanishads the great questions of man, and their answer is summed up in two words: BRAHMAN and *ATMAN*.[73]

Mascaró glosses this as comments on the "great questions of man," because he feels that any attempt to talk about the ultimate nature of things is, in finality, a human attempt. Perhaps the task for us is to remember the human attempt in which we are engaged, and to become aware, also, of the necessity of placing that attempt in a feminist framework, given the fact that more than half of the world's population is women.

Chapter 3

Dravidian India and Its Cultures

The differences in the Dravidian cultures, their languages (the government of India recognizes four principal languages—Tamil, Malayalam, Telugu, and Kannada), and their forms of worship, have impressed commentators from the first time that Europeans began to visit India.

From the beginning, the Dravidian cultures of the south struck European observers as being more closely related to what they took to be the original cultures of the south Asian subcontinent, and the darker-skinned peoples seemed to observers to be more closely related to "aboriginals." The first major translators of Sanskrit, based on their readings of the texts and their observations, came to similar conclusions.[1] Thus a tradition of commentary sprang up in the European countries in which the south of India, with its comparative lack of invasions and comparatively small number of Muslims, began to stand for Hindu "purity," and also for a number of customs that spoke to—or so the observers guessed— pre-Aryan activities and traditions.

It is clear, in any case, that the languages of the south bear no linguistic relationship to Hindi or its cousins, that the peoples of the south possess different phenotypes from those of the north, and that forms of art and architecture differ markedly.[2]

Perhaps some of the force of the differing analyses of these complex geographical areas is best exemplified in the commentary of Heinrich Zimmer, the noted German scholar whose work was first translated into English by Joseph Campbell, but whose work was done in the earlier part of this century. Zimmer is careful, in his observations, to delimit portions of the traditional Hindu worldview that he believes were derived from or owe their origin to Dravidian systems. A typical gloss by Zimmer on the importance of these beliefs is given in the following excision, wherein an analysis is provided of the origin of the notion of kingship in India:

As we know from the tombs of ancient Sumer and of Egypt, kings of the archaic period of the fourth to second millenniums B.C. were regarded as incarnate gods. This was the period, in India, of the Dravidian civilization. The principle of divine kingship survived into later Indian history in the genealogies of the non-Aryan royal houses, where descent was traced from the Sun God and from the Moon God.[3]

Here, as is so frequent in commentary that involves the Dravidian cultures, what is older is regarded as having sprung from their beliefs and worldviews, and what appears to the historian to be more contemporary or certainly not as old is frequently regarded as being of Aryan origin.

In any case, Zimmer and many of the other commentators agree on broad basics. Many of the goddess-related beliefs found in the Hindu culture, broadly speaking, seem to owe more to the Dravidian views, and certain other interesting metaphysical and ontological categorizations can be broadly carved out. Zimmer, for instance (in keeping with much of the analysis that we have already done) sees the Dravidian metaphysics as being more avowedly dualistic, in that a sharp separation is made between spirit and matter. Thus the later, classical monism that we can see in the *Upanishads*—a monism that many European commentators found moving, and that apparently inspired at least some European philosophers—is supposed to be a development that reflects the Aryan invasion.[4] If we can think of monism (and certainly monotheism, which is present, obviously, in Islam but not in Hinduism in any standardized sort of way) as being the type of belief that Western commentators would regard as an "advance," then we can see how much that was regarded as "older" is often seen—or so the story goes—in the Dravidian cultures, and thus becomes the basis for various sorts of linkages that may or may not be strongly empirically confirmed.

In any case, Flood, Zimmer, and many other commentators are in agreement on these basic principles of organization with respect to Hinduism, and their systems of categorization are fruitful for the feminist theorist, since much of what drives a remaining gynocentric strand in Hindu thought can be traced, according to most commentators, to the pre-Aryan groupings. If the feminist can make something, for example, of the older notions of *prakriti* and its dualistic opposite, *purusa*, then the Dravidian cultures can be brought into play here.[5]

In general, the areas of what is today Karnataka, Tamil Nadu, Kerala, and Andhra Pradesh are hypothesized to retain older elements of culture, and because of this there is a tendency among the commentators to shove under the rubric "Dravidian" any aspect of contemporary Hindu culture that seems either to be non-Aryan or to harken back to a culture as old as, for example, the Mohenjo Daro site (although the latter was not located in a nearby region). Flood notes the disparities in the accounts of what the distinctions between Aryan and Dravidian mean when he makes it clear that not every scholar accepts the thesis that much of contemporary Hinduism did not originate in the south Asian subcontinent. With respect to this contretemps, he writes:

> The origins of Hinduism lie in two ancient cultural complexes, the Indus valley civilization which flourished from 2500 BCE to about 1500 BCE, though its roots are much earlier, and the Aryan culture which developed during the second millennium BCE. There is some controversy regarding the relationship between these two cultures. The traditional view ... is that the Indus valley civilization declined.... The alternative view is that Aryan culture is a development from the Indus valley civilization and was not introduced by outside invaders or migrants.[6]

Flood asserts that both competing hypotheses have evidence for their support, and in the long run the notion of one hypothesis being correct may not be an important one. A point that is worthwhile for our project, however, is that much of what might be deemed to be less masculinist or less androcentric in Hindu thought almost invariably is tagged by the commentators as being a product of pre-Aryan thinking. Whatever the degree of accuracy of this line of explanation, it is worth noting, because the goddess tradition, various *naga* cults, the importance of Shaivism or Shiva devotion, and other such phenomena are linked to the Dravidian worldviews.

Still another area of endeavor in which scholars are inclined to make the division has to do with the entire nature of Hindu or Sanskrit-derived philosophical thought. Since the Sanskrit-based languages are manifestly different, it is probably safe to say that the origin is indeed outside South Asia. But it is not the origin of the languages that is so important—again, it is the philosophical thought that finds expression in the classical works composed in the various languages. The Sangam texts (Tamil and pre-Tamil) of the extreme south of India are, according to Kulke and Rothermund, filled with vivid descriptions of the "uninhibited life in the early capitals of South Indian rulers," yet the authors of these same texts required the stimulation of contact with the more northern Mauryas at a later point to develop the notion of large-scale state administration.[7]

In any case, whatever the origins of various components of the Hindu culture, certain facts are fairly much beyond dispute. The south, because of its comparative isolation from the waves of invaders, retains a kind of purity in its culture, at least from the standpoint of contact with, for example, Islam. This is no small point, since the north has had a great deal of mixing between the two cultures. What the Dravidian cultures have to offer that is distinctive from the standpoint of feminist inquiry is a worldview that has, according to many, still greater room for gynocentric principles.

Masculinism and Its Concomitants

Insofar as anything like the androcentrism or masculinism of certain portions of philosophical thought may be found in these cultures, we can again see strands of such thought in the written philosophical texts. Here again, we inevitably must rely upon commentators whose Eurocentrism is well known, and, of course, one runs the risk of overgeneralizing and failing to make points in a way that might leave them amenable to the criticisms of postcolonial analysis.

Nevertheless, although the Dravidian views are, according to most thinkers, more classically dualistic and less concerned with the overarching monism of later Hindu thought, the very fact that the texts approach questions in a recognizably philosophical way—from the standpoint, of course, of Western thought—lends them to much fine-grained analysis. As is the case with many settled agriculture, patriarchal societies with a priestly class, the early Tamil culture had already developed many of the features of stratification typical of such cultures. Kulke and Rothermund note the age of older Tamil grammars and epic poems: "The famous Tamil grammar, *Tolkapiyyam*, is considered to . . . date back to 100 BC, . . . and the great Tamil epic poem, *Shilappatikaram* . . . perhaps even to the fifth or sixth centuries AD."[8]

In other words, to reiterate, south Indian written traditions—very much resembling those of the later, more nomadic cultures—had already begun before the Christian era. The combination of a long written tradition and other features gives impetus to our analysis, and helps demonstrate precisely what the masculinist or androcentric features of the Dravidian cultures are.

In a piece on feminist method, Sandra Harding provides an inverted analysis of masculinism when she writes, "Feminist researchers use just about any and all of the methods . . . that traditional androcentric researchers have used. Of course, precisely how they carry out these methods of evidence-gathering is often strikingly different."[9] What she goes on to note is that the feminist researcher listens to women's voices and sees how women's lives are conceptualized. Her quotation gives us food for thought, for both the structure of the written cultures of Dravidian origin and other features of their social lives reveal the masculinism inherent in the societies, an androcentrism so obvious that many social scientists of a variety of backgrounds would be able to see it.

As we have seen, the Tamil culture in its older guises not only gave way to strong kingdoms of the premedieval Hindu south, such as the Chola, but to patterns of worship that themselves altered the substance of Hinduism for the more northern invaders. In her informative work on symbolism in Brahmin women's rites of passage, Vasumathi Duvvury notes, "At marriage, the gift of a virgin daughter (*kanyadan*) is said to absolve her father of the sin of begetting a daughter and to transfer the onus to his son-in-law.... It is believed that a Brahmin wife becomes assimilated through her husband and can attain salvation only through her devotion to him."[10]

Although these beliefs are common throughout Hindu society, the flatness of Duvvury's statement of them is remarkable, and underscores the tensions that we have seen previously between postmodern/postcolonial accounts of ethnography done on Indian cultures and accounts given by the informants themselves, for Duvvury is herself from the region in question (Tamil Nadu and parts of Andhra Pradesh). In any case, she authored her ethnographic work precisely because she felt that many ceremonies involving female participants in the Tamil culture were not being documented—such ceremonies are commonly held to be beneath the level of those that require the presence of a Hindu male religious authority or priest, and hence such ceremonies are often deemed to be not "serious."[11]

Since Tamil is the root language from which the other Dravidian tongues are said to have spread, documented evidence of what took place in the ancient Tamil culture leading to today is extremely important.[12] How far the notion of masculinist/androcentric biases in cultures, particularly those with written traditions, can be carried in a cross-cultural vein is a subject of much current debate. But there is reason to think, even among those whose academic specialty is myth and religious worship, that strong androcentric trends persist in almost all human cultures and can be documented.[13] Wendy Doniger and others have held that there are such common themes in human mythology and that they are cross-cultural.[14] In any case, much of the work being done now by women ethnographers in the Dravidian regions helps to establish the notion that, although masculinist tendencies may manifest themselves slightly differently in the south, they are present in abundance.

Just as the ancient Tamil philosophical thought explained the universe in terms of two principles, rather than one, we can see a range of masculinism in the social structure of the ancient societies when we look at the history of the region. The Tamil-speaking Cholas engaged in extensive commerce, and much of the commerce, especially that along the Malabar coast, long precedes the arrival of anyone from the northern cultures. In addition—as is widely reported, both anecdotally and otherwise—many people in India believe that the actual story of the *Ramayana*, particularly the parts detailing Rama's travels and his assistance by monkeys and other forest creatures, is the story of the Aryan invasion of the south and of Aryan conquests with the assistance of the indigenous Dravidians. It is noteworthy that, except for Sita, the leading characters in the tale are all male, and if this story is indeed a myth of origins, it has much to tell us not only about androcentrism within the cultures but about the various configurations of power between Aryan conquerors and Dravidian hostages. No matter how the conquest of the south is described, it is noteworthy that most observers see the mixing as exactly that—a cultural mix in which Dravidian peoples also gave something to Aryan conquerors. What they gave is itself intriguing, and can provide the focus of further analysis of trends that may not always in themselves represent androcentrism.

In general, then, the ancient Tamil-based cultures of the south already possessed similar degrees of literacy and of literary and philosophical traditions as the Sanskrit-related cultures of the north, and from a comparatively early point in time. The strength of these systems is attested to not only by their longevity and the impact that they made on the northern invaders, but by the force of their artwork, work that struck the British at the time of colonialism and in some sense had an even more pronounced effect than some of the work to be found in the north.

Specific aspects of Dravidian symbolism, already alluded to here and encompassing perhaps more attention to the world of flora and fauna and such specific icons as *nagas* (serpents) bear intense analysis and will be examined at a later point. If a strong generalization may be made, the cultures of the south in general retained more focus on goddess worship and a greater degree of pacificity than the cultures of the north. Flood repeatedly makes this point, as we have seen, when he mentions that much of the local goddess iconography in India is that of the local village goddess, and a good deal of that is found in the south.[15] That distinctions may readily be made between the cultures of northern and southern India without forcing the issue is itself testimony to the endurance of the Dravidian languages and their related cultural bases. Contemporary work done by women investigators is helping us to see precisely what might be constitutive of gynocentric or women-centered views within the culture. Insofar as the Dravidian cultures are concerned, there is much that warrants investigation.

Searching for the Gynocentric

As has been noted, there are several features of the Tamil-related cultural groups that stand out as having more relevance to the goddess principle and gynocentrism. Aside from the ubiquitous goddess herself, it is clear that more attention is paid in the south to local deities that on a symbolic level have much to do with fertility cults. Because the *naga* has a special status—shrines to *nagas* exist throughout southern India, and in some areas there is a tradition of feeding cobras and other snakes—we will examine their iconography later. In addition, as has been mentioned, the southern cultures have been widely held to be less martial (the *kshatriya* or warrior tradition is more closely associated with the north), and the original metaphysical views of the Tamil-based philosophies are, according to Zimmer and others, more dualistic and less monistic. The dualism is, in itself, probably related to the female-centered principles, and hence there is much in these cultures to flesh out a notion of respect for the feminine.

Particularly strong in the south is the tradition of local village goddesses who are associated with various phenomena, such as the once dread smallpox. Flood gives us a strong interpretation of the importance of such a deity when he writes:

> Although sometimes barely distinguishable, the ferocious village goddesses have a name and and specific location.... For example, in Kerala the particularly terrible goddess Muvalamkulica mundi is worshipped in a number of local shrines, the *teyyam* shrines, and along with other deities is celebrated in local, annual, dance-possession festivals.[16]

Flood notes that there are myths, particularly in the south, about the visitations of the smallpox goddess, and some of these myths are as heavily codified as some of the more classical myths with which we are familiar.

Serpents are crucially important in most human mythologies, but they take on a paramount importance in India, populated as it is with many poisonous snakes. In villages, the bite of such a snake can be fatal within a short period of time, and the importance of the *nagas* (in some cases, portrayed as half-human, half-serpent demigods) attests not only to the mythographical representation of the serpent within the local culture, but, more important, a respect for nature in general. It is this amalgamation of respect for the natural with an infusion of the divine that represents perhaps the most important manifestation of the feminine and life-affirming principles in the Dravidian cultures. The *naga* figure is so important that it passed over into Buddhism; the idea here is that the *naga*, being closer to the water and the earth, represents some form of divine knowledge. Metaphysically and epistemically, however, an important statement is being made when it is believed that this earth-bound spirit is knowing and wise. Far from the rarefied realms of the other beings, the *nagas* possess a special wisdom, and the fact that this wisdom is revered, particularly in the south, has a crucial importance.

Another feature of the Dravidian cultures that speaks to the issues with which we are concerned is the specific strength and utilization of the notion of *shakti* within these cultures. Again, although this notion is prevalent throughout India insofar as Hinduism is concerned, it seems to be agreed by a number of commentators that the concept of *shakti*, as embodied in the everyday traditions of women, is stronger in the south and, particularly, in the Tamil regions. Writing in an anthology titled *The Powers of Tamil Women*, the anthropologist Margaret Egnor notes:

> [I]f women have more *sakti* than men, this is ... because women stand in the position of servants with respect to men.... Viewed from this perspective, the concept of *sakti* appears to be closely linked to the strong anti-authoritarian populist streak in Tamil culture.[17]

In other words, there is a tradition of *shakti* that is particularly strong in the south of India, and it is not unrelated to other Dravidian institutions. More important, for our purposes, this particular version of what might be dubbed "the *shakti* concept" is one that cuts deep into the heart of Hinduism, because here the notion of *shakti* is fleshed out as a power derived from suffering and servitude. It is not unlike some Christian notions of spiritual strength derived through mortification, and indeed the parallels are made by many ethnographers writing on the subject. Margaret Egnor, in her fascinating study, provides biographical notes on the lives of five women informants who believe that *shakti* has had an effect on their lives, and as she herself notes, in the three cases wherein the woman is known in local circles for having the "power," it generally has to do with the instantiation of goddess-power in the woman's life through the particular suffering (frequently at the hands of men) that she has endured.[18]

A tangle of notions that might be deemed to be gynocentric in focus presents itself, then, for our perusal when examining the Dravidian world of the south. As Egnor and Duvvury both note, these concepts may very well have a stronger base in the south because of its own peculiar history and its comparative lack of contact with the north. (It is interesting to note that the state of Tamil Nadu comprises the very southern tip of India, the Cape Comorin area.) Egnor asserts, "It is clear that in Tamilnadu the woman is regarded as the power that holds the family together,"[19] and Duvvury states that "south India continues to be a strong preserver of Vedic tradition."[20] These features of the Dravidian cultures are important because they form the base for the appropriation of a number of cultural concepts, metaphysical, epistemic, and in some cases ethical/aesthetic, by women at key points in cultural narratives and in contemporary life.

In constructing a gloss on the notion of the gynocentric, Western feminists have often turned to the work of developmental psychologists, and the frequency with which the names of Dorothy Dinnerstein, Nancy Chodorow, and others appear can scarcely be overstated. But for our purposes, particularly with respect to the women of Tamil Nadu and the surrounding region, recent work on feminist philosophy of the arts and feminist aesthetics by Western feminists may prove instructive. Insofar as it can be argued—and the point has been made here earlier—that it is widely believed that the cultures of the south of India retain a greater degree of commonality with what is usually termed "indigenous" culture, a great deal of contemporary work in feminist aesthetics can help flesh out our contentions about women in Dravidian societies.

In the essay "A Gynecentric Aesthetic," the feminist philosopher Renee Lorraine writes about misunderstandings caused by the use of terms such as "matriarchal," "matrifocal," and "matrilineal."[21] Her point is that it is not terribly important whether there ever were, in fact, societies in which women "ruled"—evidence, of course, suggests that on a strict interpretation of the term, there have been no such societies. But just as the developmental theorists tell us of different voices throughout human cultures—voices that may be associated with care and nurturance, rather than conquest and domination, the use of the above terms to describe societies helps inform us of differing social structures. Lorraine writes:

It is believed that prehistoric peoples, who may not have understood the relationship between coitus and childbirth, reacted to female sexuality with awe.... [Thus, a gynecentric aesthetic may be] characteristic of a nonauthoritarian culture where the status of women is high. Notably, there is anthropological evidence to suggest that [some nonsettled agriculture cultures] also are non-authoritarian or egalitarian and tend to value rather than disparage women and female things.[22]

It does not seem recondite, then, to consider what may very well be the case, historically, with the Dravidian region of India. For a variety of reasons having to do with differing language families, geographical isolation, and intensity of cultural constructs, this region may have preserved a view of life that is a great deal more gynocentric in orientation than that of many other cultures, Indian or not.

Susan Wadley, in the title essay of the book that she has edited on Tamil women and their powers, states that it may very well be the case that we can see the women of the south in a somewhat different light from the women of the north. She claims that the Tamils allege that women have powers that need to be controlled, and she adds that "this concern for control ... is what differentiates, in part, the Tamil woman from her North Indian counterpart."[23] Given her training as an anthropologist, she goes on to talk of kinship systems and the like, indicating that a degree of inter-marriage is permitted in the south that is unusual in the north.

Whatever the explanation, commentators like Duvvury, Egnor, and Susan Wadley agree that the Tamil-derived cultures of the south (and all of the cultures of the region employ languages that are related to Tamil and of which Tamil is the chief variant) contain strong markers of the female and of ancient feminine principles. This provides a rich and fertile ground for the anthropologist, sociologist, and psychologist, and also provides such a ground for the feminist philosopher, for we can attempt to draw out, philosophically, the areas of the culture that have to do with knowledge acquisition and how women have made use of these particular instruments.

An Historical Trajectory

As has been indicated, the overall history of the south is one of mainte-nance of more indigenous strands of culture and comparative lack of influence from the northern invaders (that does not, of course, mean no influence). As we have seen earlier, a great deal of trade was carried on, particularly along the Malabar coast, but the trade seems to have been relatively pacific in nature, and the strength of warrior castes or warlike groups in the south is comparatively unmarked.

Duvvury, like other commentators, notes the comparatively late arrival of the Vedic culture in the south, but she also asserts that the Vedic rituals, once instantiated, became closely guarded. Because so many of the rituals have to do with female purity, women historically have had a (as Wadley phrases it) "paradoxical" status—they may be even more carefully guarded and watched than in the north, but this is because the south, historically, retains a belief in their strength. Duvvury's anthropological work is on Aiyar women of the Tamil Nadu and Andrha Pradesh areas, and she provides the following explanation for their group name:

> "Aiyar" is the Tamil corrupt form of Aryar or Aryan. In the *Tolkapiyyam*, the earliest and most comprehensive treatise extant on Tamil grammar, the sages or *rishis* who first introduced the various *samskaras* to the Dravidian people of South India are referred to as Aiyars and even now Brahmins are distinguished by the honorific "Aiyar" in Tamil Nadu.[24]

Very shortly after this explanatory passage, Duvvury comments on the status of women within the culture, particularly the Aiyar women. Citing the laws of Manu, she writes, "After marriage, a wife is said to become one with her husband's personality.... Men and women are considered to be complementary to each other and the wife is said to be the *ardhangini* (half-body) of her husband."[25] Again, more so than in the north, it may still be important to attempt to keep the rules literally, since there is comparatively little outside influence to bear and also—and this turns out to be very important—since part of what distinguishes the Dravidian areas culturally is their own interpretation of the Vedic rules. (Indeed, this may well be what has driven the upsurge of Dravidian political groups and even some attempts at independence movements.)

If women have been seen as vessels of purity, they have also been seen historically to possess great powers, a phenomenon that was examined in the preceding section. Yet the history of women in India cannot be separated from colonial history, for it has also been the case that much of what has transpired for women in the economic and professional areas has been related to preindependence attempts on the part of the British to "better" the lot of women in general, to form women's educational institutions, and so forth.

Postcolonial analyses of the British at work, in combination with the efforts of some Indians, have tended to focus on how the British construction of "mistreatment" of women furthered their own ends, specifically those that had judged India as unfit for independence and Indians in general as unable to rule. A number of commentators have cited the extensive documentation that bears out these claims. The tensions revolving around the status of women in India, historically speaking, are probably best exemplified in the early twentieth century by the controversies surrounding Katherine Mayo's publication of *Mother India*, a work filled with anti-Indian detail, much of it revolving around marital or sexual matters. As Kumari Jayawardena has written in her work on the role of white women in the construction of colonial analyses of Indian cultures, "Particularly insulting was Mayo's declaration that Indians were not fit for self-government because of their terrible oppression of women."[26] But while a combination of efforts to draw attention to *sati*, a practice that was more or less moribund during that period, child marriage, and general repression tended to push analysis in one direction, other factors, particularly in the south, continued the level of commentary that Tamil women were especially in touch with their *shakti*, and that they had their own modes of coping. In one of the long-term colonial twists and borrowings that has so frequently occurred in history, some of this material actually made its way into the Western view in a positive sense, since, as Jayawardena has documented, it is precisely the notions of androgyny and goddess-related notions that drove at least some Western women to admire and praise what they perceived to be the culture of India.[27]

As both Duvvury and the essayists in the Wadley volume note, greater respect for women's power in the Tamil-based cultures has frequently resulted in greater restrictions placed on some aspects of women's behavior, and also in greater attention paid throughout the culture to matters of fertility and so forth, even where some of that attention might seem to focus on male sexuality. Because of the prevalence of the notion of the divinity and his consort, any attention paid to the consort is itself an awareness of the strength of the female side of the equation. The respect paid to Shiva is especially strong in the south, and as has been asserted earlier, this respect not only yielded the Chola culture with its tremendous bronzes—the original dancing Shivas—but also gave rise to a number of iconic devotionals to Shiva that, again, linking God to goddess, as it were, are related to *shakti*. Even a more traditional commentator such as Basham is struck by this, and he presented a gloss on the importance of Shiva in the south, which is not unrelated to the southern respect for *shakti*:

But Shiva was and still is especially worshipped in the form of the linga, usually a short cylindrical pillar with rounded top, which is the survival of a cult older than Indian civilization itself. Phalli have been found in the

Harappa remains. Early Tamil literature refers to the setting up of ritual posts, which seem to have been phallic emblems.[28]

Thus we have still one more piece of evidence of the holdover of views that might be deemed to be more traditional, views that when combined with Dravidian notions of female power present a powerful influence in the culture at large.

Duvvury and other commentators also note that the construction of temples throughout the south, which was given impetus by the strains of Aryanization that proceeded in that direction, was also made more consonant with goddess worship in the Dravidian language areas than in the north. In a striking cultural combination, the purity of Vedic culture combined with these older Dravidian strands in very specific forms; Duvvury specifically mentions the temple at Kanyakumaram, the "Land's End" of India, which she cites as historically having been associated with "the Virgin goddess" and the "dwelling place of *shakti*."[29]

Historically speaking, the marriage models in the Tamil-derived cultures have also been more infused with the senses of special powers derived from *shakti* and consort energy, and the anthropologist Sheryl Daniel has written on the importance of obtaining balance within a marriage, given the distributions of power. Again, these ideas seem to be more deeply embedded in the culture of the south. The notions of special obligations in Tamil marriages are derived, Daniel has written, from a belief that "the consequences of appropriate and inappropriate actions are also conceptualized in terms of substantial equilibrium or disequilibrium."[30] Given the peculiar history of the south, the lack of overt contact with the more aggressive cultures of the north, the focus on metaphysical dualism in the south and the reoccurrence of forms of worship, such as that of the *nagas*, that are clearly related to nature and to some concept of harmony with nature, it is not surprising that the history of women in the southern cultures has been one of various forms of codification of their power—a simultaneous awareness of it and a desire to harness it.

Because colonial influence was not as strong in the south, the more modernizing tendencies represented by the various colonial colleges were muted to some extent, thus leading to twentieth-century political movements in which women might be said to have had proportionately less overt power, in a European sense, than was the case in the north. Nevertheless, it is important to note that there were, of course, women's institutions established in Tamil regions, and that some of these became very successful. Because of the strength of Tamil culture in what is today Sri Lanka, some of the first work was done in that area, and then it was easy to form links with the south of India. Writing in the *The White Woman's Other Burden*, Kumari Jayawardena notes that many European women were active in the south and that educational establishments for women were created in that region. She tells of the early work done by Dr. Mary Rutnam:

> Dr. Rutnam not only worked in the field of gynecology all her life but also pioneered numerous women's groups including the Ceylon Women's Union (1904), the Tamil Women's Union (1906). The next decade produced the first batch of graduates from Uduvil [a Tamil school], the first university graduate being Daisy Anketell.... She received a B.A. from Women's Christian College, Madras, in 1923.[31]

All in all, an historical turn toward the women of the south must both make note of the fact that the southern regional cultures historically speaking placed greater emphasis on *shakti* and women's power in general, while at the same time the comparative lack of colonial strength in the south gave the Tamil-derived cultures there own mode of functioning. Yet the paradoxical strength of women in this cultural context has, as Wadley and other investigators noted, resulted in many cases of public abnegation for women. Although this situation exists throughout India, we might be on sure ground in saying that it is fully developed and at its peak in the south.

Contemporary Women of the South

In the work *Environment, Development and the Gender Gap*, Sandhya Venkateswaran notes that, as might be expected, technology has had an impact on the women of Kerala, the Malayalam-speaking region of the south that has been noted during the twentieth century for its comparatively high levels of education. Venkateswaran writes, with respect to mechanization:

> Technological interventions have affected women in many ways, but seldom worked toward improving the quality of their lives.... Women, thus, either continue to perform repetitive, low-skilled jobs or are displaced even from such arduous tasks which because of their very nature are easily mechanized.[32]

In a similar work, titled *Kerala's Demographic Transition*, the social scientists K. C. Zachariah and S. Irudaya Rajan assert that "Kerala has been the focus of international attention for its success in several key areas including education, health and family planning. . . . The state has achieved international fame for its success in controlling deaths, especially infant deaths and unwanted births."[33] In some ways, regions of the south appear to be ahead of the rest of India, except perhaps for areas such as the Punjab, in terms of economic development and the infrastructure hallmarks that characterize stable economic growth.

But again, as one might expect, the picture for women is confused and diluted. While on the one hand certain areas of the four main southern states (Tamil Nadu, Kerala, Karnataka, and Andhra Pradesh) experience economic stability and comparatively high levels of education, the region is also marked by disparate phenomena such as a high reported level of female infanticide and use of amniocentesis to determine the sex of the fetus. In addition, although Dravidian political parties have been on the move in the south for quite some time, and as this is written are in the process of reforming alliances with such nationalist and fundamentalist parties as Bharatiya Janata, it has only been comparatively recently that women have held positions of power in these parties.[34]

It may very well be that the position of women in the Dravidian regions today is directly related to the phenomena already examined here, and noted by Wadley, Egnor, and others. The strong Tamil-based beliefs in *shakti* may make it easier for women to assume some roles, but once again the roles seem to be those that involve a moral strength gained through subservience. Thus it is no surprise that Bumiller, for example, in attempting to document the rise in cases of infanticide or abortion due to sex of the baby/fetus, found many areas in the south where such practices were known to be occurring on a regular basis, despite the fact that some of the areas she visited were not located near major cities.

While noting that the landscape near Belukkurichi, in Tamil Nadu, appeared much less harsh than in the north, and that even the villagers had a different, "gentler" appearance than many of those that she encountered in Uttar Pradesh, Bumiller found that the practice of infanticide and exposure of female infants was well established in this region, and that many of the midwives she interviewed were already aware of the common nature of the practice.

Working with a friend employed in rural development, Jaya Gokulamani, Bumiller writes:

Jaya has a whole network of contacts among families and health workers in the area, and through them we were tipped off to couples who had put their daughters "to sleep." Belukkurichi was about one hundred miles from the area in Tamil Nadu that *India Today* officials had investigated for the "Born to Die" story. Officials at child welfare agencies in Madras told me they had heard rumors of infanticide in the area around Belukkurichi, but they did not expect anyone to admit to it.[35]

Interestingly enough, as Bumiller attempts to investigate some of these stories, she finds that parents are willing to talk. As one young woman said of the death of her infant daughter, "It was better to save her from a lifetime of suffering."[36]

The status of women in the south of India may be related, in some ways, to the movements against the British that form the major portion of the historical backdrop in the early part of this century. As has been mentioned, the independence movements were centered in the north, although that is not to say that the south did not participate. But the Dravidian areas had their own concerns, and initially they were more concerned about the British leaving, or "quitting" India, than they were about independence itself. The reasons for this had to do with the long-term resentment of the south against the north, and of the north's having positioned itself as the repository of Aryan values.

Indeed, at an early point in the twentieth century, movements in Tamil-speaking areas began to try to ensure either that the British stayed, or that, at the very least, if they did leave, the south would be guaranteed its own independence. Robert L. Hardgrave Jr. writes that, in 1916, "Soon after the formation of the south Indian People's Association ... Chetty ... issued 'The Non-Brahmin Manifesto,' surveying the conditions of the non-Brahmin community and pointing out the directions for advancement."[37] The point of the movement was to try to associate all things nonoppressive and non-Brahmin with the south (although, of course, there most likely was something akin to a caste system before Aryanization) and hence with indigenous cultures. As so often happens when cultures try to assert themselves, the position of women becomes a site for debate and resuscitation of the culture. Hence anything having to do with women in the south—historical variations of *shakti* or otherwise—tended to become entrenched.

It is interesting to note, then, that with the tensions in the position of women today, stronger perhaps in some ways than those of women in other given regions, weaker perhaps in others, some of the first historical notations of the British on the situation of women in the south are compelling. One Englishwoman, on visiting areas of the south, wrote that she had reached "a strange country [where] husbands seem to be only appendages."[38]

This mixture of power and powerlessness seems to characterize much of the perception of the south today insofar as women are concerned. Writing of the Tamil epic *The Lay of the Anklet*, Mitter notes that "Every woman ... [can release] the *shakti* that dwells within her."[39] But Egnor, for instance, writing from material given to her by informants during her field work, says of her informant Chandra,

> The hardest time for Chandra is the monthly three days of menstrual seclusion, during which period she is confined to a small area and is not allowed to bathe or to do her ordinary household work. She also must avoid her son at this time, and he causes her great embarrassment by chasing her around trying to touch her, and asking what will happen to him if he does. Both mother and son end up angry and in tears after these confrontations.[40]

Nevertheless one can point to the fact that, of course, in Madras still another women's organization exists, the Working Women's Forum, founded by Jaya Arunachalam in 1978 to assist craftswomen by providing loans, and, as this is written, the actress Jayalalitha has become one of the most potent forces in Indian politics, since she is in the process of switching her alliance's votes from the BJP to Congress.[41]

Thus an overview of the status of women today reveals that phenomena similar to those of the north are in play, in that there is a tendency to try to define a "culture" in terms of the roles played by the women within that culture. The postcolonial and postmodern analyses have frequently noted the extent to which this is the case, and the parallel phenomenon of the male arbiters of the culture not being in the least fazed by the incoming of elements that benefit them and their projects, no matter how "nontraditional" such elements might be. That this phenomenon is as ubiquitous as it is may speak more to certain global threads of female conditions than to any other particular factor. Nevertheless, it is noteworthy that a great deal of what the Dravidian areas can still point to as their own in an increasingly commodity-driven and technologically adept India does, in fact, have to do with the status of women. The intoxicating combination of the historical view of women, already described here, and the various machinations against the north, and then the north and the British in tandem at an earlier point in the century, have conspired to make the status of women in the south a focal point of cultural contention.

If the status of women in the south somehow seems to smack of paradox even more than it does for the women of the north, it must be remembered that the overwhelming numbers of women in India are leading not only traditional lives, but lives that are traditional perhaps beyond most Western understanding. Most women in India are not only of the peasant and land-less groups—village women—but are illiterate or semiliterate at best, and in the south, access to "modernist" movements is largely relegated to the com-paratively small proportion who know English, since Hindi is not, despite government efforts, truly a national language. Unless a young woman of the south knows some English or happens to have relatives who have been exposed to outside ideas, her knowledge of the external world is greatly restricted. And yet that knowledge can, in some instances, be used for empowerment. It speaks well of the contemporary movements for women in India today that, no matter what their origins, almost all realize that the reality of women's lives is in some sense beyond simple description.

Feminism in the South

Although all of the factors mentioned above—the tendency for publications issued from the north to be in Hindi, the greater adherence to traditions of the south, the lack of access to English (which is, in a sense, truly India's national language) for those with little education—conspire to make the lives of Dravidian women still more tradition bound, change is taking place.

Manushi, the women's magazine with what might be deemed a feminist slant, has done a great deal of reporting on the responses of women in the south to the national awareness of dowry-related crimes and violence against women in general.[42] Although postcolonial voices have been quite right to point out that much of what Western women (and even some Western-educated Indian women) see as problematic in Indian women's lives probably reflects the hegemony of Western feminist discourse, some have also pointed out that many of the same problems have been alluded to by Indian women themselves, in many cases by those without formal edu-cation. As Narayan has said, she first heard of difficulties in the lives of women of India from the women themselves, in her own childhood.[43]

In any case, one of the most interesting phenomena with regard to self-reports by women of Karnataka and Tamil Nadu in the pages of *Manushi* is the extent to which they articulate, albeit unknowingly, some of the very difficulties and tensions that have been noticed by others.

The editors of the magazine acknowledge from the outset that "an over-whelming number of people in India, about 80 percent, live in rural areas.... Therefore, if we wish to talk of the continuing struggle of Indian women, we have to pay attention to the everyday life of these women."[44] One correspondent, a northerner, stated, "Now we must refuse to be Sitas," but she appeared to speak for many, as the pages devoted to the struggles of southern women testify.[45]

One of the most intriguing aspects of the reporting by southern women, especially in Tamil Nadu, is the extent to which the women's movement has both borrowed from, and in some cases been adversely affected by, the doctrines of the Communist Party of India (ML).[46] Many Dravidian women have become active in the movement initially because male family members chose to be active, and then a dawning realization of the relationship between women's difficulties and general issues of poverty and caste discrimination helped them becomes still more active. An issue of *Manushi* printed in 1982 and cited in the anthology contains the following:

> [Ananthanayaki] learnt a lot during prison life. She started reading newspapers and then some Marxist literature. It was in prison that, for the first time in her life, she learnt something about the "naxalites" [Marxist activists] and the ideals they pursued. She became convinced of the need to mobilize the toiling masses and to organize them into a mighty force which will sweep away the dirt and muck of our society.[47]

The intense interest in Marxism often goes hand in hand with other incidents that serve to awaken. Vijay Agnew, writing in *Women's Studies International Forum*, has perhaps given the best gloss on the intersection between Western theory and women's movement or feminist work in India, one that is especially helpful in writing about the south because much of the movement in the south has some ties with communist movements. Agnew notes that the "response [of Indian feminists to Western movements] is in part informed by discourses from Western nations, both from mainstream feminists and from critics of the mainstream."[48] In other words, unraveling the complex tangle of the impact of all sorts of Western theory—both feminist and nonfeminist—on India (northern or southern) is difficult, and may not even be possible. Although much of the theory can aptly be described using that favorite postcolonial term, "hegemonic," there is no question that aspects of the theory have been liberatory.

The women's movement work of the south is particularly difficult to analyze in any sort of theoretical terms, precisely because, as we have seen here, it is widely believed that the status of women in the south is different, both because of the history of the notion of *shakti* as a powerful notion within the culture, and because of the presence of at least a few matrifocal groups whose existence in the region, historically, very much predates any Aryanization. (These groups exist throughout India and are frequently referred to by the Indian government and others as "tribes.") One note-worthy feature of the movement in Tamil-derived regions is the extent to which it frequently emerges spontaneously in response to individualized, local events that then take on a larger meaning. Whereas the existence of organizations, centers and so forth in the north is well documented and may correspond more closely to the structure of some women's movements in industrialized nations, many of the offshoots of the movement in the south appear to be the developments of incidents reported in local regions. Under the heading "Beaten for Cultivating Her Own Land in Karnataka," the editors of the *Manushi* anthology tell of the efforts of a low-caste woman in Karnataka state to exercise her legal property rights. This incident is picked up by the Karnataka Dalit group, meaning that a protest group for the "scheduled castes" (low-caste and "untouchable" people) decided to take on her case. The story is told in this way:

> One morning while she was working on the land [which she had tried to reclaim], she was attacked by eight or ten goondas [thugs]. They took her to the centre of the village and tied her up to the pole. Some villagers tried to protest but were ignored.... The activists of Karnataka Dalit Sangharsh Samiti heard of the atrocity and decided to struggle around the issue.[49]

Because much of the work in south India is tied to other political movements, there has been an even greater urgency in asking whether such groups, tactics, and organizations can count as "feminist." Agnew has noted the importance of this question when she admits that many of the political movements that involve women and have to do with women's rights are "mass-based peasant movements," or in some cases involve organizations "which pointedly do not recognize themselves as feminist."[50]

There are, then, at least two areas of conundrum in the women's or feminist movements of the south that can be distinguished from those of the north. Precisely because these movements may tend to be more homegrown, they may directly or indirectly advert to the *shakti* tradition, but in doing so they make reference to a tradition that is already paradoxical, since as we have seen from the work done by Wadley and by Egnor, this tradition may very well define itself through the notion of overcoming by suffering. Then again, because the colonial presence in every sense was less strong in the Tamil regions than in the north, the kinds of Western-derived women's organizations that grew up in Bombay or Calcutta are found, historically speaking, in smaller numbers in the south, and thus any movement that has to do with women's causes is more likely to be tied to other movements, political or religious. Although the Dravidian political organizations are devoted to separatist notions, the very fact that they have become so powerful in national politics again affords women an arena in which to exercise some sort of power, however lacking in overt feminist structure it may seem.[51] Part of what is reflected here is simply the difference between southern and northern regional styles, a difference that is reflected in the women's movement as it is manifested in virtually every other area of Indian life. But the combination of an indigenous tradition devoted to the notion of women's power (of whatever type) and a comparative lack of colonial institutions is a heady one, and makes for an unusual combination of forces with respect to the women's movement and other feminist institutions.

Although many women's collectives and organizations for self-employment are located in the north, some are based in the south, and here, too, regional differences persist. Such collectives, sometimes working hand-in-hand with SEWA, or sometimes with agencies affiliated with the United Nations, such as its Food and Agricultural Organization, are at work in Kerala, Tamil Nadu, and Andhra Pradesh in ways that reflect the localities of women's work in these areas. Leslie Calman writes of one such organization in the south, devoted to fish marketing:

> In 1981, the United Nations Food and Agricultural Organization invited WWF [Working Women's Forum] to create a fish marketing project in Adirampattanam, a village on the coast of Tamil Nadu. As of 1984, this Working Women's Credit Society was granting low-interest credit to some 1500 women, who could for the first time be free of the middlemen who had until then dominated the market.[52]

For each of these collectives, individual and group action must be taken to reappropriate elements of local traditions, however androcentric initially, for women's purposes. Calman also cites a lacemakers' collective in Andhra Pradesh that obtained a 50 percent increase in earnings simply by eliminating the middlemen who had previously taken a very large portion of the money that would ordinarily have accrued to the women workers.[53] It is no small statement to make to assert that women of the south, long accustomed to thinking of *shakti* as a force that is generated by their suffering at the hands of men, may have come to see *shakti* in a new light.

Reappropriating the Tradition

As we have seen at earlier points, the Tamil tradition is as old as, if not older than, much of the literature of the north, and certain portions of the literature, such as "The Lay of the Anklet," have achieved a renown on a par with the other, northern Hindu epics. But if we attempt to point to specifics of the southern ontological and metaphysical traditions, as manifested in their literature, several elements appear. The worship of Shiva is stronger in the south, and according to some—especially given the presence of the bronzes from the Chola dynasty usually titled "Shiva Nataraj"—is crucial to a definition of the region.[54] In addition, the south contains a tradition of bardic verse and a strong tradition of incorporation of indigenous elements having to do with local flora and fauna in worship; hence, the specific temples and sites devoted to *nagas* and *naginis*. Speaking metaphysically, the female element appears to be still stronger in the south, and the association of water, growth, life, and power appears throughout the forms of worship. Thus the emphasis on *shakti*, which is, of course, in a sense a pan-Hindu concept, is heightened by other aspects of the Tamil-derived cultures that emphasize the male/female duality inherent in all things. In keeping with this emphasis on matter, reappropriation of power in the Tamil traditions seems to be more closely related to the power inherent in worldly things and somewhat less closely related to the notion of transcendence. Thus, epistemically, the knowledge derived comes less from an *atmanic* quest toward the *Brahman* than from the energy of *prakriti* itself and the fusion with it, which is, of course, easier for the female to maintain.

The duality of the notion of submission in order to attain knowledge or a grasp of the whole is best summarized in the various glosses on the importance of Shiva in the southern cultures. Although Coomaraswamy has often been faulted for his colonialism (and his rampant Eurocentrism), his comments on Shiva let us come to grips with certain important concepts in the characterization of the cosmic dance. These conceptualizations are crucial to southern culture.

> The images, then, represent Shiva dancing, having four hands, with braided and jewelled hair, of which the lower locks are whirling in the dance. In his hair may be seen a wreathing cobra, a skull.... In his right ear he wears a man's earring, a woman's in the left; ... What then is the meaning of Shiva's Nadanta dance ... ? Its essential significance is given in texts such as the following: "Our Lord is the Dancer, who, like the heat latent in firewood, diffuses his power in mind and matter, and makes them dance in their turn."[55]

Shiva is a potent figure precisely because the androgyny of the figure represents some fundamental understanding of the ways in which the life forces of the universe are manifested in our concepts of male and female.

Whatever title we give to Shiva's consort—Uma, Parvati, Durga, Kali—it is clear that she is, in some sense, simply his other half, and simply one more manifestation of himself. Thus Shaivism speaks to the metaphysically complex, and insofar as it is possible, from an epistemic standpoint, to enter into the ontological complexities, work of retrieval has already begun.

Although the more complex alembications of Hindu metaphysics usually distinguish between the "six systems" and the later theorizing of the nineteenth-century revivalists, including Vivekananda, whose work became known to the colonials and hence internationally, all of the schools are related, and differ mainly in their construction of the relationship of matter to reality.[56] The south Indian traditions began as sets of principles that were more intensely dualistic—Zimmer, for one, as we have seen, counts the dualistic Jainism as an offshoot of southern belief—and hence the distinction between *prakriti* and *purusha* (or personal soul) may be an important one in varieties of this tradition. Thus Shaivism, with its emphasis on androgyny, and the importance of *shakti*, make for a fertile ground with respect to epistemic retrieval in the Tamil-related areas. As in the Cartesian system, *purusha* and *prakriti* can interact in ways that are energizing for *purusha*, even if that interaction cannot be explained.[57]

Still another portion of the southern tradition that is ripe for retrieval and that has a relationship to both metaphysics and epistemology is that portion of the tradition that is folk related. The combination of the emphasis on folk poetry and music and the strength of the remaining indigenous cultures of the south gives this tradition a powerful impetus. Commentators write of the early Tamil literary efforts as being "near to the life of the people" and "realistic"; the folk tradition is strong here.

Because of a long strain of populism, the combination of the metaphysics/epistemology of the dualistic systems and an emphasis on ordinary life create a situation in which those women—frequently from the lower castes—who seem to be filled with *shakti* are actually able to accomplish much. In many cases, such women have become revered not only at the village level but in a larger political framework. In the 1980s one of the most famous cases of women involved in protest against police brutality and rape of women while in custody occurred in Andhra Pradesh, where local women sparked a large protest movement.[58] As Egnor says in her analysis of a number of Tamil women who have been deemed to have greater *shakti*,

The power acquired through suffering and servitude is a special case of the Hindu theory of *tapas*, whereby through certain forms of self-denial (called *tapas*), the individual accumulates a certain internal heat (also called *tapas*).... If the accumulated power of suffering is great enough, the rebellion may be successful.[59]

The strength of this view is seen not only in the day-to-day actions of women in their home and village but, as we have seen, may be transferred to a larger scope. Epistemically, the woman has access to a certain knowledge about relationships between form and matter derived from the cleansing that comes to her from suffering and from the "heat" or matter-changes that the suffering catalyzes. As Egnor also says, "Viewed from this perspective, the concept of *sakti* appears to be closely linked to the strong anti-authoritarian populist streak in Tamil culture (such as may be found in bhakti poetry)."[60]

It is perhaps for reasons related to these that the art of the Tamil regions, particularly the classical art of both the Cholas and the rock carvings at Mahabalipuram, teems with a life and vigor even more pronounced than that of the north, and makes strong use of animal motifs, and in particular the striking—to the Westerner—motif of the *naga*. This serpent deity, sometimes portrayed as half-human, half-serpent, and sometimes as simply a magnificent, hooded serpent, symbolizes the power of the watery realm, a certain sort of wisdom, and, of course (thinking in larger mythographical terms), the realm of the feminine and inaccessible.[61]

There are shrines to *nagas* throughout the south, and in some villages and towns actual cobras are induced to come to feeding places, and revered in the same mythological manner. On a global mythological analysis, the importance of the serpent as the realm of the feminine in opposition to the various air of sky deities and demigods cannot be overestimated. Although the *naga* figure appears to some extent all over India, it is much more common in the south, and the number of shrines devoted to it is much larger in regions of Andhra Pradesh and Tamil Nadu. At some of these shrines, elaborate stone carvings of *nagas* are placed around the entrance to the shrine, in many cases with varying details indicating the level of attention and craft that has gone into the carving. The wisdom of the *naga* stems precisely from its association with the underground, the earth and the water—in short, the realm of the feminine and female constructs. The special wisdom of the *naga* is available for those who understand its importance and who are willing to pay attention to it.

In sum, the combination of the special status of *shakti*, the preexisting populism of the Tamil regions, the different take on the metaphysical/epistemic posed by the Shaivite tradition and the emphasis on indigenous forms of worship illustrated by the *naga* shrines helps to create a refreshing tradition of feminist retrieval. The Tamil-derived cultures themselves serve as springboards for future feminist and woman-friendly theorizing.

An Overview of the Dravidian Regions

Duvvury and Wadley, both trained anthropologists, have chosen to write about "Tamil women's rites of passage" and the "powers of Tamil women" because, as social scientists and investigators, they were struck by the extra-ordinary status of women in Tamil societies.[62] Although this is not a rare happenstance—as indicated here previously, similar remarks have been made about the cultures of West Africa, for example—it is indicative of differences between the northern and southern regions of India.[63]

At the outset of the chapter, we noted the patterns of trade growth and contact for the south, and the extent to which they relied on contact with other cultures, especially along the western seaboard are, the region that is today Kerala. Because of the mountainous regions in the middle of India, and because of sea trading patterns, it might well be said that the southern portions of the subcontinent had more contact with cultures outside of the subcontinent than they did with, for example, the Aryan invaders, for a lengthy period of time.

The congruence of these factors with an independent Tamil literature—itself having pronounced differences, in terms of "populism" and "lay ballads" from the literature associated with a Sanskrit base—led to regional differences that we have categorized throughout this chapter.[64] Although the androcentric quest for a "final answer" when philosophizing was by no means nonexistent in the Tamil tradition (and although it resulted in a slightly different version of that answer, especially in the early parts of the tradition that asserted a strong metaphysical dualism), the continued emphasis on the elements of the feminine, both from the standpoint of iconography and from the standpoint of the *prakriti* portion of the dualistic view, pushed the culture in a different direction. Hence the grounding of *shakti* as a dominant force in the culture provides a basis for what may truly be deemed a special epistemic status for the woman knower: the woman who empowers herself through the sacrifice and self-lessness of *shakti* is in touch with the divine source of *atman/Brahman* as it manifests itself in our bodily matter and in each individual *purusha*, or personified form.

Oddly enough, the influx of Aryan forms of worship seemed only to consolidate some of the indigenous forms, especially among the masses. It is for this reason that, as Robert Hardgrave points out, strong populist political movements were already afoot in the south at the turn of the century. This particular juxtaposition has resulted in a number of small, folk-oriented movements that are either led by women or that have women as revered figures. Even the women interviewed by Egnor—lower-caste women, in almost all cases—were the recipients of a kind of local respect for the empowerment that they had received after endurance of perilous hardship.

Thus the openly political feminist movements of the south, perhaps more so than is the case in the north, are sensitive to the needs of, for example, fisherwomen and carriers.[65] Whereas portions of the women's movement in the north have tended toward "kitty parties" and get-togethers of women from the better-off groups, several incidents involving demonstrations against police conduct in the south have been sparked by mistreatment of lower-caste and outcaste women. As has been noted, the combination of the political tradition, embodied currently in a number of parties, the largest and most active of which is probably the DKM, and other local traditions constitutes a heady brew, and, as this is written, various national-level coalitions are having difficulties reconstituting themselves because of the force of the Dravidian parties.[66]

As seems to happen so frequently on a global basis, the northern/southern split in India seems to reconstruct various differences of power and prestige that actually predate colonizing and may have their origins in cultural differences that predate written artifacts. Whatever the ultimate source of the differences, it is noteworthy that the persistence of the differences not only makes southern India, according to many visitors, a singularly attractive region, but also makes it an especially fertile ground for social science investigation into the relationship of mythologies to local organizational structures, the forces of kinship in anthropological family accounts, and so forth.

The Dravidian cultures not only have a history, with which we have already become acquainted, but the intense focus on poetry and written works of the early Tamil-language cultures provides us with a worldview that, as has been analyzed here, is distinctly different from that of the north. Visitors to Kerala, for example, are often struck by the presence of an old Jewish community in Cochin.[67] But this community, rare as it may seem, given that it is located on the Malabar coast of India, is but one example of a number of visits and interactions between the south and other, non–South Asian cultures, over a period of time. Each of these transactions left its mark, and these exchanges, plus the comparatively small strength of Islam in the south, have made for a completely different region.

In writing about *shakti*, Susan Wadley and the other anthropologists whose work is the focus of her monograph have taken the time to spell out the importance of *shakti* for everyone who lives in the south, and not just for the female inhabitants.[68] Male informants regularly told her and other social scientists of the importance of women in the Dravidian regions and of the powers they were supposed to possess. But as the researchers noted, much of the power that is exhibited comes from a sort of withstanding, a sort of abnegation, a sort of withholding—it is a power of overcoming, which then has the potential to transform itself into something else. Wadley probably sums up this power best (a power which is, of course, also found in the north, perhaps to a lesser extent) when she writes:

> This female generative force is fundamental to all action, to all being in the Hindu universe. The goddess, as *shakti*, as *devi*, as the *amman* of South India or as one of her more concrete manifestations, such as Durga, Kali, Parvati or Laksmi, provides a backdrop that is fundamental to understanding Hindu women, their status, roles and powers![69]

Wadley tells us something very important here—the roles of the goddess provide us with philosophical tools to analyze both women's oppression and possible paths out of that oppression. Thus when we remember the greater relationship between *prakriti* and the female role, and when we understand not only the greater attention paid to all goddesses in the south, but also the origins of transformational Shaivism in the south and in the classical Chola culture, we can see that women possess a closer ontological connection to the dualistic split. Because women are closer to matter on this view, they can achieve a greater force when they harness this particular energy.

The philosophical differences between the early southern cultures and the later (especially nineteenth-century) Hindu revival, with its overarching focus on the transcendental and its palpable monism are seldom discussed in the literature, although Zimmer and Flood allude to these differences.[70] But the upshot for theorizing is that, on a large view, the traditional southern cultures—at least in their priestly articulations—are less androcentric, and this matrifocality is apparent throughout the culture. It may be the case that other differences (such as the comparative lack of contact with British institutions during the colonial period) keep some of the feminist growth that might have taken place from developing a more recognizably Western form, such as clearly happened in the north, but on the whole the powers of women are more obvious in the southern cultures.

As we have seen from the material given to us by *Manushi*, movements springing up throughout the south not only provide impetus for future feminist theorizing but alter women's day-to-day lives.[71] But women have stories to tell throughout India, and we have focused at earlier points on the strength of Bengal and the classical Bengali writing forms. This culture, both the Hindu and Islamicized parts, eventually gave way to the Bengal of the partition, and, finally to Bangladesh. We will next visit the women of that contemporary Bengal state.

Chapter 4

Bangladesh and Islam

The Islamic state of Bangladesh is one of the many creations of the British empire. The partition of India had left the subcontinent with two nations, Pakistan and India, and Pakistan, implausibly enough, was divided into two parts. The eastern part comprised roughly half of the former Bengal, and was completely different culturally and linguistically from the western part, taken from the former Punjab. What joined the two parts was a sort of Islam, and yet all agreed that, by temperament, the Bengalis displayed an attitude toward Islam different from that of their western counterparts.

Today the former eastern Pakistan is the state of Bangladesh, having won its independent status in a war that drew massive international outpourings of aid in 1971. As Akbar Ahmed has noted, "[The war] fed into the international image of Pakistan as a brutal military power oppressing its own people. India orchestrated the campaign. Global sympathy was created for the Bengali cause. Even the Beatles performed for them."[1]

Today the culture of Bangladesh is a rich mix of Bengali pride and nationalism (itself a mixture of the influence of the British on the Bengali Hindus, felt also to some extent by the Muslims), Islam, and the remnants of certain political organizations, many of which go back to the Raj. Despite its poverty and its relatively large population—hundreds of millions live in an area the size of one of the midwestern states in the United States—Bangladesh has performed one remarkable feat: it has caused an international reputation for programs aimed at reducing rural poverty, and particularly programs aimed at women.[2]

Although in general Bangladesh has been spared the fundamentalist Muslim agitation that, in its turn, is now helping to create fundamentalist Hinduism in India, Islam was, of course, crucial in the formation of its identity as a state, and was originally the glue that held the state of Pakistan

together. Although India had at one point, before the partition, seen clashes
between Shi'a and Sunni Muslims, and although such clashes have, to some
extent, continued in what is now Pakistan,[3] the largely Sunni Bangladesh
has, in general, been free of such troubles. It has not, however, been free of
droughts, floods, typhoons, and drownings of entire villages and their populations. This, plus the overwhelming crowding and population density (to
be found, to be sure, in its neighbors, but probably not to quite the extent
that these factors are found in Bangladesh) has made life in Bangladesh
since its independence far from easy.

Islam, perhaps the most misunderstood of the world's major religions in
the West, is an intensely monotheistic belief system with a strong emphasis on justice, morality, piety, and compassion.[4] The lack of representational
images in the artwork of Islam has likely contributed to the confusion in
non-Islamic circles; with the exception of Judaism, other major religions
generally do possess such images, and they may become a focal point of
worship. (This is, of course, a major point of separation in the rituals of the
Hindu and Islamic systems.) In addition, although Islam demands little in
the way of male/female separation that is not asked of the adherents of
other systems, again such as Judaism or Hinduism, this has also become a
focal point of commentary in the West. It may well be that the comment on
this topic has reached the level that it has achieved largely because this feature, combined with the lack of representational images, provides something that can be discussed in terms familiar to Westerners.

In any case, it is difficult to sort out, in contemporary Bangladesh, the
influence of what might be termed religion on the one hand and a large
variety of cultural forces, including Bengali nationalism, left over from previous times. Originally, some thought had been given to having two independent Islamic states at the time of partition—Mohammed Ali Jinnah, the
political spokesperson for India's Muslims, had understood that the varying cultures of the Punjabi and Bengali regions did not provide much of a
common bond for the formation of an Islamic nation.[5] Nevertheless, such a
nation was created, and the ethnic and regional hostilities began immediately. As is generally known in political circles, by the time of Bangladesh's
war for independence, there were rumors circulating that it was a moral
duty for Punjabi soldiers from the western part of the state to rape and
impregnate Bengali women.[6]

The long tradition of Bengali literacy meant that, although the Hindu
population may have been the main beneficiary of some of the educational
changes that were instituted by the British, all Bengalis, Hindu or Muslim,
to some extent identified with the Bengali cultural tradition and its inter-

nationally renowned proponents, such as Rabindranath Tagore. Thus, except for a very few prominent families that speak Urdu, even the wealthier Muslim families of Bengal have traditionally spoken Bengali, and hence a sense of Bengali national pride (or, more properly, "Bangla" national pride) has been a leading feature of life in the region and in the formation of Bangladesh.

The Islamic life of Bangladesh has also been noted by many observers to be of a somewhat different type from that of many Islamic nations, and certainly from that of West Pakistan, or what is today simply Pakistan.[7] Craig Baxter notes that Islam is more a personal matter in Bangladesh, and, although it certainly has marked the life of the people, the tradition of *ulama,* or Islamic court of law, is not instantiated in Bangladesh to the same degree that it is in Muslim nations of the Middle East.[8] Nevertheless, of course, one fact remains: Islam was important enough to the Muslim inhabitants of the region of Bengal at the time of the partition of India that they chose to remain, for more than twenty years, a part of what was an artificial hodgepodge held together by Islam and Islam only.

If a combination of Bengali national identity, Islam, and the remnants of some British institutions taken together constitute core parts of the Bangladeshi identity, it is also worth note that some of that identity comes from the remarkable geography and topography of the East Bengal region. The area is marked by a confluence of three or four major rivers—two of them, the Ganges and the Brahmaputra, being among the most important of the South Asian region—and it also has the geographical accident of being the center for enormously powerful storms that drench the region during monsoon time. It is indeed such a typhoon that, in a sense, was the precipitating factor in the creation of the Bangladesh state; December 1970 saw a storm that, through flooding, caused what was believed at the time to be approximately 200,000 deaths. The national government of Pakistan was extremely slow to respond and this, in combination with other factors, probably hastened the creation of the state of Bangladesh.[9]

If it is true that the status of women in South Asia tends, unfortunately, to be marked across the subcontinent, one difference that might emerge in Bangladesh is that Islam, in whatever forms, is a belief system of extreme monotheism and no representation. In other words, although a Westerner may be hard put to discern how the goddess tradition of Hinduism makes a difference in the daily lives of Hindu women, there is no such tradition in Islam, and there is little outside of local custom and the portions of the *Qur'an* that specifically mention women (those, for instance, that have to do with marriage) to guide the lives of women.[10]

This has resulted in a society in which at the village level, by their own admission, women have perhaps even less say than in some other areas of South Asia. As has been the case with other regional identity battles, the lines seem to be drawn for the formation of Bangladeshi identity by appealing to traditional Bangla life. But traditional Bangla life revolves around the oppression of women.

The Male-Centered Point of View

Perhaps it is no exaggeration to say that the "religions of the desert," Islam and Judaism, are marked by the greatest degree of androcentrism and the least influence of matrifocality. Although Judaism does have mention of some few traditional women leaders, such as Esther and Judith, in its core documents, the same cannot be said for Islam.

Thus the double austerity of Islam—at least as seen in the eyes of the nonbelievers, who, of course, have written most of the commentary upon it that is available in the West—comprises both the nonrepresentational monotheism that underlies some of the most eloquent and profound *surahs* of the *Qur'an* and the unspoken but overwhelmingly strong male centeredness of its doctrines. Kenneth Cragg and Marston Speight, in their *Islam from Within*, quote some longer passages of the *Qur'an* that at least mention women. Many of these passages have to do with marriage; but the coincidence, in many Islamic regions, of local custom and the comparative male centeredness of the doctrine has resulted in extraordinarily difficult lives for many women.

If, as many Eurocentric commentators have remarked, part of androcentrism is the focus on the overarching, the conceptual purity of Islam with its pronounced repetition of the doctrine of one God reaches heights of what might be termed the transcendental quest. Here the realm of particularity is doubly displaced: there is no place for it in the doctrine, because there is "no God but God," and there is no place for it in vehicles of worship, since the ban on representation also results in mosques marked in their construction by a remarkable degree of structural rigor and purity. It is indeed such rigor and purity that yields Islamic art its peculiar flavor.[11] In any case, whatever the origins of the conceptualizations at work, most commentators on Islam are struck by the combined influence of these factors. Insofar as a given Islamic culture is concerned, many other factors may be at work—and, as we have seen, this is certainly the case in Bangladesh. But even a comparatively weakened or truncated version of classical Islam, whether Sunni or Shi'a, will undoubtedly leave its imprint on the lives of women simply by virtue of the unstated but understood androcentrism both of the doctrine and of its instantiations.

If, as many contemporary feminists have contended, the realm of epistemic androcentrism is signified by the detachment from the emotions that is the hallmark of the male intellectual style, some of the flavor of this purity and detachment, insofar as Islam is concerned, is evident even to the beginning observer. Cragg and Speight introduce *Islam from Within* by asking the reader to begin to read portions of the *Qur'an*, as they have said, "Arabic style," from the back. They remark,

> Certainly the last two pieces, by the actual order, immediately introduce one to the atmosphere of Muhammad's world of listeners, while the third from their last states, in ringing terms, the core of his affirmation about God.
>
> In the name of the merciful Lord of mercy. Say:
> "I take refuge with the Lord of the daybreak
> From the evil of what he has created,
> And from the evil of the enveloping darkness,
> And from the evil of those who bind their spells
> From the evil of the envier and his envy."
>
> Surah 113 [12]

The style of this particular excision might put a reader in mind of the Old Testament, or for someone familiar with the Judaic tradition, certain portions of it or its commentary. In any case, the style is spare, and the lines somewhat severe. It is noteworthy, as we can see from what the authors have written, that Cragg and Speight have chosen this particular Surah because of its authenticity and introduction to atmosphere.

If the male-centered point of view of Islam itself is fairly easy to demonstrate, it is perhaps even easier still to describe the manifestations of the mix that we have already cited: the peculiarities of Bengali culture, the position of women in general in South Asia, and Islam. Bangladesh, perhaps even more so than India, has become the focal point for numerous non-governmental organizations concerned not only with rural development but specifically with the status of women. Hence there is no dearth of documentation about the lives of rural women in Bangladesh: several works are available that discuss, for example, the Bangladesh Rural Advancement Committee, a large, multinationally funded NGO that began work in Bangladesh in the 1970s.[13] No matter what cultural base is involved, of course, women are not unaware of the conditions of their own lives, and the women of Bangladesh are no exception. As Martha Chen notes,

> At one BRAC-organized workshop for women, the participants were asked to list their problems as women. They listed the following in no particular order:
> —oppression by mothers-in-law
> —differential feeding as a child
> —no education
> —no inheritance[14]

(It is interesting to note that the list, not quoted in full here, goes on for approximately a dozen more items, including violence and dowry.) Although many of the traditions encountered in Bangladesh that affect women's lives may simply be variations on local custom, it is the combination of these features with Islam, with the topographical peculiarities of the Bangladesh region, with population density, and so forth, that makes for a remarkable constellation for women, and one that has been seen by almost all observers as overwhelmingly oppressive.

Added to this is the feature, mentioned earlier here in our citation of the growth of educational institutions in India under the British, that postcolonial education has been the preserve of men. Although the Calcutta Presidency, of which all of Bengal was a part during the colonial period, was among the first to develop colonial colleges, the elite attending these colleges tended to be both male and Hindu. This leaves the women of the Bengali region in a situation analogous to women of color in many developed nations: they are oppressed both by gender and by religional/cultural identity.

Chen, in her analysis of the BRAC work done in Bangladesh, cites the extent to which, because of the various factors cited above, many observers from a variety of backgrounds would see the women of Bangladesh as suffering from extensive oppression. She summarizes this situation when she writes:

> When people describe the status of women in Bangladesh, more often than not they refer to the custom of *purdah*. *Purdah* means, literally, curtain. *Purdah* is used, figuratively, to mean the veiled seclusion of women within the four walls of their homes and the veiling of women when they move outside their homes.[15]

Although, as has been indicated, the form taken by Islam in Bangladesh is far from fundamentalist—and as Craig Baxter indicates, there appears in fact to be little or no interest in such fundamentalism in Bangladesh—certain features of life for women in Muslim societies tend to large similarities.[16] *Purdah* must count as one of the most obvious of these areas to persons from Western backgrounds, and, as Chen is indicating, the perception of its existence and its importance is a crucial one, for it affects the various ways in which women of Islamic South Asia are seen by those in a position to render assistance, particularly from NGOs. In any case, one thing is clear: at least some of what is traditionally associated with Islam in the West affects the women of Bangladesh, even if a postcolonial analysis of the situation might well reveal some exaggeration. As is often the case in Muslim societies, a mix of local tradition and mandates both scriptural and from the *ulama* probably account for the various levels of treatment afforded women. In this sense, the women of Bangladesh are no different from the women of many or most Islamic cultures.

Realms of the Feminine

Although it may well be the case that one would have to make a great effort in terms of analysis of Bangladeshi society to find areas that retain the hallmarks of female-centered or gynocentric influences, much of what can be found is probably within the sphere of the home. The combination of the general status of women in South Asia with, again, the peculiarities of Bengali Islam has meant that women are associated with the home and with familial activities to an even greater extent than would be the case, for example, with Hindu India.

Since Western commentators often confuse regional custom and lore with the teachings of the *Qur'an* or officially sanctioned Islamic law, it is important to assert what such law actually says that bears on the lives of women. Cragg and Speight claim that, for all intents and purposes, much of the commentary governing both the Shi'a and Sunni communities, especially with respect to marriage, is similar and even identical. Quoting extensively from a Shi'a theological text on marriage written in the twelfth century, the editors state, "The norms concerning marriage in the following selection do not diverge in general from the Sunni ideal."[17] A brief excision from some of the commentary on the selection of a wife is as follows:

Except for Islam, there is no greater benefit that a man can have than a
Muslim wife who gives him joy when he cares for her, who is obedient to his
command, who protects her reputation in his absence, both by her behavior
and by taking care of his possessions.[18]

These lines are helpful because they provide what might be deemed to
be an official statement of key aspects of the position of the Muslim wife—
she is obedient, protective of her reputation, and a caretaker in the home.
Within this framework, a woman may exercise much authority, and it is
here that, given the monotheism and formal severity of the Islamic tradition in general, a woman may choose some degree of control.

Within the home, a woman may make crucial choices, and her style may
come to demarcate the lives of others in the home, especially her children.
She may make all of the decisions in matters relating to food, the treatment
of other women in her home, cleanliness, religious observance, and so forth.
Chen notes that older women, especially mothers-in-law, have a great deal
of power within the home, and that the mother-in-law exercises not only
authority, but also "considerable domestic respect with this seniority."[19]

Because so much of what is done in the home is a form of service to
others, the care taken in the preparation of food, the rites of religious observance, and the health of others becomes, perforce, an arena for the remaining
foci of gynocentrism within the Bangladeshi woman's sphere of life. If, as
has been maintained by standard contemporary feminist theory, a crux of
gynocentrism is the notion of relating to others, the Muslim woman in a
home in Bangladesh will exemplify the praxis of this notion to a high degree.

Chen documents the extent to which women from a wide variety of
backgrounds in rural Bangladesh each confront the roles for women. The
situation is exacerbated, of course, by social class—women from better-off
rural backgrounds are allowed to remain more within the home (their labor
is not so necessary) and hence they are better able to fulfill traditional
women's roles. But in any case, in the home or outside of it, the Bengali
Muslim woman is working within the framework of a variety of roles that
revolve around serving others. Although the original work of western feminists has been derided by many as having been structured from the lives of
middle-class white women (particularly the developmental work, such as
that of Chodorow and Dinnerstein), other feminist commentators, such as
Patricia Hill Collins, have written of women's relatedness and connected-
ness in other racial and ethnic contexts.[20] In any case, the notion of relatedness and its place in the lives of the women of Bangladesh is certainly an
important one and yields a place for epistemic gynocentrism.

In marginal or poor households in rural Bangladesh (and the reader must bear in mind that these terms are relative—"wealthy" village households in the rural part of the country are well-off only in comparison to other village households, and are poverty stricken by developed standards) women are forced, by economic necessity, to work outside the home. Chen writes, of one such woman living in a poor household:

> Kamala's husband owns no land or fruit trees or cow.... She used to work in other people's houses or do cane work or stitch quilts or do whatever work she could find in the village.... Kamala and her husband live in a dilapidated one-room bamboo hut with thatched roof.... Kamala and some other women decided to cultivate paddy on a plot of land they were able to lease. Kamala explains her decision: "If I stay hungry, no one will feed me or my children. Hence, I do not work because any one forces me to. I work because of my own zeal."[21]

Kamala has taken it upon herself to do nontraditional work—work that would not be done by the better-off women in the village—because she feels a sense of responsiblity for her family. This sense of responsibility, resulting, in many cases, in Bangladeshi women doing work considered so inappropriate that it may result in extreme loss of status, is found throughout the interviews and life histories that Chen took as a result of her work with BRAC. Although a nongovernmental organization such as BRAC may result in what a Westerner would doubtless term "empowerment" for the women involved, it is important to note the extent to which Bengali women take responsibility for their own lives and the lives of their family members even when such responsibility is far from what would be dictated by religious authorities.

The conflict, in an Islamic society, between the idealized view of the woman's place as found in scripture and the actual situation of those in poverty is often made manifest in the decisions of religious authorities. Unfortunately, what a rich woman can do (even if it occasionally takes her outside the home) may be deemed acceptable, while in the case of a poor woman, almost no behavior is actually acceptable. In describing the decisions of the *mullahs* over such cases, Chen observes:

> [The *mullahs*] do invoke the norm, I am told, but at the behest of the rich and the elders. The elders sit on the local mosque committee which elects the local *mullah*, sets his tenure, and determines his stipend. The *mullahs* have some say about religious norms, but the elders have the final say about them.

The *mullahs,* upon request from the elders, will start the rumour that such-and-such action or behavior is *bepurdah* [outside the bounds of *purdah*].[22]

This passage is crucial, for it indicates the extent to which even religious law, frequently cited as the arbiter of what is proper in Muslim countries, can be subverted at the behest of others. In other words, while women of all groups are required to serve—and while most women are adept at constructing their lives around this relating-to-others—some service is considered acceptable, from a *Qur'anic* point of view, and some not. Unfortunately, those who are able to determine what does and does not count as acceptable are often those who have the most money and the most power. Thus, a group of older, better-off men may condemn younger, poorer women whose every endeavor centers around the fulfillment of the type of commentary alluded to here earlier in the scriptural comments on marriage and service. While the better-off woman may be able to provide the caring and relating required of her within the home, because her husband is able to support her, the poorer woman may show the utmost devotion by exhibiting the caring in ways that save her family economically but place her beyond the confines of what is religiously acceptable.

Mainstream feminist theory in developed countries has taken many forms, but perhaps one of its strongest points is its mixing of the literal and the metaphorical. In writing of issues having to do with feminist aesthetics and male dominance, Beth Dobie has written that there is a suggestion of "both a literal, physical oppression and an oppression exercised through the masculine definition and control of women's sexuality through images and myths."[23] In Islamic Bnagladesh, the masculine definition and control is, as Dobie writes with respect to another topic, exercised both literally and metaphorically. But within this sphere of masculine dominance, women can choose to establish relationships and webs of social structure that go some distance toward articulating a more gynocentric point of view.

Unfortunately, how a woman is placed in such situations is often not her choice, and the other decisions to be made frequently are made under duress or are not actually the woman's decisions. Because the sphere of activity allotted to women is small, the NGOs and other agencies and institutions that have attempted to assist women in rural Bangladesh have counted it as a small victory if a woman is able to leave her home to attend a meeting, for example, or if a woman feels free to bring literature into her home from one of the assisting organizations.[24] Although the women of Bangladesh seem to have precious little to which they can turn, each woman creates the relationships in her own life which allow her a sense of fulfillment within the cultural confines in which she finds herself.

The History of Bengali Women

As we have examined at an earlier point, the history of Bangladesh until fairly recently is inseparable from the history of colonial Bengal as a whole, and, at a slightly later point, the nation of Pakistan. Because everyone who lives in Bangladesh is a Bengali first ("Bangladesh" means "Bengali state"), for both the relatively small group of Hindus still living there and the majority of Muslims, identity in terms of Bengali culture is highly important. When Islam came to the region, it was in general the poorer people who were the converts, and the type of Islamic culture that evolved in the northwest of India did not occur in Bangladesh.

Bengal was ruled during the British period from the arena known as the Calcutta Presidency, and as we have seen this area was crucial to both British institutions and to the emergence of some Bengali cultural movements.[25] Because of the importance of Bengal, British women activists such as Margaret Noble went out of their way to work with both Hindu and Muslim women, and by the turn of the century much had been done to form educational institutions for women in the area and to use the importance of Bengali culture as a basis for further organization. Jayawardena writes, with respect to some of the activity of this period,

> In 1904, Nivedita [Margaret Noble] toured India again, lecturing against Lord Curzon's Universities Act which brought higher education under government control; she also spoke on the need for Hindu-Muslim unity. She was in touch with many Bengali activist religious and political groups, speaking at their meetings, giving them books on the Irish struggles, the American revolution and the lives of Garibaldi and Mazzini [fighters for Italian independence].[26]

The combination of these elements and their continued presence in Bengal up until the time of partition made for a potent and heady brew. This ferment, however, touched the lower classes little, and it is from the lower classes that most of the population of contemporary Bangladesh springs, for as indicated the Muslim conversion in this part of India was mainly to untouchable or *shudra* (fourth-caste groups).

Nevertheless, it may be said that any region with as rich a history as that of Bengal has created a dominant culture that affects, to some extent, everyone within a given geographical region.

The same kinds of splits that typified Bengal before partition remained after, albeit in different guise. After the creation of the state of Pakistan, the splits in power between West and East—the East being, as has been noted here, considerably weaker in almost every area—created a situation in which different versions of Islamic culture were forced to attempt to work together, united only by the fact that they could always posit a common Hindu enemy. Another fact of partition, deleterious to all Bengalis, but especially to women, was the retention of Calcutta and its surrounding area as part of the nation of India, rather than Pakistan. Thus Pakistan received what is known as "East Bengal," which then became "East Pakistan." Metaphorically, it seemed that each halving resulted in an exponential decrease for the Bengali population.

These dislocations are not, of course, the only fracturings suffered by Bengal or by the Muslim population in Bengal. At a much earlier point in the history of India, the entire north of the region was under Islamic subjugation from the Mughals, and during this period many of the features of Mughal courtly existence found their way into the subcourts or smaller regions of princely rulers in the Bengal/Bihar area. Here, also, what took place inevitably affected women, albeit in a variety of ways. In his history of Bangladesh, Baxter notes that several of the cities of what is today that state were already important during the Mughal period, and indeed they even played a role in the contemporary mythology. The courtly life of women, we can assume, was much the same throughout the north of India. With respect to the areas of Chittagong and Sylhet in what is today Bangladesh, Baxter writes:

> Sylhet's is surely the more interesting tale, although surely much is mythological. It is said that one Shah Jalal Mujarrad, a preacher and a soldier, in 1303 conquered the city's Hindu ruler, having gained access to Sylhet by crossing the river on his prayer rug. His preaching is said to have converted the people of the city and its region to Islam.[27]

The mythological content of this tale mirrors the lives of many of those Muslims and Mughal leaders who found themselves at the main courts in the parts of India that are now Uttar Pradesh. Because we know that the women of these courts led lives that are now associated with a great many concepts with which we are all familiar—the harem, enclosure, and so forth—we can assume that these same sorts of lives were led by the wealthy Muslim women of early Bengal. A commentator on the Mughal Emperor Akbar noted that "The imperial palace and household are therefore in the best possible order."[28] The order, of course, is the ordering of women's lives, and this element of commonality, as we can see not only from commentary on Islam in general, but work by current relief agencies in Bangladesh, cuts across social classes and time periods.

While upper-class Bengali women led lives that were simply sheltered, we can guess that the daily rounds of poorer women in Bengal, both before partition and after, were very similar to such lives today. In these cases, of course, no cloistering at the court is necessary—rather, the cloistering takes place in the comparative lack of freedom and the constraint that is placed on women even in the smallest villages. Chen reports in her work on BRAC that giving women the courage to begin to transgress these rules is one of the most difficult obstacles facing the development of interior Bangladesh. More so perhaps than is the case for Hindu women, custom, law, and poverty conspire to leave poorer women in contemporary Bangladesh at the mercy of the wealthy classes and their control of the *mullahs*.

Because so much of the history of Bengal is tied both to the British and to the Hindu culture of Calcutta, it is difficult to separate the Muslim history of the region, especially as it pertains to women, from the region's general history. As we have seen at an earlier point, the twentieth century brought a strong surge in Bengali culture, and the arts of the South Asian area are still believed by many to have their home in Bengal. Because of the importance of the work of those such as Tagore, whose influence was international, much of British power and prestige was situated in Calcutta, and this inevitably had an influence on Bengali Muslims. Many Bengali Muslims—largely male, of course—did benefit from British educational institutions, and many Bengali Muslims were active in the independence movement and were key players in the Muslim League. Once again, however, these individuals tended to be from the better-off groups, and in many cases they had adopted Urdu as their language in order to facilitate an identity with Islam across northern India.

But in a sense the not-so-well-off Bengali Muslims retained a greater sense of identity with Bengal as a whole, and here again we can see how, for the women of Bengal, this mixture has proven to be definitive in setting the course of their lives. When Craig Baxter notes that "Bangladesh is unique among the countries of South Asia in that it is unilingual: All Bangladeshis, save for the Biharis and some tribals, have Bengali ... as their native tongue,"[29] he is making an important statement. Martha Alter Chen observes that one woman, in describing the changes in her life that had

come about because of BRAC, said, "We can speak better Bangla now."[30]
That brief but poignant statement from a woman at the bottom of
Bangladeshi society is an indicator of how the cultural forces of the region,
particularly a sense of Bengali national identity, have affected all of those
living within the region.

Because of the work of major relief organizations in Bengal, the social
structure for women in rural areas is now beginning to change. Each move
of women away from their dwellings is a victory, for it is fought for and not
achieved easily. Although many contemporary commentators have warned,
and quite rightly, against confusing local custom with prohibitions on the
conduct of women that actually occur in the *Qur'an*, there are verses that
make strong suggestions about the conduct of women. Some of this material, even in attenuated form (and sometimes in stronger form) may be
found in the lives of the women of Bangladesh. Wiebke Walther writes,
with respect to what is actually said in the *Qur'an*:

> Much has been written and said about the wearing of the veil by women in
> Islam. Basically, there is no binding prescription for this in Islamic law, but
> there are suggestions, as in the 33rd Sura, which says, "O prophet, say to thy
> wives, and thy daughters, and the womenfolks of the believers, that they let
> down some part of their mantles over them; that is more suitable for their
> being recognized and not insulted." (33:59)[31]

Thus, although variations on the veil may well be local custom, at least
some of the notion of covering for women is indeed found in the *Qur'an*. In
any case, even given the exigencies of local custom, many of the restrictions
on the conduct of women which Westerners, rightly or wrongly, have come
to associate with women do exist in Bangladesh, and it is a struggle for the
average woman to move beyond these restrictions, particularly when it
seems as if they are arbitrarily used against poorer women. Chen and
others have documented cases of women involved with movements such as
BRAC being addressed as prostitutes. But as one young woman replied,
"OK, BRAC female staff are also prostitutes, that is why they have printed
books for us poor people."[32]

The Current Status of Women in Bangladesh

As has been documented, the overwhelming majority of the population of
Bangladesh is rural, and there is only a comparatively small urban and
well-off class. Baxter and others have noted the extent to which the Muslim

population of Bengal that was indeed originally better-off chose to remain in the greater Calcutta area at the time of partition, and this area, of course, remained part of India. Ironically, as has been noted here, much of what is associated with the Islam of South Asia more properly belongs to the northwestern and Punjabi areas of the subcontinent, and thus today pertains to the various cultures of Pakistan. The Urdu language and the Mughal-derived cultural viewpoints that gave us some of the finest relics of Indian art and architecture do not, in general, bear much relationship to the Islamicized Bengali population that forms contemporary Bangladesh.[33]

Chen, remarking on Bangladesh's reputation as an "international basket case," characterizes the population as follows:

> Indeed, more than half of Bangladesh's people do not eat enough each day. Some ninety million live in 55,000 square miles, in an area the size of Iowa or Wisconsin. Nine out of ten Bangladeshis live in her villages.... Among the poor, the plight of women is harder still.... The average rural woman will experience 11 pregnancies but only 6 live births.[34]

The statistics go on and on, but the combination of the statistics and the individual life stories documented by many of the NGO workers is indeed overwhelming.

Since literacy is a problem for so many in Bangladesh, one of the first tasks of most of the workers involved in the self-help organizations that have now, to some extent, come to define Bangladesh on the international scene has been to increase literacy for the village women or at least to make use of the literacy available. Given the strength of Bengali culture, there is no dearth of printed items, and we can guess that the lives of better-off women in Dhaka, for example, are probably very similar to the lives of Muslim women in Calcutta. But at the village level a book is a rare commodity, and for a woman to read a book or attempt to acquire knowledge is seen by many as an act of rebellion.

Thus tradition, poverty, and the peculiarities of the local interpretations of Islam bow many Bangladeshi women down to the extent that they are afraid to leave their own homes for fear of village gossip and ridicule. Although reading hardly seems to be an activity characteristic of prostitution, as we have seen, obtaining reading material can in and of itself constitute a revolutionary act. The documentation of this acquisition of knowledge on the part of Bangladeshi women is indeed moving, and an ample literature has now been developed by various aid groups to provide just such documentation.

The first step frequently consists in making the literature available. Although BRAC is just one of dozens of NGOs at work in Bangladesh, and although it has evolved through the years with many projects, including oral rehydration, reading and literacy for women is one of its chief goals. Another BRAC observer, Catherine Lovell, notes that the organization "is known worldwide among education professionals for its innovative and successful approach to primary education for the poorest rural children, particularly girls. It is also known worldwide among development management specialists as a prototype of the 'learning organization.' "[35]

When BRAC literature is made available, a woman who leaves the home to participate in a group—where, in addition to literacy, she may learn new ways of thatching a roof or preparing rice—is almost always the object of controversy in the home and may be the object of violence. Despite *Qur'anic* injunctions to caring and provision of responsibility, involvement in such endeavors is almost never interpreted in this way for the Bangladeshi woman or girl, who generally will have to fight almost all the males in her family and often other females as well to acquire more knowledge.

Lovell notes that although most of the statistics for rural people in Bangladesh are sad to begin with, the statistics take on a special poignancy in the case of women. Organizations such as the World Bank and the Population Crisis Committee have provided NGOs with the following information, according to Lovell:

> Of the ninety-nine countries studied, Sweden was ranked first and Bangladesh last on data derived from five areas: health, marriage and children, education, employment, and social equality....
> Although women live longer worldwide than men, the average Bangladeshi woman lives to be forty-nine, two years less than the average man in a culture where birth males get better care than females.[36]

Nevertheless, a woman's attempting to make a small move in the general area of betterment is frequently interpreted in a negative manner, both by religious authorities and by those around her. Many of the women interviewed in the Chen anthology report initial reactions toward their attending literacy and self-betterment groups ranging from hostile remarks, attempts to prevent their attendance, and allegations of promiscuity (this reflects the extent to which women are not supposed to leave the home) to general disbelief that it is possible for women to accomplish anything.[37] As Chen indicates that one informant remarked, "What is a group? Can a group be run by women?"

That the emphasis on knowledge and self-help by those who have worked with the rural poor of Bangladesh—who make up the overwhelming majority in this nation—benefits everyone has been documented even by the Nobelist Amartya Sen. Sen's recent work in economics has been dominated by studies of famine and other contingencies in South Asia; in *Resources, Values and Development* he did groundbreaking work on the distribution of food during famine. His work has been hailed because he has conclusively shown that starvation occurs so frequently in Bangladesh and other nations of the region not simply for lack of food, but because of a maldistribution of food. Rural laborers are among the first to suffer, and women form a high proportion of the group of rural laborers at any given time, despite the fact that, of course, they are not supposed to labor outside their dwellings.[38] He has also found evidence of sex-bias malnutrition in small children, and, although such bias may vary wildly within a region, there is no doubt that it does occur and is a chief cause of death and debilitation in girls five and under.[39]

The combination of what we know about conditions for women in rural Bangladesh and the restrictions placed upon them may seem overwhelming, but it is heartening to note that women themselves are often able to surmount these restrictions, after effort, by making an appeal to the acquisition of knowledge. If, as the commentary from Al-Hilli which we had quoted before had noted, the woman in marriage was to be "virtuous … and one who will be most careful in taking care of … possessions,"[40] it is sometimes possible for women to be able to make the argument that, by acquiring knowledge of better homemaking, frugality, care of possessions and livestock, and so forth, they are in fact fulfilling their duties in new and more virtuous ways. The condition of women in Bangladesh is such that international organizations cry out for assistance in developing programs that would ameliorate, even in minor ways, the tradition-bound misery of the poorest women in the most marginal groups. Each individual success story, then, reflects the efforts of many to make a difference in the lives of a few. The fact that women who have participated in BRAC groups and similar efforts have glowing tales to tell of what they have learned and how it has empowered them and has bettered the lives of their family members is indeed a testament to the workers who have developed such groups in thousands of villages throughout the nation.

Women are indeed at the bottom of every social measure when applied to Bangladesh, but the fact that this has been recognized by international organizations is a step in the right direction. Bengali women, particularly Bengali Hindus who remain in what is today India, are by no means

without some power in their own society. Indeed, the social history of
Calcutta, rich as it is with literary, philosophical, and artistic traditions,
contains allusions to twentieth-century women poets, thinkers, and writers who have added to the life of that city. But, as we have said earlier,
Bangladesh was created in such a manner that not only is the country
overwhelmingly Muslim; it is also overwhelmingly poor. The combination of the fact that the lower-caste Hindus were the most likely converts
to Islam in the region and that the wealthier families tended to identify
with the Urdu culture of the Punjabi regions left Bangladesh with a peculiar social structure.

As Lovell reports, BRAC-led groups had to focus on women because,
simply put, in the past there had been virtually no recognition of women's
lives. She notes, "The separate groups of poor women allow women to
address their own problems as women with limited autonomy and power, as
well as to address their own special economic and social problems."[41]

A Nascent Feminist Movement

We can think of the women's groups begun by BRAC and other NGOs as a
beginning step toward feminist movements in Bangladesh. Although the
Dhaka area almost assuredly possesses some groups led by wealthier
women that would correspond more dramatically to their western counterparts, the rural groups are engaging in the kinds of efforts toward growth
and change that we standardly associate with feminism. It is easier, perhaps,
in India for such movements to carry an avowedly feminist label; in Islamic
Bangladesh, and among the poverty-stricken, the feminism springs more
from tasks accomplished than from the actual stated orientation of some
groups.

Nevertheless, as has been stated here, the general recognition by outside
and internal observers that women are especially oppressed in Bangladesh
has created a powerful impetus toward work for them. Among projects led
by NGOs, health projects, literacy endeavors, and general self-assistance
groups at the village level have been paramount.[42]

Many of the groups have as their aim one general goal: to break the stran-
glehold of the *mullahs* on village life, and especially to try to stop the cycle
of fear that is perpetuated by women's refusal to go outside or participate in
activities beyond the home because of a belief that they will be castigated for
breaking *purdah*. This work creates enormous difficulties, because the denial
of the importance of the *purdah* tradition is, of course, a denial of key

portions of the tradition that are either directly Islamic, or that follow local custom in accordance with some variation on an Islamic theme.

A postcolonial analysis of Western responses to Islamic cultures is sure to focus on the demonization of Islam at the expense of other barriers to women around the world. Nevertheless, what is striking in so many of the first-person accounts of women in Bangladesh is that, once they have been freed from the complete force of the belief system—which, of course, works largely to benefit males—they overwhelmingly express relief at the change in their lives, and many do indeed express resentment at a system that, by their lights, has cost them a great deal. The paradoxes here are many, because as was made clear earlier, not all of the difficulties that women face in the village are directly related to Islamic belief or even to historically traceable custom. Nevertheless, the reality of the situation for many village women in Bangladesh has been that *mullahs* have consistently refused to allow women to participate in literacy projects, and that, in some cases, women who have participated in such projects have been verbally or physically attacked.[43]

If we think of a definition of "feminism" as it might be presented to undergraduates, for example—perhaps something along the lines of "a doctrine that promotes the moral and legal rights of women"—then the work that is being done in the villages of Bangladesh is, of course, radically feminist, because it challenges the disempowering structure of daily life where it actually occurs. Thus a woman's leaving the home to obtain a small notebook written in large-type Bengali is a victory for her and for other women, and will be so viewed.

Many of the theorists who are working in contemporary feminist theory of knowledge have written of communitarian criteria for knowledge acquisition from a gynocentric point of view.[44] If we can distinguish empowerment and finding voice on both individual and group levels, then one of the most pronounced features of the work by NGOs that might be deemed to be feminist is its emphasis on women working together. The dynamics of village life tend to create situations in which rivalries and jealousies become a dominant theme of life, and a woman may frequently find herself isolated, or perhaps with only one or two friends in a village.

BRAC and other groups working in Bangladesh have succeeded in altering social structures, at least on a small-scale level, to a remarkable extent. Women have succeeded in forming small informal self-help groups, such that if one woman's bamboo needs thatching or replacement, other women will help her.[45] Assistance in repayment of the loans that are often a core part of the self-help groups is common, and has become a regular feature of life in some villages. Chen notes the importance of such features of feminist change when she writes:

> Before the women had few opportunities to socialize beyond the home and the family. Now BRAC-supported women come together, to meet and to discuss mutual problems. The new experience of sharing develops new loyalties. Many of the women expressed an affection for the other women in their group. This affection very often translates into small gestures of helping and sharing.
>
> —If anyone is staying hungry we inquire after each other. We inquire house to house about the group members.
>
> —When Asia's son was getting married she had no money. I had 54 takas which I gave to her.[46]

In a society in which women have so few alternatives, group organization of women can be seen as a profound movement. It is particularly striking given the tendencies, well documented in the literature, for older women to engage in behavior toward younger women that exacerbates, rather than heals, long-existing wounds. Because the older woman—in her capacity as mother-in-law, most likely—often finds her authority over younger women to be one of the few areas in which she has direct say, the fact that women of all ages are able to come together in groups and then transfer that solidarity and knowledge in daily activity is a remarkable feat.

Perhaps one of the strongest indicators that NGO groups initiate moves that are feminist is found in the overt change in attitudes toward *purdah* and similar customs found in many villages once the women have begun BRAC (or some other) training. Because *purdah* (again, in its broadest sense, adhering to the norms of enclosure and covering) represents such a strong cultural force, it is always difficult to discuss violations of *purdah* in an Islamic context without making it seem as if an entire culture is being attacked. Nevertheless, many of the poorer women are aware of the fact that *bepurdah* (violations of *purdah*) are commonly disregarded if the woman is wealthy enough or if she has powerful people behind her. It seems that, in function, *purdah* exists largely to stifle poorer women. Some of the changes in attitude that rural women working in groups experience toward *purdah* can be quite striking, especially considering the power of the *mullahs*. Martha Chen writes of these alterations:

And they begin to look at the rich in a different way.

—We do not listen to the *mullahs* anymore. They did not give us even a quarter kilo of rice.

—If there is no food in our stomach, *purdah* does not feed us. If there is no food, then no one looks after us.[47]

Although the importance of the stature of the *mullahs* and the general sanctity attached to *purdah* in the Islamic cultures can scarcely be overestimated, most commentators see these aspects of Islam as holdovers from an earlier, more overtly patriarchal time, in the same way that contemporary commentators on Orthodox Judaism or Gnostic Christianity are able to discern the misogynistic tendencies of cultures in the first millennium. The fact that illiterate women who, in many cases, have scarcely been outside of the home might come to see the power of orthodoxy in a new way is a remarkable fact in and of itself.[48]

Feminism is also at work in the ways in which portions of the tradition that can be interpreted in ways to aid and empower women are often reappropriated by women working in groups, a fact that will be examined in greater detail in the next section. But while on the path to such reappropriation, women participating in the self-help groups started by NGOs frequently have to band together in at least one other way, and that is the commonality that is required in order to fight back against overt hostility directed toward them by other villagers.

Chen has amply documented not only the ridicule and failure to conform to *purdah* that dog women who participate in the groups, but other tribulations as well. In a section of her work titled "Pattern of Interference," she begins the relevant remarks with the following sentence: "*Rumors* are spread through the village or directed at the households of group members."[49] She then goes on to say:

We asked the women what else is denied, what else must be endured. Under this temporary banishment all the normal, small village reciprocities—the offer of a cup of tea, the loan of a bowl of rice—are denied. Those who are ostracized are prevented from bathing in the ponds, collecting water from the tube-wells.[50]

Obviously, women who are going to endure such treatment must find ways to band together, and this is, of course, one of the accomplishments of the group, even if it occurs under unhappy circumstances. What is intrigu-

ing, however, is the extent to which the violation of prohibitions on women's
going out—even comparatively minor violations, such as attending a meeting of other women where locally produced Bengali literature is distrib-
uted—constitutes a grave, and in some cases even life-threatening, offense.

Feminist Reconstitutions of the View

At an earlier point in this chapter we noted the difficulties with trying to
attribute strands of gynocentric thought to classical Islam or even its offshoots. Although comparisons between worldviews are difficult, particularly in the "writ large" terms in which such comparisons are frequently
made, few belief systems prominent on a global scale can be deemed to be as
androcentric as classical Islam, a fact noted by almost all commentators.
Misogynistic attitudes prevailing in the pre-Islamic societies in which the
system took root, along with some of the material in the *Qur'an* and, more
important, the scholarly compendia and commentary upon it, resulted in a
series of coalescing cultural views in which women are allowed little movement beyond the home and the sphere of close interpersonal relationships.

Nevertheless, within this sphere of relationships, much can be accomplished, and the Western feminist theorist finds fertile ground when
attempting to articulate how it is, within the structure of the Islamic Bengali society that is Bangladesh, that women reappropriate portions of the
tradition for themselves and for knowledge acquisition. In general, the
Islamic tradition holds that genuine knowledge is the product of divine revelation and must bear at least some relationship to material found in the
Qur'an. Cragg and Speight quote Khalifa Abdul-Hakim, an Indian Muslim
writing in the 1950s, on epistemic views of Islam:

> According to the *Qur'an*, the entire creation is a realm of reason and order,
> but reason and order work at different levels of existence.... Revelation
> which according to the *Qur'an* is supreme source of guidance may be natural,
> instinctive, or supra-rational.[51]

According to the classical view, it would be much more likely that such
revelation would occur to a man, since many of the commentators held dis-
paraging views about women's souls, as was the case, of course, in early
Christian communities and among the ancients.[52]

Nevertheless, the existence of extensive commentary in Islam helps us
to understand how nascent reappropriation of parts of the tradition may
begin for women, and especially for the women of Bangladesh, living in a

society less harsh in its construction of Islam and less fundamentalist than many other contemporary Islamic societies.[53]

The commentary on the *Qur'an* is extremely important, given both the comparative brevity of the document and the dispersal of Islam to a broad range of societies. Walther distinguishes four main sources of Islamic law, with, of course, some variation between, for example, the Sunni and Shi'a traditions.[54] In addition to the *Qur'an*, the *hadith*, or officially compounded commentary, is crucial, she notes. It is this commentary, in many cases, which has allowed for the buildup of certain attitudes toward women.[55] She also cites as authoritative the *ijma*, or unanimous consensus, and the *qiya*, or method of analogous reasoning. The latter, of course, does have epistemic import.

Given the comparative looseness of the social structure of Islam in Bangladesh, we can recapitulate epistemic moves that might be made by Bangladeshi women in the context of their growth in groups largely on the basis of what we know about existing pan-Islamic traditions. Certainly, as the commentary by Chen indicates, *mullahs* frequently find the behavior of poorer women who are drawn to such groups intolerable and objection-able.[56] But our concern is with how the woman can justify to herself, within the context of her society and the social sphere in which she grew up, alter-ations in her behavior.

One easy answer is that the knowledge that she obtains through the groups aids her precisely in the core areas of functioning that are prescribed by Islamic law and custom. In other words, although any given act may not be in accordance with local edict, by her own version of *qiya* and by her own interpretation of the intent of *hadith* and sections of the *Qur'an*, she can come to an understanding of what she is doing. Peter van der Veer has emphasized, in his work on religious nationalisms in South Asia, the extent to which mysticism, or Sufism, originally informed the acquisition of Islam in Bengal.[57] If it is true that this part of the tradition, with its emphasis on the individual coming into contact with the divine, and thus with knowl-edge, was paramount in the original formation of an Islamic culture in Bengal, then perhaps portions of it remain in the culture, even in diluted versions. In any case, it seems clear that the women of Bangladesh are determined to articulate their knowledge acquisition within the framework of what they see as a viable part of their tradition.

Many of the women emphasize how their new knowledge helps them in their familial tasks, or in relationships of caring, an area which, of course, is seen as a central part of their task even in traditional commentary.[58] One woman remarked to Martha Chen:

After I joined the group I acquired knowledge gradually. How to bring up my son in a decent way. How I can bring about changes. How I can live better. If I did not acquire knowledge, how could I say all these things?[59]

This woman clearly sees her new knowledge (and she refers, of course, to specific accomplishments, such as the acquisition of literacy, or the knowledge of ways to make for greater cleanliness and hygiene) as within the framework of duties that she already feels to be hers. Far from finding her new steps to be disgraceful or *bepurdah*, she is able to articulate how they enable her to be a better Muslim wife and mother.[60] Even though it may be the case, initially, that *ijma*, or consensus, does not reflect well on the women, there is enough flexibility in Islam that almost always some part of the tradition can be seen as empowering and validating for the steps that the women are taking.

We can employ some commentary from contemporary sources on the concept of veiling to do some theoretical work here. Many commentators, including Walther, go out of their way to remark upon the fact that forms of veiling are very much local custom, and vary greatly throughout Islamic regions. Of variants on this view, she notes:

Opponents of veiling, such as the freethinker Jahiz in the ninth century, have also pointed out that while on a pilgrimage, one of the "pillars" of Islamic faith—in the state of *ihram* (ritual consecration), as it is called—men and women are required to uncover face and hands.[61]

Just as there are many times when veiling and covering are not called for, there may be times when learning that proceeds from sources outside the home is called for. In any case, it is clear that the women interviewed by Chen and Lovell feel that what they have accomplished makes them more fit for various parts of Islamic tradition.

Much that is written in the postcolonial vein, especially insofar as the commentary has to do with Bengal proper, encourages us to look for new ways to approach epistemic categorizations by Bangladeshi women. Even where such categorizations may be more or less unconscious, there is a long history in colonial Bengal of mergings of various cultures to achieve various points of view. Partha Chatterjee, in a well-known postcolonial analysis of Bengal titled *Texts of Power*, claims that the rise of science in Bengal in the nineteenth century occurred as a synthesis of British and Bengali culture (at least some of which, of course, must have been Muslim). He notes that if one discusses the hybridization of the English and Bengali cultures, one is not "rejecting hybridization but asserting the right to define 'the native stand-point' for selecting the appropriate hybrid."[62] In a sense, the women of Bangladesh, in their appropriation of knowledge through emerging women's groups, have achieved the same hybridization. They have learned how to be "most careful," as the Al-Hilli commentary enjoins them to, in guarding the household and those within it.[63]

Summarizing the Bangladeshi Situation

As indicated earlier, Bangladesh is a much more rural nation than India, with the vast majority of its citizens still leading agrarian and communal lives in the countryside. Because of this, the large majority of Bangladeshi women do not have access to the kinds of urban groups or organizations that characterize Calcutta, Bombay, Delhi, or even Dhaka, the capital of Bangladesh.

Within this large area denominated as the countryside, most of the advances for women have been achieved through NGOs and spin-offs of governmental agencies and relief programs that emerged when the nation broke away from Pakistan in 1971.[64] Hence any movement that might in any sense be labeled "feminist," however inappropriate that western label may seem in some cases, is most likely either related to one of these organizations or is a lineal descendant of it.

Groups such as the Bangladesh Rural Advancement Committee usually have three or four statedly separate goals, which are, of course, interrelated. The goals include the establishment of at least minimal literacy, the encouragement of small cooperatives and cottage industries through small loans, training for better hygiene and health, and, in some cases, education on contraception. The greatest goal, however, is frequently subsidiary to or subsumed under many of these other aims—the goal is to enable the Bangladeshi woman to leave her home under her own power and to attend a group meeting, something that many of the women have never done.

As we have seen, although the form of Islam currently practiced in Bangladesh is less stringent than, for example, many of the more overtly fundamentalist Islams practiced in nations of the Middle East, Islamic identity nonetheless almost always requires restrictions on women's dress and behavior, even if many of the restrictions are related to local procedure. This is also true in rural areas of Bangladesh, and what it has meant in reality for many women is that leaving the home causes adverse comment, hostility, and shunning. It may cause local *mullahs* to indicate that the woman in question is *bepurdah*, and if the edict stands for any length of time, it can cause serious difficulties for the woman and her family.[65] Thus it is all the more remarkable that, over a period of time, thousands of such groups (from a wide variety of NGOs and initial parental organizations) have formed across Bangladesh. Their work has become internationally known and widely reported.

After working their way past the initial hostility, most women not only come to see the group as an important part of their lives, but, all the more remarkably, many are able to persuade friends and relatives to change their minds. And, perhaps most important, the very restrictions on women—the roles into which they are cast by Islamic and local custom—can be retrieved and turned toward something else. Many of the women interviewed by Chen and Lovell indicate that the growth in knowledge that they have experienced as a result of attending a women's group, initiated by BRAC or some other source, has led them to become better mothers, caretakers, and homemakers. Statements such as these, from women living in a society that frequently castigates those who form the initial groups as "prostitutes,"[66] are indeed noteworthy.

The knowledge traditions of Islamic societies are overwhelmingly male based and tend to revolve around divine ordinance as found in the *Qur'an* and *hadith*. Although Sufism and some other movements may indicate a role for the individual believer,[67] women in general have not had access to these traditions. Hence the daily knowledge of a woman in rural Bangladesh, if it is augmented by new ideas based on group work, must fit into the general conception of a woman's life if the woman is to survive in the society.

The women of Bangladesh who have participated in women's empowerment groups have, in general, internalized their growth and valorized it according to Islamic and local tradition, to a remarkable extent. Literacy, for example, not only helps the individual woman, but every woman realizes that it helps make her a better mother or relative to someone else's children, if only because it means that she will then be in a better position to pass on the rudiments of literacy. A bamboo-thatched home, particularly if poorly thatched in the first place, may be vulnerable to storm and wind, but a home put together with new techniques makes a better home for everyone in the house. Water-borne pollution through animal and human feces is an especially acute hazard in rural Bangladesh and the cause of much illness, but learning how to carefully separate contaminated areas from other areas is a boon to every single individual in the surrounding area.

In addition, as we have seen, appropriation of knowledge for caretaking has resulted in a growth in good relations between individuals and households in those areas where many residents in a given village belong to a group.[68] Poverty tends to increase every ill of human social relations, and the villages of Bangladesh are frequently marked by disputes, large and small, over children, animals, water, contaminants, and so forth. Learning the value of taking care of or helping out another greatly assists in cutting down on the incidents that mark poor relations. Many of Chen's informants indicated that their "knowledge" had assisted them in setting right old wrongs and, in general, maintaining better relationships.

The women of rural Bangladesh lead lives that are greatly constrained by tradition and custom, much of which, as has been remarked here, is regional, and some of which is characteristic in one or more ways of Islamic societies. Wendy Doniger, who has done so much work on the mythography of India and of the Hindu worldview, has edited a collection that contains material on women's headwear and the symbolism of hair and head coverings for women.[69] Writing of the Islamic Turkish society, the essayist Carol Delaney notes that "the contemporary debate [on headgear], and Western analyses of it, ignore such elementary questions as: (1) Why covering? (2) Why is it women's heads that are covered?"[70]

Delaney goes on to analyze the mythic and symbolic elements of hair, sexuality, the upper portion of the body, and so forth. Certainly some ramifications of hair will alter from society to society, but some, we can hypothesize, will remain comparatively invariant. Bangladeshi women are discouraged from leaving the home, called names and insulted when they do leave the home, and warned against letting their heads go uncovered.

Part of what it means, then, for women to be able to participate in movements outside the home is that they violate restrictions on modesty that implicitly have to do with sexuality—this is well documented in the remarks that we saw earlier about the BRAC workers being "prostitutes." But the women of rural Bangladesh are starting to make their own decisions about what "care" consists of and what constitutes the best interpretation of the Qur'anic role assigned to them.

In making these decisions they necessarily become their own interpreters of law and custom, overriding—in some cases, very blatantly—the *mullahs* whose judgment they no longer trust because the *mullahs* seem so often to endorse the movements of wealthy women but fail to acknowledge or support activities of poor women. But as we have seen, Islam is filled with *hadith*, much of which is fragmentary, contradictory, or susceptible to numerous interpretations.[71] In addition, although we cannot claim that it has a formal role here, the Sufi or mystical tradition enjoins the believer to act alone. (Interestingly enough, Van der Veer cites Sufism as originally having been a major formative influence in the Islam of Bengal.)[72]

The women of Bangladesh who participate in women's groups and reappropriate even small parts of their tradition, for whatever knowledge-bound ways, are their own interpreters of an old and androcentric tradition. In this sense, they have become arbiters of what is meaningful in their lives. The living tradition may perhaps best be modeled in the lives of these iconoclastic Muslim women.

Chapter 5

Nepal and the Himalayan Societies

The historiography and mythology of Nepal are significantly different from those of the other nations we have examined so far, both because of Nepal's isolation and because of the conditions under which they were produced. The long period of comparative isolation from other cultures formally ended with the British arrival in India, but Great Britain used Nepal more or less as a buffer state and had little direct influence on the area. Historically, a few Nepalese, especially those from the Kathmandu Valley area, made their way to other regions, particularly India, but again this did not occur in large numbers until approximately the last two centuries, when Gurkha soldiers, recruited by the British, became well-known fighters and participated in battles around the world.

Much of the rest of the material which an historian of religions or a scholar of comparative religion might want to employ about Nepal is also conflicting and difficult to assess. Nepal is the planet's only Hindu kingdom, but the Hindu influence is, again, found primarily in the Kathmandu area, and thins to near nonexistence as one travels in the traditionally Buddhist mountain areas. Thus, although the numerical majority of the population has perhaps been exposed to elements of both belief systems—and has even created an amalgam of them—many living in the hinterlands are involved in traditional Buddhist modes of worship that are probably best described as being close to Tibetan Buddhism.[1]

For a large proportion of the population who remain close to great villages, or within walking or traveling distance of Kathmandu or Pokhara, religious life is a combination of Buddhist and Hindu beliefs, with features of both. On the surface, this might not seem surprising, particularly when we remember that Buddhism is an historical offshoot of Hinduism, in the same way that Christianity emerged from Judaism. But there probably is no other cultural area of any size today in which these belief systems exist side by side or in which they have actually merged—there is almost no overt Buddhist influence in contemporary India, and little Hindu influence in the other Buddhist Asian nations.

The combination of Nepal's landlocked geography, its mix of cultural and indeed ethnic physiological types (Leo Rose and John Scholz describe the stock as "Indoaryan" on the one hand, and "Tibeto-Burman" on the other),[2] and its long history—written histories in the Tibetan-derived scripts go back many centuries—provide for it a unique vantage point on the world scene. In the middle of this heady brew we find attitudes toward women, again a compound of various cultural features and some ideas no doubt more recently imported. Visitors to the Kathmandu area are often astonished to see details of the search for a young girl to embody "Kumari," the living goddess kept in a compound near central Kathmandu; this search is in itself a rich mixture of the various religious traditions.[3] On the other hand, women of the hill areas, more centrally Buddhist and with a history of having engaged in trading by traveling around Nepal, are often cited as leading lives of comparative equality. Indeed, many such women have become entrepreneurs in the climate of the current Nepal, which has, of course, been much affected by international tourism and the general economic upswing of areas in Asia.[4]

Insofar as Buddhism itself is concerned, the Mahayana Buddhism of Nepal reflects a great many of the aspects that have come under investigation by contemporary scholars in religious studies. The emphasis on the notion of the Bodhisattva and the extent to which "salvific" elements, from whatever sources, have crept into Buddhism in this region provides fertile ground for investigation. Because so much of the artwork that is actually influenced by Buddhism simultaneously reflects a great Tibetan influence, anything produced in the Nepalese hill regions is in great demand, and, by the same token, undiscerning Westerners frequently cannot tell work from one region from another, and a market in such commodities has sprung up in other Asian areas.[5]

We have already seen the extensive goddess influence on Hinduism, and this influence, of course, remains in the Kathmandu area. Noteworthy, however, are the practices of Buddhism that allow for the participation of women—historically speaking, there have always been a few holy women in almost every Buddhist tradition, and in some areas the concept of Buddhist "nuns" is employed. It may be that market-driven forces have something to do with the comparatively greater freedoms, but the women of the hill regions seem to be equal participants in many aspects of daily life. It is also the case that, again given the hybrid nature of much of the religious worship, elements of goddess-derived worship have probably sprung up in many of the local cultures.

Because of the mixed nature of the religious cultures of Nepal, and the general miscibility of the belief systems, important points are frequently lost on those who attempt to make generalizations about Nepal or about a general Nepali culture. As Frederick Gaige, a University of California researcher who has done extensive work on Nepal, has noted, the majority of the inhabitants of Nepal—because the plains are so much more heavily populated than the hill regions—are Hindu, but the popular imagination, and to some extent varietals of the local cultures, is seized by the Buddhist elements. He writes:

> Many of the hill tribal groups are still primarily influenced by religions they practiced before the advent of Hinduism into the region. The hill tribal religions are Mahayana Buddhism, a Tibetan religion called Bon, and local variants of animism.[6]

Each of these traditions affects the other, allowing for (in some areas) a sort of modified Hinduism, with a much less rigid caste structure, or a Buddhism with some elements of caste and of other, pre-Buddhist beliefs.[7] In any case, the brew is further mixed by the fact that some hill groups have spent enough time in the *tarai*, or plains regions, to form a caste among local Hindus, despite the fact that their beliefs may, at least statedly, be somewhat at variance with Hindu beliefs.

Nevertheless, all of these traditions mesh to form lineaments that are particularly fruitful with respect to noting feminist knowledge belief systems, for each of the major traditions has at least some elements of a woman-centered tradition. Much work has been done in recent years on such traditions within Buddhism itself, and the work on Hinduism centers, as we have already seen, on the goddess-related elements and the force of such traditions at local levels and in local lives. The Tibetan Mahayana Buddhism which informs much of Nepalese practice, having originated, of course, in India, allows for a number of roles for women, and does indeed possess a tradition of women renouncers and officiators.[8] As so frequently happens, it seems that greater structure allows for more rigidity in practice, and hence for more misogyny. Joanne Watkins asserts that "many Buddhist scholars have noted that the more positive attributes of female gender and views of women are found in the Mahayana tradition, particularly among the Tibetan tantric sects."[9]

Nepalese belief systems have long been attractive to foreigners, perhaps for these very reasons. Thus it is the case that since Nepal was opened to the West in the early 1950s, seekers and travelers from a wide variety of backgrounds have gone to the region, and at present the Kathmandu Valley area has, of course, many signs of foreign influence and a wealthier class of persons who are, in many ways, leading Western lives.[10] Nevertheless, the attractions of Nepal remain, probably because although there are other regions that might be thought to bear some cultural resemblance and remain comparatively untouched—such as, for example, Bhutan—these areas are still almost inaccessible and require great effort, and even some influence, in order to prepare for a visit. Nepal is open to the visitor.

Articulating the Male-Oriented View

Our work here will be more greatly concerned with the Buddhist elements of Nepalese tradition, since Hindu-oriented traditions are so well documented, at least with respect to India. But as is so often the case, and as was noted above in the citation from Watkins, the more stratified elements of Buddhism, and the more formalized and codified portions of religious worship, are decidedly male and in that respect resemble many if not all of the world's great religious traditions.

Mahayana Buddhism uses the notion of the Bodhisattva, or Buddha-becoming—one who has forsaken individual salvation (salvation here consisting largely in a move away from the influence of the senses and toward individual internal growth) for the prospect of helping others along the path—as a central focal point in its pronouncements. Although most such figures are male, there are a few female figures who might be deemed to be Bodhisattvas. Many beliefs that remind the investigator of parallel beliefs concerning women found in other societies are also present in much of the Tibetan Buddhism that has flavored Nepal. As Watkins reports,

> Negative images of women in the ... Mahayana ... literature seem to be derived from women's association with reproduction, with "nature," with worldliness or attachment, desire and pain.... The subordinate moral status of women may also be reflected in the Buddhist belief that the female body is a lower form or less desirable rebirth.[11]

In general, the forms of Buddhism that are associated with Nepal are more relaxed than those associated with some other regions—particularly such countries as Sri Lanka and Thailand—and so the types of generalizations that might be made about Buddhism and gender there do not necessarily apply in Nepal. Nevertheless, many portions of the Buddhist tradition tend to link that which is most transcendental to that which is also male. To the extent that any one subgroup has been able to overcome the history of this conceptualization, real work has been achieved. Because the sort of discipline that is needed to overcome bodily drives and engage in genuine meditative practices in Buddhism is key to much of the tradition, that discipline tends, in many places, to be deemed male. Again, some observers, such as Watkins, feel that these associations are not as strong in many of the northern areas of Nepal as they are in other cultures. Still, she also notes that:

> [one author,] writing about Tibetan migrants to the Gyesumdo region south of Nyeshang, states that in that community "female birth is thought to be a sign of having committed more evil deed ... in previous lives.... Lamas can be heard to urge the deceased to at least gain a male rebirth."[12]

Another set of symbolic representations that is prevalent in the Mahayana Tibetan Buddhism that permeates northern Nepal is that of the hunter. Although these images are clearly taken from elements of the pre-Buddhist local culture, they are indeed powerful and, to the extent that village life is, as has been maintained, a mixture of pre-Buddhist, Buddhist, and some Hindu elements, they are powerful elements indeed. Many village ceremonies reenact hunting rituals, and in earlier times, according to several visitors to the region, much bloodletting was involved and a great deal of animal sacrifice. The role of the hunter is still an important one metaphorically in northern Nepal, and the extent to which this permeated colonial India is noteworthy because of the British appropriation of such martial traditions with specific communities, such as the Gurkhas.

The Buddha is, of course, a male figure, and the power of transcendence—the same sort of transcendence at work in a great deal of the Hindu tradition, since Hinduism precedes Buddhism chronologically—is a power that attempts to detach itself from the body. To the extent that the body and the body's needs interfere with this transcendence, the body must be denied. Because of the traditional association of the body with that which is female, much of the most important part of the Buddhist tradition from the standpoint of codification and formality is, of course, male oriented.

Nepal is now, in many ways, a thoroughly postmodern society, if there is such a thing, and much of what transpires in any Nepalese mountain community is affected by the influx of a great deal of foreign material, and especially by the influx of groups of tourists particularly interested in trekking or mountain climbing. Because this industry has affected virtually all parts of Nepal, it is safe to say that at the current time there is probably no area in Nepal that has not been influenced by it or by the commercialization that it inevitably brings. Thus the point is that there is still more of a foreign influence on Nepalese culture—already a mixed bag—than would have been the case fifty or sixty years ago. Nevertheless, some areas of commonality with preceding forms of communal structure remain, and in these areas we can see remnants both of the pre-Buddhist traditions and of more recent amalgams of Buddhism and Hinduism.

Almost all of the commentators on the mountain Buddhist traditions have focused on the comparative looseness of these social structures, again when taken in contrast to Buddhist societies of the south, where there is still a marked distinction between laity and the priesthood. Watkins reports that even such activities as switching sects and moving from one (marked) form of worship to another made little apparent difference to her informants in the Nyeshangte area north of Pokhara. As she notes in her text, "When asked about switching to another sect and another *dgon pa*, Pema just shrugged and said, 'It makes no difference to my parents, nor to me.'"[13] This comparatively lax attitude about matters that might be deemed to be more serious in other forms of Buddhism has repercussions for most of what can be thought of as gender roles in the mountainous northern regions of Nepal, especially insofar as those gender roles intermix with more traditional forms of worship or with anything not originally codified as Buddhist.

The two male-oriented traditions that we have seen referred to here—the general notion of the transcendental as being male defined, and the emphasis in many traditional mountain groups on a history of hunting that becomes glorified and revered—combine to a give a powerful male cast to much of what is thought to be traditional in such societies. If androcentric forms of knowing in the Hindu/Buddhist cultures are frequently identified with the capacity for transcendence, it has been difficult to find places in the tradition where woman's capacity for such knowing/action is valorized or even explicitly formulated. Nevertheless, despite what many commentators have referred to as "Buddhist texts['] ... consistently patriarchal and androcentric attitude toward women,"[14] there are elements in the tradition that help us to focus on gynocentric possibilities for knowing.

Areas of commonality across the Hindu/Buddhist worldview, and very much manifested both in Nepalese folk tradition and in the use of a number of texts, seem to encompass male possibilities for transcendence, the leadership of the male in the household, the male's consequent leadership role with respect to religious duties, and the original (in Buddhism) position of the Buddha with respect to female renunciants as one of "hesitancy."[15] All of these formulations tend to empower males and to disempower females, but there are, of course—as always—paths out of the obvious. Watkins notes, with respect to Nyeshangte ceremonies, that it is frequently the business of males as householders that may interfere with their attempts to be better celebrants, thus opening the door for females:

> Although the decision to host a large-scale [Thonje, or redistribution] ceremony is usually made jointly by spouses, it is often the senior woman in the household who sets the actual process in motion: recruiting friends, neighbors, and relatives in the village to help. In contrast, men, unless they are approaching their retirement years, are often too preoccupied with their business pursuits to keep track of village affairs.[16]

Whenever men are too "preoccupied," the door is opened for women. Thus there is much within the Tibetan/Mahayana Buddhist systems of northern Nepal that allows women to become agents and knowers.

Female-Centering within the View

Commentators seem to agree that there is a female-centered tradition within Buddhism, and in some sense, because of the variants in codification, it may be more explicitly set out than is the concomitant tradition in Hinduism, for example. But the difficulty is in articulating precisely how this tradition interacts with women's lives.

In a scholarly analysis of the *Therigatha,* "the only canonical text in the world's religions that is attributed to female authorship and that focuses exclusively on women's religious experiences,"[17] Kathryn Blackstone takes note of the fact that "struggle pervades the experiences of the *theris* [female renouncers]."[18] It is not easy, as a woman, to have the goal of achieving *nibbana* [nirvana]. But there is much in the daily lives of women in Nepal that allows them to fulfill aspects of the goal in other ways. Women are crucial to much of the ritual that is created within the Buddhist/Bon/animist context, even if that ritual was originally designed for men, and women are also crucial (as is so often case) to the maintenance of the home and family bonds that allow others to participate in these rituals.[19] In many cases, women have—by default, to some extent—appropriated roles that may have originally been intended for men, but that have become women's roles because women have the energy and the time to put into them. Thus not only is there a tradition of the Buddhist nun or renouncer in the northern Nepalese culture, but there is also a strong tradition of the woman who organizes and puts together important local festivals of sacrifice and worship. Watkins summarizes the strength of women's roles in this regard when she writes:

> In a society where adult women occupy positions of authority and power within the household, it is not surprising that their responsibility for the everyday welfare and well-being of their families extends beyond the economic domain, and involves managing or controlling the supernatural domain as well. Senior women have the primary task of keeping their houses in order, and that includes keeping evil forces at bay and keeping household gods (*thin lha*) in a contented state.[20]

For purposes of the Thonje or redistribution ceremony documented as part of the Nyeshangte culture, women not only, of course, do the requisite amount of cooking and cleaning, but they frequently select the *lama* to participate in the ceremony, prepare the site for purification, and in many cases actually do the redistribution of cash or goods that is one of the chief parts of the ceremony. Although codified Buddhism may have some trouble with the notion of "women's bodies," as we have seen at an earlier point, women's actual bodies do a great deal.

Even within the codified tradition, however, there are decidedly different views on the status of women and on the possibility for women to overcome desire and thus place themselves on the path to Buddhahood, or to becoming Bodhisattvas. The Bodhisattva tradition is part of Mahayana Buddhism, itself the larger umbrella under which the more or less Tibetan Buddhism of northern Nepal finds itself. Within this tradition, unlike the purer Theravada Buddhism of Sri Lanka or parts of Thailand, Buddhas-to-become choose to remain on the earthly plane in their activities, leading others toward enlightenment. A Bodhisattva is thus, to cast the notion in terms with which we may be more familiar, a sort of Buddhist saint.

It is important to attempt to work through notions of the feminine in Buddhism, because unlike Islam, with its monotheism and much less frequent mention of women, there are *sutras* (works alleged to have been composed by the Buddha for instruction) and folk tales in the Buddhist tradition in which women are prominently mentioned. The scholar Diana Paul has become well known for her work in this area, and she has compiled a lengthy collection of *sutras* and stories that feature women in prominent roles. She is acutely aware, however, of the duality of the feminine in Buddhism. Much of Buddhism emphasizes a transcendence of worldly desire such that it might be thought that the gender of the initiate is irrelevant. On the other hand, as we have seen, much of the tradition is related to an underlying Hindu foundation that sees the female body as corrupt. Paul assigns a paradoxical status to much of the commentary and tradition of Mahayana Buddhism insofar as sex and gender are concerned:

> It is only when sexuality remains a criterion for enlightenment that feminine images of Buddhahood are untenable. The enduring association of the feminine with sexuality becomes a "double-edged sword" in images of Buddhahood. When sex is conceived as an important factor for attaining Buddhahood, the perfect sex is always masculine. The inconsistency in beliefs and values is readily apparent in maintaining the elimination of sexuality as essential to Buddhahood, but adhering to masculinity as the ideal state rather than one of asexuality. By definition, feminine images of Buddhahood are a contradiction in terms if asexuality denotes the masculine state.[21]

Paul is right on target, especially since much of the tradition asks adherents to fail to take notice of the worldly, or to act as if the realm of the senses were one from which a person could, with effort, make a withdrawal. But it is precisely this "inconsistency," as Paul puts it, which is important for our purposes, since it is manifest in much of the daily lives of Nepalese women. The association of pollution with the female body is never far away, but by the same token the images of Buddhist nuns, female Bodhisattvas, or those who transcend, like Queen Srimala, glorified in the text for which Paul's comments above serve as an introduction, are never far away. Thus perhaps more so than women in either of the traditions that we have examined in the immediately preceding sections, Nepalese Buddhist women remain caught in a swirl of contradictions that are not susceptible of easy resolution.

As is the case to some extent with the concept of *shakti* in the Hindu tradition, it may well be that the contaminants associated with the female body allow for the possibility of greater transcendence, although it is not clear that there are portions of the tradition that specifically spell this out. In any case, it is clear from ethnographic commentary and observation that many Nepalese women are in charge of a variety of activities, in and outside of the home, and that the tradition does not seem to be as disempowering for them as, for example, portions of other traditions are for some women in South Asia. Wherever Western commentators go, they are struck by both the level of activity of women and the comparatively high status that many women are accorded within their specific groups. As is the case with the scriptural views to which Paul alludes above, much is contradictory, even on an everyday level. Broughton Coburn, an American photojournalist who spent a great deal of time with the Surung people in the hills near Pokhara, captured some of these contradictions in *Nepali Aama: Portrait of a Nepalese Hill Woman*. Aama, to give her the motherly title of respect by which Coburn addresses her, is not strictly Buddhist, since she belongs to a group that has become Hinduized in the sense that it is close enough to urban areas to have become "low caste." Nevertheless, her observations tell a great deal about the life of someone who is simultaneously respected and not respected because she is a woman. But her life also tells about change in Nepal. She says:

> At my husband's home I couldn't even blow my nose when the in-laws were around, and that's just when my nose would run—I was that scared of them.... [Y]oung girls now refuse to be married off at an unripe age. They probably want to wait and see which of the village boys will get rich or be accepted into the army.[22]

The lives of the Nepali hill women revolve, to a great extent, around the lives of other women and of small children, as is the case in many South Asian societies. Although a postcolonial analysis might deem it to be irretrievably Eurocentric to cast such lives in terms of any part of Western feminist theory, new work by contemporary feminists emphasizes the extent to which woman-woman relationships are often overlooked in the mythologies or mythographies of many cultures.[23] Because such relationships tend to reinforce patterns of thought that have been deemed by many to be gynocentric—patterns that are relational rather than dominative, or are cooperative rather than exploitative—they have tended not to figure in the official histories of various cultures as those histories are written and codified.

But the women of northern Nepal lead lives in which such relationships are prominent, and they may become (as appears to be the case in many familial situations throughout India) the defining feature of a woman's life. The older woman lives to be in a position where she can comment on and guide the behavior of the younger woman, and this is what we see in, for example, the quotation from Aama above. Reflecting back on her life and the lives of other young women of her age group, she is able to make comparisons and to ask questions about what young women are doing right now. She becomes a teacher and mentor, in both official and unofficial capacities. The extent to which these gynocentric relationships are the hall-

mark of the lives of many Nepali women is one that is only now being documented in the literature.

The Nepalese Woman's History

Nepalese history is both ancient and modern, in the sense that there is, of
course, a lengthy history that precedes anything like what Europeans refer
to as the "modern" era, but there is also a surprising amount of contact—
even for an Himalayan kingdom—with the West and with India, in particular, during the so-called modern period.

In addition to the history of truncated contacts with Great Britain, any
historical overview that would attempt to serve the purpose of placing
women within a chronological framework has to make note of the continued conflict between the hills and the *tarai*, the district of Nepal that,
because it is closer to India and comparatively flat, yields most of the arable
land and thus is the source of most of the nation's food and tradeable goods.

The sense of independence that the Buddhist-oriented hill people (and,
especially, the women in these groups) may well feel no doubt owes a great
deal to the continued conflict between the *tarai* and the hills in Nepal, a
conflict that continues to this day. As has been indicated, the "official" religion is Hinduism, and there is an "official" Nepali language, promulgated
by the government in much the same way that Hindi is promulgated in
India, but not much headway with any of these projects has been made in
many of the mountain regions of Nepal.

Gaige aptly summarizes much of the pre-twentieth-century history of
Nepal, to the extent that it can be chronologized in Western terms, as one of
the "hill kings cast[ing] covetous eyes on the *tarai* for centuries."[24] This
seesawing back and forth between rulers who maintained hill contacts or
loyalty and those who more firmly identified with the Hindu culture of
northern India no doubt increases the strength of hill women as traders and
negotiators, since any period of prolonged conflict and battle tends to take
men away from a given region and to increase the negotiating power of
women. Watkins, in her work with the Nyeshang, noted the extent to
which a long history of comparative independence had made a number of
patrilineal models of social organization and descent somewhat less than
useful in looking at the hill society.[25] As is the case with much else in the
societies of northern Nepal, what is available to the observer presents itself
as a bit of a hodgepodge (much like the religious or linguistic situations
previously referred to), and Watkins notes that, with respect to marriage,
for example, "it is important to note how different rules and different

meanings are invested" in that notion, meaning that attempts to categorize the status of women here (or of men) invariably suffer from Western institutional bias.[26]

In any case, it is clear that a number of factors have combined to make a profoundly complex situation, both with respect to Nepalese history in general and with respect to the status of women. The comparative levels of strength for women would apply, as has been noted, to the hill societies, whereas the Newar and caste society of Kathmandu, in particular, have a social structure much more similar to that of northern India. Making the complexity even greater is the fact that much that is written about Nepal is based on the *tarai* or flatland society.

But since our concern is with the Buddhist-oriented hill groups, it is worth noting that observers focus now on two areas: the first is, as we have already noted, the comparative egalitarian strength of the societies with respect to gender roles, and the second is the relatively rapid pace of change that is now encompassing such groups, with many of the more mobile members of the groups not only going outside Nepal to India (as has been customary for centuries), but also flying to Bangkok and other areas in Asia to trade on a regular basis. This has not only broken down categories within the social structure of some groups, but has actually encouraged—at least in some cases—a move back from egalitarianism, as more restrictive gender roles and stereotypes associated with other groups have been seen and adopted by some members of the hill groups.

Historically speaking, the time-honored tasks of planting, gathering firewood, and participating in Buddhist rituals (the cycles of life, so to speak) continue in most of the hill regions with only minor adjustment. Watkins, a trained anthropologist, was struck by the free-and-easy ways of the Nyeshang with respect to gender, and came to feel that the greatest genuine prohibition on a woman's outdoor activity was against plowing (although this, too, was violated in some instances). She observes that:

> Although there may be strong cultural prohibitions against particular kinds of activities, there seems to be a great tolerance in Nyeshang toward wayward behavior and individual eccentricities, as well as a sense that people should not interfere unnecessarily in the lives of others.... In many rural homes I have seen young men (and women) who were *not* household members help with various chores without being asked.[27]

The point that Watkins is making here is that this breakdown of gender-related activity seems historically to have been the case among the Nyeshang. Even with the consolidation of Nepal during the eighteenth and nineteenth centuries, a consolidation that was precipitated to some extent by the presence of the British in India, hill life continued relatively unchanged, and the patterns of which Watkins writes seem to have been around for a good deal of time. Thus again there is the paradox that the more Hindu-oriented culture of the *tarai*—also the structure that has, until recently, received more exposure to the West—probably has a greater differentiation among gender roles than the hill cultures. Watkins points out in her observations that some change currently due to the travels of various Nyeshang who go to the West or Bangkok on a regular basis may have resulted in the notion that " 'housework' has become synonymous with . . . 'girls' work.' "[28]

Because of some cross-Buddhist concepts such as those associated with the Middle Path, the emphasis on self-control and good works in the hill societies may have historically led to a situation where a comparative degree of independence from the *tarai* groups was maintained in the societies, along with a comparative egalitarianism, for this egalitarianism allows for the accumulation of good works. Watkins notes that greed, selfishness, and laziness have historically been among those traits most devalued by the Nyeshang.[29] Some types of work that needed to be done in the traditional hill societies were indeed associated with the accumulation of merit, possibly because such work allows for periods of solitude or meditation. Herding is one such activity, but again with change much herding is now being done by outsiders who actually are from Tibet or Bhutan.

Under the Rana leaders of the nineteenth century the hill peoples, such as the Nyeshang, were able to bargain for concessions in order to maintain a degree of independence from the growing power of the Nepalese state.[30] But now that most Nepalese have had at least minimal exposure to the West—and certain hill groups have had a great deal of exposure, since they have become focal points for the ubiquitous mountain tourism—the notion that the society as a whole retains an imbalance in favor of the Newars and the *tarai* is somewhat antiquated. In any case there is no question that, as Coburn, Watkins, and others have documented, an uneven borrowing of some ideas from the West persists, along with a tendentious battle against such borrowings in some quarters. Coburn's Aama states:

> With many of the city jobs now, you earn money at someone else's loss, sometimes by unfair means or trickery. Children don't learn this in school, but they study there for ten years and then lose their appetite for farm work. . . . Office people have anxieties to deal with, and they have to make decisions that affect many people.[31]

Coburn's hill woman has seldom been away from her village, but she has heard from those who have, and she has her own opinions about city life or nontraditional life. Her testimony is a remarkable demonstration of the extent to which hill Nepalese have been affected by the movements of others around them, and the extent to which alterations in belief are taking place in a climate of rapid change.

The Nyeshang are not alone in their comparative independence, and in the way in which that independence has fostered women's courage and a certain egalitarianism. Rex Jones and Shirley Jones report similar kinds of phenomena with respect to women's roles in the Limbu, and again the history of Nepal, with its strife between hill and valley, seems to have abetted the situation. The Joneses write of the life of the Limbu woman:

> The actual division of labor between the Limbu man and woman is recognized by the people themselves as extremely flexible. Women are never "put down" by Limbu men because of their childbearing role and their domestic labor; on the contrary, the men respect them the more for their contributions in these spheres.[32]

Limbu women, like their Nyeshang counterparts, engage in extensive trading, a role that has probably received more impetus because of the unique social position of the Nepali hill groups vis-à-vis the valley.

If the history of the hill woman is, then, one of comparative independence (just as the history of the hill peoples themselves might be placed in this category), the movements of women today in Nepal show a remarkable amalgamation of Western and traditional views. It may be easier for the Nepalese woman than either her Indian or Bangladeshi counterpart to take information that has come from abroad and use it to alter her life. In any case, Nepal is filled with women who have either been abroad—even if only to India or Thailand—or have relatives who have been outside Nepal. The most interesting story in Nepal is the tale of the Nepali hill woman today.

The Nepali Woman: A Contemporary Look

Throughout our text we have made a distinction between the lives of the traditional women of the Kathmandu Valley area (many of whom belong to the Newar culture), and the flatlands, or *tarai*, and the women of the more Buddhist- or Tibetan-oriented hill groups. The *tarai* and Kathmandu Valley area is, as has been said, Hindu, and the lives of women from these areas are much more similar to the styles of living employed by women in northern India. Indeed, a recent work in cultural anthropology by Steven Parish on the city of Bhaktapur, near Kathmandu, is titled *Moral Knowing in a Hindu Sacred City*.[33]

But the roles of women in the hill groups are affected not only by the comparative freedom of the juxtaposition of Hindu, Buddhist, and animist beliefs that might best be described as the foundation for their lives, but also by the history of trading and of traveling-beyond in which these peoples have engaged. Because women in these groups have a long history of trading, in general, and because of their comparative freedom with respect to other roles—in the past, women were often herders, for example—changes for women now are coming rapidly. Watkins writes of the unusual mélange of cultures that is to be found among the hill groups, as they pick and choose from among a variety of items to which they have been exposed:

> In the course of their excursions out and about on the Asian continent, Nyeshangte encountered (and learned to deal with) not only Chinese warlords, British colonial officers, Western tourists, and American GIs, but also on occasion came face to face with their favorite Western icons. One of my acquaintances in Kathmandu proudly showed me a photograph in his office that was taken in Chiang Mai [in Thailand, where he had gone to trade]: he and his younger brother were dwarfed by a smiling Sylvester Stallone, who stood between them with his arms draped around their shoulders. Apparently, while filming on location in Northern Thailand, Stallone had visited the family's souvenir shop and posed for the photo with the two Nyeshangte brothers.[34]

What makes the story almost more remarkable is the subtext—many Nyeshangte traders in Thailand are posing as regional hill people (that is, Thai people) for the benefit of Westerners, and selling crafts that are so demarcated! This fact is mentioned by Watkins on the same page, and, although it may not pertain to the Stallone familiars themselves, it is an indicator of how the breakdown of categories has come to affect the entire Nepalese area and alter social relationships.

The Nyeshang women interviewed by Watkins are currently leading quite independent lives, moving about Nepal as traders and exposed—as has just been mentioned—to an enormous variety of outside influences. One of Watkins's informants, on being taken to see the Oliver Stone film *Platoon*, remarked that she wondered whether or not the film was quite accurate, because she, a young Nyeshangte teenager living in Nepal, had always been under the impression that the Americans won the war in Vietnam.[35]

Some of the Buddhist tradition of reference to women in contexts that allow for female growth is no doubt configured in the explanation of the comparative strength of Nepalese hill women. Although it is difficult to pinpoint with any precision what parts of what tradition might have taken hold in a given area—particularly since, as we have seen, Nepal is noteworthy for its religious mix—Paul and other scholars have noted not only the female tradition of the Bodhisattvas, but a role for females as spiritual guides as well. According to Paul, there is a "good daughter" tradition in Buddhism that allows for daughters, as well as sons, to take their place as fomenters of spiritual growth. Paul writes:

> The good daughter who is virtuous teaches others about the Dharma and may qualify as a "good friend" ... although the good daughter does not necessarily have to be a good friend. To be a good daughter presupposes one has had a good friend who shows the Buddhist path by example and who instructs in the teaching of the Dharma.[36]

It may be that many hill women, in addition to performing a variety of duties that would, for example, probably be outside the sphere of the Bangladeshi woman, are living out the example of the "good daughter," in the sense that they have become instructresses. Whatever the accuracy of this statement, there is much in the observations of those who have lived in Nepal to support the notion that the non-Newar, non-Hindu women are leading lives relatively unconstrained, and where the strength of the trading model may have actually opened some doors.

A feature of the lives of contemporary hill women, particularly those who have either traveled beyond Nepal or who have relatives who have traveled beyond Nepal, is that they are often the first to bring back styles and modes of living that, even though Westernized, may ultimately result in an amalgam between the Western and the Nepalese. Watkins was constantly struck during her stay in Kathmandu by the changes that had been wrought not merely by tourism, but by specific patterns being adapted by Nepalese women and then spread to other regions. She recounts that one of her Nepalese hosts, a young woman, was constantly mistaken for a foreigner, even by Nepalese, because sufficient exposure had altered her manner, even though she thought of herself as Nepalese.[37] Hill women, living in the region of what has become known as the "Annapurna Circuit," have set up on their own "tourist shops," and some of them have opened lodges or begun catering to tourists in other ways. In some cases, these women are unmarried, and this is strictly a female-only enterprise.[38]

The combination of business acumen, the changes wrought to Nepal by the booming "mountain" industry, and the somewhat stronger emphasis on the female in Buddhism than one finds in some other religious traditions can be a heady mix. As Watkins notes of the Nyeshang, the Joneses also assert that, within a traditional society the Limbu woman has a greater degree of autonomy than a naive observer might expect. Again, the autonomy extends in several directions: it may have to do with tasks performed, with roles in ritual, or even with relationships in marriage. The Joneses characterize contemporary Limbu life and the woman's role as follows:

> We have noted the changing role of the Limbu woman, her contributions to Limbu economy, her authority within the household, her covert and overt powers within the decision making process, and the ambiguous and often difficult situation of marriage in a patrilineally organized society. Nowhere is her role more active, however, than in the dissolution of a marriage.... [W]e try to explain the part she plays in divorce.[39]

In many ways, of course, the lives of both Nyeshangte and Limbu women are constrained by tradition. As is the case in the other South Asian societies we have examined, the marital institution is driven to a great extent by the cares and wants of the mother-in-law, and in many situations the change in a woman's status over time from daughter-in-law to mother-in-law herself is one of the greatest changes that a woman can experience. The Joneses perhaps understate the case when they say, with respect to the mother-in-law, that "she tests the young bride daily."[40]

A combination of ritual, tradition, and new ways retrieved from foreigners or from contact with the mountain or tourist trade now shapes and guides the lives of many Nepali hill women. The ability to take the new and transform it into the familiar is a hallmark of change, of course, and the hill woman is now, in many cases, adept at this task. It is not at all uncommon for visitors to Nepal to find material taken directly from Western "junk" culture lying on top of, or mixed in with, sacred objects or objects that would have a completely different sort of appeal. This postmodern mix may say a great deal about contemporary Nepal.

Watkins probably provides the best look at contemporary Nepali hill women who have moved into the Kathmandu area when she describes her interaction with young women who are themselves appropriating the postmodern mix and the tradition of business acumen to alter their lives.

Watkins illustrates the conundrum that is the life of the contemporary woman of Nepal—especially the contemporary woman who has had some exposure to Western culture, which is, of course, not unusual—when she writes:

> The actual existence of this partial or scrambled knowledge was especially hard for me to fathom at first, since many of my young Nyeshangte friends in Kathmandu seemed at times so worldly, so sophisticated (yet paradoxically so Americanized) in language, dress and mannerisms. They also seemed generally more self-possessed and more widely informed than many of the youths I had known in California, friends of my teenage son. But I came to realize that this fragmented knowledge was quite pervasive and that it occupied a central place in the imaginations of Nyeshangte youths.[41]

Paul's analysis of the notions of the feminine in the Buddhist tradition helps us to come to grips with the lives of Nepali women today, but a fuller understanding is achieved if we think of their lives, in particular, as related to the current postmodern notions of bricolage or mélange. The Nepali hill woman who has been exposed to the urban areas of Nepal—or any other urban areas—is frequently acting out several traditions at once: traditions of the Buddhist woman of compassionate action, the hill market woman, and traditions of the Western active woman picked up from the general ubiquitous influence of the Western media and Western culture. Such a woman may find herself in a bit of a state of flux as she moves from one role to another, but of one thing we can be assured—move she will, as motion seems to be a chief component of the lives of many contemporary Nepalese women.

Feminist Beginnings in Nepal

Among the Newar women of the Kathmandu Valley, there doubtless are contemporary feminist groups cast in the Western mold, just as we can hypothesize that there are such groups in Dhaka in Bangladesh, for example.[42] But Watkins, the Joneses and other observers report work in the hill groups that may be nascently feminist, as was the case with the BRAC-related work that we encountered in Bangladesh. Whether or not hill women have achieved a self-consciousness about their status qua women appears to be another matter. Such consciousness was born in the BRAC groups partly due to the efforts of the group leaders and partly, we can hypothesize, because the Islamic culture may have placed women in such a position that it virtually demanded some thought from the woman who first begins to read and write or experience a direct awareness of her culture.

Hill women may experience some awareness of what we would label "feminism" when they begin to participate in activities that put them in greater touch with Western culture, or when they experience episodes stemming from the involvement of a male household member's awareness of such culture. Watkins, as we have noted, has reported that men who have traveled abroad may actually bring back the notion of "men's work," and that this may cause a given situation to become less egalitarian than it otherwise would have been. As she notes, the category "ketiko kam" is one that involves the conceptualization that certain tasks are women's work, but this category is one that appears to come into play largely when the males in question have been exposed to the "traditional" gender division of labor through other cultures.[43]

In any case, there appears to be at least some awareness within the various hill cultures of divisions (no matter how more egalitarian hill groups may actually be) within the culture that work to the detriment of women, and at least some nascent movements toward alteration of this situation. The Nepalese government has experienced a number of tensions arising from the longtime attempt to implement a "panchayat" system, rather than direct democratic representation, and more recent attempts, especially during the past decade, to achieve a governmental structure more on a par with other nations, even other monarchies.[44] Because of the acrimony engendered by such efforts, and the ongoing strained relations between the Hindu *tarai* community and the mountains, many government mediators have found themselves in situations of ongoing mediation with hill groups. In various formats, the concerns of women have come to the fore, and women have frequently been vocal about expressing indignation over criticism they have received if their efforts to do work on behalf of their regional group have come in for criticism.[45]

Still another area in which beginning feminist stirrings are felt is the work having to do with Nepalis in the sex industry. Because of the open India-Nepal border, a situation that is virtually porous with regard to both human beings and goods has developed, and many young women from the mountain groups (and some Newars and other Hindus from Kathmandu and Pokhara) have wound up in brothels in India, primarily in Bombay and other large areas. Women who have been involved in the work have formed the United Nepali Organization for the Relief of Suffering Women, and reports generated by them and by others can be found in the work of

Human Rights Watch.[46] It is currently estimated that there are approximately 20,000 Nepali women involved in prostitution in the Bombay area alone. The Watch reports that:

> Despite the abundance of legislation aimed at preventing trafficking and other forms of slavery, neither India nor Nepal has adequately enforced existing laws, investigated reports of official complicity in the trafficking industry or prosecuted officials found profiting from the trade.[47]

Interestingly enough, much of the information that Human Rights Watch was able to obtain on this topic came from Nepali women themselves who had either been or were currently involved in prostitution.[48] Because early marriage is still the norm in many villages, and because marriages tend to be arranged, it is possible for young men to present themselves in a village as interested in marriage, or simply interested in friendship, and to wind up abducting young women to regions outside the village and, ultimately, outside Nepal. Increasing numbers of girls and young women who have become victimized are becoming activists after their return to Nepal, sometimes after they have been infected with HIV.

The doubled-edged sword that we have examined earlier with respect to Nepal seems to run through the lives of Nepali women, affecting both their circumstances and the manner in which they choose to fight their circumstances. The modernist and postmodernist cultural spaces that have been visited upon Nepal in rapid succession have yielded a bewildering variety of changes, in dizzying speed, with little if any infrastructure designed to assist in dealing with the changes. Thus the paradox remains that, partly due to the comparative egalitarianism of hill groups, new practices, such as those just described, can be instituted in such a way that it may not be immediately apparent exactly what has transpired. Hill women are accustomed to travel, as has been noted, because trade has always been such a large part of their lives. Approximately 70 percent of the sex workers in India who are Nepalese are thought to belong to one of four groups, according to Human Rights Watch—the Tamang, Gurung, Magar, and Sherpa.

Still another form of interaction with foreigners that may have odd twists and turns for the Nepalese is that engendered by the visits of various American assistants from aid groups, such as the Peace Corps and other such organizations. Barbara Scot, in her largely anecdotal account of a year spent teaching in Nepal, writes of some of her encounters with local women:

I rise to wash before it is light. I walk a quarter mile to the village well. Other women are already there with water jugs. They are used to me now and even take my bucket and fill it out of turn. I say thank you in English since there is not really a word for it in Nepali—only *danybaad*, which is used by foreigners. There is not even a concept for it in Nepali, because you do not expect to be given thanks for doing what is required of you by your *dharma*.[49]

Scot's encounter marks, of course, a two-way intersection. As she learns more about Nepalese culture, she is in a position to comment on notions of duty and respect. But what is happening simultaneously is that the women to whom she is talking are learning, perforce, more about Western cultures and are receiving lessons in other ways of being that they would never have had. Thousands and thousands of such incidents, repeated all over Nepal because of the promotion of the tourism and mountain industries, have resulted in a much greater degree of exposure than would be the case, for example, in Bangladesh or in most of India's villages, particularly those that are not located near any well-known shrines or large cities.

Thus the exposure to Western ways brings, in many cases, new forms of oppression—such as the notion of "women's work," or the burden of the sex industry—but it also brings the tools with which to fight this oppression. And it may yield the thought, on the part of at least some Nepali women activists, that certain cultural patterns need to be examined in light of their predisposition to lend themselves to abuses. There are signs that this is even now emerging in Nepal.

In this chapter we have focused almost exclusively on Buddhist-derived traditions for the mountain communities of Nepal, since the Hindu culture of the *tarai* and Kathmandu Valley is very similar to that of northern India. Nevertheless, one salient point emerges. If it is the case, as almost all commentators agree, that the Hindu and Buddhist views mesh and merge to a great extent in Nepal, and that there are other holdovers as well (Tibetan animism, for one), then much of what has infused women's movements and lives in northern India must be playing out to some extent in Nepal as well. That is to say that elements of the goddess-related tradition lead us, as usual, in two directions: there are "evil temptresses" and benign or helpful deities, and the existence of the temptress tradition is mentioned in Paul as being concomitant with codified elements of Buddhism.[50] Because of this, we can hypothesize that elements of these traditions are at work in Nepalese culture in ways that are parallel to the assessments that we have already made about portions of Indian culture.

But that which is truly unique about the Nepalese hill groups whose existence we have described here is a kind of Buddhism that retains its primary focus while still having admixtures from a number of other traditions. This, as has been indicated—plus the decidedly postmodern mix of the tourist/mountain industry and the emphasis on trade that was already a part of the mountain cultures—yields a potent source for cultural analysis and has been the subject of a great deal of contemporary commentary. The Buddhist tradition has an epistemics of its own, and women are a part of this knowledge-related set of practices. How women participate is a subject that now yields to rigorous analysis.

Women and the Knowledge Path

As is the case with the doctrines of some well-known thinkers in the Western tradition, the knowledge path in Buddhism requires withdrawal and an awareness of the transitory nature of all phenomena. One of the first parallels that comes to mind in the Western tradition is with the thought of Spinoza, since his distinction between partial and other causes asks for a focus on *sub specie aeternitatis*.[51] In a chapter titled "The Bodhisattvas Without Sexual Transformation," Diana Paul makes a similar point when she says:

> The *Diamond Sutra* summarizes the metaphysics of these [canonical Buddhist] texts most appropriately in the following quatrain which concludes the sutra:
>
>> As stars, a fault of vision, as a lamp,
>> A mock show, dew drops, or a bubble,
>> A dream, a lightning flash, or cloud,
>> So should one view what is conditioned.[52]

In any case, it is clear that at least a strong part of the Buddhist tradition enjoins us to forget about worldly distinctions, since they have nothing to do with the capacity for transcendence. In Paul's work she spends a great deal of time analyzing the tensions between the older, more classical part of the tradition—some of it dating back to the Buddha's own commentary—which sees sexual differences as important, since women presumably have different roles, and a different sort of tradition that indicates that sexuality/gender is unimportant.[53] One assertion that can be made is that the tradition as a whole allows for the existence not only of nuns, but of female Bodhisattvas and of other enlightened beings who might in some sense be demarcated as female. But this leads to still another difficulty: given that the actual Bodhisattva path is a rare one, and that it does not make sense to try to categorize even dedicated, hardworking women along these lines most of the time, how can the lives of women within the Nepalese Buddhist tradition be conceptualized in a way that is connected to traditional Buddhist epistemic practice but that is not question begging?

As indicated earlier, there are also traditional levels of assistance along the path toward knowledge acquisition that do not themselves entail such severe renunciation. One of these is the "good daughter," a path that we have already analyzed. The "good daughter" is capable of much, but one of the tasks that she is specifically assigned is "teaching and respecting the Dharma."[54] In this sense, there is much that represents an appropriation of this particular knowledge tradition in the lives of both Nyeshangte and Limbu women, as we have seen from the work of Watkins and the Joneses.

Fortunately, Buddhism, with its respect for life, already lends itself to lines of analysis that Western feminist theorists might deem to be feminist friendly. Kathleen Okruhlik, in her *Women and Reason*, provides an analysis of why the work of Carolyn Merchant and others on the nature/culture distinction has become so important:

> Merchant argues that the view of earth as a nurturing mother brought with it moral constraints against exploitation—as, for example, in mining, which was often identified as a sort of rape of mother earth.[55]

This view is by no means foreign to the Buddhist outlook in general, and is a view that informs much of what Paul identifies as the "good daughter" or even female Bodhisattva approaches. In general, an epistemic that asks one to divorce oneself from the senses and to approach reality in a meditative way is consistent with much of Buddhism, and although this particular outlook declined in the West with the advent of the Renaissance, the rise in science, and so forth, it is identifiable in many Hellenistic traditions, and, as we just indicated, in certain thinkers such as Spinoza.

Watkins identifies the current ramifications of such views in the work that she sees Nyeshang women doing in their villages and in rituals performed both inside and outside the home. It is not necessary to formally become a renouncer or a nun, of course, to embody this outlook. Rather, the "good daughter" or "good friend" is one who uses her skills to try to set others on the right path. One of the points that Watkins makes is that, in the odd mix that has become "tradition" in contemporary Nepal, it is now more common for young men to be drawn outside of Buddhist traditions and to fail, in some sense, to perform their duties. This has led an even larger number of young women to assume such duties, and it also allows for women to assume roles that in the West might be more strictly gender defined. Watkins writes of the exodus of young men and the arrival, so to speak, of young women:

> It is largely because of this "monk exodus" from the community that the number and duties of nuns have expanded in recent years. In addition, with the influx of trade money, many village residents are commissioning household and community rites more often, and this too has led to an increased demand for ritual specialists. As a result, many locally trained nuns are replacing monks as officiates and are undertaking ritual activities—funerals, consecrations or playing the drums and cymbals—that traditionally were performed only by male monastics in other Tibetan Buddhist communities.[56]

The "good daughter," then, is a figure who appropriates some of the knowledge path for herself and also helps or teaches others, as the material from Watkins indicates. As remarked earlier, Paul identifies two separate strands of the tradition that illustrates the roles that women have in Buddhism. One strand emphasizes the Buddha's own sayings, usually demarcated as *sutras*, and indicates that the Buddha had outlined what would be regarded as traditional roles for women, as caretakers in the home, preparers of household goods and services, and so forth. The second part of the tradition, however, indicates that because the inner core doctrine of Buddhism is beyond gender—these "accidents" of the body, in Western philosophical terms, not being crucial for roles having to do with renunciation and liberation—the gender of the novice or would-be knower or renouncer is not important. Paul has separate chapters to indicate how, insofar as the concept of the Bodhisattva is concerned, all of this is relevant.[57]

In any case, for purposes of our analysis, it is interesting to note that not only is it the case that the epistemic paths of canonical Buddhism allow for roles for women, but that the infusion of the postmodern in Nepal has, if anything, actually increased the number of roles. A slight rise in the number of women becoming nuns or officiating, as Watkins indicates, may actually be discernible because of the influx of Western ideas insofar as those ideas affect the more mobile young men.

Although the question of the ultimate possibility of "Buddha nature" in the female may never be answered fully from the texts,[58] the crucial Buddhist notion that adoption of a certain attitude is the key factor in moving toward the Bodhisattva role (or, for that matter, the "good daughter" or "good friend" role) makes it easier for notions that in the West might be considered androcentric to be adopted for a variety of uses. The withdrawal and speculation that European tradition sees as the hallmark of the philosopher—and thus, of one who has begun a quest for ultimate knowledge—are, in the West, seen as activities characteristic of males and not of females. Thus the lengthy commentary on the defects of females, dating back to Plato and Aristotle both, ensures that even in Enlightenment times the work that women did of an intellectual nature was not taken seriously.

In general, this problem does not exist in the Buddhist tradition to the same extent that it does within the European tradition. We can see the evidence, in the lives of the mountain women of Nepal, of a female-driven articulation of knowledge patterns at work.

The Nepalese View

Our work on the hill women of Nepal has focused on two main areas: we have looked at the fact that cultural patterns for the Nyeshangte and the Limbu, as spelled out by ethnographers, already indicate a high degree of movement within the culture for women in these groups, and by extension many groups that are in the Buddhist/Tibetan/Bon traditions. By the same token, we have also been able to see that Buddhism—unlike some other major religious traditions—has a greater history of roles for females that are specifically articulated as such. The combination of these factors, plus the somewhat unusual mix of modernist and postmodernist elements found in contemporary Nepal due, at least partly, to the mountaineering and trekking businesses, has made the roles of women in Nepal somewhat more fluid than they are in a number of nearby regions.

For purposes of contrast, it may be recalled that much of what we found to be taking place in the villages of Bangladesh, for example, that allowed women a reappropriation of certain roles was driven by the intervention of BRAC workers who attempted to get Bengali Muslim women to leave the home for small periods of time and begin to make decisions about their lives. In general, no such inhibitions mark the lives of most Nepali hill women, and many of the women have routinely traveled and traded and taken on traditional religious roles for quite some time. Nevertheless, there are, of course, some restrictions. As we saw earlier, Watkins reported that plowing was forbidden to women, and women who took on the task were quite aware of violating a number of prohibitions.[59] In addition, and perhaps more important, many women were reported by Watkins as having to cope with a new phenomenon: the notion that some work was "women's work" (in some cases, this was work that had not previously been demarcated as women's work), a concept imported by male Nepalese who had traveled abroad and who had actually picked up the concept in their travels.[60]

Finally, although it is clear from a perusal of both Kathryn Blackstone and Diana Paul that there is a specific gynocentric tradition within Buddhism,[61] the existence of this tradition is itself bifurcated by a notion, on the one hand, that women are best seen as "temptresses"—a notion not unfamiliar to other traditions, obviously—and a notion on the other hand that much of what is positive in their role may be seen as helpmate or guide. There is much within traditional Buddhism, as within almost every major religious tradition, that tends to preclude the participation of women in many ways, and to fail to acknowledge this is to err with respect both to Buddhism and to the practitioners of it.

The Nyeshang and Limbu women are women of hill trading cultures that have a lengthy history of contact with India and with other regions, dating back in some cases before the British intervention in India, and certainly forwarded by the intervention. Part of the historical conflict between power in this region has to do with the notion that the most economically valuable part of Nepal, the *tarai* or flatlands region, could not be dominated without at least some assistance from the hill regions. Thus, in a paradoxical twist, the mountain people became important in colonial circles even as it was recognized that their land was not nearly as valuable or profitable as the flatter, more arable areas.[62] As Gaige notes in his historical overview of relations between the British and the Nepalese, mountain groups were forced into the *tarai* regions both because of their importance strategically and because of their worth to the British. This constant influx of activity no doubt increased trade levels and made the roles of traders in the hill groups—male or female—more active and more attuned to nonlocal happenings than they otherwise would have been.

In writing of the Nyeshangte and the Limbu, the authors whose work we have examined are continually struck by the comparative egalitarianism of both groups. The Joneses note that the Limbu function in such a way that knowing the patterns of the women involved is the crux to an understanding of what transpires in their society:

> [A]n understanding of the Limbu woman's active role in society is crucial to an understanding of Limbu family life. In Limbuan nuclear family households predominate, the bridewealth payments are extensive and drawn out, and the Limbu have a relatively high rate of marriage instability and divorce.[63]

From an ethnographic standpoint, understanding the roles of women can only become this important if women are already accorded a status in the society that may well not be found in many comparable groups. As has been indicated here, this status is a combination of factors, two of which—the trading history of the mountain peoples, and the history of canonical Buddhism itself—have become intertwined to a remarkable extent.

To cite Paul one more time, the controversy within Buddhism about the importance of the type of sexed body in which one is born (male body or female body, as "body-of-this-lifetime") sheds light on the overall conception of the roles open to an individual. Paul has extensive discussion of both female Bodhisattvas and the "good daughter"/"good friend", but she also has a closing chapter on the concept of the female Buddha.[64] Here is Paul on this topic:

> If women were truly capable of having a Buddha nature in this lifetime without undergoing any sexual transformation, this would implicitly indicate that women were not biologically determined as religiously, psychologically and physically inferior to men....
>
> Other commentaries on the *Lotus Sutra* also indicate that there is no necessity to undergo sexual changes prior to Buddhahood. For example, the ... commentary claims that if an individual has attained the patience to understand the Emptiness ... of all phenomena, then there would be no necessity to relinquish one's present physical form for another.[65]

Thus women have an unusual status within Buddhism, a status that, as we have seen, is probably significantly different from that of most of the world's other major religious traditions. Although Buddhism certainly has texts and commentaries that are malecentered, the existence of the material cited by Paul is significant and places Buddhism outside of the main arenas of sexist text development, at least insofar as the possibility of taking part in major religious psychological transformation is concerned. Christianity, Judaism, Islam, and, as we have seen, Hinduism are all more straightforwardly misogynistic in their espousal of doctrine. What Watkins cites, then, as the remarkable independence of Nyeshang women is just another example of the juxtaposition of religious traditions, economic necessity, and the unusual terrain and topography of Nepal. All of these have combined to allow the Nepalese mountain woman working within the Buddhist/ Tibetan/Bon tradition a degree of freedom and place in the culture that is rare throughout South Asia.

Our overview of four cultures in South Asia—northern India, southern

India, Bangladesh, and Nepal—would not be complete without at least a minimal contrast among these varietals. As we have seen, the women of Bangladesh work against the greatest combination of obstacles: not only is the poverty of Bangladesh probably the most extreme (a fact that is regularly reported by organizations such as Oxfam and UNICEF), but the juxtaposition of the Islamic tradition and the levels of rural poverty combines for massive oppression. Although the women of northern India might be thought to have been exposed to a greater number of outside influences than those of southern India—especially when the effect of British colonialism and its construction of schools and universities is taken into account—the *shakti* tradition actually appears to be somewhat stronger in southern India, and however paradoxical the effects of this tradition, it makes itself felt more keenly in areas that are more purely Hindu and where the local culture is less an amalgam of influences. Both southern and northern India provide women with a variety of goddess models, but ethnography informs us that the appropriation of these models, and thus the epistemic effect of them, seems to be stronger in the south.

Nepalese women of the *tarai* and valley areas close to Kathmandu and Pokhara are frequently Hindu, and their culture, by all accounts, is very similar to the culture of the northern Indian plains, particularly Bihar and the area adjacent to the Nepalese border.[66] Our work here, then, has focused on women of the Nepalese mountain cultures, specifically the Nyeshang and Limbu cultures, as documented by extensive contemporary ethnography. Watkins, in particular, has helped us to see the lives of these women as a postmodern mix: in some cases, as she has mentioned, roles that might initially be thought to be more egalitarian are actually changed for the worse by exposure to Western culture.[67] The Joneses document the extent to which life among the Limbu was a surprise for them; little that they had seen in previous trips to South Asia prepared them for the comparative ease of the situation of women within the Limbu society.[68] Zimmer himself writes of the degree to which Nepal, India, Afghanistan, and other areas are aligned in the great South Asian traditions.[69] Perhaps the most noteworthy statement that can be made about the hill women of Nepal is that they stand out.[70]

Part 3

New World Focal Points

Chapter 6

Mexico and the *Mestizaje*

Descriptions of the culture of Mexico almost always focus on its *mestizo* origins and the tensions between the Spaniards and indigenous peoples that have been a hallmark of the Mexican geographical region for hundreds of years. It is important to note, however, that well before the arrival of the Europeans long periods of warring and conquest had come to only a brief halt with the completion of the Aztec empire.[1] Continued struggle among various groups, and among the Europeans themselves, was a regular feature of life in the early period of Mexico's European settlement, often referred to as "New Spain."

If the origins of *mestizo* Mexico can be said to have begun with the arrival of the Spaniards and their cohabitation with indigenous women, it is also the case that one of the other great features of Mexican culture, the reliance on religion and faith, can be said to have begun in a similar fashion. Stories of the Aztecs' beliefs in the supernatural capabilities of the Spaniards sound apocryphal, but historians agree that the year of Cortes's arrival was by chance precisely the year foreordained for the return of Quetzalcoatl or a harbinger of the deity.

Robert Ryan Miller notes some of the complexity involved in getting clear on what the Spaniards could have meant to the Mexicans:

In 1515, rumors that Quetzalcoatl had returned circulated throughout Anáhuac. Reports filtered up to the highland plateau about large watercraft, "temples in the sea," that had been sighted along Mexico's eastern littoral. . . . After much discussion, the majority of the leaders, concluding that the intrusion was the return of the Feathered Serpent god-king or his disciples, appointed a welcoming committee. . . . The next year was 1519, or One-Reed, the year of Quetzalcoatl's prophesy. Indeed, the bearded strangers embarked that year and made plans to visit Tenochtitlán, thus initiating one of the most fascinating cultural confrontations in all of recorded history.[2]

In other words, an odd mixture of the supernatural, human greed, natural curiosity, and a desire to explore marked the arrival of the Spaniards, and similar remarks might be made about much of the rest of their early stay in New Spain.

Alternating movements of priest, and nuns—the first convent appears to have been established in 1547, thus giving women an earlier role in the Church than some may have guessed[3]—interacted with the Native Americans, and the motivations of the Spaniards as a whole seemed to have moved back and forth between trying to attain wealth and a genuine desire to produce converts to Catholicism. In some cases entire religious orders walked barefoot from points of disembarkation to the interior of Mexico, and the respect that was shown by the Spanish military toward the friars and priests no doubt made an impression on the indigenous population.[4]

There was little about this unusual cultural combination that did not speak of male dominance, however, whether one conceptualizes the dominance in the form of war or religion. Aside from the nuns, the women present at the time were overwhelmingly Native American women, who were obviously at the mercy of the Europeans. More important, perhaps, a tradition began almost immediately for the Spaniards to take multiple "mistresses" (Cortes alone is said to have had eight), so that the number of offspring produced by these liaisons was from the beginning very high. It is because of these facts, as well as the historical position of La Malinche, or Doña Marina, that Octavio Paz and others have labeled Mexico's culture as fraught with the knowledge that the people are "hijos de la chingada" (children of the one who was violated). Rapacity, overt hostility and aggression, and the continual desire to build Catholic churches on the sites of Indian temples of worship marked the early years of the Spanish conquest.

Howard Cline, Robert Ryan Miller, and others agree on the violence and chaos that both preceded and succeeded the arrival of the Spaniards. Cline notes, with respect to the period of Aztec consolidation and attempts at hegemony immediately before the Spaniards, that "discontinuities outrank continuity and homogeneity in the aboriginal epochs."[5] It is also the case, however, that within approximately sixty years the Spaniards had established effective control over a huge area, encompassing regions far south of contemporary Mexico. *Encomiendas*, or land tributes exacted from the Native Americans, allowed an Iberian system of agriculture to flourish, and Cline notes that by around 1580 "Mexico had settled down to its main colonial occupations."[6]

The emphasis on the other-worldly found in both the indigenous cultures in Mexico and in Catholic Spain itself combined, in the case of the construction of the *mestizo* culture, to create a metaphysical overview reliant upon speculation and an almost mystical sense of communion with reality. Although a number of commentators have emphasized how thoroughly nineteenth-century Mexico was influenced not only by Spain, but by France and to some extent even by Great Britain,[7] there has been little, historically speaking, in the Mexican temperament that has been empirical or even positivistic in the sense of Comte's nineteenth-century philosophy. By the time of the consolidation of the Mexican state under Porfirio Díaz, much of what was constitutive of Mexican culture was contained in the original *grito*, or cry of independence, "Viva la Virgen de Guadalupe!"[8] This sense that Mexico contained a special destiny, encouraged in part by the plain historical fact that the region surrounded by Popocatépetl and other volcanoes was the home of two or three great cultures, became enshrined in Mexico's own articulated philosophy during an earlier portion of this century, that of José Vasconcelos.[9] Vasconcelos argued that the creation of Mexico had forged a new race, which he termed the "*raza cósmica*" (cosmic race), and that, among other things, this new group was marked by a gift for the aesthetic and a propensity to see the beauty in life. Vasconcelos writes, in comparing the "Mexican soul" with that of its European counterparts:

> The basis of white [Anglo or British] civilization is fuel.... The rude fight against the environment forced the whites to devote their aptitudes to the conquest of temporal nature, and it is precisely this that constitutes their contribution to the civilization of the future.... The English, who see only the present in the external world, do not hesitate to apply zoological theories to the field of human sociology.[10]

The fact that a leading Mexican intellectual felt free to articulate what he took to be key points of difference between his culture and other cultures by citing British empiricism as a counterpoint tells us a great deal about the construction of Mexican thought in the twentieth century.

In addition to Mexico's spiritual heritage, with its complex ramifications of both European and non-European points of origin, Mexico has been greatly influenced, of course, by its proximity to the United States. Especially later in the nineteenth century after the Mexican War, the United States was an entity against which Mexico chose to define itself, and this was comparatively easy to do because technology had not yet reached the point of near-instantaneous communication, nor was global capitalism in such a position as to create a near-insatiable market for consumer goods around the world. More recently, however, the proximity of the United States has proved to be a factor that must be taken into account in every aspect of Mexican culture, and much ink has been spilled on the notion of the "border culture," a zone that extends on both sides of the border for hundreds of miles and certainly to a depth of penetration of approximately fifty to a hundred miles on each side. Contemporary Mexico is, to rephrase Porfirio Díaz, "too close to the United States."

Macho, Male-Centeredness, and Dominance

As almost all commentators agree, the creation of present Mexico has much more to do with the emergence of the *mestizaje* than it does with any political movement or even any war, battle, or rebellion. Before roughly the middle of the nineteenth century, persons either born in Spain (*gachupines*) or of purely Spanish ancestry, although born in Mexico (*criollos*), held most positions of power and defined the nation culturally. After roughly the time of Benito Juárez, to be Mexican came more and more to mean to be a *mestizo*, someone whose ancestry literally was traceable to both Spanish (or other European) and indigenous elements. Perhaps most important of all, as Enrique Krauze writes, "The decisive *mestizaje* had been neither ethnic nor biological but cultural. The conquest of Mexico can be seen as a long process in which the cultures of the conquerors and the conquered flowed together in a new synthesis."[11]

But the creation of the *mestizaje*, however it is defined, is itself an act of male dominance and conquest—one might say the ultimate such act. When Cortes landed he was greeted by two Spaniards who had been left inland years before after an unlucky sailing from Cuba. One of the two had already taken an indigenous woman and had children resulting from the union, certainly the first mestizos of whom we have record. That many of these unions were no more voluntary than the master/slave mixings that mark the creation of the black American culture can scarcely be denied.

If one were to try to be specific about the various elements that comprise the androcentrism of Mexican society, one could scarcely be more precise than to note the blend of the masculinism of the sixteenth- and seventeenth-century Roman Catholic Church (especially as it made itself felt in post-1492, Moorless Spain), the aggressive warrior mode of much of Aztec and Aztec-dominated pre-Columbian Mexico, and the uses to which this masculinism was put in the classic development of Mexican history, the Revolution.

The androcentrism of the Church might be thought not to require much articulation, but it must be remembered that the Church, along with Iberian culture in general, reached Mexico at a time when it was fresh from one of its greatest triumphs, and so its traditional teachings were strengthened and enforced. The Church of the Inquisition and of the expulsion of the Moors and Jews from Spain still relied heavily on the teachings of the Fathers, and the speculative and transcending philosophical commitments of those teachings, in which denial of the body was paramount. Augustine, in the *Confessions*, wrote that in seeking answers he had "found the unchangeable and true eternity of Truth."[12] His commentators refer to his intellectual journey, the kind of journey engaged in by many in the Church, of course, as a "prayerful ascent."[13] These elements of Catholicism, untempered by the types of commitments Catholicism later made, met a powerful counterposing force in the mythology of the Aztecs and other indigenous groups. Most commentators emphasize the sacrificial nature of much of Aztec worship, and the stringency of Aztec dominance over other groups.[14] The meeting of these two worldviews meant that, in an odd way, they reinforced each other. Each already possessed a hierarchical, exalted, and quite explicitly androcentric overview.

The power of androcentric constructions in Mexican society has already been alluded to with respect to the formation of the *mestizaje*, but it had a stronger impetus in more contemporary times. Although Mexico had achieved a national sense of itself during the latter portion of the nineteenth century, it took the Revolution (1910–1920) to give the country still greater self-definition, particularly insofar as the peasantry and Indians were concerned. The Revolution itself seemed to mirror much of Mexican society, not only in its violence and chaos, but also in its recapitulation of social relations.

Women were actors during the Revolution—*soldaderas* were not uncommon, and many popular ballads or *corridos* that have become enshrined in the pantheon focus on them, such as "Adelita." But their roles, unsurprisingly, became highly sexualized, and once again they became the crucible in which a sense of national identity was formed by competing groups. For a period of a decade or more, armed parties led by various national and local leaders, including Zapata, Villa, Huerta, and others moved across the country, seizing land, destroying property, killing, and burning. As Miller notes, the Revolution built slowly, and once Diaz had been ousted and Madero gained power, "It then appeared that the Revolution was over, but it was just beginning."[15]

The role of women in the Revolution, particularly its early stages, is best summed up by Miller in the following:

> They [groups of peasants] fought in bands of thirty to three hundred, obtained guns from the enemy, and counted *soldadas* (women soldiers) among their leaders. Unarmed women who cooked for the soldiers, shared their beds, and nursed the wounded and ill were called *soldaderas* (camp followers). They formed part of most guerrilla bands and part of the regular army as well.[16]

At a later point Villa expelled most of the women who were with his particular group. Although there is no question that the situation demanded as many bearers of arms as possible, and that many of the photographs of the period document women with rifles and weapons, there is also no question that their role was in general secondary and highly sexualized. Thus once again possession of women became a defining element in the formation of crucial aspects of Mexican culture, especially since it is indeed the Revolution—with its notion of redistribution of land to those who had before been landless—that is the crux around which contemporary Mexico, however haphazardly, forms itself. This redistribution itself comprises the notion that each man has a piece of land, a woman, and a home.

The Revolution was a turning point for Mexico like no other, and the "institutionalized Revolution," that is, the PRI as it is known (*Partido Revolucionario Institucional*), became the only political party in Mexico for a period of some sixty to seventy years (until very recently—this structure has been altered in a meaningful way only in this decade). This political and social apparatus managed to institutionalize not only the Revolution, but much of what had transpired in *mestizo* Mexico before its occurrence; the systems of patronage, the family structure, and male dominance were all codified within the terms of the Revolution so that they came to be seen as symbols of progress. Doubtless this is in some sense accurate, since the Mexico of the preceding period was (especially before the 1860s) more a society of *criollos* and Indians, and to an even greater extent a society of *ranchos* and *patrones*. But the difficulty with the mythology created by the Revolution and the PRI was that anyone who tried to fight against it looked less than progressive—and this system proved to be very difficult to break.

Indigenous societies, as has been noted here, have frequently been seen by European anthropologists as containing more elements of the feminine than more industrialized societies, and globally speaking this may be the case. The Aztec culture, which had already come to dominate Mexico before the advent of the Spaniards, had perhaps something less of this structure than many other groups, even Native American groups. More important, as we have maintained, the Aztecs featured human sacrifice and outright aggression as prominent aspects of their way of life. The combination of this set of traits with the already extremely stylized and hierarchical life of the Catholic Spaniards was a particularly forceful and domineering one. Perhaps because of the literal creation of the *mestizaje*, the constructs within the Mexican culture that emphasize either point of origin have always underlined the most masculine aspects of the culture. Nevertheless, there is, of course, a counterbalancing force. There are decided elements of the gynocentric within the *mestizo* culture.

Female-Centeredness and Its Focal Points

Each separate element of the *mestizo* view—the Spanish Catholic world of the fathers, and the Indian world of the mothers—constructed the female in its own way. It might be thought that due to the patriarchal dominance of Catholicism, there has always been a strong Marianistic strain within the Church, which many feminist commentators have seen as an attempt, albeit unconscious and with ancient roots, to tap into some of the goddess-related cults of preceding eras of worship. This strain became extremely important in Mexico, of course; the rise to prominence of the figure of the Virgin of Guadalupe is merely one example of the importance of this Marian line of thought in Mexican Catholicism.

More intriguingly, perhaps, the goddesses of the Aztecs (and here we focus on this particular indigenous group, as they had already achieved a degree of consolidation before the arrival of the Iberians) are a particularly mixed collection. A listing of major deities of the Aztecs by Cottie Burland shows seven goddesses or goddess-like figures out of twenty-two mentioned deities;[17] in some sense these figures are standard, as they include more than one version of an Earth goddess figure, and at least one goddess related to phases of the moon. The number of goddesses listed is perhaps somewhat small, but we cannot know what criteria prompted the delineation of "major."[18] What is most remarkable, perhaps, is that only two or three of the goddesses listed seem to be related to aspects that might be thought to be beneficial or even benign. At least four of the goddesses (Chalchihuitlicue, Coatlicue, Itzapapalotl, and Tlazoteotl), can be construed as part of the darker forces, or as an observer of Hindu societies might say, of the fiery forces. Thus there appears to be a tendency to construe the female in terms of the demonic or death related. Given the fascination with brutal death that most commentators agree was an aspect of the Aztec culture, this construction of notions of the feminine has a powerful juxtaposition with devotion to Mary and to other female Christian figures. The result is a combination that places emphasis on females as having the power of life and death, and that perhaps strengthens connections of the female to death itself, transcendence, and overcoming.

As was mentioned earlier, nuns arrived in New Spain fairly early, although of course the overwhelming number of persons from the Iberian peninsula was male. But Mexico would have been ripe for a combination of Marian devotion and goddess worship, and this did, of course, occur. In Miller's version of the story, the Virgin is allied with a goddess not mentioned on the list compiled by Burland:

> One factor that aided the conversion of Indians in New Spain was the cult of the Virgin of Guadalupe. According to tradition, the Virgin Mary appeared three times in December, 1531, at the hill of Tepeyacac near Mexico City, a site that was an ancient Indian sacred place identified with Tonantzín, "the mother of the gods." Here the Virgin conversed with a Christianized Indian named Juan Diego and asked that a church be built on the hill.[19]

The fact that the seer was Indian is, obviously, crucial to this tale. If it is the case that the indigenous is categorized as the "feminine," it is also the case that much of what has occurred in Mexican history has aided this particular categorization. Lourdes Arizpe, a contemporary Mexican social scientist, has employed notions of the gynocentric in her conceptualizations with respect to Mexican peasant culture, and we can see some of these notions not only in the contemporary categories she uses, but also as historical holdovers from the original period of the creation of the *mestizaje*. She notes that there is much in the lives of peasant women (created, of course, from the same groups that originally gave rise to the vision of the Virgin) that speaks to us of the realm of that which is female:

> It is not that they [peasant women] have not spoken, only that their words have not been recognized. Because their words are discomforting when they denounce exploitation; disturbing when they display a deep understanding of the world not shared by their city sisters; ... and because, being women's words, they are not important to androcentric history.... Within the wide range of integrating philosophies of the peasants, "being" is not restricted to humans. Each element derives its existence from its relation to the whole.[20]

Although the indigenous cultures may not have engaged in the form of goddess worship that in some other cultures has been most closely allied with the gynocentric, Arizpe's comments make clear not only that the agrarian life cycle is today associated with the realm of the feminine and the natural, but, of course, that such associations would have been made at an earlier point in time. Thus, as has been argued here, the combination of the elements of Catholicism that led to a rise in interest in Marianistic devotion in Mexico, the Coatlicue- (and other-goddess) related material in the indigenous cultures, and the agrarian nature of *mestizo* life all combined to create a strong, if sometimes overlooked, gynocentric strain in Mexican thought. That this gynocentric strain had to contend against an even more pronounced strain of the masculine is, of course, true, and it is interesting to note how even cultural and literary critics have categorized the post-Revolutionary period, in particular, as being marked for its interest in the *macho*.[21] Perhaps this constant battle against masculinism has in some sense helped to define the gynocentric in Mexican culture.

In any case, it is worthwhile to note the extent to which the type of gynocentric thought referred to by Arizpe has strong analogues in contemporary mainstream feminist theory. Here it is not necessary to do as much conceptual work as might be required with an Asian society, for example, since much of what is located in Mexican culture is clearly of European origin. Arizpe is, in fact, using such categories in her own approach. But all of this material, taken together, helps to underscore the type of contention made in the introduction to Kathleen Lennon and Margaret Whitford's *Knowing the Difference: Feminist Perspectives in Epistemology:*

> Feminism's most compelling epistemological insight lies in the connections it has made between knowledge and power. This, not simply in the obvious sense that access to knowledge enables empowerment; but more controversially through the recognition that legitimation of knowledge claims is intimately tied to networks of domination and exclusion.[22]

Since it is clear that masculinism and Eurocentrism worked in tandem in Mexico throughout its history, it is easy to see why the gynocentric strains, though always present, might legitimately be said to have been dominated and excluded. Retrieval of such strains, then, is a feminist project of overwhelming importance.

Just as there has been a number of elements in the general culture that pointed to female-centeredness within the Mexican outlook, there is also

another strain that has been of somewhat greater assistance than might originally have been realized. As mentioned earlier, because of the presence of at
least a few nuns in Mexico from the very beginning of the Spanish possession, at least some literary work was always under female production. The
importance of Sor Juana Ines de la Cruz to Mexican culture on the whole can
scarcely be overestimated, and her work has always received recognition.
Here again two lines merge: the Catholicism that we have come to associate
with masculinist elements of the European tradition does indeed find a different sort of outlet in the work of nuns and women thinkers in the sixteenth
and seventeenth centuries, and Sor Juana's work is noteworthy not only for
its piety but for its articulation of a female point of view.[23] Since Sor Juana
wrote at a time when the literary output of New Spain was still comparatively small, her early voice helped to define that literary output and she herself becomes emblematic of the creation of Mexican writing and literature.
As one translator has it, one of her "Redondillas" begins:

> Stupid men, quick to condemn
> Women wrongly for their flaws,
> Never seeing you're the cause
> Of all that you blame in them![24]

If it is true, as Arizpe has suggested, that we can define at least some
gynocentric elements by advertence to an epistemic of indigenous and
impoverished women in Mexican history, then it is also clear that many of
the elements that we have alluded to here push us in that direction. Rebellious nuns working against masculinist Catholicism, some strains of the
indigenous culture itself, and Marianistic devotion as an intersection of the
Catholic and the indigenous—all of these form a powerful nexus of gynocentrism, and help to establish a view that distances itself from the overarching, the transcendental and the patriarchal. As Janna Thompson writes,
the claim that women reason differently in the moral sphere is at bottom a
claim that can be simply stated: "[Those] who make it are suggesting that
women reason differently about moral matters, or have a distinct and different moral perception of the world. This amounts to a claim that the difference is an epistemological one: that it has to do with the way ethical
beliefs are acquired or applied, or how ethical judgments are justified."[25]

There are several strong gynocentric strains in Mexican thought, and as
we have seen they have much that is distinctly androcentric against which
they must push. But contemporary feminists who theorize in Mexican
terms have much material to mine, and the mining is already taking place.

Despite the predominance of *macho* as a theme of the Revolution and post-Revolutionary culture, the icon of Mexico is the Virgin of Guadalupe. As Mexican citizens move throughout the New World of North and South Americas, the ubiquitous Virgin, symbol of all things *mestizo* and Mexican, moves with them.

Searching for the Historical Roots

There is a good deal of reason to believe that Central Mexico was settled early by Native Americans and that cultures there engaged in crop-growing agriculture several thousand years ago. Miller notes that human artifacts from as far back as 20,000 years ago have been found, and that settlement in one area—a major change where human cultures are concerned—had already occurred near or before 2,000 BCE.[26] Many of the cultures form the period that we now think of as "classic," with Mayan, Toltecan, and other groups holding sway, although this period had passed by the time of the Spanish conquest. As is the case with virtually every human society that is reliant upon seasons and crop cycles for its sustenance, these communities also exhibited a full array of religious beliefs, gods and goddesses, and appeals to the supernatural to guide them in their daily lives.

As has been mentioned, the history of women in Mexico cannot be separated from the figures who have come to be iconic—for whatever reasons and with whatever consequences—for Mexican women. La Malinche, or Doña Marina, becomes of double importance in the history of Mexico, not only because she is represented as having betrayed her own people to the Spaniards, but because this betrayal, rightly or wrongly, comes to be seen as a sexual matter—and so the colonizing of Mexico by the Iberians is seen literally and figuratively as a rape. Even before Cortes's encounter with her, as we have discussed at an earlier point, at least one Spaniard had already begun to cohabit with an indigenous woman, resulting in the first known *mestizo* offpsring.[27]

La Malinche herself becomes iconic for a complex variety of reasons that might be thought, at bottom, to stand symbolically for the female-writ-large. She had been sold by her own family and was living with a Tabascan- or Mayan-speaking group when encountered by Cortes. Her first task was to translate from one Indian language to another—still another person had to translate into Spanish. As Miller describes it,

> Moreover, she became a loyal friend and advisor of the conquistadors, saving them from several embarrassing or threatening situations. At first Marina

was given to Alonso Hernández Puertocarrero, but when, a short time later, Cortes sent him to Spain, Don Hernán took Doña Marina as his mistress.[28]

Like the indigenous cultures themselves, then, La Malinche is sold, exchanged, and traded on more than one occasion and violated physically and mentally. The knowledge that she has is put to use in the service of others who will ultimately make use of that knowledge to endanger and eradicate that which is hers. Her story is, in a sense, the story of all indigenous women and the children they bear, who as the Nobelist Octavio Paz has said, describe themselves as "hijos de la chingada."[29]

At the same time that La Malinche comes to stand for the female/indigenous cultures, the male-identified Spanish culture has at least one rebellious woman who can be identified with it, and who thus provides a point of departure for the history of *criolla* women in Mexico.

From the standpoint of what might now be termed a postcolonial analysis, and to recapitulate, Sor Juana's contribution to Mexican culture and thought is emblematic not only because of her position as epistemic agent of much of the peninsular and creole thought, but also because of her position as a woman in a society in which few women were able to receive formal education. Although some women from the upper classes attended convent schools from the birth of New Spain, virtually no Indian women, and few *mestizas*, were allowed to receive formal education. As Miller writes, "A wide social gulf separated the elite from all other ethnic categories."[30] Into this heavily Catholic atmosphere, with its reliance on *zambos, indios, mestizos,* and poorer *criollos* for manual labor, and with its emphasis on the Thomistic and Augustininan categorization patterns that later were challenged by Descartes, Sor Juana's own work has come to be seen as a battle cry of freedom. One critic dubs her "the outstanding poet of New Spain;"[31] in one of her most well-known compositions, usually translated as *The Reply to Sor Filotea*, Sor Juana explains to the clerics why she will not try to rein or restrain herself intellectually, and why she feels free to pursue a life of the mind without the impediments that the Church wishes to impose upon her.[32] In some of the best-known lines of the *Reply*, she also explains her feelings about the life of a married woman, the expected life of her time:

> I became a nun because although I knew the religious state in life had many things (I mean the accessory things, not the formal ones) that were repugnant to my nature, nevertheless, owing to my total disinclination to marriage, it was the most fitting and suitable state I could elect, anxious as I was to

assure my salvation. My petty whims were such that I would have preferred to live alone, to have no duty or occupation that might interfere with my freedom for study.[33]

As Arizpe says with respect to the epistemology of the silenced peasant woman, "Silence, when not deliberate ... could be anger or wisdom, or simply, a gesture of dignity."[34] But Sor Juana was not silent, and her deliberate voice became a beacon for women in New Spain, one that still echoes.

While Sor Juana and a few other women were studying, most women were either in the home or serving in other homes.[35] A few wealthy women were, of course, having others serve them, but this did not negate their constrained lives, which would have been an imitation, so to speak, of those of wealthy Spanish and Portuguese women at that time on the Iberian peninsula. Historically speaking, progress for women as a whole came much later, under the time of Porfirio Díaz—the latter part of the nineteenth-century— and, of course, after the Revolution. But the combination of Catholicism, the Spanish peninsular culture and the position of women in the indigenous cultures has, historically speaking, proved to be a heady mix.

Octavio Paz, in *The Labyrinth of Solitude*, has noted the metaphorical importance of women in Mexico, even when few women were in a position to make a statement of open rebellion, such as that made by Sor Juana.

> When we shout, "Viva México, hijos de la chingada!" we express our desire to live closed off from the outside world and, above all, from the past. In this shout we condemn our origins and deny our hybridism. The strange permanence of Cortés and La Malinche in the Mexican's imagination and sensibilities reveals that they are something more than historical figures: they are symbols of a secret conflict that we have still not resolved. When he repudiates La Malinche—the Mexican Eve, as she was represented by José Clemente Orozco in his mural at the National Preparatory School—the Mexican breaks his ties with the past, renounces his origins, and lives in isolation and solitude.[36]

In other words, the juxtaposition of a wide variety of forces combines to make the position of women in Mexico strongly mythographic, even while denying, in many cases, their actual rights. The prevalence of the "hijos de la chingada" attitude even in contemporary Mexico provides testimony for the peculiar psychological construction of the Mexican personality, which, as Paz has it, is one that is burdened by an historical sense of oppression.[37]

While twentieth-century Mexico has, like most nations, undergone a political transformation that has attempted to redress wrongs done to women, comparatively few women have been able to achieve national prominence or positions of prestige or power. Nevertheless, university attendance by women is no longer uncommon, and some of Mexico's best-known intellectuals are women and have come to be spokespersons for a variety of progressive causes. Elena Poniatowska, for example, has written extensively on student revolts and on the various political maneuvers that Mexican governments have employed to deny students power. Some of these students are female—certainly many more so than in the past. Poniatowska writes of the government-led firing on students that occurred at the Plaza de las Tres Culturas in October 1968:

> Why? The story of what happened at Tlatelolco is puzzling and full of contradictions. The one fact that is certain is that many died.... All the people in the plaza—casual bystanders and active participants alike—were forced to take shelter from the gunfire; many fell wounded.[38]

As Poniatowska goes on to add, many women were among the killed and wounded; women were also among those who were able to comment in print and in the media.

Some of the greatest changes for women, from the standpoint of legal rights, were pushed through in the early 1950s. During the presidency of Ruiz Cortines, women were formally granted the right to vote, and as one historian adds, "Within the next two years five women legislators had been elected; others were appointed as ambassadors, magistrates, and high-level bureaucrats."[39] It is remarkable, nevertheless, how comparatively late Mexico was in granting women the legal rights that most European countries had granted much earlier; the first presidential election in which women were allowed to vote occurred in 1958.

Like many other nations in the Americas, Mexico has also experienced waves of immigration from other countries. A number of European Jews immigrated to Mexico in the late nineteenth century. Perhaps Margo Glantz sums up their experience best when she writes: "My parents were born in a Jewish Ukraine quite different from today's and more different still from the Mexico where I was born."[40]

Mexican Women Now

The status of women in Mexico today very much reflects the other divisions within the nation, and to a remarkable extent parallels difficulties for women that might be thought to adhere largely to the status of women in more developed countries. Mexico is considerably better off than many of the nations to its immediate south, and indeed, than many of the nations of Latin America taken as a whole. Despite the economic setbacks of the 1990s, Mexico retains a strong infrastructure in the cities, and Mexico City itself is known as one of the world's great capitals.

The division between the wealthy and the poor within Mexico, however, is increasing, and this, according to many commentators, is one of the most glaring facts about its current economic state. This division is, of course, mirrored—perhaps in a way that is most obvious to other observers—in the status of women within the nation. Miller describes this division as "two Mexicos": "the world of the well-dressed versus the threadbare; fine houses in one section, shanties elsewhere; well-educated people and illiterates; those with good jobs or incomes alongside the jobless or underemployed."[41] Although one might be tempted to say that this split follows that between the urban and the rural, it is, of course, more complicated than that, because a great deal of the poverty is urban.

Within this world of poverty, the lives of many or even most Mexican women are still very constrained. Because of *machismo*, a great number of Mexican women still devote their lives to childbearing,[42] and enormous amounts of time and energy are spent in food preparation, especially since the call of traditional dishes, including maize and the preparation of *masa*, is still strong. While women belonging to the better-off groups now attend university in large numbers and are doctors, lawyers, and themselves university instructors, rural women and poorer urban women live as almost all women did centuries ago. In addition to the foregoing splits, there is the fact of the remaining large indigenous population in Mexico—much greater, of course, than that in the United States, it still numbers, by government estimates, several million.[43] Because of the force of the remaining indigenous group, other political movements (which have, of course, led to still further episodes of violence), such as the Zapatistas, refuse to die down.[44]

There is a continued commodification of women within the culture that reflects other, more dramatic psychological chasms within Mexico. As is the case virtually everywhere, women are used on posters and billboards in Mexico to advertise products—but in Mexico many of the women shown on the billboards and oleographs are blonde, displaying features that are very rarely found within Mexico itself. "*Bella como una rubia*" ("Beautiful as a blonde") was the motto of one brewery during the 1960s and '70s, and as American-made products continue to flood Mexico, a turn against the obviously *mestiza* appearance of many or most Mexican women seems, if anything, to be gaining fuel. Because the nation itself suffers from a split, the split becomes magnified in the case of women/commodities.

The *maquiladora* movement (the creation of small factories close to the border used by multinationals for manufacturing purposes) and the general growth in labor in Mexico have altered conditions for women of the more impoverished groups to some extent. In many cases, such jobs represent the first real opportunities that females have had to work outside the home in regularly paid labor. Nevertheless, the double standard continues to persist, and many Mexican women workers are paid a great deal less than their male counterparts. They must, of course, continue to perform most of the domestic tasks and tasks within the home. As Sue Charlton indicates in her study of working women in developing countries, the situation for women in Mexico recapitulates problems already encountered in other nations:

> A study of a strawberry agribusiness in Mexico shows both the advantages and the problems of agroindustry for rural women. The strawberry production near Zamora, Michoacan, is completely dependent on multinational (U.S.) investment. The majority of the workers at the eighteen packing and freezing plants are young women, who typically come from the villages around Zamora. Although the demand for workers fluctuates and all the plants are closed from four to six months a year, more than three-fourths of the strawberry workers interviewed for this study made more money than they had in their previous employment.[45]

Charlton goes on to note that, as might be expected, women workers are preferred at such plants because of their "docility." Although their employment may result in a slight increase in their disposable income and may allow them to purchase a few items from time to time, in most cases it scarcely results in anything that can be termed an overall benefit. Charlton also indicates that street-vending, along with prostitution and its concomitant activities, remains one of the most important modes of employment for women in Mexico.[46]

The association of "feminism" with the *yanqui* culture, so close geographically and always a threat to Mexican identity, may have the effect of prohibiting the type of development of feminist thought that has already been seen in other Latin American countries. In any case, although there is a feminist movement among educated women and in university circles, much of the popular culture still derides rights for women as feeding into some sort of masculinization of women. This view, in combination with the *machismo* of the culture and the working conditions for women just described, yields the effect that women are still encouraged to act only in ways that are safe for home, family, and men. Carola García Calderón, in an excellent review of popular magazines for women published in Mexico, titled *Revistas Femeninas*, writes:

> Las revistas femeninas juegen un importante papel como difusoras de ideas y formas de pensar que ayudan a conformar la mentalidad de algunas mujeres de la sociedad.... Las revistas ... ofrecieron su "liberación." Esta liberación se proponía dentro del personal y reducido mundo de la mujer, el hogar, su universo y el centro de sus problemas.[47]
>
> [Women's magazines play an important role as producers of ideas and forms of thought that assist in having women conform to society.... The magazines ... offer a "liberation." This liberation situates itself in the realm of the personal and the smaller woman's world of the home, the woman's universe and the center of her problems.][48]

In other words, contemporary women's magazines in Mexico for the most part have dealt with women's problems in the age-old way, by attempting to help women become more attractive, become better wives and mothers, and so forth. Needless to say, the combination of these media effects and the reality of women's employment in Mexico is overwhelming.

As most contemporary commentators indicate, the catastrophic split in Mexican society between the haves and the have-nots exacerbates the already severe situation for women. Perhaps a visualization of the scene when government troops shot students and others in Mexico City in 1968 is helpful: according to Elena Poniatowska, an eyewitness was quoted as saying, "In a few minutes the whole thing became a scene straight out of hell.... The bullets were shattering the windows of the apartments ... and the terror-stricken families inside were desperately trying to protect their youngest children."[49] It might help to think of the women in the apartment as employed in some of the capacities described here—as street vendors, or as workers in someone's *maquiladora* or even as seasonal pickers. Add to this the notion that any form of media to which such a woman is exposed is likely to be along the lines of that analyzed by García Calderón, and one has a good indicator of the potent and heady social mix into which today's Mexican woman is plunged on a regular basis.

From pre-Columbian beginnings, through the colonial New Spain period, to the Revolution and finally the contemporary period, Mexican women have had to shoulder a wide variety of roles while simultaneously serving as the "mothers" of a new race, the *mestizo* group of people whom José Vasconcelos was ultimately to term *la raza cósmica*. These historical roles, as is so frequently the case, serve in paradoxical capacities: while it is true that in many ways the role of women in Mexico has always been limited by *machismo* and an overwhelmingly agrarian culture, as we have seen there are exceptions at every turn, from the roles of the goddesses to the writings of Sor Juana and finally to the contemporary women's movement. If part of the work on global feminist epistemology demands an accounting of how it is that women have taken opportunities, both curtailed and otherwise, and used them to fashion new modes of knowing, then Mexico is rife with possibilities for analysis, since the images of women are, if anything, perhaps more driven to extremes than in many other cultures. One thing is for certain: there is no lack of images of women in Mexico. The ubiquity of women in the chromo art calendars so often found in Mexican households is perhaps the most eloquent testimony to their place in the popular imagery.[50] Wherever Mexicans have traveled, they have taken images of females with them, from the medals and posters of the Virgin of Guadalupe to the snaps of *soldaderas* and the oleos of calendar girls. A new generation of Mexican women is trying hard to make the images available to the women of Mexico reflect a greater range of options and choices.

The Mexican Feminisms

The feminist movement in Mexico today is neither as strong nor as vocal as in some other Latin American countries, notably Argentina and Uruguay, which have much greater populations that are largely of European ancestry, and perhaps a greater level of contact with European nations. Nevertheless, the movement proceeds apace on more than one front: a number of feminists are working with politically progressive leftist groups, and while they may not always call themselves "feminist" (for a variety of reasons), their work is feminist in nature. A smaller, more vocal group is in touch with feminist movements around the world, and at least some publications overtly feminist in nature, such as *Fem* and *Debate Feminista*, are on the market in the major cities.[51] It is a noteworthy feature of much of the work currently being done, however, that is draws not only on the Revolutionary tradition of social change, but on the general leftist atmosphere of redistribution of wealth and criticism of existing social institutions that permeates the Mexican left, particularly the parties (aside from the conservative PAN) that challenge the PRI. Elizabeth Maier, who helped found an organization known as *Benita Galeana* around the time of the Mexican presidential elections of 1988, explains why it is important for Mexican feminists to adopt a more socialist perspective and work within a framework for greater change:

> Well, it took quite a long time to set up *Benita*. . . . Shortly after that we drew up our manifesto in popular but "feminist" language, presenting the whole situation from a woman's point of view and from our own standpoint. . . . [O]ne of our main aims is to make the link between gender and class. . . . I'd describe these meetings as feminist meetings but they don't use the word, feminism, because it tends to put people off here. The mass media encourage people to think that feminists are all lesbians, burn their bras.[52]

Here Maier tells us that, in a society derived from Iberian Catholicism and its intermixture with indigenous cultures, holdovers are strong enough to prevent ardent feminists from using the word "feminist" in public. But it does not, of course, prevent them from doing the theoretical work: part of what Maier is saying here is that the overwhelming majority of the poor women—urban and rural—who form the natural part of her constituency are not yet ready, psychologically, to use the word "feminist," but their realization is that their social class demands and demands as women are interlinked.[53] Thus much of the feminist movement has become linked to the PRD, the party formed by the leftist candidate Cuauhtémoc Cárdenas, son of Lázaro Cárdenas, the Mexican president of the 1930s who probably did the most to nationalize various services. The party was formed specifically as a result of the 1988 election, which led to the presidency of Carlos Salinas de Gortari, who later fled Mexico.[54]

The combination of this leftist activism, the strong proportion of women represented as employees in the *maquiladoras* and the tradition of rebellious women (the *soldaderas* and others whose images fill popular culture) has created a climate for change in Mexico. Aside from the more theoretically oriented groups formed in the cities and run by women who might have an intellectualized basis for identifying with the feminist movement, small groups are springing up all over the country, and making political differences at the local and village level. In this sense, the development of feminism in Mexico is similar to that in other so-called Third World countries, including those of South Asia. Many commentators have noticed the extent to which even comparatively uneducated village women can draw—sometimes consciously—on preceding traditions that further gynocentric notions, and that this can be done effectively. The social scientist JoAnn Martin writes:

So goes the story of how Buena Vistan women [of Morelos] became involved in politics. . . . In the story women draw on gender images from historical events to place themselves at the center of politics. . . . By building their politics on existing cultural themes women effectively established themselves *both* as astute political actors and newcomers to the political theme.[55] [Emphasis in original.]

Martin goes on to note the explicit establishment of both images of the Virgin and of Malinche as tools for women's power. Because, as she asserts, these emblematic notions of female power are so deeply embedded in the *mestizo* Mexican culture, any movement by women is bound to draw on them. She makes this claim forcefully when she remarks, "Both [images] unite the public and the private. . . . The power of both is imbued with the mystical forces of the female body."[56] Thus village women who begin to march or protest, or who leave their homes at night to attend political meetings (to which they may not have been invited, and at which they may not have been expected) are using these concepts of female force, in many cases in a knowing and not unconscious manner.

Still another realm of endeavor for Mexican feminists has been the publication of journals for the dissemination and promotion of feminism, although so far this has been achieved on only a rather limited scale. Marta Lamas, one of the editors of *Debate Feminista*, also takes the view that feminism in Mexico cannot afford to divorce itself from the general movement for political progress, a movement that has its origins, of course, in the battle to give less power to the PRI and more to the opposition parties. Lamas writes of the crux of theorizing over *mujerismo*, a notion difficult to translate directly into North American concerns, but meaning generally a form of feminism that attempts to separate itself from other political and social concerns. Although this notion is a topic of debate in Mexico, Lamas finds it devoid of meaning appropriate for the Mexican situation. She tries to make clear the relationship between the different types of oppression when she claims, "It is only because women as a social group . . . find themselves in specific conditions of discrimination, repression and exploitation, that it is valid to do specific work on their behalf."[57]

In the early 1990s, Claudia Colimoro, who specifically identified herself as a prostitute and as someone who had been forced into sex work by economic oppression, ran as a candidate for the Mexico City parliament on the slate of an extreme left-wing party. By this time many women candidates from a variety of parties had made a national appearance, but Claudia's boldness was indeed unusual in Mexico.[58] Again, her interest was sparked by awareness of the very specific needs of women sex workers, and by participation in a grass-roots organization devoted to health needs. As she stated in her recounting of how she came to run for office:

> Four and a half years ago I got involved in the fight against AIDS. We needed to teach the other girls about the causes and consequences of this dreadful illness.... We founded the citizens' alliance, CUILOTZIN, which fights for healthcare and civil rights for prostitutes of both sexes and street children.... I was even visited by representatives of the World Health Organization (WHO).[59]

Two common themes seem to run through the various Mexican feminisms: one is an attempt to draw on the strength of traditional figures, particularly where rural groups are concerned, and the second is a desire to ensure that women's concerns are not divorced from other concerns or other forms of oppression. The strength of the images, then, particularly as recounted in Martin's appraisal of a spontaneous political movement involving women in the state of Morelos, is that women can see themselves engaging in the same kind of work as that done by every follower of the Virgin and, indeed, insofar as the Virgin was a "helper" of the poverty stricken in early New Spain, by the Virgin herself. Whatever view is given to Malinche, she is a powerful figure from the early period who clearly made decisive moves while at the same time, insofar as she was Cortes's mistress and the mother of his children, also being immersed in traditional roles. Mexican women of today see themselves as cast in much the same mold, and the appropriation of these images becomes a source of strength and power.

There are, of course, multiple efforts along the lines of Mexican academic feminism, and some of these efforts have seen the light of day in American philosophical journals, such as *Hypatia*.[60] In general, new movements have included postcolonial and postmodern accounts, and at least a few accounts of hybrid American and Mexican efforts to cooperate in the teaching of feminism or women's studies in Mexican universities.[61] Although it may very well be the case that a number of other Latin American nations have pursued academic feminism at a greater pace than Mexico, this may in large be a reflection of the Eurocentric origins of the cultures of these nations. It is probably for these reasons that Griselda Gutiérrez Castañeda, a well-known Mexican feminist scholar, has chosen to articulate a postmodern point of view in her work. Mexico, with its mixed heritage and revolutionary introduction to the twentieth century, eschews a univocal voice. As

Gutiérrez writes in her piece "Feminist Movements and Their Constitution as Political Subjects":

> The motto taken up by feminist movements, the personal is political, as positive as it may seem, can be the subject of different, even antagonistic, representations.... But there is a new problem faced by this ... struggle: how is it possible to build a new collective order while, at the same time, affirming plurality?[62]

Gutiérrez reminds us of the dangers of overgeneralization and of construing women in useless and groundlessly essentialist ways. Mexican feminism displays—and will doubtless continue to display—great sensitivity toward the richness of women's experience.

Mexican Feminist Reconstructions of Knowledge

What has been bequeathed to us as epistemic paths by Mexican women can be categorized in several rough-and-ready ways: advertence to the goddess relationships of the ancient cultures, recapitulation and reappropriation of the Iberian Catholicism of the New Spain period, particularly as articulated by women thinkers of that time frame, and the new reliance on the voice of peasant and Indian women in their rural lives, which might be thought to lend itself to a version of naturalized epistemology. Here we will focus particularly on the second and third strands of this interweaving, as there is much material for fructification in both the Catholic and more contemporary rural traditions.

At least one version of the reappropriation of epistemic categories relies heavily on Sor Juana Ines de la Cruz and her role in Mexican culture. As we have seen, Sor Juana stands out not simply because she was Mexican, female, and writing during the seventeenth century, but also because her stand encompassed strands of rebellion that, while seemingly anti-Church, were, of course, derived from the very Catholic tradition in question. Today, many Mexican women see themselves as contemporary Sor Juanas; they are concerned, as Christians and Catholics, about the welfare of others, while retaining a framework of intellectual independence within the reflective and rationalist Catholic tradition.

Gerard Flynn reminds us that Sor Juana's initial letter was an attempt to state a basis for agreement with some of the writings of the Jesuit Antonio de Vieyra, a thinker who had gone against some of the teachings of both Augustine and Aquinas. Although by no means all of the doctrines in question involved women, we can infer that many did, for "Mulieres in ecclesia taceant" (Let the women in church be silent) is one of the leading themes of both Sor Juana's letter and the bishop of Puebla's reply to it.[63] Although many are now more familiar with Aquinas's thought, since it is so heavily reliant on Aristotelian doctrine, it is worth examining Augustine briefly, since his works would form not only the backbone of both Sor Juana's and Vieyra's commentary, but in some sense might also form the basis for an epistemic reappraisal. We can sense that Sor Juana herself must have felt that she could indeed engage in such an appraisal, for she repeatedly cites the authority of Scripture and other thinkers in developing her reply.[64] In at least some of Augustine's work, we can see the notion that a rationalist sense of union with the divine is driving him, and that it is possible that it may lead him in a variety of directions. In one well-known part of the *Confessions*, he writes: "But Thee, O Lord, I imagined on every part ... as if there were a sea everywhere ... and it contained within itself some sponge, huge."[65] Robert McMahon notes the importance for Augustine of the personal and of the metaphorical, both ways through which he appropriates a rationalist knowledge tradition of inquiry to himself.[66] Just so, we can think of Sor Juana as validating and using those parts of the Catholic line of thought that enjoin her to create her own sense of union, which may evoke a sort of intellectual independence. As Flynn notes, she says in her letter, "[F]or love is union and where it is there are no opposite extremes."[67]

A second large strand of gynocentric epistemics in Mexican thought can be categorized as intersecting with what many American feminists are labeling naturalized feminist epistemology. Such intersections are never perfect, of course—nevertheless, because of the kinds of training available at universities in Latin America, much feminist theorizing (and, indeed, much intellectual work in general) may be more closely related to patterns of thought found in the United States and other European-derived cultures than is the case, for example, with cultural thinking found in Asia or in some parts of Africa.

That this may very well be an accurate assertion can be substantiated by looking at the work not only of Mexican feminists, but of theorists who have done work on rural Mexican women. Indeed, a few thinkers, such as Arizpe, seem to fall into both categories. Contemporary naturalized feminist epistemology has asked us to look at new work in epistemology *simpliciter* that is already naturalized (that is, work that proceeds in accordance with information from the social sciences/cognitive sciences) and apply it to feminist concerns and gynocentric conceptualization patterns.[68] This work would emphasize women's ways of knowing within, for example,

Mexican rural contexts insofar as those modes relied on empirical and day-to-day intellectual operations, rather than speculative ratiocination. Insofar as the juxtaposition of two traditions may be found here—for example, the speculative thought of Sor Juana and the daily reality of the life of a woman in a village—they are not necessarily in opposition to each other. However, for our purposes here we can spell out a differentiation, as this helps us to come to grips with different epistemological devices and styles.

To recapitulate, Arizpe in "Peasant Women and Silence" is close to the development of a mode of knowing that intersects with what we have called naturalized feminist epistemology.[69] Part of what she is trying to say is that peasant women perform a wide variety of tasks embodying folk and other kinds of knowledge—derived from their daily life—that are seldom recognized. Such knowledge may involve work with crops, knowledge of plants and their healing powers, and so forth. As Arizpe writes, "It is said that women discovered agriculture while men went out hunting."[70] Although much of what Arizpe writes may be taken metaphorically, she is also speaking of communities of knowers.[71] This concept is one that is familiar to feminists in American and English-speaking countries, and it is a concept that has played a key role in the development of a gynocentric naturalized epistemology. Folk medicine, folk science, and folk wisdom all attain their epistemic status through such communities, but they frequently lack the validation of some "higher" epistemic authority.

Because we can hypothesize that knowledge of crop cycles, for example, among peasant women is a strong example of knowledge that may be passed down orally and that receives great empirical confirmation based on the availability of food, much of the contemporary work in naturalized feminist epistemology points us in the direction of thinking of this sort of example as one of communal validation of knowledge acquisition. Much of W. V. O. Quine's work has been cited by feminists because of its emphasis on the acquisition of constructs in social contexts; such emphasis severely undercuts what, in certain circles, might be thought to be the observation/theory distinction.[72] Lynn Hankinson Nelson, for example, has written of communities of knowers, and consolidates the importance of such a take on epistemology in general when she writes:

> I use the implications of feminist science criticism as well as central features of Quine's empiricism to argue against the view that "knowers" are individuals and to support the view that knowers are communities. Communities, not individuals, "acquire" and possess knowledge.[73]

The new emphasis, then, on the groups and bonds formed by Mexican peasant women lends itself to a naturalized feminist epistemology at the same time that it also points us in the direction of those more metaphorical notions often used by feminist theorists, such as acquisition of voice and the effect of silencing. The network of ties, both actual and iconic, available to Mexican women ensures that they can hold patterns of female knowledge acquisition in front of them, so to speak, as they go about their daily lives. More important, perhaps, as is the case in many of the nations of Asia, Africa, and other areas of Latin America, the actual welfare of various members of the household is in the hands of the women of the house, from the drawing of water to the preparation of food to the making of clothing. Thus the rural Mexican woman stands both literally and metaphorically in a strong tradition of knowledge, and one that is receiving current crucial emphasis from Mexican theorists.

Recounting the Mexican Worldview

Retrieval of the gynocentric strands of Mexican culture is a task of more than average interest, for as we have seen there is much in Mexican culture that would tend to prevent such a retrieval. Although the ancient cultures of other parts of the world (Malta, Greece, the Basque regions, to employ but a few examples) often seem to employ a great deal of matrifocality and goddess worship, this does not seem to be the case to as great an extent with many of the indigenous Mexican cultures.[74] In addition, the conquest of Mexico itself helped to reify notions of *conquistadores*, and the Iberian Catholic culture of those conquerors was itself, of course, already intensely androcentric.

Given all of these factors, it might well be said that the merging of the lines we have seen here—the emphasis on Marianism in the form of veneration for the Virgin of Guadalupe, the tradition of commentary by learned nuns and other women, such as Sor Juana, the recapitulation of the tradition of the rebellious woman or *soldadera*, and the recasting of the Malinche story—represents some sort of triumph. JoAnn Martin, in her study of the political action of rural women in Morelos, recounts how the notion of the Virgin and Malinche came to unite, so to speak, for some women:

> The separation between the Virgin and Doña Marina was the work of Ignacio Ramirez. . . . But the importance in popular imagination of the separation and

the dual images it produces may be exaggerated. Speaking of Tlayacapan, in Morelos, Ingham observes that "there are, then, two Eves: the innocent Eve, and the Eve of the Fall, *although both are one.* These considerations may explain why young girls dress as Malinches for the fiesta of the Virgin of Guadalupe.... The practice implies that Malinche is identified with the Virgin and indeed 'Malinche' is the diminutive form of Mary."[75]

This passage is noteworthy because Martin's analysis focuses on the extent to which rural women in the state of Morelos have found figures with whom they can identify for power; the figures, however, alternate between the "acceptable" Virgin and the not-so-acceptable Doña Marina. Maybe women have already discovered what scholars have struggled to articulate: Malinche is simultaneously as much a hero/ine as many of the other female figures of Mexico, since the line between victim and traducer is indeed a very fine one. She is also, in a literal sense, the mother of the nation, even if this mothering was not a voluntary act.

Although Paz has been roundly criticized for the masculinism of his analysis of Mexican culture, it may simply be the case that, on a transparent view, much of what he says is accurate in that it reflects the power of the male in the daily life of Mexico and the extent to which the male defines himself against that lack, the female. Thus, in the passages analyzed earlier, the *chingada* is not only victim, but personification of emptiness, and—as it happens—originator of the national *mestizaje.* Hence there is a wonderful move in the retrieval of the ultimate *chingada* as a figure of power. In a spirit somewhat similar to the very different cultural construct of *shakti* in Dravidian India, the *chingada* becomes powerful partly through accepting, enduring, and transcending. But this is, of course, to some extent the story of the indigenous in Mexico themselves. As Krauze and others have indicated, much of what constitutes the Mexican culture of today is more Indian than not.[76]

In writing of the well-known author Nellie Campobello, associated with Revolutionary themes, Poniatowska quoted a line about her to the effect that she "is part of a generation which carries images of the Revolution stored in memory in the way that others carry childhood songs."[77] In a sense, this applies to the general Mexican culture, and insofar as the notions of "Adelitas" who saved the day for the Revolution and its future are concerned, it applies most strongly, perhaps, to most Mexican women. It is this carrying forward of two traditions, one housed in the speculative philosophical views of the Roman Catholic Church, and the other in the everyday tasks that women in rural and poverty-stricken areas have to face all over the world, that marks the situation of women in Mexico today. It might naively be thought that there would be little or no intersection between these two threads, but one such intersection is found throughout much of Latin America, although it in many cases has a focus that is by no means overtly feminist, and that is liberation theology. Here again a tradition originating in pure rationalism and with a long history has been welded to more contemporary views, many of which are either more naturalistic, or which hearken back to the views of those in the Church who might be thought to have a greater interest in the natural.

Because of the proximity of the United States, the influence of feminist and postcolonial theory in academic circles here, and the concomitant growth of such theory in at least some other parts of Latin America, feminist and other progressive theorists in Mexico are now being subjected to a steady diet of commentary that is miscible with their cultural concerns and that does not, in most cases, present an insurmountable obstacle to possession or reformulation. Some of this commentary, insofar as it deals with Mexican/Latin concerns, is more appropriately labeled Chicana/o, and we will examine it in a later chapter. It is obvious, as we have seen, however, that many Mexican feminists are now ready to draw on this theorizing, and that other feminist social scientists, such as Martin, are ready to examine conditions in Mexico and for women with a feminist eye. The combination of the continual cultural onslaught on Mexico from the United States with the development of *maquiladoras* by multinationals may indeed mean that there is no "post" in "postcolonial" for Mexico. In any event, a steady array of images and commodities from north of the border and from other areas penetrates Mexico, leaving many Mexicans now with a hodgepodge of traditions for holidays, worship, and so forth.

Just as the iconography of Mary/La Malinche emphasizes the dual aspect of the female, a feature of most cultures perhaps, but certainly marked in Mexico, the contemporary Mexican woman is using the traditional power of the feminine to navigate between these areas of her life and the lives of those around her. The new metaphorical usage of "border" that is so common in reflections on the state of United States/Mexico relations and the *frontera* in general is, in many ways, apt for all of Mexico. The porousness of the actual border means that all sorts of exchanges—physical, cultural, health related, and other—are taking place all the time. Changing attitudes toward female roles filter into Mexico, and women who have worked in the United States, in whatever capacity, and then returned to

Mexico are in a good position not only to bring some of the attitudinal changes with them, but to translate them into reality. As Antonia Darder says in a recent piece on biculturalism,

> Biculturalism as a critical perspective acknowledges openly and engages forthrightly the significance of power relations in structuring and prescribing societal definitions of truth, rules of normalcy, and notions of legitimacy which often defy and denigrate the cultural existence and lived experiences of border groups.[78]

Although Darder is writing here of the area immediately surrounding the border, her remarks might be thought to be applicable to much of Mexico. The European influence—Iberian in its origins—that has always run Mexico from the top commingles with a number of other lines of influence to ensure that there is still a tension between city and village, European or *mestizo* on the one hand and *indio* on the other, and "modern" versus traditional. Thus almost all Mexicans participate in a sort of biculturalism in which one side of the polarity is valorized at the expense of the other.

The contemporary Mexican woman thus functions at a crossroads, and waves of global feminist theory mark her progress, both in her daily life and in the stated and articulated feminisms that emanate from Mexico. But the epistemic heritage of Mexico entwines two intensely opposed ways of knowing: Catholic ratiocination and a natural/agrarian-based empiricism. As the women in Martin's village in Morelos demonstrate, it is possible to work, in a sort of code switching, between these two frameworks. Perhaps code switching, with its connotations of the linguistic and the multilingual, is the most powerful metaphor for the daily activity of the Mexican woman today.

Chapter 7

Guatemala and the Indigenous

The history and intellectual patterns of life in Guatemala are inextricably tied to the indigenous cultures, particularly the Mayan groups. Although Guatemala borders Mexico on the latter's southern end, Mexico is an industrialized giant in comparison to Guatemala, where a very large percentage of the population still speaks Native American languages and where persons of mixed ancestry are comparatively few in number.

The combination of Guatemala's comparative poverty and relative lack of industrial development has meant that the role of the Indian cultures is much greater with respect to the country's overall sense of itself than one might expect. It is for these reasons that Guatemala—in contrast to Mexico, or even some of its Central American neighbors—represents a waiting area of investigation for the categorizer who wants to see how contemporary cultures deal with both a past and a present that are largely Native American.

In addition, and to complicate matters, contemporary Guatemala has been in a state of war or subject to some sort of violence on and off now for dozens of years. Most recently, publicity was given to both the violence and the plight of the indigenous peoples when Rigoberta Menchú's purported autobiography detailing her family's battle with the army and other forces received international attention, leading to her being awarded a Nobel Peace Prize.[1] As of this writing, other works, including a book reviewed extensively in a number of well-known publications, have come out alleging that most of what is supposed to be fact in the Menchú book is at best an amalgam of detail gleaned from a variety of sources and not something through which Rigoberta Menchú actually lived.

In any case, one fact can be ascertained and agreed upon: even today, Guatemala is a largely indigenous nation with many pockets in which virtually no persons speak Spanish. Indeed, the speaking of Spanish is taken as a sign of acculturation.[2] Because of this, the Guatemalan worldview, if there may be said to be such a thing, is heavily reliant upon indigenous patterns. Here it can truly be said that a number of strands of thought having to do with land cultivation patterns, worship of and respect for local deities, and a sense of the richness combined with agricultural life to create a worldview which, although it has a Spanish overlay, is much more rife with traditional patterns, some of which are gynocentric, than that of many other nations of Iberian conquest.

In addition to this, because of the publicity given to the region by the Nobel Prize and the surrounding controversy, Guatemalan and Guatemalan Indian cultures have already begun to receive extensive feminist commentary.[3] Although it might very well be the case that the Menchú controversy was the catalyst here, it is obvious that the conflict between the Indian cultures and the more Westernized and Eurocentric Guatemalan state forces has become a focal point for theorizing in a highly contemporary vein. For example, Irene Matthews has written:

> Additionally, the forces of "conquest" (or control) in Central America were often comprised of young men coopted from the indigenous population itself.... The outraged body in *I, Rigoberta Menchú* is not that of just "any" Indian woman (although it might be almost every Indian woman).... [T]hey are now also punished not because of their chastity ... but ... for their assumption of a voice.[4]

In another words, much of what has been written that reflects on the current situation in Guatemala already has the flavor of contemporary theorizing, and given the force of postmodern/postcolonial attempts to conceptualize about such matters, it is inevitable that this kind of theory is brought to bear here in abundance.

Contemporary Guatemala consists, then, of large land holdings, usually termed *latifundias*, worked by indigenous peoples and under the at least nominal influence of a central government. Aside from the capital, there are few cities, and many who live in the mountainous regions have rarely traveled outside of their villages. Writing from the standpoint of a cultural geographer, Lovell reports in 1992 that entire areas of Guatemala, particularly the highlands, have been undervisited and underinvestigated.[5]

Because of the small number of persons who identify with a Eurocentric view, many commentators on Guatemala have said that the nation as a whole retains an indigenous outlook. Peter Calvert, in fact, reports that "no separate stratum of native born citizens of European stock emerged";[6] he also notes that outside the capital, there has been little European influence.[7] The metaphysics and ontology of the Quiché-Maya, then, prevail; most commentators emphasize the extent to which they retain a great deal of their traditional elements, and are based on an intricate calendar pattern for ceremonies in conjunction with crops, village festivals to appease local spirits/deities, and so on.[8] As is the case in other societies still closely tied to the land, a comparative egalitarianism in gender matters has been observed, along with a profound belief in the nondualistic (employing European terminology) view that spirit pervades all things. The anthropologist James Sexton has an excellent triad of works that are diary transcriptions of his informant, Ignacio, an Indian who has traveled widely in Guatemala and is familiar with many social sectors.[9] The importance of local fiesta days and the type of work Ignacio does to help out his family is underscored in the following passage:

> I didn't work on the principal day of the fiesta because previously I had worked three days, continuously making bread for the people who have little money, but I was like a *mozo*—they gave me the materials needed. Also my son José worked three days and three nights. We earned Q35 and we made some bread to sell but we sold little, because the people did not have money. But this was the case with all the bakers, since we observed bakers that came from other towns to sell bread during the fiesta.[10]

Such activities constitute the daily life of almost all Guatemalans, except for the relatively small *ladino* class, mainly living in the capital. As Calvert also notes, "[T]he country has one of the largest proportions of people of indigenous descent in its population in the Americas."[11]

Finally, wars, guerrilla actions, and general upheavals have been a way of life now in Guatemala for at least twenty or thirty years, depending upon the source. A variety of right-wing and occasionally left-wing factions has attempted to overthrow various governments, and almost always the indigenous groups are the first and most obvious targets of the violence. Although there have been sporadic patches of civilian rule, the pattern has been one of military juntas taking over the office of the presidency and then imposing force. The latest rounds of violence are said by many to date back to the assumption of the powers of this office by General Rios Montt in 1982–83. It is the level of violence—continual and by any standards brutal—that has led to the publication of works such as the Rigoberta Menchú book and to the concern of human rights organizations all over the world.[12]

Guatemala today, then, exhibits an interesting and perhaps unique mix of European and indigenous elements, with the indigenous predominating. Because of the social structure's time-honored and traditional elements, it is possible to examine in Guatemala a number of ancient views stemming from agriculture societies that have existed in comparative freedom for hundreds, even thousands, of years.

The Androcentric Outlook

What parallels most closely the *macho* standpoint exhibited in other Latin American countries—Mexico in particular—is found in the *ladino* culture of the cities. Calvert notes, "To the [*ladino*], the capacity to exercise power is primarily sexual in character. A man succeeds because he is truly male (*macho*), possessed of sexual potency.... In the twentieth century, as the members of the *ladino* elite have emerged as the unchallenged leaders of their country ... their appetite for power has grown."[13] Thus the *ladino* outlook, like that of *mestizo* Mexico, presumes a dichotomous world in which the gender roles have their place and in which reason and power automatically accrue to the male, and in which reason, in particular, does not accrue to indigenous persons. Because *ladino* society does in fact shape the political life of the nation, we can assume that there is some direct influence of these beliefs throughout the country. Nevertheless, however, they clash to some extent with the indigenous worldview, in which strains of androcentrism might be said to be more subtle. In the indigenous views, because of the importance of crop growth and cultivation, there is more room for strains of the feminine, and Calvert notes of the Indian woman that "unlike her *ladino* [sic] counterpart, she will expect to participate fully in making decisions."[14]

A great deal of the Spanish-language culture of Guatemala is confined to the capital and its environs, as we have said, but this is, of course, the politically potent area of the country. Perhaps one of the greatest manifestations of a kind of masculinized aggression throughout the culture has occurred in the wave of governments, very few elected democratically, during the course of the twentieth century. The army has more or less run Guatemala. Thus it has been difficult for democratic governments to survive any length of time without the support of the army, and it has been all too easy to lose that support. A sort of fascist glorification of things military permeates much of the life of the capital, and influences all of the other institutions. A table compiled by Peter Calvert for comparative purposes indicates twenty-four separate governments during the period

1931–1984 alone, only eight of them chosen by election. Calvert notes that even insofar as legal niceties have been preserved, it must be remembered that because these traditions stem from those of Roman law and Iberian custom, they do not, in general, resemble those of Anglo-Saxon law. He articulates the paradox at the heart of Guatemalan government in this fashion:

> Guatemala is, then, constitutionally a strongly centralized state, in which the president legally holds overwhelming power, including the right in case of emergency to suspend the constitutional guarantees of individual citizens. The Hispanic tradition of legalism means that as long as the letter of the law is observed, e.g., elections are held and ballots are counted, their substance need not be, as there is no effective check to a president backed by the agreement of the army and supported by an effective centralized police apparatus.[15]

In addition, several other strains in the *ladino* society militate against a softening of the strong androcentrism that seems to permeate it. Once again, of course, the role of the Roman Catholic Church is paramount—in Guatemala the Church was particularly strong during the New Spain period, and the Inquisition was brought to Guatemala in 1574.[16] In general, the Franciscans played a leading role in the development of both the Guatemalan Church and state. Unlike in Mexico, successive mountings of liberal protest against clerics seem not to have effectively reduced the role of the Church. Thus the army and the Church together, it might be said, run *ladino* life.

As so frequently happens when indigenous cultures are exposed to the Eurocentric tradition, some of the attitudes adopted most readily seem to have to do with the roles of women. Thus Indians who have been exposed to the urban culture may actually treat their wives in a way that is nontraditional from the indigenous perspective and is worse than what would normally be accorded to a woman in the original culture. Ignacio, the informant of Sexton whose work is now well known in the portrayal of indigenous life, remarks:

> In the afternoon of this same day, the wife said that two *judicia policial* arrived in San Martín la Laguna to investigate the case of each prisoner [cases in which Ignacio was personally involved because of his local position] to see whether it's true that they have two to three wives and to see whether their houses and offices are well-furnished.[17]

One does not need a great deal of imagination here to see that the statement that is being made is that acquisition of wives is on a par with the acquisition of furniture. Both accruals would signify that the male in question had bettered his status.

All of the above elements (the power of the army, the comparatively small size of the Spanish-speaking group, the influence of the Church and its history, especially during the sixteenth century) converge to give contemporary Guatemala, at least in its urban areas, a highly masculinized culture. It is for these reasons that still another related factor is often noted by commentators: the culture as a whole is extremely conservative, even to the point of xenophobia.[18] Attempts to bring in foreign works of art are usually discouraged, except where they "support rather than alter an essentially conservative worldview."[19]

Because the *ladino* group constructs itself against the Indians, hallmarks of the Indian culture may be seen, as is so often the case, as exemplars of the culture's "backwardness." In any case, it is clear that much of what is highlighted as indigenous serves a useful purpose for tourists (particularly in the Chichicastenango region) without playing more than a dress-up role in national life. This explains why it is the case that the "death squads" (which can be either left- or right-wing) so frequently take out their hostilities on the Indians. It is this historical aspect of Guatemalan power politics, along with the fact of its largely indigenous population, that has led to the contemporary interest in the region.

Still another way of making clear the masculinist structure of the *ladino* society is to note the extent to which the indigenous society is consciously identified with the female, and urbanization/culture/Eurocentricity (signaled by adoption of the Spanish language) with the male. Matthews reports, as have other commentators, that the incidence of rape, killings of male spouses, and general degradation of the female seems, if anything, to be higher in Guatemala than elsewhere. Those who have not understood this, she says, have failed to grasp much about contemporary Guatemalan life:

> Violence specifically directed against women would seem [to some] to have little political import in this climate of virtually total control. Once again, however, I would supplement Todorov's interpretation that widespread rape is a signal to raped women's menfolk, to argue that it is an act of triumph and bonding among the "conquerors" and a symbol of contempt to other women.... [For purposes of economic growth] a few of the captive population [have been] permitted to preserve their ethnic identity and archaic cultural production in favor of the other foreign currency earner in Guatemala—

international tourism for the picturesque (especially women and children in traditional costume).[20]

In Guatemala, as in virtually every Latin American nation to some extent, the original "conquest" was one of Iberian males, speakers of Spanish and Portuguese and bearers of European culture, cohabiting with/ raping/absconding indigenous women and their traditions to produce a new *raza*. In many countries, such as Mexico, the *raza* ultimately triumphed, and the national culture—as constructed during the late nineteenth and twentieth centuries—became one that statedly belonged largely to the *mestizaje*. In Guatemala, this sequence of events never took place. Instead, a large group of millions of indigenous persons remains, with a small, Spanish-speaking stratum at the top. Thus, to a remarkable degree, the original construction of "culture" as European and "primitiveness" as Native American remains, and that culture is, of course, male.

The Gynocentric and the Traditional Culture

Almost all commentators agree on the pervasive influence of the ancient Mayan worldview on the contemporary indigenous societies of Guatemala, almost all of which are related to the Maya or possess Mayan-influenced languages. The complexity of the Mayan cosmogony is such that one can only scratch at its surface, but again most commentators seem to converge on the importance of the cyclical, as manifested in the complex calendar system, the significance of corn as symbol and ritual producer, and the comparative gender egalitarianism of the society. As it happens, these cultural elements are important for Mexico today, too, since much of what is transpiring in the south of that country is related to the same Mayan influences that today abound in Guatemala. But in any case, as we have noted, in Guatemala these influences are paramount.

Miller notes the importance of the Mayan counting system and its accuracy;[21] Krauze explains that in the late nineteenth century the "ancient chronologies and cyclical prophecies" were still important in fights against Eurocentric dominance in the region.[22] Lovell asserts that throughout the entire period of the Hispanic conquest, and up to and including the present, key elements of the Mayan belief system remain in place: the importance of the agricultural cycle and natural worlds, the traditional belief that the "first father" and "first mother" were of cornmeal dough, and the general emphasis on fertility/germination.[23]

That these elements are all related to early-settled and presettled agricultural patterns of gynocentricity and respect for female power hardly needs to be stated. Yet it is interesting to contrast the strength of these beliefs with various other patterns even within Native American groups, or, cross-culturally, with other groups of whose god/goddess patterns we are aware. Despite the grand scale of its architecture, and the intensity of its development of mathematics, Mayan culture retains elements of the force of goddess worship that tie it to presettled agriculture beliefs. In comparison with many of the societies examined by Marija Gimbutas, for example, Mayan beliefs more closely resemble those of preclassical Greece or even earlier periods.[24] It is no doubt partly for these reasons that the comparative gender equality of the indigenous communities has been commented upon, for example, by Calvert:

> Unlike *ladinos*, Indians see husband and wife as working partners, enjoying a rough equality within marriage. The wife may own land on her own account, but even if she does not, the herd animals are regarded as joint property, and she continues to own the movable property that she brings with her to the new home.[25]

It is also noteworthy that feminist anthropologists have seen some of the same evidence for traditional gynocentric modes, even if it is acknowledged that anthropological work of the past was not always straightforward about categorizing this evidence. Nancy Black, in her piece "Anthropology and the Study of Quiché Maya Women in the Western Highlands of Guatemala," is at pains to try to give an analysis of Quiché society that foregrounds roles played by women. In so doing, she is able to tie together—albeit in a more standard sociological manner than might be done by a thinker focusing on the symbolic—a number of strands of Quiché life that are intriguing from the standpoint of feminist epistemics. Weaving is not only a staple of the women's lives, but is a staple of Quiché life in general. Thus weaving becomes iconic for the indigenous life in Guatemala, and the importance of women's work is highlighted.

Black finds that although gender roles cannot be described as strictly egalitarian—human cultures being what they are—the tie in the culture to the land and the importance of women's fertility is pronounced enough that it has even made its way into the more standard literature. As in many traditional cultures, children spend most of their time in physical proximity to their mothers until they are four or five years old. Bride price is still traditional in many communities, and this emphasis on the groom bringing goods to the bride's family, rather than the other way around, reinforces some features of status. Although the family unit is patrilocal, the tie to the land helps reinforce some elements of gynocentrism.

A combination of factors defines the family units, but these factors taken together still push in directions substantially less androcentric than that of the urban, *ladino* society with its coded elements of the *macho*. Black writes:

> While the family unit may vary in composition, the household is the basic structural unit for Quiché Maya socialization, production, and consumption. Social integration and coordination are based on clearly defined divisions of labor by sex and relative age.... Marriage for women is generally more stable among Indians than for the non-Indian population. [S]ocial disapproval in San Sebastián Lemoa is a strong deterrent to unacceptable behavior.[26]

In general, then, a number of factors promote gynocentric strands within the traditional Guatemalan cultures. The juxtaposition of vestiges of Mayan cyclical thinking, ties to the land, respect for crops and divine forces/images related to crops, and the importance of such traditional female tasks such as weaving creates a matrix of the gynocentric within the culture. It is for these reasons that commentators such as Matthews and others writing about the campaigns of various Guatemalan governments against the indigenous have cast those campaigns as being against women both literally and metaphorically.[27] Matthews sees the various incidents of destruction of indigenous villages carried out, of course, not only by burnings and lootings, but by systematic rapes and other specifically female-related violations, as part of a denigration of things female/indigenous where it is clear that the indigenous is signified to some extent by the female (and vice versa). Because the period of settlement for Mexico, Guatemala, and the other regions of Latin America included the conquest of the indigenous female body on a literal level—and the establishment of a new *raza*—indigenous has come to mean *"chingada"* and Hispanic/Iberian/*Ladino* *"chingón"* in a number of different ways and on a number of different levels. Thus in a sense Paz's writings, although specifically intended for Mexico, are not inappropriate for some aspects of Guatemalan culture. The crucial difference with Guatemala is that the indigenous factors are writ large, so to speak, and the *mestizo/ladino* factor writ small. Matthews ably summarizes the inscription at the core of *ladino* destruction of Indian villages in the following:

While the very public nature of Guatemala's state terrorism against the populace emphasized the devaluation of human life, it also confirmed the impunity enjoyed by those who perpetrated the official violence. Violence specifically directed against women would seem to have little political import in this climate of virtually total control. Once again, however, I would supplement Todorov's interpretation that widespread rape is a signal to raped women's menfolk, to argue that it is an act of triumph and bonding among the "conquerors" and a signal of contempt to other women.[28]

Matthews goes on to note that women's "submissive production" is essential to the culture.[29] Although this statement might apply to a number of cultures/locales, it is especially important in a situation such as the one in Guatemala where it is clear that the majority of the population is still statistically identifiable as Indian and where any movement against the indigenous population by those in power makes an extremely forceful statement.

The importance of these statements with respect to the position of Guatemala internationally can scarcely be overestimated. On the international scene, Guatemala has become a rallying point for a number of causes tied to indigenous persons and their status within the greater Latin American societies. Because of the publicity surrounding the receipt by Rigoberta Menchú of the Nobel Peace Prize, and the controversy surrounding her work, which will be examined shortly, it has not been possible to divorce the notion of Guatemala as a nation or country from the status of the indigenous population. Thus the easy conflation of the realms of the feminine/female with the realms of the indigenous/natural becomes more important in terms of the commodification of a culture on the international scene than it might otherwise have been.

Most observers have been careful to state that the situation in Guatemala has the seemingly odd concomitant that a move from the Indian culture of the countryside to the *ladino* culture of the city is actually a move from a more egalitarian gender-role situation to one that is less egalitarian.[30] Thus the conflation that we have articulated here is one that more or less can withstand empirical confirmation. As Tracy Ehlers says in *Silent Looms*:

In line with this cultural dichotomy, [traditional/Indian] marriages lie somewhere between the mutual complementarity of and relative equality of marriages among traditional Mayan peasants and the full-blown *machismo* that characterizes marriages of middle-class *ladinos* in which men maintain dominance through female economic dependence.[31]

The point that Ehlers makes is one that has been made by many observers. The ubiquitousness of this type of commentary underscores the strength of gynocentric strains within the culture.

Historical Tie-ins and Their Importance

The comparative power of the indigenous societies in Guatemala and the corresponding lack of power of the Spanish-speaking elite—especially in comparison with some other Latin American nations—is probably related to the topography and geography of Guatemala, its highlands, and the parallel depredations suffered by the Spaniards in their conquest of the region.

Because of the relative lack of level land or plains in Guatemala, Spaniards on horseback encountered a great deal of difficulty in simply making their way physically across the land. Even now, the northeastern extremity of the nation, known as El Petén, is scarcely settled and, for all intents and purposes, remains in the state it was at the time of conquest. Lovell notes that an account authored by Pedro de Alvarado indicates that the land was "so rough that the horses could scarcely climb," and, for whatever reasons, Spaniards in this area encountered more and fiercer opposition than they had in some other areas.[32] Indeed, one feature of the Spanish attempt to dominate what later became Guatemala was that it took decades, and featured highs and lows, including actual Spanish losses and reversals. As Lovell indicates,

> The military phase of the Spanish conquest may, therefore, perhaps be regarded as beginning with Alvarado's *entrada* in 1524 and ending around the time of the *conquistador*'s death in 1541. It thus took almost twenty years, by fire and sword, before the various native peoples of highland Guatemala were brought under Spanish rule. During this prolonged period of conquest, several Indian groups were not only superior in resisting the forces of imperial Spain; some actually inflicted defeat, albeit momentarily, on the European invaders.[33]

The combination of mountainous land, strength, and (by Spanish lights) ferocity of the native population, and lack of a place from which physically to gain a foothold meant that, from the beginning, the conquest of Guatemala proceeded in a fashion different from that of neighboring Mexico, or even Peru. Because of this, many Mayan traditions were left virtually undisturbed, and rural areas continued along traditional lines until very recently.

Within the indigenous households, weaving and the growing of crops for cash and sustenance on small patches of land have been the staples of life. Because women have been such steadfast producers, particularly of products from the loom, the role of the woman in the indigenous household has always been one of comparative egalitarianism. Whereas men have often traveled away from their villages to work on large plantations, women have generally remained within a given area, traveling perhaps only to the nearby market regions to sell goods. Women traditionally have grown fruits and vegetables, engaged in weaving and knitting and small shopkeeping, and sold items door-to-door. These patterns of life, predating the time of the conquest, remain in almost all of the nonurban areas of Guatemala.

Ehlers documents the historical importance of weaving for the Guatemalan highland communities by noting that the simple change from the stick loom (pre-Columbian) to the foot loom (introduced by the Spanish) made an enormous difference in the amount of weaving that could be done by one woman. Because weaving traditionally was an income generator in the highland communities, the change brought about by introducing the foot loom meant that much more income could be generated in a shorter time. Since the work of males has largely been on the *latifundias* or plantations, female income is often the only sure income in the home. This factor alone increases the status of the woman in the non-*ladino* households. According to Ehlers,

> Like other Guatemalan towns ... that have historically engaged in commercial production of woven articles, the volume of San Pedro's textile trade has for many years been based upon utilizing the four-harness footloom introduced to the region by the Spanish in the seventeenth century. The production of fabric on a footloom (also called the treadle loom) is rapid and simple when compared to its predecessor.[34]

In a given region, the work produced by women has almost always been the mainstay of the family, and this pattern is only now beginning to change, and even with contemporary economic conditions, the change is most pronounced in the *ladino* communities. Thus there is a known historical trajectory in the indigenous communities from pre-Columbian times to the present that includes women's work and production as absolutely central to the lives of the household. Ehlers and others comment on the *ladino* pattern of attempting to demonstrate middle-classness by not allowing the wife to work or to pursue money-earning activities. Obviously, this is a pattern which most Guatemalans have not had the luxury of examining at close range.[35]

The domestic production of crafts by women and the selling of these items as means of commodity exchange must be viewed against the history of the breakup of traditional landholding of indigenous communities by the Spaniards. The consolidation of land under the Spaniards meant that *haciendas* became forms of tribute to the Crown, and those who worked on haciendas were forever in some form of debt. In the seventeenth and eighteenth centuries the form of land merger was a function largely of the Church and the few other wealthy Spaniards who possessed the personal temerity to endure the hardships of life in colonial Guatemala. Although a strong attempt was made to resettle Indians in areas that were under Spanish legal title, such resettlement seldom became permanent, and many pockets of land remained completely under indigenous control. Thus the pattern emerged that was to mark the growth of Guatemala as a nation— attempts at Europeanization, only partially successful, due to geography, climate, and the strength of the local cultures. Lovell describes early efforts at land breakup in the following:

> Under the policy of *congregación*, the Indians [who] resettled at a new town site were legally entitled to an allotment of land from which to derive basic subsistence. Included in this allotment were both arable tracts and an area designated *ejido*, uncultivated land held in common by the Indians and used by them for cutting firewood, grazing livestock, hunting animals and gathering the various products of the forest.[36]

As is so often the case, it may very well be that males began to feel a greater sense of displacement and disempowerment under the Spanish than did the females—and this pattern of felt disempowerment might then lend itself to a variety of stratagems of overcompensation once the opportunity availed itself. As we have seen in an examination of the Nyeshangte culture of Nepal, once the more Europeanized elements have established themselves, European-like "status" is often signaled by a concomitant loss of power for women and a demeaning of traditional female-oriented activities. Thus a dispossessed indigenous male, if he at a later time is to acquire more wealth, may signal his more *ladino*-like place by refusing to let his wife engage in even the most time-honored activities, activities that signaled the strength of gynocentric elements within the traditional society.

The history of Guatemala, then, has been the history of the attempt by the

Spaniards and other Iberians to conquer a highland-filled and mountainous region inhabited by persons very determined to defend themselves. Unlike in Mexico, where a rapid population mix was able to at least unsettle the European dominance by the middle of the nineteenth century, Guatemala today is still a traditional society with a few pockets of Eurocentric culture. These pockets have comparatively little to do with the rest of the country, which no doubt accounts for the strength of government-led violence.

Grant Jones, in his extensive and prize-winning work on the Maya, emphasizes the difficulties that the Spaniards had, in general, in conquering the Maya, and the immense strength of the Mayan social structure. The group to which he refers as the "Itzas" were the dominant group in Chiapas, Campeche, Quintana Roo and a good part of what is today Guatemala until finally put down by the Spanish at the end of the sixteenth century. Jones writes:

> Far from being naive about Spanish methods of conquest and colonization, the Itzas demonstrated awareness and understanding of their enemy. At the same time they acted in the context of an ancient and highly traditional culture, purposefully retaining political, military, social and religious institutions that had served them well before the sixteenth-century conquest that had isolated them in a sea of Spanish colonies.... While patrilineal descent remained the most important organizing principle, a limited form of matrilineal descent may have constituted the critical marker of the nobility's right to rule.[37]

Jones is merely recapitulating what has been said by almost every historian and current-day social scientist on the subject. The strength of the Mayan culture is intense, marked by a comparative egalitarianism, a strong sense of ties to the land, and an unbending respect for ritual. It is because of these factors, according to many, that the Guatemalan government sees the Mayan culture as so threatening, and perhaps also due to these factors that it is an indigenous woman, rightly or wrongly, who has come to symbolize most of Guatemala's current grievances.

The Contemporary Guatemalan Woman

Ehlers has well documented the changes experienced by one highlands town, San Pedro Sacapequétez, in her *Silent Looms*. Although traditional life continues to a great extent unabated, there have, of course, been changes due to regional transport and a wide growth in schools. Thus some girls now attend primary school, and many young men travel much farther away from the village. The tradition of "female family business" continues, with a great deal of the work for each small business—sewing, crafts—being done by female members of the immediate family for little or no recompense. Since government assaults against the indigenous peoples continue on a sporadic but irregular basis, some areas have remained relatively peaceful, while others have seen great violence.[38] In any case, Ehlers is able to track extensive evidence that traditional activities abound. One of the most telling examples she employs, not only of traditional crafts, but of poignant aspects of the culture, involves a woman who makes her living simply by sewing specially decorated shrouds for the dead. In a culture with a high infant death rate and a great respect for tradition, the woman is one of the most prosperous individuals in her village.[39]

In addition to creating an international spokesperson in the form of Rigoberta Menchú, the government has succeeded in turning many other Guatemalan women into activists. Rosalina Tuyuc amply documents how the continued violence has to some extent broken the back of the traditional notions that limited women's involvement in certain activities. Tuyuc notes that approximately 50,000 Guatemalan women have lost their husbands due to the recent killings and "disappearances," but that there is now a decline in the notion that "there's always been this *machismo*."[40] The government has had the effect of shaking up traditional views of women, and of indigenous persons, for that matter.[41]

Indian men have had to work outside the home, frequently away from the village, at least since the time of the Spanish invasion. Although a typical scenario involves the male member of the household (whether husband, brother, or son) promising to send money back, such payments are often sporadic at best and nonexistent at worst. Thus all female members are frequently more than willing to pitch in to keep the small-scale family businesses going, and, in the process, they hand down traditional knowledge and recapitulate the lives of previous generations. In one story told by Ehlers, her informants had been contracted to bake a special cake for the "*quince años*" party usually given for girls as they turn fifteen, and the cake was so large that they borrowed an electric beater for it. But the beater broke down, and all the female members took turns working on the cake for hours to produce it on time. In the end, as Ehlers notes, it "took six people all afternoon," and they earned ten quetzals.[42] Needless to say, this is not the type of task that would have been performed by male members of the family under any circumstances. Yet no female member of the family would dream of complaining or of failing to help out.

As is the case in most agrarian societies, a series of basic tasks that must be performed for the immediate family fills the early day of most Indian women. Nancy Black reports that basic daily responsibilities include "food procurement and preparation, fetching water, gathering firewood, tending small domesticated animals, marketing, weaving, pottery making and child-care."[43] Because these tasks are performed by female family members in addition to running the ubiquitous family businesses, female members literally work all day. They may or may not occasionally relocate with male members when the men are able to find work on the coastal plantations, but if they do relocate, all of the other tasks must be taken with them. Then, of course, it is the responsibility of the women to turn the new area into some kind of a home. Black reports that women who accompany their husbands or male companions in the search for paid employment outside the village are frequently exposed to DDT levels that are hundreds of times higher than that deemed to be acceptable in more developed regions. Black categorizes the conditions for women in these areas in these terms:

> Women laboring on plantations usually work with their youngest child strapped onto their backs, and earn less than males for the 14-hour work day. Women are still responsible for the regular food preparation, laundry, and childcare in addition to the work of harvesting. Wages remain exploitative, although a workers' strike in 1980 resulted in minimal daily wages being increased by the government from $1.12 to $3.00.[44]

The importance of the shelling, soaking, pounding, and overall preparation of maize for tortillas is so great that in the rare cases where women are unable to complete this time-consuming series of tasks on a regular basis, husbands generally express great embarrassment.[45]

As mentioned earlier, ritual is so important to most indigenous groups that preparation for ritual—whether actual seasonal ceremony, or wedding, birth, death, or other such event—again takes up extraordinary periods of time, with all females helping out to make sure that such tasks are carried out properly. Within a nondualistic worldview, to fail to do this is to show a degree of disrespect for one's ancestors and the land in general which is intolerable. Given the gynocentric patterns of belief in harmony, the importance of fertility, and rituals to ensure fertility, Indian groups in general will form social structures around these important days.[46]

The extent to which daily life revolves around these activities is shown by a more or less typical set of brief entries in the diary of Ignacio, part of James Sexton's well-known trilogy on the Maya. Ignacio, who in general reflects high levels of thoughtfulness and some education and awareness, is very traditional in many of his beliefs. The diary excerpts, which were taken mainly in the mid- to late '80s, reflect the importance of traditional living structures. Speaking to Sexton about how proud he was of his sons, who were to take part in a torch-carrying portion of the national independence day ceremonies, Ignacio notes, "My wife was working very hard, preparing food for our three sons."[47] At the same time, Ignacio recounts an interesting episode of having been scared by a spirit on the road, as he says, which reminds him of the fact that other members of his family had also encountered a spirit during the same place in previous travels. He had traveled to Antigua to help out a friend who had a sick baby, and on the way back he had an unusual experience:

> On the path from San Martín to San José, we were frightened. At times I didn't believe in these things, but this time we were scared. Well since 1950, when I was nine years old, my grandfather, Ignacio Bizarro Ramos, was spooked in this same place when he went to San Martín at night. When he had to return, he didn't have the courage to pass by it again. I thought they were lies, but now I believe it.[48]

When Sexton questions Ignacio about what precisely happened, he is somewhat vague, but mentions that he heard some "shouting," and that "they started to move the stones and the trees."[49] Ignacio finds that one of the factors that is helpful to him in recovering from the episode is indeed the memory of having been told by other family members that the place in question was haunted, and then recounting to himself their specific stories about what happened to them when they passed through the given area.

The juxtaposition of traditional life, respect for ancestors, intense labor on the part of families with little recompense, and government violence has led to the formation of some groups specifically aimed at women. Although many of the groups are for *ladinas* and are in the cities, Rosalina Tuyuc and others have formed the National Coordinating Committee for Guatemalan Widows (CONAVIGUA), an organization of activists for the widows of the "disappeared."[50]

To say that the Guatemalan woman of today is pulled in many directions at once—even more so than many of her sisters in other regions—is an understatement. Indigenous women are exposed now more than ever to the *ladina* culture of the cities, and the international movements to assist Guatemala, combined with the levels of violence, have meant that there is virtually no one who is unaware of the peculiar status of her nation and history at this point in time.

In speaking with women from largely indigenous backgrounds in her recent work in Guatemala, the feminist theorist Margaret Randall, known for her writing about Latin America, characterizes her experience as follows:

> Today—and it's been a very long today—painful poverty, terror, and loss are central facts of these women's lives. In whatever their language, words like *torture, disappearance, strategic hamlet, hunger,* have become stalwarts of their vocabulary. The *feelings* such conditions engender are expressed by words and in hard-to-translate silence.[51]

Randall here is at pains to make the point that traditional Mayan lives now have an overlay of factors that would have been unthinkable a few years ago. As has been documented, the brutality of the events seems to fall disproportionately on women, a fact of which most of the women interviewed by Randall seemed painfully aware. Other researchers have done specific work on the occurrence of post-traumatic stress disorder among Guatemalan women refugees, and its direct traceability to the events propounded by the army and the national government.[52] To be a woman in Guatemala today is to be the target of severe and extreme oppressions.

Feminisms of Guatemala

The awareness of the larger community of NGOs and assistance givers has helped establish in Guatemala a network of organizations, some overtly feminist and some not, that speak to the specific issues faced by Guatemalan women. What is encouraging about the intellectual structure of such organizations is that many, like those reported by Randall, Black, and Menchú, are using the gynocentric patterns of conceptualization and growth already inherent in the Mayan-derived cultures to help establish strong voices for women.

In addition to CONAVIGUA and COMADRES, which was originally based in El Salvador, groups such as GAM and others are making an appearance not only within Guatemala, but within the international community.[53] Many of the groups, unlike some of their counterparts in other regions, have been able to establish levels of dialogue that are specifically and overtly feminist and communitarian in knowledge structure and engage issues that relate the intricacies of various forms of oppression. Randall and others cite the growing importance of awareness about the effects of the original colonization on the indigenous, and both Randall and Menchú note the feminist efforts to tie resistance to the Quincentenary (the 1992 "recognition" of arrival in the New World by Europeans) into general resistance to the dominance of the *ladino* culture and other specific acts of oppression.[54]

Randall writes of meeting with a group of indigenous women who only the previous week had been themselves talking to Spanish women who were in Guatemala to try to plan ceremonies of "Reenactment." The persons with whom she spoke were only too aware of the connection between the acts perpetrated by the government, from which they currently suffered, and acts perpetrated in the past. Randall tells us:

> Margarita [her informant] knows we are on a mission of solidarity and she hopes to bridge some part of the distance between us by telling us this story about other women of similar intent: visitors from Spain who recently sat on these same benches.... [Margarita] looks from one to another of us and repeats: "I was silent.... Finally I told her: I am not going to be able to be gracious about your commemoration.... For us these five hundred years have brought us nothing but abuse, rape, genocide. The death of our cultures."[55]

Women such as Margarita are easily able to make the connections because the *ladino* patterns of overt violence, male dominance, the importance of *machismo*, and lack of respect for the natural world and growing things are patterns that she sees every day. Although no indigenous culture represents a Golden Age to which persons might rationally yearn to return, there is no question that the Mayan cultures, particularly as lived before the conquest, exhibited belief systems and philosophies that were focused on respect for natural cycles and ecology in general simply because such respect was necessary for survival in a hostile world. The mountainous terrain of much of Guatemala, reported on by George Lovell, Peter Calvert, and James Sexton, and well known as a topic of discussion among the sixteenth-century Spanish chroniclers, demanded a respect for the natural world simply in order to be able to grow enough food for daily sustenance. The changes wrought by the Iberians reinforced a general concept of brutality that, as Margarita notes, reverberates in multiple cultural patterns.

In a sense, a number of the groups mentioned here may be considered feminist groups—this construal is made in the large sense, of course, that the groups are composed mainly of women, and that the women are using gynocentric patterns from their own lives to accomplish tasks that would not otherwise be accomplished. GAM, CONAVIGUA, and UNSITRAGUA, one of the largest unions, are all led by women and persist in the strength of women's cooperative principles. In a region where the patterns of the *huipil* or *traje* of traditional clothing indicate to the viewer the bearer's village or point of origin, the persistence of women's points of view is strong indeed. Margaret Hooks, in *Guatemalan Women Speak*, has many examples of women-dominated social commitments or small groups that come to have more power and more say in a given situation than they might originally be thought to possess.[56]

It is important to note that, frequently, a stand is taken by women on a more-or-less spontaneous basis, and the stand may well precede any type of formal organization. Village women, in particular, understand that if most of the men in the village have been killed or "disappeared," the women have only each other to turn to.[57] Thus the emotional bonding and communicative networks that are so important in indigenous groups for the weaving and growing projects in which they would ordinarily be engaged become a source of strength and mode of learning and knowledge acquisition when circumstances change. María de los Angeles, another of Hooks's informants, describes what happened when she and some of her workmates decided to stop accepting the insults and physical abuse of their superiors at their workplace and to organize themselves:

> From that day on the management began to separate us from the rest of the plant. We were put into a kind of alleyway behind the factory, which we called "the chicken coop" because it really wasn't suitable for 65 people to work in.... There was no ventilation whatsoever; it was like a cauldron. When we couldn't bear it anymore we soaked our clothes. They would dry within two or three minutes, so you can imagine how hot it was.[58]

María had to tolerate, of course, strong criticism from some persons for her actions, including members of her own family who accuse her of endangering her children's safety and welfare by staging a strike. But as she says in her interview with Hooks, "I *am* on my own and my work supports my kids."

Because the *ladino* culture of the urban areas so heavily reflects the original Spanish culture of the conquest, it is not difficult to make the assertion that it also reflects the more ingrained and overtly patriarchal values of a Catholicized society. It may be for these reasons, even if they are sometimes unarticulated, that so many indigenous women resist elements of the *ladino* culture, even when they have received heavy exposure to it, or when its adoption would seem to benefit them in other ways. One of the most intriguing interviews that Hooks presents is with a *ladina* woman who is a member of the elite group and hence a supporter of the army's most right-wing tactics. She articulates a view common among *ladina/os*—it is better for the indigenous to learn Spanish and "abandon their customs and their language."[59] Interestingly, however, she, too, is aware of feminism and the lack of opportunities in Guatemala even for women of her social class and education. She indicates that the discrimination against women (here, of course, she means in wealthy or educated circles) is a source of constant anxiety to her. Intriguingly enough, however, she does not link discriminatory attitudes toward women's participation in politics and the government to the *ladino* attitude toward Indians and traditional cultures.

The most interesting feminisms in Guatemala, then (as might also be said, as we have seen, of Bangladesh) are those that arise spontaneously from women's desire to achieve despite enormous obstacles. One informant who told Hooks of her village's rabbit-breeding project specifically mentions the confusion and fear that she and the other female villagers felt when they realized that almost all of the men in their village had been killed and that they were now alone. But as she says, people in another village "told us to get together with other women in the same situation. And so we got started."[60]

A number of commentators, of course, have made the connection between the patriarchal and androcentric structure of *ladino* society and its repression of the indigenous. It might seem, on analyses both traditional and radical, that such repressions are indeed constitutive of what "masculine" and *macho* mean, on certain construals. One does not need French poststructuralist theory here to see that part of what the phallocentric reading of a culture means is that women and other males—especially males whose cultural background is different from that of the dominant culture—need to be dominated in order for the full expression of the male-in-power to take place. This is what Matthews, for example, intends when she says, "The soldiers in the Guatemalan army were themselves positioned very precariously on the ladder of social and sexual security. [It has been observed that] the most common sign of upward social mobility is acquiring a woman from the social stratum to which the man has risen."[61]

Thus the position of women overall in Guatemala today is defined by the actions of the male army. The better-off *ladina* women, comparatively few in number, in many cases support the government or possibly do not fully understand the nature of the atrocities.[62] The indigenous women have employed the same modes of functioning that they have always traditionally employed for ceremonies, *maza* preparation, and general daily functioning to try to establish a bulwark against the violence. A recent journalistic piece on a proposed new translation of the Popul Vuh indicates the extent to which this later-composed piece of Mayan mythography relies on the notion of the sacred power of corn.[63] It might well be said that, in a society in which it is believed that humans originated from the divine maize, the powers of reproduction and of growth are greatly venerated.

Reconstituting Knowledge

It seems almost too facile to speak of gynocentric traditions in indigenous societies, since it is widely believed by scholars that a great many, if not most, indigenous societies adhere more to the generalized goddess traditions that are associated in the West with the pre-Mycenean and Minoan cultures.[64] But the general paths of knowledge acquisition must be more carefully delineated if we are to indeed make sense of feminist epistemologies and if we can attempt the difficult work of moving in such directions cross-culturally.

In a sense, such work is more dangerous and smacks more of Eurocentric appropriation and dominance in cultures with a lengthy tradition of literacy and the establishment of written records, such as some of those of South Asia, for here we understand that we are pitting a firmly articulated Sanskrit tradition, for example, against a Eurocentric tradition that is taken as the norm. Because so much of what transpires in most indigenous societies is passed down orally, the analogies are probably somewhat looser to begin with, and, oddly, this may make it easier to attempt to make assertions about such societies.

Controversy has always surrounded the Popol Vuh, since, according to some, it was not put in writing in anything like its present form until after the arrival of the Spaniards.[65] Thus it is simpler, and probably more accurate, to cite glosses on practices as they are known in the Guatemalan highlands region, without a great deal of concern over whether such practices are codified or written down. Some facts are obvious: that the Mayans did in fact have a hieroglyphic form of writing and an extensive system of calendars is known, and the existence of many ceremonies having to do with crop growing and fertility cycles is also known. The general reliance on the notion of small communities, the *huipiles* of which designate the community in question, is also extensively documented. Current notions frequently employed by Western philosophers, such as "communitarian," might then seem misplaced when applied to the traditional communities, until it is remembered that, in some sense, such notions are derived from such communities.

Harding, in a gloss on contemporary feminist standpoint theory, as articulated by Nancy Hartsock, political scientist and feminist theoretician, reasserts the extent to which the theory owes its origins to a Marxist-derived account of the importance of labor and the material in constructing the epistemology of our everyday lives. She writes: "The argument here is that human activity, or 'material life,' not only structures but also sets limits on human understanding: what we do shapes and constrains what we can know."[66] Here we are best off almost returning to basics, so to speak: the notion of a feminist epistemology or feminist epistemologies came about in more recent Western scholarship precisely because it was intended to counter the view-from-nowhere epistemics that grew up and was articulated by privileged males in such social structures. Males having the power, time, and capital to pursue lives of intellectual inquiry developed epistemologies, to be sure, but their views on theories of knowledge frequently reflected the concerns thrown up by male personality development and male individuation, overlooking the fact that their concerns themselves could be described in terms of their social roots and origins. Masking such origins, they pretended to have none. Harding's work, and the work of other feminist epistemologists, has reminded us that every construction or theory of knowledge has discernible roots.

When looked at this way, much can be said about indigenous knowledge patterns. The calendars and prophecy patterns of the Maya were so striking that they were among the first cultural features noted by the Spaniards. Jones, in his work on the last viable Mayan kingdom, which lasted well beyond the time of the first wave of Spanish conquest, notes: "As for the royal wedding conflict, Roys believed that it was the same event as one mentioned in the Maya chronicles involving a banquet, a love charm, and treachery."[67] Although prophecies have been part of many ancient cultures, the specificity and ubiquitousness of the Maya prophecies in general tie them to notions of time that are deeply related to observed cycles of growth and fertility. In other societies, time might come to be measured in ways more divorced from such events—from the time of the birth of a "divinity," for example. The wholistic approach of the Itz'a calendar referred to by Grant Jones shows an extensive sense of gynocentric time measurement.

Although it has become something of a cliché to write of feminist epistemics or, indeed, other types of feminist theorizing as failing to employ oppositions in their philosophically standard way, the insight that such oppositional constructions have much to do with standard androcentric categorizing is a valuable one. Caroline Whitbeck, in her "A Different Reality: Feminist Ontology," provides one of the most succinct characterizations of oppositionality in Western philosophical thought patterns:

The self-other opposition is at the heart of other dualistic oppositions, such as theory-practice, culture-nature, spirit-matter ... that figure prominently in "western thought." The feminist ontology outlined here yields a distinctive, nonoppositional, and nondualistic conception of these subjects.[68]

It is not only the case that we can see strands of this nondualistic ontology construction in the Mayan take on time, but we can also see a much less dualistic construction in the patterns of personal organization, particularly among women, to which we have already referred. Ehlers's Violeta, for example, to whom we were introduced in *Silent Looms*, is able to employ herself and others full time in the making of funereal items because each member of the community is seen as deeply tied to others in ways that we might have trouble understanding.[69] It is too naive, of course, to suggest that some constructions of the ontology of the person are seen entirely as "individualistic," and others as the "self-in-relation-to-others," but it is not too naive to indicate that splits along something like these lines tend to be more characteristic of some cultures than others. Violeta involves herself heavily in the mourning rituals for every person for whom funereal items are sold. Cynically, it might be thought that her motivation is financial, and it may well be partly financial, but Ehlers makes it clear that Violeta is genuinely involved in the community in ways that would be uncommon in other cultures. In this sense, her shop and her seamstress skills have involved her in rituals, largely with other women, that give new meaning to gynocentric ontologies, themselves, of course, related to feminist epistemologies.

In writing of the new translation of the Popol Vuh that Greenwood Press hopes to commission under the editorship of the University of California at Davis scholar Victor Montejo, Ramirez quotes one of the extant editions as saying, of the creation, "[The flesh of our first mother and father] was made of white and yellow corn. The arms and legs of the [first] men were made of corn meal."[70] Many creation stories provide precise mythographic details of the origins of the first humans, but it is somewhat unusual, perhaps, for the details to include the fact that the humans were made of one of the constituents of the most important crop available in the region.

Here once again, we can see elements of the kind of analysis provided by both Whitbeck and Harding in their work on gynocentric metaphysics and epistemics. A society that has divorced itself from reliance on crop growth can afford to develop a more overtly dualistic (or even monistic, but nonmaterialistic) metaphysics. Spirit might be hypothesized as something completely apart from matter if some have the leisure to speculate on such topics (and if the labor that supports their speculation is provided by others). But cultures such as the Mayan culture almost always have seen matter and spirit as intermixed and intermingled: spirit is in everything, so to speak, all matter, because it is all matter from which human beings have sprung. Some contemporary philosophers have expressed difficulties in pronouncing such views philosophical, but this, of course, is the very point. If philosophy is thought of as a speculative activity produced largely by leisured males, it will result in speculations frequently divorced from daily reality and, in many cases, unconfirmable. Where human beings are in daily contact with the sources of life, such speculation is unlikely and unnecessary.

The Mayan Mythos

According to Robert Ryan Miller, "ecological adaptation" was a principle upon which the classic Maya civilization was founded.[71] What we know today about this world of ritual and orderly chronology is concomitant, to a surprising extent, with the lives of the Mayan-descended peoples in the three main regions of contemporary Mexico and Guatemala in which we still find them: the highlands regions of Guatemala, the Yucatán area of Mexico, and the El Petén tract in Guatemala.

In many parts of the world where ancient cultures flourished, visitors seem disappointed to find little evidence in contemporary times of the former societies, but with the Maya this is not the case. Contemporary people in the region not only visibly resemble the friezes that we have of their ancestors, they also retain the interest in ritual and cycle that permeated the lives of the ancients. Miller notes that the daily life of the classic period showed the importance of music ("drums, trumpets, flutes, whistles, rattles") but many of these same instruments are used in ceremonies by contemporary Maya, and the importance of these ceremonies has been documented.

This worldview, with its respect for nature and its gynocentric adherence to ecological adaptation rather than blind conquest, might be thought to constitute a philosophy in and of itself, but it is instructive, especially when viewing cultures through the inevitable Eurocentric lenses, to ask how the term "philosophy" came to be used. In our quest to make note of patterns androcentric or gynocentric in differing cultures, we are thrown back, especially for purposes of postcolonial comparison, on the region that usually yields, for Western thinkers, the first "philosophers."

G. S. Kirk and J. E. Raven are the authors of the text that frequently is cited, in philosophy courses, as containing the work that demarcates mytho-logical/mythographic thinking from philosophy.[72] The opening chapter of their work contains various cosmogonies of the Greek pre-Classical period, but the text turns toward the first recognizable attempts at philosophizing, according to the Cambridge scholars, when we encounter the work of Thales. They write:

> Although these ideas were strongly affected, directly or indirectly, by mytho-logical precedents, Thales evidently abandoned mythic formulations: this alone justifies the claim that he was the first philosopher, naive though his thought still was.[73]

But what is it about Thales's thought that merits the label? According to Kirk and Raven, translating from the Greek and relying also on mention made of Thales by Aristotle and others, it is Thales's conceptualization of water as the first "principle" (the Greek here is generally *archon*) that dis-tinguishes his work from what might be regarded as mere tale telling.

It is important to note these distinctions, for just as, according to Kirk and Raven, there is the "naive" view of the Minoan or Mycenean groups that preceded the Greeks of whom we have written record, there is also the naive assumption, by Westerners, that there is a hard and fast demarcation between "myth" and "philosophy." Actually, as the authors implicitly sug-gest, the distinction is far from hard and fast.

Although their record-keeping is not usually deemed "philosophical," and although their language is not directly related by conquest and history to the European languages that later came to dominate the planet, there is much in the meticulousness of Mayan thought that suggests at least as much "philosophy" as the work of Thales and many other pre-Socratics. In any case, the important notion is the one that asks us to view these societies somewhat differently than we have in the past. Perhaps, after all, they have more in common than might have been asserted. And if they still do not have a great deal in common, we might wonder if it does not have to do with the other labels we have employed.

For the thought of the philosophers preceding Socrates, in their single-minded attempts to provide the Complete Account, already bears the hall-marks of a culture that will become profoundly androcentric, so much so that ultimately Plato will devalue the companionship of women and insist that the highest form of love and knowledge seeking—for he runs the two together—can occur only between men.[74]

The cultures of Central America, including the Maya, were perhaps not so single-minded. A more fluid take on reality suggests, we might guess, that they suspected reality of being too complex for easy formulation. This part of the Mayan worldview either does or docs not deserve the appellation "philosophy," depending, of course, on one's point of view.

Our brief digression into the use of the term "philosophy" highlights some of the problems involved in applying terms of European origin or expressive of Eurocentric concepts to non-European cultures, issues also discussed here with respect to other nations. More important, it suggests that at least some of what drives the application of such notions has to do with the perception on the part of the dominant or dominating culture that some sort of "advanced" patriarchy is alive and well in the subaltern culture. As we have seen, the rhythms of daily life of the indigenous people of Guatemala are driven by women and involve groups of women working closely together. The *ladino* culture of Guatemala City is, of course, "advanced"—after all, it is derived from the equally "advanced" cultures of the Iberian peninsula, the home of the original conquerors.

But it is perhaps expressive of some of the strength of the international movements on behalf of women, indigenous persons, and ecological concerns in general that there is now a developing awareness, even in industrialized nations, that First World countries may not be so "advanced." The controversy surrounding Rigoberta Menchú may, in fact, be related to this.[75] Although David Stoll finds it important that some details of the original tale, as purportedly told by Menchú to Elizabeth Burgos-Debray, are not literally true, many defenders of Menchú and of the Mayans in general have indicated that what is important here is the larger point. If the story is taken as emblematic—and indeed this seems to be the way in which it is being taken by many—what Menchú intended to accomplish has already been accomplished.

The right-wing women cited by Hooks in her interesting compilation genuinely feel that they are working for a more sophisticated Guatemala, one that can hold its head up in international circles. Part of what this means, of course, is that fewer and fewer of its indigenous persons would lead traditional lives. Guatemala, the rightists hope, would eventually come to resemble more and more a First World nation (a hope also articulated, incidentally, by Mexico's ruling class). Hooks's *ladina* informant, cited earlier, states:

> It is also important to have enough authority and popular support to control crime. Everywhere you go in Guatemala people's main protest is, "We are so insecure! We are being assaulted all the time! We are being robbed." If you

go into the city centre your car is likely to be stolen. It never used to be this bad in Guatemala. And crime affects the lower classes more, because they live in areas that are vulnerable to attack.[76]

It does not seem to occur to the speaker that by far and away the largest amount of violence in Guatemala comes from the ruling group, and is directed toward the same persons she mentions in her last sentence. It is not the likelihood of having one's car stolen that is the greatest danger for most Guatemalans. Most Guatemalans do not have cars. It is the likelihood of having one's culture stolen.

Guatemalan women today are using some of the same patterns that they have traditionally employed in the production of crafts and woven items to forge movements that have become international symbols of resistance. GAM, UNRG, and other such organizations in many cases exhibit the same communitarian patterns of knowledge acquisition and transmission that inform, for example, the lives of many of the women interviewed by Ehlers in *Silent Looms*. In a traditional culture the ontology of which differs significantly from the more particularized, individualistic, and in some cases metaphysically dualistic ontologies of other cultures, communitarian epistemologies express significant features of the society. Whitbeck noted in her work on feminist ontology that, in a more gynocentric worldview, "the distinction between the self and an other does not turn on an opposition."[77] The lives of many Guatemalan women today are demonstrating the fact that it is possible to create a culture in which distinctions, thought by many to be so important a feature of human functioning, do not turn on oppositions, but rather on connections.

Chapter 8

Chicana/os

The Chicana/o cultures of the American Southwest present a new area for theorizing about feminist constructions of knowledge, and they have given us a metaphor that appears to be resonant with many, that of "border-lands."[1] The theorizing derived from the Chicana/o groups is particularly exciting, since it represents a potential for work that is truly postmodern and yet still retains—insofar as it relies on work from Mexico—ties to a discernible and describable past.

What is today described as Chicana/o culture of the area taken from Mexico in the War of 1848 is itself a hybrid of Mexican culture, Anglo-American thought (especially, it seems, Anglo-American consumerism), and some remnants of American culture that are themselves taken from cultures of color. Before approximately World War II, it might well be said that a great deal of Los Angeles, for example, had a distinctly "Mexican" flavor, but since that time the influx of immigrants combined with the establishment of a distinctly homegrown culture by those who have been in the United States for generations has combined to create a completely new cultural force. The opening up of American universities and the rise in theorizing of many groups originally deemed to have been "marginal" has meant that there is now self-conscious Chicana feminist epistemology, and even in cases where no such construct has been articulated, many other theoretical moves of interest have taken place.[2]

Another factor that gives rise to a great deal of interest in Chicana thought within the space of Chicana/o thinking is the obvious fact, acknowledged here earlier, that Chicana theorizing derives from an inevitably androcentric and patriarchal starting point, and one that is, if anything, perhaps more intensely androcentric than it might have otherwise been due to its having been dislocated into the hostile United States. Thus, as noted earlier, insofar as an awareness of things "Chicano" emerged in the postwar United States, it did so largely under the auspices of militant student movements, themselves run almost entirely by males, and with little notice of the presence of females. Thus the obvious emergence of an articulate and aware feminist movement from such origins provides a noteworthy focal point for many sorts of discussions.[3]

Persons of Mexican ancestry have been coming to the United States in a sense both before there was a United States and before there was a nation/state of Mexico—the presence of the chain of missions in California attests to that.[4] The more recent wave of movements, however, started around the time of the Mexican Revolution, and gained during the Cristero Rebellion of the late 1920s and early '30s and then again during World War II and its aftermath. Current immigration is from many countries other than Mexico, and it is probably true now that immigration from Mexico— as opposed, say, to El Salvador, Nicaragua, or Guatemala—is actually somewhat less a percentage of the total than it has been in times past.

Immigrants from Mexico brought with them, of course, the *machismo* of that culture, and patterns of women's work that revolve around the preparation of dishes, child care, sewing, weaving, and so forth. But a new kind of androcentrism awaited them in the United States, particularly after World War II. Women who might have done a number of things in a village or small-town atmosphere were now exposed to the ultradomestication of the postwar American economy. The notion that families who could afford it did not have wives/mothers who worked outside the home meant that a sort of double whammy of patriarchal thought greeted a number of young women of Mexican ancestry living in the United States during the 1950s and '60s. As is the case with a number of the other cultural patterns to which we have alluded, the combination of "developed" patriarchy and the already existing variety is a powerful juxtaposition. The few Chicanas who attended college in the '50s and '60s, like their Anglo-American counterparts, may well have expected not to have to work after marriage, and were encouraged by the larger culture to think of this as some sort of goal.

It is particularly ironic, then, that much of the contemporary Chicana/o movement is related to the labor awakenings of the 1960s that took place among farm workers in California and throughout the Southwest. César Chávez, Dolores Huerta, and others helped to spark an awareness of labor conditions at the same time that they gave birth to a sense of "Chicanismo." The result was a heady and potent brew.

Some of the cultural artifacts of the Grape Boycott of the United Farm Workers (UFW) came to symbolize *chicanismo*, and, intriguingly enough, they put new twists on remnants of the Mexican culture. Chávez originally titled one of the main walks from Delano, a small California agricultural town, *"La Peregrinación."* This Spanish word refers, of course, to pilgrimages and other walks with a statedly sacred Catholic theme—one might make a *"Peregrinación"* under more ordinary circumstances to a shrine of the Virgin, such as Lourdes or the basilica of the Virgin of Guadalupe. But Chávez clearly chose to use this icon of Mexican culture for political ends; his initial marches were overtly political and economic, and not statedly religious. Yet the somewhat postmodern use of *"Peregrinación"* did not seem out of place, since his workers were almost all Spanish-speaking Catholics for whom anything associated with the Virgin had become a cultural symbol, rather than simply a religious one. Chávez and Huerta together also created a logo for the UFW that incorporated stylized elements of the Mexican eagle as taken from Aztec/Toltec legend and as appearing on the national flag of Mexico. Once again, not every worker was even of Mexican ancestry, but the important point was that the power of symbols was being drawn upon in a new and forceful way. In creating a labor movement, Huerta and Chávez also helped to create an explicitly Chicano movement, where American-born persons of Mexican ancestry could feel for the first time that their political/cultural needs were being expressed.

José Antonio Burciaga, in his *Drink Cultura: Chicanismo,* writes of the origins of artifacts now specifically associated with *chicanismo,* that is, with a culture that is of American origins and with a Mexican ancestry. Yet he admits that, in some cases, tracing the ancestry has proved to be difficult if not impossible. This is what gives the contemporary Chicana/o movement its decidedly millennial flavor. Of the graffito symbol "c/s," usually taken to stand for *"con safos,"* he writes:

> It is not a Mexican symbol, but a Chicano, a Mexican-American symbol. Its origin is unknown, but like the *Pachuco,* it probably originated in South El Paso's *Segundo Barrio.* The c/s sign-off means *con safos,* and translates literally as "with safety." It was meant as a safety precaution, barrio copyright, patent pending.... But [the Chicano dialect] is the combination of a few basic influences: Hispanicized English; Anglicized Spanish; and the use of archaic 15th-century Spanish words.[5]

Like *caló,* the dialect of which Burciaga writes here, the Chicano culture of the 1960s–'70s was a rich mixture of not only the obvious Mexican and Anglo-American influences, but borrowings from the past—in many cases from pockets of Spanish-speaking cultures left in the New Mexico region from before the period of the development of Mexico as a nation—and traces of the commodification culture of the United States and the Americas in general.[6] Then feminism, as both a cultural and literary force, moved into the movement with still a further transformation, obvious from the way in which the movement has been identified here. Before 1980 or so, "Chicanas" received scant reference. The movement is now generally known as "Chicana/o," and some departments and political programs have altered their titles to reflect this change.

The Masculine and the Chicano

Things "Chicano" gradually began to have a different designation, as indicated above, partly because of a growing realization that the movement was extremely masculinist. Once again, this reflected not only the labor origins of the movement (although Dolores Huerta was a leading figure from its start), but the *macho* culture of Mexico, which, if anything, seemed to become reinforced rather than weakened in the United States. Thus many observers have noted that the "low-rider" subculture of East Los Angeles, long defined as a Southern California Chicano hallmark, flagrantly uses the female body as a symbol of desirability and commodification, and does so in ways that might very well not occur in Mexico or in other Latin American areas. It has long been a staple of feminist commentary that, where cultural constructs threaten male identity, androcentrism may take on stronger forms in an attempt to restore male esteem and pride. The mix of the actual Mexican culture itself, as Paz and other commentators have insisted, reflects the degree to which Spanish colonialism involved the degradation of the Indian mother. Original Chicano cultural constructs featured proud emblems of *"la familia"* and "The Motherland," and many other potently male symbols—eagles, weapons, warrior trappings—abounded. Possession of the woman has been a staple of the chromo or oleo art that is constitutive of Chicana/o definition, even in contemporary terms.[7]

Here again, lines of analysis taken from standard views of the mixture of things Mexican and things American merge with some contemporary postmodern analysis, yielding a bit of an anodyne for those suffering from the cultural blues. Aida Hurtado, in a sharp analysis of some points concerning gender relations in *chicanismo*, notes that one of the staples of the Chicano movement, Luis Valdez's Teatro Campesino (originally part of the farmworkers movement) simultaneously revealed the core of *machismo* in the movement while, if anything, propelling that core by relying on *actos* with stock stereotypical characters.[8]

The original idea behind the formation of the theater was to try to urge potential members to join the union by presenting skits. These small plays, or *actos*, however, were not merely exercises in dramatic art—as Hurtado notes, "Teatro Campesino's goal was to represent the collective social vision of Chicanos and to reflect all that is valued in these communities: family ties, ... Chicano culture ..."[9] But the *actos*, Hurtado contends, relied to a startling degree on sharp dichotomies where women were concerned; these were dramatic skits written from, as she notes, "a man's perspective."[10] Although many of the *actos* involved female characters, these characters were, if anything, even more stereotyped the male characters. In a series of gender twists, the few women characters who were allowed more than the traditional "virgin" role fell into a category termed by Hurtado "*media cabrona*." Because, according to the cultural construct, the virgin can do so little, the only female characters allowed to achieve any independence were, according to Hurtado, "potential whores." ("*Cabrona*" is a feminized term for the more standardly used male *macho* term "*cabron*," a man who engages in all kinds of standard masculine bad behavior, much of it sexual.)

As Hurtado says,

> The femme-*macho*, unlike the virgin or the whore, can either be attractive or unattractive. A strong personality is what characterizes her. The strength of the femme-*macho* does not lie in her racial/physical appearance [earlier she had been characterized as "Indian-looking"] but rather on remaining emotionally uninvolved, though sexually active.[11]

Hurtado's point in recounting some of the standard dramatic characterizations used in Teatro Campesino is to indicate that, if anything, the Chicano male has become hypermacho. Possibly in an attempt to ward off discomfort caused by cultural clash and the devaluation of all things Latino or Mexicano, the cultural constructs employed in much of the Chicano cultures (especially before the new wave of *feminista* activism) exaggerated or strengthened male categorizations that were already present. This exaggeration is especially pronounced when one remembers the comparative strength of the female in indigenous cultures, many of which are strongly present in Mexico itself.

If it is the case that, in order to mobilize farmworkers living under conditions of degradation in valley towns in California such as Delano and Visalia, dramatic action must be taken, then it is remarkable that so much of the action relies on an astoundingly androcentric take on things Chicano. As Hurtado also says, El Teatro "reproduces the intra-group gender dynamics found in Chicano communities."[12]

From zoot-suiters to low-riders (the former movement was itself originally a rebellion and culture clash occurring during World War II Los Angeles, the style being adopted throughout the Southwest), the masculinized
Chicano culture has adopted a number of exaggerated and hyperintense
characteristics, many of which are familiar from the popular culture insofar
as they are staples of urban scenes, much like the contemporary black male
"gangster." But if core elements of standard feminist analysis that insist on
the notion of "stylistic aggression" as a response to individual growth patterns of maturation and individuation are correct, the Chicano male adopting these intense patterns may well be engaging in defensive aggression to
thwart the dynamics of the larger oppressive culture. In any case, whatever
the trajectory of its development, the androcentrism of early Chicano
activism was pronounced and manifested itself in a variety of ways, from
Teatro Campesino to the papers found in the journal of Chicano studies
Aztlán. If the Chicano male was battling the forces of the white man's
society, then he probably found the adoption of a threatening persona a ready
way in which to do battle. This forced the Chicana/o movement to then take
steps to repair the damage—a move perhaps somewhat belated, but finally
assisted by the developing awareness in contemporary feminist theory of the
comparative lack of theorizing by women of color. All of these forces con-
joined to give the movement a new sense of growth and dynamism from the
1980s on—but this time the growth did not come at the expense of the Chicana. More properly speaking, she was the impetus of the growth.

Like other cultures within the New World context that have suffered
degradation, the Chicana/o culture might be demarcated as one in which
males, because of the oppression, have become still more "male" as a
defense mechanism, thus causing certain kinds of behavior to be more
accepted, pronounced, and simply more frequent within the culture. Such
allegations have frequently been made—and by black feminists—about the
black American culture, and they may well also be accurate assessments of
much of what has transpired in the United States for persons of Mexican
ancestry. In any case, conquest of women, abuse of substances, and overt
violence have, in many areas, become rituals of male growth and prestige,
and these factors, combined with cultural misunderstandings, harassment
by law officers, outright discrimination, and the victimization of poverty,
have led to high incarceration rates for Chicano males. Indeed, the California prison population, the largest in the country, is overwhelmingly composed of black men and men of Mexican/Latin ancestry.

But despite the strength of male-oriented cultural views, there is much
within the Chicana/o cultures that promotes a certain sort of gynocentrism

and that speaks to women's ways of knowing. Historians like Samora have written of the "popular" nature of Mexican-derived culture in the United States.[13] The strands of the folk culture valorize the female at crucial moments—moments of religious inspiration, of family festivity, and of quiescence and solitude. All of these moments can come together for political and social action. In the 1960s, this was the path taken by many Chicana/os in the United States.

A Woman-Centered View

Three focal points of the gynocentric/female present themselves in the various Chicana/o styles, and because they emerge so rapidly upon view of the culture they are not difficult to articulate. The Catholicism of Chicanos has historically been informal—Julian Samora has documented the reluctance of the Catholic hierarchy (including the bishopric) to serve in regions such as the Texas border area, and thus the official Catholicism even of Mexico City developed new tones within the Mexican/American areas.[14] The Sor Juana influence of Mexico does not make much sense within the Chicana/o cultural context; here, the reliance on folk practices, many of which are pre-Columbian, in combination with elaborate festivities for Christmas and Easter, means that there are already gynocentric strands within Chicano Catholicism that are separate from official Church doctrine.[15] The laity are more important in Chicano Catholic practices than is the case in many areas, and within the laity women have a powerful role.

A second obvious strand is closely related; *chicanismo* has always been aware of the power of the *curandera/o*, and these folk healers, using a number of tools—some of which are overtly Catholic in origin, and some not—are a powerful presence in the Chicano community. Because of the traditional ties of women to healing in most cultures, the female presence in *curanderismo* is strong. This phenomenon in and of itself ties to the third area in which a strong gynocentrism pervades the culture, and that is the presence of the mother figure within the home. This is more important than is at first apparent, for it must be remembered that, for the vast majority of Mexican families that came to the United States, particularly in this century, the "home" was anywhere the mother was; in many cases, a barn, a shack, or someone's discarded (and previously used) railroad boxcar had to serve as a dwelling.[16] The preparation of food and traditional meals (especially those involving the preparation of *masa*), the importance of holidays/festivities, and the power of healing gave the traditional mother figure unparalleled scope within conventional areas of knowing. That these areas were later to merge in the 1960s farmworker movement is testimony to the strength of the traditional images and the celerity with which they metamorphosed into something more than the mundane.

This combination of healing, worship, and mothering creates a powerful web in Chicana/o worldviews, and parts of these views are transmitted in popular legend to small children, thus reinforcing their overall strength. Almost all children of Mexican ancestry know about "La Llorona," the weeping woman who roams at night searching for her children. But not only does she represent that focal point of the female/feminine that in many cultures we have associated with the "dark" goddesses, in some versions of this story, particularly Chicano versions, she is something more. She may be La Malinche; "replaced by a high-born Spanish wife," she is driven to acts of revenge and kills her children.[17] The symbolism of killing the *mestizo* children is overwhelming, and already tells us much about the sufferings of the *hijos de la chingada* as they moved from Mexico to other areas.

Notions of folk healing have also been powerful throughout the culture simply because of the difficulties of making one's way in a new land. For the newly arrived Mexican-originated family in the United States, home was frequently where the calendar was hung—literally.[18] The garages, shacks, boxcars, and even cardboard contraptions that housed railroad, farm, and crop workers were made "homes" by the efforts of the women in the family, usually either the mother or an *abuelita* (grandmother). At the same time, as the historians have documented, conditions were so poor that illness was rife, and few Chicano families could escape extreme sickness, and in many cases, death, particularly of children and the vulnerable.[19]

Females in the household were powerful figures in the sense that they could "create" a home, and at the same time they knew what to do in case of trial or sickness. West documents, for example, the extensive use of aloe vera within Mexican-originated households: "It is kept in most Mexican-American households for use in many medical situations."[20] At the same time, many folk remedies relied on a combination of food, herbs and novenas—saying special prayers for nine days, or in some other ways asking the intercession of the saints.[21] Of course, the most popular "saint" upon whom to call was the Virgin of Guadalupe.

The strength of the Virgin and of female or gynocentric elements in the folk culture is also signaled by the growth of variations on the traditional system of beliefs regarding the Virgin. She is frequently spotted in natural objects, and other manifestations of the Virgin have appeared that are specifically associated with the Chicano migrant (rather than Mexican) culture. In cataloguing the numbers of beliefs within the Chicano community that are at variance with official bishopric beliefs, Samora notes:

> Along with the Sacred Heart, she is also enthroned in the homes of Mexican Americans throughout the Southwest. Another important representation of the Virgin Mary is Nuestra Señora de San Juan de los Lagos located in San Juan, Texas. Mexican American migrant workers make the shrine the focal point of the beginning and the end of their entry into the seasonal migrant stream; it is a tradition for many migrant families to have their vehicle blessed at the shrine before the beginning of their northern journey.[22]

Since the Chicana/o movement has become more self-conscious and has taken hold in ways both academic and nonacademic, a good deal of writing and theorizing has taken place about the importance of woman-centered spiritualities in the Chicano tradition, and how some of the obvious has either been ignored or simply omitted. Lara Medina, writing in the anthology edited by Carla Trujillo, mentions the obvious roots of a spirituality that is both gynocentric and multiply *mestizo*.[23] As Medina notes, despite the patriarchal structure of traditional Catholicism, "*consejeras, curanderas, rezadoras, espiritistas* and even *comadres* practiced and still practice their healing ways."[24] Although much of the tradition, as was indicated, is alive and well and constitutes a folk tradition that developed against the grain of the Church, other portions of the tradition are being rearticulated, or in some cases, invented, by Chicanas who now are a great deal more aware of the tensions within the culture. As Medina indicates, a better take on the notion of *mestiza* means "Indian, Spanish, African, European American"—and delineated in this way, the heritage on which the Chicana can draw is even richer. Even ordinary celebrations like the Día de los Muertos take on a flavor through the conscious involvement of women and, ironically enough, seem to become more popular as a result.

The combination of folk/Catholic practices that already have strong tones of gynocentrism, the importance of the mother/*abuela* within the home, and the power of the *curandera* is one of *potencia*, as it is said, and this is not lost on Chicana activists and thinkers of today. As is so often the case, a conscious retrieval is needed in order to be able to reproduce or recapitulate all the strands, but Chicanas—particularly those whose awareness has expanded since the male-dominated movements of the '60s—are aware of these difficulties. Mexican-originated people would not have been able to survive in the United States without the intense work of women, many of whom received no special reward or recognition. The taken-for-grantedness of the female-oriented elements of the culture tells us not only about the androcentrism that informs it, but also tells us about the conditions of scarcity and hardship in which most Chicano families have had to survive. West is able to document page after page of practices constitutive of Mexican-American folk healing simply because, in most cases, newly arrived immigrants were not able to consult with a doctor because of language or money. The practices originated with and were driven by the concerns of women—and at this point many women are making this clear, both through the written word and other actions.

One point is clear. In this male-dominated culture, the features of which are more variable than any cultural construct in Mexico simply because of the interaction between a multiracial society such as that of the United States, the media, and the original cultural constructs, women have been responsible for the transmission of those aspects of the culture that have survived and for their reemergence in the Americas. As was mentioned earlier, insofar as there are homes for people constantly on the road—and this describes the early lives, at least, of the vast majority of Mexicans who came to the United States—the homes were created by *madres, comadres, abuelitas,* and others who took the time to try to fashion something of warmth, comfort, and memory from whatever was at hand. As the catalog for "La Patria Portátil" indicates, home is where the artifacts are that bring to life the Mexican culture in a new land:

> Far beyond the months and years for whose illustration they were conceived, some of these prints endured as national icons which crossed borders: a portable homeland which traveled to the north with migrants and, freed from calendars, became tattoos, graffiti, stained glass, arts and crafts decorations and street murals.[25]

The chromo is something that was found, treasured, and "freed" in many cases by women. Photographs of some of the unsung heroines who established *hogares* on the basis of little more than a bedstead and a calendar appear in the "Portátil" exhibit.[26] Their names may not be remembered on an individual basis, but the women involved were creators of the Chicano culture.

History and the Chicana/o

In a sense, Chicano history precedes the formation of the United States, since the intermixture of Spaniards and Indians involved in the founding of the California missions is the same mingling that later produced Mexico itself and California—and the entire Southwest—which were part of Mexico until the Treaty of Guadalupe Hidalgo in 1848.

But it is widely believed by most commentators that the creation of what we now think of as the Chicano culture of the Southwest came in two large waves: the first was in the years immediately following the Mexican Revolution, and may have been heightened and intensified by the Cristero Rebellion of the late 1920s to early 1930s. As the federal government of the newly revitalized Mexico attempted to demolish the last vestiges of institutional power of the Catholic Church, pockets of resistance from staunch Catholics began to appear, and violence led many to flee. Still more important, the Bracero agreement (begun during World War II, and based on the labor shortage in the United States created by the war) and its aftermath created the second and largest wave.

Although, as we have just seen, women were the creators of many of the conditions that allowed Mexican families to become Chicano families, women are remarkably absent from some of the classic "histories of the Chicano" of this period. To an extent, this simply reflects historiography of the time. To a greater extent, however, it probably reflects the ways in which Anglo Americans, or some acculturated Mexican Americans in social positions that allowed them to write "histories," saw the Chicano culture.

Carey McWilliams, for instance, in his classic *North from Mexico*, seldom mentions women as actors or agents anywhere in his work.[27] McWilliams is a sympathetic commentator, and well able to discern the underlying racism in incidents such as Los Angeles's "Sleepy Lagoon" debacle, which itself gave rise to the notion of the *pachuco* or zoot-suiter, and according to some, many elements of *chicanismo*. But women scarcely figure, even in supporting roles, in his recounting.[28] Similarly, another classic of the beginnings of "Chicano history," Samora's *La Raza: The Forgotten Americans*, virtually fails to mention women in its important "The Migrant Worker" chapter, even though the section, quite rightly concerned with such issues as education, has a subheading titled "Child Labor."[29]

One might be inclined to chalk all of this up to Anglo insensitivity were it not for the fact, mentioned earlier, that the combination of the androcentrism of Mexican culture itself and the stress felt by males in a new land may very well have meant that, to the outside observer, women in the realms of migrating Mexicans and their families were nearly invisible. Invisible though they may have been, however, they were still active, not only in the sense of being the creators of the homes that fostered such cultural growth, but in many other ways as well. Throughout the 1940s through the 1960s, Mexican-American or Chicana women, like their black counterparts, were forceful in organizations designed to promote awareness and political resistance.

In the early 1960s a number of social scientists saw the enormous numbers of persons of Mexican ancestry already in the Southwest and questioned why they had not yet become an organized political force. The articles and scholarly publications at that time tell a great deal about the history of Mexican Americans in general, and they also indicate much by elision. Because women are seldom mentioned, we can assume that they did indeed play active roles where the investigator takes the trouble to mention them. Paul Sheldon, in one of the pieces of the widely cited *La Raza*, edited by Samora, notes that several organizations, including the Mexican American Political Association, the Community Service Organization, and the American G.I. Forum, had been active on the Mexican-American political scene since the end of World War II.[31] For at least one of the organizations, American G.I. Forum, he specifically mentions husband and wife participation, and even cites participation by wives as a factor in reversing trends toward declining membership.[32] There was already at this time, especially in the Los Angeles area, tension between black groups (referred to in the text as "Negro" organizations), and those for Mexican Americans, so Sheldon is in a sense quite right when he remarks on what he sees as a problem:

> Organizations of other ethnic groups have their differences, but they seem to be able to work together more effectively than do Mexican-Americans. Reportedly there is little mutual affection between the American Jewish Congress and the Anti-Defamation League and yet they are able to present a strong front.[33]

What Sheldon sees as a lack of cohesiveness may, however, have been the result of patterns of entry for persons of the Chicano community, as well as a wide variety of injustices—none of which, on its face, was as great as some of the legal injustices suffered by the black population, and many of which seemed to take place on a sporadic basis.

If women are a somewhat neglected part of pieces such as those that comprise *La Raza*—even though we know of their potent force within the home, and their ability, in many cases to create a home—they are also present only as silent witnesses, at best, in the classic recounting of one of the most publicized instances of bigotry against Mexicans in the Southwest during the war, the so-called Sleepy Lagoon Incident. This case, involving an unsolved murder, community resentment (at least according to the press) against persons of Mexican ancestry, and newspaper overreaction and headline building, probably did more than any other single incident to unite Chicanos, especially after the war was over and decorated veterans returned.[34] But in McWilliams's entire recounting of this case, including details about the young men charged with the murder and their families, there is virtually no mention of females (not even female relatives). The most unusual comment comes at the end of the chapter when McWilliams, trying to describe the origins of the *pachuco* look that, according to many Anglos, will for a while characterize Chicano styles in Los Angeles, notes that there is a special style for young *pachucas*: "for the girls, black huaraches, short black skirt, long black stockings, sweater, and high pompadour."[35] As might be expected, the Chicana is a creature who is best mentioned under the rubric of "style."

Nevertheless, as the Samora book was being written, women were beginning to take a more active and visible role in the Chicano movement. Dolores Huerta, who had worked with César Chávez in Community Service Organization groups, assisted him in the early stages of striking and was a visible presence. One of the most publicized marches to gain support for what was later to become the UFW wove from Delano to Sacramento, the state capital, and culminated on Easter Sunday, 1966. Thousands were involved in the march at various times, and many women participated, along with children. Appropriately, the march was dubbed a *"peregrinación,"* and the banner of Our Lady was at the forefront. This rich symbolism was not lost on the commentators, and the Rev. William Scholes, writing in *La Raza* notes,

> At this writing the strike still continues, and the boycott has been shifted from Schenley to Di Giorgio products. The Spanish-speaking farm laborers who carried the emblem of Our Lady of Guadalupe from Delano to Sacramento have persevered longer than anyone thought possible, and have received more support from the public than even they dreamed of.[36]

It is a poignant irony that, with a few exceptions, the women marching under the banner of Our Lady received little overt credit, yet they were, of course, those who by their daily work and caretaking of all involved made the march possible.

The history of women of Mexican ancestry may have been left out of most of the books, but at least some contemporary Chicana historians have undertaken the task of retrieval. Vicki Ruiz gives name and face to many women who were active in the labor movements of the 1930s and '40s that preceded the UFW:

> As a twenty-three-year-old member of the Workers' Alliance and secretary of the Texas Communist Party, Emma Tenayuca emerged as the fiery local leader. Although not a pecan sheller, Tenayuca, a San Antonio native, was elected to head the strike committee.... Known as "La Pasionaria," Tenayuca, in an interview with historian Zaragosa Vargas, reflected on her activism as follows: "I was pretty defiant. [I fought] against poverty, actually starvation, high infant death rates, disease and hunger and misery. I would do the same thing again."[37]

Ruiz, combing through archives and newspaper records, is able to find many women like her. The important fact, of course, is that later movements could not have gotten off the ground but for these foremothers, many of whom were moved by the plight of their fellow workers and especially by the spectacle of children working. Ruiz is able to find records of Mexican and Chicana women leading strikes and picketing as far back as 1903, and doubtless there are more to be found.[38] The fact that the Chicano movement of the 1960s, insofar as it incorporated ideas that would themselves become leading conceptualizations for academic departments, was largely male oriented and male defined speaks to one of the lacunae with which Chicana/o studies departments are now having to contend.

The Chicana Today

Patterns of employment and education for Chicanas are changing, and the awareness generated by the discipline of Chicana/o studies has helped in this regard. So, too, oddly enough, has increased immigration from Mexico and Central America. The sheer massive increase in numbers has ensured that many more immigrants are now from the middle and even upper classes, and this has helped Anglos and others to see that people of Mexican ancestry come from a wide variety of backgrounds.

Although many Chicanas are still stuck at the low end of the employment spectrum—and Ruiz notes that in Los Angeles, this may mean wages of $4.25 to $5.35 per hour—the difference is that, now, few are earning these wages without at least some level of raised consciousness.[39] As is the case in the black community, many young women who have attended college have made a personal decision to "give back" to the community, so the Chicana (or recent Mexican immigrant) who is working at the kind of employment that used to be traditional is much more likely now to be confronted by a union organizer who is herself a second- or third-generation, college-educated Chicana. "Justice for Janitors," and SEIU Local 11 in Los Angeles have benefited from the services of Maria Elena Durazo, who, according to Ruiz, is organizing specifically because she believes that she must "go back to her community."[40]

Catholic activism, labor radicalism, and a rewriting of Chicano/a history are only some of the activities in which better-educated Chicanas currently engage. Although there would be no need for the radicalism were it not the case that many Chicanas are still severely underemployed, other Chicanas are actively working as feminist theorists to try to alter the status of contemporary American feminist thought. In this they have been more than successful—Gloria Anzaldúa and Cherrie Moraga, among many others, have become well-known names in feminist theoretical circles and have opened the doors to a good deal of thinking that does not take the privileging of the white heterosexual woman for granted.

In his important work on contemporary critical race theory and Chicana/o culture, Carl Gutiérrez-Jones cites Anzaldúa, among others, for the centralizing of La Malinche as a site for discourse and movement.[41] According to Gutiérrez-Jones, work on the notion of La Malinche is crucial to understanding new Chicana/o theory, and it is theorists such as Anzaldúa who have largely been responsible for making this move. This move—which has, of course, been made by Mexican theorists as well—is, according to Gutiérrez-Jones, one that "build[s] on the theory and practice of translation—with all the productive betrayal implied by La Malinche as a Chicana feminist cultural force."[42] If a Mexican theorist can reappropriate La Malinche as the founder of *la raza*, the Chicana theorist can reappropriate this original border crosser as a postmodern token of what it means to be Chicana in the United States today.

Postmodernism, then, becomes the theoretical tool that speaks most clearly to Chicana/o theorizing, since it reminds us of the divorce of signifier from master narrative and referent—a divorce that, for the Chicana/o, has happened over and over again. Because of this, much of the Chicana/o literary production of the moment hearkens to familiar symbols used in unfamiliar and unusual ways.

Reappropriation of Malinche has been a theme even among Mexican feminists, but among Chicana feminists the reappropriation has been writ large. Part of the seemingly endless possibilities transpiring from Malinche revolve around the fact that she is not only the "mother," but that she in a sense herself represents postmodern spaces because she is the harbinger of that which is "mixed" and crosses borders and breaks types. Without a Malinche or many Malinches, Mexico could not have come to exist; the *raza* needs a parent who is indigenous in order to become the *raza*. Since the Chicana/o culture represents that which is mixed again—a culture originally of Mexican derivation and functioning in an Anglo-American space— the power of Malinche as a symbol is, if anything, increased.

Thus Ruiz is able to write that:

> Given these symbolic meanings, one of the first tasks Chicana feminists faced was that of revising the image of La Malinche. Adelaida Del Castillo's path-breaking 1977 article provided a new perspective by considering Malinche's captivity, her age, and most important her conversion to Christianity. What emerges from Del Castillo's account is a gifted young linguist who lived on the margins and made decisions within the borders of her world.[43]

From "traitoress" to "gifted linguist" is big leap, and one that, in a sense, has not even been made in Mexico, where the racial intermixing of Malinche is paramount. Perhaps it is only from the Chicana perspective that all of Malinche's "transgressions" can best be understood.

Working within the paradigms of collective awareness, the importance of the home, and the appropriation of traditional symbols (even if the appropriation takes decidedly nontraditional shifts), parts of the Chicana feminist movement have affected young Chicanas today even in areas/spaces that are still hostile to overt displays of feminism. Thus a Chicana in downtown Los Angeles is, paradoxically, probably more likely to be exposed to this intriguing cultural mélange that is a postmodern/feminist/cultural construction than are some of her non-Chicana sisters to be exposed to other varieties of feminist thought in other settings.[44]

Although young Chicanas in urban areas are still likely to follow a path that includes less-than-adequate schooling, underemployment, and, too often, early motherhood, they are being exposed to a wide array of cultural artifacts, particularly in the greater Los Angeles area, where part of the brew includes wide exposure to a number of Third World cultures and styles. Local media have repeatedly reported on the phenomenon of intermarriage not merely between people of Mexican ancestry and Anglos, but between persons of Mexican ancestry and individuals from all over the world—including most of the nations of Africa and those of Asia. One news article featured an analysis of marriage between persons from Guatemala and Thailand, neither of whom knew English well, but neither of whom, understandably, could speak the language of the other.

The Chicana today has also benefited enormously from new awareness of cultural issues in education. Starting with the movements in downtown Los Angeles that culminated in the Chicano boycott of March 1968, the schools have been forced to admit the importance of Mexican/Chicano issues to the curriculum.[45] Currently, of course, one of the biggest issues in California is bilingual schooling, now shelved, at least temporarily, by the passage of a statewide proposition in June 1998. But if bilingual education is not currently an option—at least not in the sense in which it was being attempted as recently as a few years ago—bicultural education still carries on, and it is now a commonplace to see literature reflecting Mexicano/Chicano cultural viewpoints in classrooms all over California and the Southwest. This is a far cry from the sort of education that was imposed upon preceding generations of Chicana/os and Mexican immigrants, when rapid "sink or swim" instruction not only in English but in Anglo culture as a whole was the only pedagogical mode.[46]

Perhaps because of the attraction of the notion of the "border," work that was originally done by Chicanas has become a staple of many interdisciplinary offerings—including LGBT studies and almost all of women's studies. Again, such work has filtered down at least to the high school level, and in some cases below. Ruiz cites no less than four anthologies on Chicana lesbian theory that have achieved national renown and that have become important offerings in the American higher education curriculum.[47] Gutiérrez-Jones's work reflects a similar concern for the notion of "border" as one that is permeable, literally and metaphorically, and that can be put to good use in a variety of academic contexts.

The Chicana today in a given community is more likely than not an "activist," even if in some cases her activism is unofficial. The Chicana scholar Mary Pardo writes of women who have formed organized groups in East Los Angeles specifically designed to combat what they see as patterns of misuse of the community based on Anglo perceptions of what a "Mexican" community could or should be.[48] As so frequently happens, communities of color in the Los Angeles area have become "dumping grounds," literally and figuratively, for aspects of life that are deemed to be too unsanitized for the Anglo community to bear. Local mothers, such as Juana Gutiérrez, who formed Mothers of East Los Angeles (MELA), have often found the courage to simply refuse to tolerate any further abuse. As Juana herself says, "Yo como madre de familia, y como residente de East Los Angeles, seguiré luchando sin descanso por que se nos respete" ("I, as a mother, and as a resident of East Los Angeles, will continue to fight—without tiring—so that they will respect us").[49]

Although Chicanas today are living in the East Los Angeleses of many parts of the country, and not merely California barrios, a tradition of activism and of refusing to be victimized—even if it has not always been recognized by the larger culture—propels them. The contemporary Chicana may well be faced with some of the same obstacles faced by her sisters at an earlier time, but the difference is that she now has a number of foci of resistance to aid her. The Chicano movement, continued immigration, and patterns of resistance in the past have all coalesced and made her life one that is less likely to be the site of unacknowledged struggle.

A Chicana Feminist Outlook

Contemporary Chicana feminism itself divides into two broad strands. One strand, as said earlier, merges with previous activism, but in a way that is more marked and less likely to go unrecognized. The other, more academic strand, has affected not only Chicana/o studies but many other disciplines, and has drawn on a rich diversity of poststructuralist and postcolonial studies to make its points.

Each of the two strands is, of course, concerned with empowerment, a phrase that has now become something of a hoary code word and that, at least in some circles, is devoid of meaning. The difference parallels a distinction now being drawn in feminist circles throughout the United States and other industrially developed countries; while on the one hand it might well be argued that real change necessitates community action, many (particularly academics) have felt that altering styles of discourse in the sphere of the published is itself a step in the right direction.

In each case, Chicana feminism has reappropriated symbols and modes pertinent to the Mexicano/Chicano community at large, and even, in a few cases, the larger American Latino community.[50] Insofar as activism is concerned, the key notions of the family, the importance of the mother/*abuela* and the significance of symbols such as the Virgin remain unabated. Because of the strength of the family, and the desire to keep it intact and to retain its power in a comparatively undiluted form, many Chicanas have gone beyond the mere "double duty" syndrome of a large number of American women and have undertaken a wide variety of tasks entailing countless hours of work both in and outside of the home. Mary Pardo writes, for example, of Gloria, who became a leader in her local UNO group after taking a look at the problems of her neighborhood.[51]

Gloria was not working for wages at the time, and she held leadership for four years. Like the women in MELA, to avoid domestic disruption she continued to meet her household responsibilities. When I asked her how she managed to balance her household work with her activism, she acknowledged that it was difficult. Her strategy was to take care of household chores very early or very late in the day:

> To avoid conflict in the home, I would get up at 5:00 in the morning, clean house, prepare dinner.... I would come home from meetings, and be ironing at 11:00 at night.[52]

Although there is a sense in which many women will probably identify with Gloria's plight, it is also in a sense somewhat atypical. The fact that Gloria gives new meaning to the phrase "double duty" signals to us how intense her drive is to transform all of her roles into one role that is still in accordance with the gynocentrically driven importance of the *madre* in the home. This appears to be a point of pride with Gloria, and it is unclear whether any set of circumstances could reduce her desire to meet a set of standards so internalized.

Both working-class and middle-class Chicana and Mexican-American women have been involved in the local activist movements that are now transforming Los Angeles. Just as Juana Gutiérrez and others have been working in Boyle Heights, so the Monterey Park area is being transformed by the activism that takes its roots from communitarian and *comadre* concerns. What groups of women activists from many barrio communities have in common is a desire to defend their community from the negative perceptions of outsiders, and from the damage that actions caused by the outsiders' negative perceptions impose.

Pardo recites an interesting and telling example of a specific form of community activism with strong feminist overtones. Not only did MELA, led by Juana Gutiérrez, attempt to move against the building of a prison in an East Los Angeles neighborhood; the group also had to take action against movie crews. Gutiérrez and other mothers noted at an early point in their activism that film and movie crews, intent on making "true-life" *barrio* films, were actually defacing traffic barriers, underpasses, and buildings in their attempt to make scenes look more authentic. The truth was that in many cases the actual structures in question had never looked as bad as they came to look immediately before filming. According to Pardo, Erlinda Robles and some other activists devised a unique method of getting the crews to stop their work:

Upset by such unfair representation of the community, the women on the
block first tried individual resistance strategies. Erlinda explained how she and
one other woman attempted to disrupt the work of the filming crews: "We
would come by honking the car horns. And you could hear them saying, 'Cut,
cut!' I would go out and call real loud ARMANDO! DANNY! EDUARDO!
[the names of her three sons]."53

Mentioning the children helped to contextualize the situation—it
showed the film crews that, despite their preconceived notions, the community was one of at least some caring families and mothers. In this way,
women of MELA managed to disrupt or alter the production schedules of
filmmakers who wanted to try to create more moneymakers like the 1980s
film *Colors* at the expense of the well-being of the local community.54

Vicki Ruiz does a superb job of tying together the various strands of
activism, feminist and traditional, in which many Chicana women are now
engaged when she cites the theorist Chela Sandoval at the same time that
she writes of activist groups such as Mujeres Mexicanas, active in the
Coachella Valley.55 This group, run very largely by local campesinas, many
of whom are active UFW members, has undertaken everything from voter
registration drives to the distribution of condoms and free pamphlets on
AIDS. Although some local college-educated professionals have some connection with the group, they do not attempt to lead it. The idea is to try to
make sure that the women in control of the group are working farmwomen
from the Valley area. As Ruiz is recounting the group's successful activities,
she notes that "feminist theorist Chela Sandoval has adroitly distilled 'the
differential mode of oppositional consciousness' that underlies 'concrete
action.'"56 Ruiz, still quoting Sandoval, uses the phrase "self-consciously
choosing and adopting the ideological form best suited to push against
[power] configurations."57 This gloss on the situation from Sandoval not
only seems to describe the work of Mujeres Mexicanas, but might also
describe the work of MELA as well. What better form of "push" could be
chosen by a group of mothers who are outraged by film crews' abuse of
their neighborhood than to disrupt the filming by calling out the names of
the children who live there?

Ruiz and Pardo both emphasize the communitarian and mother-oriented
models of behavior regularly adopted by Chicana activists, even those who
might not be willing to commit to the "feminist" label. The point is that, in
contradistinction to what some might see as the individualism of white
women activists who would indeed identify as "feminist," Chicana/
Mexicana activists seldom embark on activities that do not impact on the

community as a whole. This is often done in the face of personal danger and the real possibility of genuine personal disaster, such as job loss. One of the most moving testimonies found by Ruiz has to do with activism in the El Paso area by Chicanas against the local Farah factory, or *maquiladora*. Toward the close of her last chapter, Ruiz quotes Estela Gómez in a letter to the editor:

> A lot of people in the El Paso community ask quite often, with all of these good benefits Willie Farah provides at his factory, why did these people walk on strike? ... These benefits were only there for the good of the company, not for the worker.... What good was the vaccuum [sic] cleaner he gave us for Christmas, when a lot of us didn't even earn enough to afford a carpet.[58]

Leading or participating in a strike is not only physically dangerous; it is psychologically dangerous as well, particularly if the women strikers understand that they will be perceived (at least in the short run) as going against the immediate goods of their children, their families, and themselves. But the women in the Chicana/Mexicana movements have fashioned a vision of their community that encompasses themselves, their families, their children, and the future. Working on the basis of their social networks of support, they have come to the conclusion that short-term gains are not preferable to those that might be deemed to be long term; further, they have realized that long-term gains can be had only through sacrifice.

What Ruiz and Pardo are at pains to emphasize in their works is that the Chicana and Chicana activism have been omitted from almost all accounts or histories of the Chicana/o community. Given that such histories sprang up, in general, only as recently as the 1960s, it might not be surprising that first efforts were simply that—preliminary takes on what was constitutive of the community, what had taken place in the community, and what the future was for the community. But Ruiz and Pardo are both sensitive to the fact that, perhaps more so than for other American communities of color, the difficulties the Chicana/o community faces because of the extremely patriarchal views imported from Mexico and added onto here are enormous and require special articulation. Thus emerge works that address the "unsung" among the Chicanas who have assisted their communities all the way along. It probably tells us a great deal that it is most likely a combination of the emergence of feminist theory, Chicana/o studies as a discipline, and French poststructuralist/postcolonial strands of thought that has allowed for these volumes to be written. Whatever their origins, they are badly needed and are enormously helpful in uncovering the multifaceted roles of Chicanas.

Reconstructing Ways of Knowing

We have been at pains, with Chicana/o theory, to try to emphasize a variety of points of origin because the feminist construction of knowledge, in this case, is a particularly nonmonolithic one and reflective of diverse areas of background.

In the postmodern take on symbols that has become increasingly prevalent as a mode of analysis in cultural studies, the Chicana feminist knowledge path has proved to be a bonanza. If we can discern at least three or four foci for Chicana knowledge modes—"border" as a metaphor, appropriations of the Virgin/Malinche, communitarian frameworks, and labor activism/collectives—it is especially intriguing to see how these foci might interact with other forms of feminist theorizing that have been deemed to be feminist epistemologies. After all, it could be argued, isn't it the case that much of what passes for postmodern analysis is far from constitutive of an epistemics or epistemology on any grounds? And doesn't it make sense to think that, at bottom, what might work as a Chicana feminist epistemics is closely related to (or even the same as) what might be said to be a Mexican feminist epistemology?

Least problematic are the communitarian frameworks and labor collectives as important sites for knowledge acquisition, since these fall within the frame of reference of what contemporary mainstream feminist epistemology has dubbed "collective ways of knowing," and they are, in any case, closely related to some of the modes that we have examined here in other chapters. Insofar as some of these might have a special "folk" appeal that transcends their Mexican background—we can imagine a mix of Mexican, "American," and other categories here—they still are susceptible of analysis along the lines of much work already done in feminist epistemology. When West, for example, tells us about folk remedies that are passed from mother to daughter or from woman worker to woman worker, the material being described is very similar to what Vrinda Dalmiya and Linda Alcoff analyze in their essay "Are 'Old Wives' Tales' Justified?"[59] Thus far, the problems addressed are similar to those with which feminist epistemologists have already grappled, and precious few theoretical surprises seem to be in store.

More problematic, however, is the use of the "border" construct (especially when one considers the sheer number of borders being crossed, so to speak) and the sliding and slipping of previously exclusive categories such as Virgin/Malinche. In the use of these symbols, which has permeated a number of areas of cultural studies above and beyond those having to do with Latina/o cultures, we find areas of difficulty for the articulation of an epistemics, precisely because one scarcely knows where to begin.

A place to begin here might be some of the work that has been done on the general notion of marginality and developing an epistemology. Bat-Ami Bar On, in her essay "Marginality and Epistemic Privilege," has tried to pick out areas of difficulty for such theorizing, given that, originally, many feminists thought of Marx as an embarkation point because of his work on the standpoint of the proletariat and the possibility of their construction of knowledge.[60] But as Bar On indicates, there are difficulties with attributing some sort of special epistemic status to a group simply on the basis of its marginality. She notes:

> The attribution of agency to a marginality that is not at the same time a centrality problematizes the attribution of epistemic privilege to the socially marginalized subjects.... Epistemic privilege then becomes a function of the distance from the center.[61]

But which center? As Bar On indicates, women (and here she has not even begun to refer to the problem of women of color in America as a separate subcategory) do not constitute a "class" or "group" in the same sense that the proletariat does, and in that way it is moving in the wrong direction to try to use Marxist theory as an origin for the notion of some kind of female epistemic privilege.

Here we can see a way around, or a way to theorize about, the kinds of problems constituted by Chicana ways of knowing, and the specific use of the "border" metaphor in its most postmodern sense. The problem here is: which border? If the Chicana indeed inhabits the "borders," and if they become her reference points for knowledge construction, it is unclear what the center is. The center could be Mexico, or the United States, or Aztlán, or some as yet unidentified indigenous standpoint. In any case, the notion of borders in some sense assists and in some sense hinders the development of Chicana feminist epistemics. Everyone is at a border of some sort; women of color no doubt more than others, but this seems like another way of saying that women of color in the United States are doubly oppressed, or triply oppressed, or whatever the relevant rubric is.

Bat-Ami Bar On ends her essay by observing that the notion of "epistemic privilege" in and of itself seems like another one of the master's tools which, as Audre Lorde is frequently quoted as having said, will never dismantle the master's house.[62] In any case, one thing seems clear: the "borders" concept is simultaneously powerful and dangerous—perhaps, of course, that is its appeal. It pushes any theorizing that employs it in a direction that is ultimately quite individualistic and probably not susceptible of group interpretation, except at short bursts. But this may simply be a reading of it that fails to do justice to its historical, Chicana/o ancestry.

Finally, the Virgin/Malinche imagery plays with a number of different concepts at the same time, much in the same way that the borders metaphor does. Within Mexico, we might guess that a sharper separation has been kept between the uses of the symbol of Malinche as a kind of mother and the uses of the symbol of the Virgin herself, particularly since the one symbol is, after all, an importation from the Spaniards' religious culture, whereas the other symbol remains indigenous. Chicana theorizing, however, has turned the opposition into still another version of the classical madonna/whore opposition, and in that sense has made the opposition something to which every woman can relate, again as a mode of knowing. Because these symbols are carried over to the United States in a somewhat deracinated fashion—and because they are also liable to commodification in the United States, as is nearly every other symbol—they become tropes-of-the-moment, so to speak, and some of their original power and mystery is no doubt lost. But since every Chicana has the potential within her to use the symbols, they can indeed become foci for liberation.[63]

Chicana feminist epistemology then cuts across most of the more standard appropriations of feminist epistemics that might be encountered in the academy. As has been argued here, in its communitarian and labor-related aspects, and in its reliance on intense networks of validation and confirmation (as well as oral tradition), it bears a striking resemblance to portions of naturalized epistemology/feminist theory, especially as articulated by some contemporary feminist theorists of knowledge. But although this sort of theorizing has already been put to some use within Mexico itself, especially by Lourdes Arizpe, the more postmodern aspects of Chicana theorizing yield an intensely individualistic mode of knowing that, in a sense, is not group oriented. The "border" may be literal, or it may itself be intensely metaphorical, and it may refer to language, gender, sexuality, or a more general notion, such as personal life/belief systems. It is intriguing to note the titles of some recent essays in the Trujillo anthology that explore the borders concept: among them are "Border Perspectives desde las Fronteras: a Reading on Rosario Sanmiguel's 'El reflejo de la luna'"; "La Virgin de Guadalupe and Her Reconstruction in Chicana Lesbian Desire"; and "Mestizaje as Method: Feminists-of-Color Challenge the Canon."[64] The titles provide an indication of the range of uses of the conceptual apparatuses under examination. Perhaps the most lasting contribution of Chicana theory, particularly as applied to feminist epistemology, will be the virtually inexhaustible latitude supplied by a notion as permeable, liquid, and hospitable as "borders."

The Chicana/o Trajectory

We have been able to make ample use of postmodernism in examining Chicana/o cultures because of the chiaroscuro-like impression created by the mixture of U.S., Mexican, and other influences. As we have seen in the preceding section, Chicana feminist theory in general has been enormously helpful to other areas of cultural studies simply because so much has transpired within it that can be reappropriated for other groups.

But if the power of Chicana/o thought in the United States has a great deal to do with its multifacetedness, a tolerance for theoretical mix is certainly needed. Unlike the other cultures examined thus far, each of which was situated within a geographical area that might be thought to be its home, so to speak, the Chicana/o cultures draw on areas none of which are uniquely central to their development, but all of which are more or less equally important. Thus the androcentrism of Mexico and of the Latin cultures in general meets plain old American sexism, so one might be inclined to say, and the result is "low rider" chauvinism. The strength of Mexican women—whether of the *soldadera* or *comadre* variety—joins up with American labor organization tactics to produce the Chicana farmworker and activist. Finally, and perhaps most important, because of the already phenomenal growth in knowledge-category scholarship among U.S. academics (particularly feminists), standard feminist epistemology confronts women-of-color epistemics, and powerful new tropes are generated.

Chicanas may indeed feel marginalized, not only because of their precarious position in the United States, but also because, until recently, a number of other theoretical positions even among American women of color seemed to be foregrounded. But the new scholarship, driven by a variety of theoretical views, has allowed for the development of a Chicana/o overview that propels not only cultural studies but critical legal and race theory in new directions. Carl Gutiérrez-Jones summarizes this situation when he writes:

> The guerrilla writing offered by Williams and López [critical legal studies work] ... has important corollaries in the literary realm, as evidenced in the works of minority authors who serve witness to the more pragmatic effects

of the legal and educational institutions. . . . Like the legal scholars discussed
above, these artists appropriate rhetorical options in order to alter a cognitive
framework and in so doing recondition reception itself.[65]

It may well be the case that a number of artists of color in the United
States see themselves as consciously aiding in the effort of redefining the
canon, or as altering cognitive frameworks, but Gutiérrez-Jones's larger
point in his work is that the Chicana/o artist is in a unique position to do so.
No other persons of color grouping in America has the strength of numbers of the Chicana/o community while at the same time the power and
position to draw on historical memories of another culture situated in
another land. The effect of this situatedness lends a swirling, kaleidoscopic
quality to much Chicana/o theory, and, as we have seen, places the Chicana
in an especially powerful position, since she is able to theorize feminism
and feminist epistemologies from a multiplicity of directions. Although as
Bar On has written there may well be reason to question the notion of
"margin," if the notion has any merit at all it is put to assertive use in Chicana theory, since so many margins are involved.

It is for these reasons that the newest uses of Chicana/o theory seem to
go against the grain of standardly construed "liberatory" theorizing. Some
of the work shown in the *Patria Portátil* exhibition referred to earlier seems
to self-consciously mock committed Chicana/o power: historical views of
the chromo works as seen in the United States meet up, at the end of the
exhibit, with contemporary photographs of East Los Angeles gangbangers,
their tattoo work, and, in one instance, a send-up of the Popocatépetl-
Ixtaccihuatl myth in contemporary Chicana/o terms.[66]

In urban areas, particularly in California, the Chicano has frequently
been seen in criminal terms—among the other stereotypes affecting his
worldview has been, as Gutiérrez-Jones notes, the "seductive yet criminally
prone Chicano . . . within a society that politically underdevelops [its] real-
life counterpart."[67] Still another twist on this view, and one that has been
appropriated by Chicanas as well, and hence has become a part of Chicana
theory, is that of the urban rebel who sees the contemporary reformulation
of the Virgin/Malinche symbols in the young women around her, many of
whom are living lives that might, in some sense, be drawn from the film *Mí
Vida Loca.*[68]

If the Chicana/o today is the product of a number of movements of the
1960s, including the labor movement and a response to the perception of
the Chicana/o as criminal, there is an interesting unexplored junction
between more naturalized feminist epistemologies and the poststructuralist/

postmodernist twists of which we have been writing. At this point it is not difficult to capture the relevance of naturalized epistemology in its feminist vein; our citation of such theorists as Lynn Hankinson Nelson and others has helped construct how a reliance on lived experience, communities, networks, and information exchanges inform the knowledge-gathering techniques of women in many areas. One citation from Nelson is especially apt for much of what has transpired in the labor/Church/movement activities of Chicanas:

> But although our epistemological communities are not monolithic or stable, such communities also do not "dissolve" into "collections" of knowing individuals. By virtue of our membership in a number of such communities, as well as by virtue of our experience as individuals, we can each contribute, and uniquely, to the knowledge generated by our various communities.[69]

Nelson was writing here of communities of investigators in the academic arena, such as women primatologists, but the quotation remains apt for our purposes. Knowledge transmitted through labor and community organizations can serve in much the same way; some of the knowledge may have to do with conditions of labor, some may have to do with modes of work, and some may have to do with modes of communication. In any case, all are likely to be "unofficial," and hence to represent differing takes and constructions on official patriarchal knowledge, especially when that, within a Mexican-derived tradition, has to do with the Church. The fascinating twist that is put on all of this by contemporary Chicana/o theorizing and intellectual activity is that "signifiers" and "signs" are being moved about in a loose and fast manner that virtually assures a Foucauldian overturning of knowledge hierarchies. As indicated at an earlier point, the continual use of the "borders" construct is but one example of these rapid shifts; another is the appropriation of a number of stigmatized activities, such as lowriding and gangbanging, as cultural symbols in continual acts of reinvention and reappropriation.

What the Chicana/o population has in common with, for example, the American black population is that much of what has happened to it has been involuntary. It is true that persons of Mexican ancestry have voluntarily come here—the simple statement of this fact, however, ignores the conditions of their lives once they arrived here. Instances of overt discrimination of the type lodged against the black population abound; although it may well be the case that no codified body of law on the state level has ever existed against persons of Mexican ancestry, much *de facto* or even municipal segregation has been recorded.[70] Because of the extent to which internalized oppression can affect members of a group subjected to this degree of overt harassment and exclusion, any act of cultural retrieval on the part of the group in question usually represents a step in the right direction.

Although the Chicana/o community had been taking such steps years before the '60s (and frequently, as we've seen, under the leadership of women), the greatest single move may well have been the formation of what later became the UFW under the leadership of Dolores Huerta and César Chávez. The use of the concept of *peregrinación*, the construction of the Virgin of Guadalupe as patron, and the reliance on a notion of giving as a force for spiritual transcendence and change all positioned the Chicana/o community in such a way that there was no turning back. The Chicanas who led this fight saw something that many others had not seen: the strength of the Virgin belongs in the fields, the roads, and the march as well as in the home. She represents that force for change that takes us out of ourselves and into something larger, a community of believers. In that sense, a community of knowers was created, and at the same time, a Chicana epistemics for the twentieth century.

Chapter 9

The African Diaspora in the United States

The resurgence of scholarship in African diaspora studies, black history, and the black American cultures in general has reaffirmed the importance of what has long been known, but often not articulated frequently enough—black American culture in general is a product of the West African cultures from which it was derived, and has much in common with other African-derived cultures throughout the New World. Although historians such as John Blassingame and Sterling Stuckey have been very careful in their citation of what groups of persons were transported to which region, W. E. B. Du Bois probably said it best in *Black Reconstruction* when he explained that black Americans came from almost all regions of Africa, as, over a period of time, virtually every region became represented to some extent in the slave trade.[1]

Even if we hypothesize, as seems to be borne out by the records available, that some groups are much more highly represented than others—among them the Wolof, Bambara, Hausa, Igbo, and Yoruba—each group would have imparted its particular cultural characteristics to the brew that was mixing in the seventeenth, eighteenth, and early nineteenth centuries in the contiguous United States. We know not only from American records, but also from contemporary work in the Caribbean, where many of the African-derived cultures are stronger, that the metaphysics and ontologies of many groups, particularly the Yoruba and Igbo, affected the belief systems not only of the black South, but also of the white American religious institutions that came into contact with them. Thus a traceable lineage for many important elements of black culture exists, and black literature, particularly of the past twenty years or so, has made an attempt to incorporate much of this material.[2]

Much of what we now know about the importance of the metaphysical for West African cultures helps form the basis for any contemporary analysis of the role of the black Church in American life, or for the importance of preaching and religious activities in general. In his analysis of the salience of Yoruba *orisha* for the black cultures of the New World, Robert Farris Thompson writes:

> The Yoruba remain the Yoruba precisely because their culture provides them with ample philosophic means for comprehending, and ultimately transcending, the powers that periodically threaten to dissolve them. That their religion and their art withstood the horrors of the Middle Passage and firmly established themselves in the Americas (New York City, Miami, Havana, Matanzas, Recife, Bahia, Rio de Janeiro) as the slave trade effected a Yoruba diaspora—reflects the triumph of an inexorable communal will.[3]

Thompson's citation of a range of New World cities—both in the United States and in Latin America—underscores the importance of the notion of diasporic change for an understanding of black cultures, and also signals areas of commonality for such societies throughout the Americas. More important for what we do here, the new scholarship gives meaning to such expressions as "black philosophy," because it increases the number of possible referents; such philosophy is now not only contemporary philosophy produced by Africans or by blacks in other parts of the world, but is also, increasingly, the thought of African cultures when analyzed along lines that would allow for the notion of a developed metaphysics or for stated and articulated ontologies.[4]

To take the Yoruba metaphysics as but one example, as Thompson has done, any precisely formulated statements about it will have to take into account the importance of the notion of "spirit" and the admixture of spirit and the material that is the hallmark of many non-Western belief systems around the world. Unlike the dualism so prevalent in the periods of Western philosophy frequently emphasized in the classroom, Yoruba thought (and much other West African thought) posits spirit in everything—lakes, trees, the earth, stones, and other material objects. Perhaps in Western terms we should think of this worldview as being closer to a vitalism; although many reject the notion that Western terms are helpful in discussing African philosophies, they may do a certain amount of work. In any case, such a term will help us construct a rough-and-ready analogue that may get us to a certain conceptual place.

A great deal of the scholarship that is currently being done on African-derived metaphysics underlines not only the tie-in to New World cultures, but the specific elements of the West African cultural views that might be thought, even within the sometimes narrow confines of Western scholarship, to constitute pronounced ontological structures. Kwasi Wiredu, for example, has provided excellent work on these philosophical issues in a recent piece titled "African Philosophical Tradition: A Case Study of the Akan." Because postcolonial arguments remind us of the simplicity—and in some cases, the stupidity—of trying to cut metaphysical views in such a way as to make them consonant with Western views, what Wiredu has to say on this score with respect to the positions of the Akan-speaking peoples is instructive. He gives us commentary, for example, on two concepts from the Akan that might be thought to be related to the Western concept of "soul." The first is the *okra*, which he glosses as "life principle," and the second is the *sunsum*, a "personality ingredient" which cannot withstand death. Here is Wiredu:

> The difference in ontological character, then, between the *okra* and the *sunsum*, on the one hand, and the *mogya* and the bodily frame as a whole, on the other, is only one of degree of materiality, the body being fully material and the other constituents only partially material in the sense already explained. Carefully to be distinguished from this conception is the Cartesian notion of a material body and an immaterial soul. On this latter conception, any talk of the incarnation of the soul is simply self-contradictory.[5]

Wiredu's work here is important, for it already speaks to large issues. When we make the simple gloss, as was done here at an earlier point, that "spirit" suffuses, we are being too crude in our formulations. Depending upon the cultures involved, views of greater or less complexity than the ones Wiredu expounds may be brought to bear; one fact emerges, however. If a "philosophical" view is one that is supposed to provide an "explanation," or an "account of," it is clear that many West African cultures do indeed possess philosophical views about personal identity, even by somewhat recalcitrant Western standards.

To try to articulate a black feminist epistemics in terms of the black American culture or cultures requires that we cover a now familiar array of conceptual grounds and spaces: we need to try to set out what might be deemed to be androcentric or masculinist in those views which, statistically speaking, are likely to have been most predominant in the slave cultures transported to the New World. We will not, for example, in general concern ourselves with Ethiopian philosophical views (although much work has been done on them), for the simple reason that comparatively few Ethiopian people were taken in slavery. A great deal of work indicates that many of the West African cultures held complex views of spirit and matter similar to those indicated by Wiredu when he writes of the Akan peoples.[6] In setting out portions of the views that might, even in more standard terms, be deemed to be those leading to the creation of a gynocentric epistemology, we will be addressing new areas of scholarship that have touched on this very issue. The scholar Oyeronke Oyewumi, for example, has recently published a work contending that what constitutes "woman" is in fact a Eurocentric construct that, in some ways, is scarcely applicable to African cultures.[7]

Tracing the Androcentric

As we have indicated in our work on other cultures, there is always a danger in applying Eurocentric concepts, and yet we can scarcely proceed in analysis without doing so—particularly since a great deal of scholarship that is now being done in the cultures in question does in fact use such categories. The fact that the West African cultures in question possess categories of analysis that may, in many respects, resemble categories with which we are already familiar pushes us, initially, in a certain direction. The categorization referred to by Wiredu, for example, indicates a desire to give an account of personal life and the possibility of an afterlife in the speculative, somewhat transcendental terms that, in other cultural views, we have come to associate with male development, androcentric theorizing and a quest for Complete Accountism. Yet in the West African cultures, one is initially tempted to say, the situation is a great deal more complex. It may well be the case that a great many griots, for example, were, historically speaking, male, but it is also true—and now extensively documented—that in many such cultures women held a degree of power and authority not comparable to the station of women in almost any European society. Thus any attempt to flesh out the notion of androcentrism must proceed carefully.

The important point is to attempt an examination of the cultures in question with an eye to gender positions and genders, as authorities and commentators, within the cultures. Within the African diaspora as it is commonly examined for purposes of developing notions of black American history, two masculinist foci stand out: not only are there philosophical/mythographical stances that remind one of those of other cultures that might be thought to be androcentric, but the concept of kinghood is crucial for many of the cultures that were transported to the New World, including, for instance, most Kongo-speaking cultures.[8] In addition, as we examine the diasporic growth over time in what is now the United States, we are struck by the fact that certain sorts of masculinist trends become stronger once daily contact with European cultures is established—Paula Giddings, for example, writes of the tendency in Reconstruction-era southern groups for the male-headed household to assume a transcending importance.[9]

Although the importance of the notion of kingship varies from group to group—and is comparatively less important, for our purposes, in those groups that exhibit strong matrilineality—its overall strategic qualities cannot be denied. Thompson notes that, as was the case with the Yoruba, the Ki-Kongo were able to achieve a greater degree of coherence in the New World than many other groups, and it certainly is fair to say that many aspects of their culture survived, and did so in a straightforward and readily identifiable manner. (Thompson asserts, for example, that partly due to strength of numbers, when Kongo speakers came together in the New World. "They fostered their heritage.")[10]

The concept of the king and the king's access to a privileged supernatural realm was crucial to the Ki-Kongo culture. Although these male-initiated beliefs are found to some extent in virtually every human culture, the aspect that often receives comparatively little attention is the direct tie to the realm of the sacred. Thompson gives us some idea of the importance of these beliefs when he writes:

> For the Bakongo envisioned their capital as an ideal, noble place where "a strong chief, supernaturally inspired, assures every citizen his due." ... A newly elected king would make a circular tour of his domain, symbolically passing through the worlds of the living and the dead, thereby acquiring mystic insights proper only to a Kongo king.... The religion of Kongo presupposes God Almighty, (*Nzambi Mpungu*), whose illuminating spirit and healing powers are carefully controlled by the king (*mfumu*).[11]

Various groups within the New World would have been able to maintain these belief systems to a greater and lesser extent—Thompson writes, for example, of the strength of the Ki-Kongo cultures in Latin America.[12] But what is true—and which has varying degrees of influence on the notion of androcentrism, depending upon the point at which one is in the chronology, so to speak—is that the conditions of slave societies in the New World in many cases were such as to undercut male influence and authority in slave households.[13]

Because the black male was seen as a potential threat, and because of the sexual commodification of the black female, black men lost an enormous degree of influence in the various slave cultures.[14] At the same time, insofar as Christianity had a rapidly spreading influence on slave societies (and this, of course, was largely a product of force), the model that was held up to African-derived households was one of male dominance. The upshot of this somewhat incongruous historical juxtaposition was that newly freed slaves in the period immediately after the Civil War were often anxious to establish households that adhered to the only norm with which most of them were familiar by that time: the norm of the male-headed, Christian nuclear family.[15] Thus a combination of beliefs that, traceably, tend to occur throughout human societies having to do with male divinity and male epistemic access, and other beliefs, acquired and reinforced at various historical junctures, led to attempts at strongly patriarchal families and leadership structures in the black American cultures of the latter part of the nineteenth century.

The strong line taken by feminist scholars on an international basis— that societies with written languages and post-hunting and -gathering cultures tend to produce androcentric constructs and worldviews—is certainly recapitulated in the African slave trade cultures that had been exposed to Islam within Africa itself.[16] Although estimates vary as to how many persons from Islamicized backgrounds could have been taken in slavery (and, clearly, it is only a comparatively small percent of the total, partly for geographical reasons), there is extensive documentation of slaves in the New World who had a working knowledge of Arabic and who were sufficiently literate to be able to read the Qur'an and to compose in Arabic at the time of their arrival. Blassingame's narrative of Abduhl Rahhahman is but one such example.[17] We can hypothesize that this influence was, of course, quite androcentric, although we cannot be sure how much overall influence slaves from such cultures actually had. The fact that they were literate certainly would have given them a high degree of say in certain circles.

Finally, we can note that, just as a certain sort of metaphysics is capturable from some of the Akan societies, such societies also possessed a notion of a Creator-deity with remarkable similarity to some of those found in the monolithic, patriarchal religions. In some crucial respects this deity is dissimilar; as Wiredu notes, "he" cannot go against his own laws. But the very fact that such a metaphysically speculative question arises is an indicator of the extent to which this sort of thought already existed in at least some West African societies. Wiredu tries to explain the status of the creator in the following:

> It should be stressed that the idea is not that God just decides not to forestall this or any other death, but rather that, by the very nature of the laws by which he fashioned the cosmic order, he cannot do so.[18]

This sort of debate—reminiscent of medieval debates about whether the Christian God can create a stone so large that he cannot move it—is the no-holds-barred metaphysical theorizing of societies where some (usually privileged males) have the time and the leisure to think about such issues. In any case, this much can truly be said: the androcentric tendencies of a number of West African cultures, although possibly truncated or ameliorated in the early years in the New World, may have sprung back with renewed vigor at a later time. How much those tendencies were shaped and reinforced by the surrounding patriarchal Eurocentric culture is impossible to say. But as Giddings and others have noted, a sad irony of the post–Civil War situation in the United States was that, for many African-American males, vindicating manhood, a race, and a people included "establishing conventional patriarchal relationships."[19]

Unraveling the Gynocentric

That matrilineality and matrifocality are properties of many West African societies is beyond dispute. A number of commentators have written at length on this feature of such cultures, and there can be little doubt that at least some of this emphasis on female power within a given society must have carried over into the New World African-derived societies. Oyeronke Oyewumi, for example, writes of the extent to which the Yoruba culture possesses few of the gender markers widely assumed by many Western feminists to occur in most human cultures.[20] In such a society—and there are several West African groups that possess many of these characteristics—age is the predominant social distinction; gender is of comparatively little importance, and in many social situations gender is not alluded to, either directly or indirectly.

In addition to matrilineality and matrifocality, another important aspect of many of the West African cultures suffering depredations through the slave trade was the extent to which god and goddess figures retained comparable levels of strength throughout the culture. This is no mere curiosity; if it can genuinely be said that a goddess is perceived as being as forceful (if not more so) than a god, a great deal is being stated, for, as we have indicated earlier, this is probably not the case, for example, in the Greco-Roman tradition.

In his portraits of the major *orisha* of the Yoruba, Robert Farris Thompson routinely gives equal time to goddess figures. He explains their importance when he writes:

Yoruba-Americans, outwardly abiding by the religious practices of the
Catholics who surrounded them, covertly practiced a system of thought that
was a creative reorganization of their own traditional religion. Luminously
intact in the memories of black elders from Africa, the goddesses and the gods
of the Yoruba entered the modern world of the Americas. They came with
their praises (*oriki*), extraordinary poems of prowess that defined the moral
and aesthetic reverberation of their presence.[21]

From the divination system of Ifa, to the worship of Nana Bukuu and the
riverain goddesses, female power is an important source of strength in
Yoruba life, and the goddess is positively not seen as a mere consort or coac-
tor to a divinity.[22] Because of this, an interesting twist to much of the
Yoruba cosmology and theogony as it appeared in the Americas is that the
Catholicizing of the deities—resulting, of course, in *vodun* and its variants—yielded some intriguing gender switches. In some cases, goddesses
became male saints, and vice versa; gender was not nearly as important here
as power itself.[23]

This combination of matrilineality, emphasis on the goddess, and lack
of emphasis on what have come to be known as "traditional" gender
roles exerted a powerful influence in the New World. But we cannot
escape an analysis that juxtaposes this combination with the plain fact
that, during slavery, men of African ancestry were disempowered on a
regular basis. This, plus the additional obvious point that both male and
females slaves had to engage in hard physical labor most of the time
meant that the gender-driven division of labor—probably seldom the
same as in European societies, in any case—played out differently in
black households.

Angela Davis has provided one of the most politically astute analyses of
African women during the nineteenth century in her classic *Women, Race,
and Class*.[24] Although Davis does not spend much time on the type of
material used by Oyewumi or Thompson, for example, she does give us fuel
to make the conceptual add-ons to these lines of argument that would yield
an overarching analysis. In an oft-cited passage in the first chapter of her
book, Davis notes the conditions of labor for American black women in the
1800s. Here we can theorize readily enough if we remember that the vast
majority of these women would have been one or two generations removed
from West African societies, many of which had social structures similar to
those that we have examined. Davis writes:

Required by the masters' demands to be as "masculine" in the performance of their work as their men, Black women must have been profoundly affected by their experiences during slavery. . . . A traveler during that period observed a slave crew in Mississippi returning home from the fields and described the group as including

> forty of the largest and strongest women I ever saw together; . . . they carried themselves loftily, each having a hoe over the shoulder, and walking with a free, powerful swing like chasseurs on the march.[25]

Patricia Hill Collins makes similar points in her own work on Afrocentric feminist epistemology, when she notes that those who, more contemporarily, derided black families for their "matriarchal" structure, failed to note the historical antecedents, the relevant social conditions, or any cultural constructs. As she says, prior to the 1960s, "an ideology racializing female-headedness as a cause of black poverty had not emerged."[26]

Still another factor giving rise to elements of gynocentrism in African-derived American culture is the employment status of black women throughout the period after the Civil War and even up to the present in some communities. The same set of factors that relegated the black man to a feared status—and one that left him vulnerable to lynchings, murder, and reprisals—left the black woman in a space that was comparatively undisturbed. Because of this, it was frequently much easier for black women to obtain employment than black males. Although Giddings notes that this employment, especially in the latter part of the nineteenth century, led to an increasing number of semiprofessional positions for black women, much of it was, of course, domestic.[27] Although this led to larger cultural perceptions of "mammies"—images that, of course, did tremendous damage and which Collins, for one, is concerned to decry—it is also true that the prevalence of black women's work throughout various social strata reinforced the power of black women in certain kinds of tasks. In any case, one thing is certain: there is no lack of female-centered foci in the African-derived New World cultures.

If all of these lines of analysis yield a picture of black women as dynamic and active, as indeed they do, we would expect, historically speaking, that a number of the most important social movements in black circles have been led or managed by women, even if this was not obvious at the time. This, too, turns out to be the case. Giddings devotes several of the last chapters of her book to the work done by black women activists that, again, infiltrated almost all circles of activism, even if it was not acknowledged at the time. Despite the fact that we may associate the Montgomery bus boycott, for example, with the organizational powers of men who later became well-known on the national scene, women were extremely prominent players at the time. Giddings attributes all of this not only to the factors that we have explicitly mentioned, but to something that is at least implied in the excision from Davis. Work, of whatever nature, may lead to an increase in coping skills—even if, perforce, one did not want to initially gain such skills, or at least gain them under the given conditions. But black women have always had "role models"; they have always seen women doing things, because it was in general not possible for a black woman in America to lead a life of leisure. As Giddings says of the young women who helped to propel SNCC thirty or more years ago, "At the least their mothers worked, and were usually capable of coping with *any* situation that could affect their children's lives."[28] It was not necessary, therefore, for a young black woman to feel that she was breaking the mold—she was indeed part of a long line of women who had been "active" for centuries.

However active black women have been, and however much it has been the case that there are traceable gynocentric patterns in the West African cultures (and strong patterns at that), the development of a black feminism/womanism in the United States has been problematic. The theorist Joy James indicates that part of the problem is what she refers to as the "limbo" of the black woman's position. In some ways in the forefront, in other ways completely marginalized, her position is difficult to describe. James notes:

> The criticism that black feminisms are not "feminist" enough simplifies the existential dilemmas of black women's lives and struggles in a racist state. The liberation of black women as a group rather than as atomized individuals is inseparable from—but not identical with or reducible to—the liberation of their peoples or communities of origin, what some label a black or an African community.[29]

This particular dilemma has always been at the heart of black women's movements, and is one which will affect the burgeoning developments of black feminist epistemologies, as we will see later. In any case, when James says, as she does slightly earlier in the same text, that black feminists are "suspended midway between eurocentric or postmodern feminism and afrocentric masculinism," she is hitting at a core part of the analysis. History, theory, political forces and plain geographic space are all necessary components of an analysis of black women, their worldviews, their feminisms, and their epistemics.

Black Women's Histories and Their Impacts

Black women's history in what is now the contiguous United States is a story of the movement from slavery to Reconstruction, antilynching activism to the civil rights movement, and beyond. But it is also a story, unfortunately, of the commodification of black women as sexual beings, and the creation of different classes or groups of black Americans on the basis of skin color, phenotype, and perceived white ancestry. While the black woman struggled during slavery to create some sort of home—at the same time laboring with back-breaking vigor on a daily basis—she was also frequently held up as an object of sexual pleasure, and, of course, a few black women were selected for other kinds of labor on just such a basis.[30] While nineteenth-century race theoreticians criticized the creation of a group of "mulattoes" on the basis of their supposed shortcomings as biologically constituted human beings, black women were being seen as the instigators of the interracial liaisons that gave rise to the birth of such children, and were being blamed for their lasciviousness.[31] The black woman as sexual creature (while simultaneously, in many cases, hard laborer) is an inescapable image from the preceding centuries and is part of the history of black cultures in America. Naomi Zack quotes the sociologist Reuter writing in 1918:

> Reuter had complicated speculations about the origin of the superiority of mulattoes among blacks that involved the "choicer" of black women deliberately seeking liaisons with low-class white men to further the life chances of their children among blacks. These black mothers of mixed-race children, Reuter claimed, never objected to and personally sought out the interracial liaisons: "It was never at any time a matter of compulsion; on the contrary it was a matter of being honored by a man of a superior race. Speaking generally, the amount of intermixture is limited only by the self-respect of the white man and the compelling strength of the community sentiment."[32]

It would be helpful to be able to report that a view such as Reuter's here was in a decided minority, but, of course, it was not. Thus black women have labored under a staggering number of burdens regarding their "femininity," their sexuality, their capacity to labor, and so forth, that, as Joy James said, have made the development of a specifically black feminism difficult at best.

Nevertheless, such development has occurred, and we can see its roots, also, in the nineteenth century, especially with the rise in authorship by black women in the era immediately after the Civil War and Reconstruction. This period, characterized by the rapid growth of Jim Crow laws and the frequent public lynchings that became a staple of life throughout the South, was also dominated by the work of many black journalists and correspondents, several of the most noted being women. Their work stands as testimony more than a hundred years later to the beginning development of black feminism/womanism. Among the most prominent were Ida B. Wells and Mary Church Terrell. Wells's work alone constitutes a veritable outpouring of thinking about the black community, the importance of lynching as a tool of oppression, and the need for black women to unite for the betterment of their community and themselves. Much of the work that was accomplished by literate black women in this period, especially those who were in an authorial position, was done because of the rising black bourgeoisie, whose wealth and privilege—in many cases, of course, related to lighter skin color—enabled them to obtain money from white benefactors and to begin the numerous black institutions that were to serve the population throughout the late nineteenth and earlier twentieth centuries.

A small bourgeoisie had long been in existence, however. Among of the most poignant documents of the Civil War period written by a black woman are the *Journals* of Charlotte Forten Grimke, daughter of Robert Forten and member of one of America's most prominent free black families in the period before the war.[33] Foreshadowing the type of work done by Wells, for example, Grimke details her daily life, but with a strong emphasis on her concerns with respect to abolitionism, the enactment of fugitive slave laws, and so forth. Her writings are all the more remarkable in that they are among the few documents we have from that period that testify to the lives of black Americans who were not enslaved. Charlotte fulfilled, to some extent, the role for middle-class white women that Angela Davis has referred to as "angel of the house"; she had the leisure to pursue reading, embroidery, and the piano.[34] Nevertheless, the startling difference in Charlotte's case is that she did not allow her comparative luxury to deflect her from her larger purpose. On one occasion her diary notes "Another fugitive from bondage has been arrested";[35] on still another she writes, "read again today as most suitable to my feelings and the times 'The Runaway Slave at Pilgrim's Point.' "[36]

A nexus of factors, including the rise of the bourgeoisie, a small but sturdy tradition of black female authorship (which we may say began with Phillis Wheatley, before the Declaration of Independence), concern for the establishment of the family but equal concern for women's rights, and a powerful antilynching movement all propelled black women forward in positions of activism during and immediately after Reconstruction. Unfortunately, black women frequently were unable to count on a solid alliance with white women activists in areas of either race or gender equality. This obstacle, combined with the notion, already articulated here, that the black family must be reconstructed along "healthy" patriarchal lines, made the plight of the black woman activist a difficult one. Nevertheless, she persevered. Ida Wells herself wrote, with respect to the general white backlash against black enfanchisement and economic power:

> Nobody in this section of the country believed the threadbare lie that Negro men rape white women. If Southern white men are not careful, they will overreach themselves and public sentiment will have a reaction. A conclusion will then be reached which will be very damaging to the moral reputation of their women.[37]

Shifting alliances between white and black women yielded a kaleidoscopic array of causes and activities. During the 1880s and 1890s, the black women's club movement became firmly established as a way for women of color to accomplish something for the race and themselves at the same time. In some cases, organizations were offshoots of abolitionist and suffragist organizations that had originally been integrated; in other cases, they were black organizations from the start. The Women's Christian Temperance Union (WCTU), for example, constantly veered back and forth between at least some integration in its northern branches and complete segregation in its southern regionals. Led again by Wells, and also by activists such as Anna Julia Cooper and Josephine St. Pierre Ruffin, nationwide organizations such as the National Federation of Afro-American Women and the National Association of Colored Women were formed in the years 1895–96.[38] Giddings notes that black women activists often felt a call from on high, as it were, to forward movement of the race; as she indicates, Cooper herself had written that black women were "the fundamental agency under God in the regeneration ... of the race, as well as the groundwork and starting point of its progress upward."[39] It has been a staple of commentary on the American black woman that she is doubly oppressed; the forerunners of today's activists, however, might have said that she was doubly gifted.

Black women also became active in that most un-American of American political organizations, the American Communist Party.[40] This group, and other related organizations such as the International Workers of the World (IWW), were among the first to achieve something like genuine integration, and black women communists such as Claudia Jones were at the forefront of their activities. (And this at a time of complete Jim Crow segregation in the South and *de facto* segregation in the North.) Controversially, some black women communists were vocal in their promulgation of a very socialist line; the main enemy was class discrimination, not necessarily race discrimination.

But for a large part of the last hundred years, black women activists have focused on race and uplift. Again, it is Ida B. Wells who probably stands out most prominently around the turn of the century as someone who was able to place the focus where it should be—and who did this despite the handicap of her gender. Wells's writing not only galvanized the club movement, but stands even today as a paradigm of its type. She ferociously waged a battle and gave no quarter; her articles are filled with statistic after statistic about lynching, racial sex crimes, and atrocities committed against the black population. From an historian's point of view, Wells's greatest accomplishment may have been serving as a catalyst for others to till the same soil. In "The Reason Why the Colored American Is Not in the World's Columbian Exposition," Wells and several others (among them Frederick Douglass and Wells's husband) provided a startling catalog of the achievements of black Americans during the some thirty year period after slavery. Most of those whose achievements were being listed were, of course, male; yet Wells, a woman, is the leader of those who put pen to paper in an attempt to chronologize the accomplishments. As she says in one of the subsections of "The Reason Why" which she personally authored:

> [F]or nearly fifty of these lynchings no reason is given. There is no demand
> for reasons, or need of concealment for what no one is held responsible. The
> simple word of any white person against a Negro is sufficient to get a crowd
> of white men to lynch a Negro.[41]

These stark sentences sum up, unfortunately, much of black American life in the Reconstruction period and immediately thereafter. They were written by a black American woman.

Contemporary Black Women

The American black woman now, perhaps a great deal more than her male counterpart, has been able to benefit to some extent from the changes wrought by the 1960s and the civil rights movement, and statistic after statistic attests to her greater enrollment in college, for example, or to her greater pro rata share of success in the professions.

But more so than these accomplishments, black women's voices have made enormous inroads in literature, the arts, and, in general, in feminist theory and in any academic area that has been impacted by feminist theory. In a sense, these moves are phenomenal—to name but a few areas, the novel, poetry, film, and straightforwardly developed feminist theory have all been changed enormously by the voices of black women. Yet, as is true for the Chicana, it is probably the case that the average black woman has remained relatively untouched by these developments in her daily life, since the same indicators that show market growth in the U.S. economy show the black population's decline in terms of absolute standing.

Perhaps the greatest move, aside from the disproportionate share of black women in higher education (that is, in comparison to black men) has been in literature and the arts. Until the early 1970s, only the comparatively little-known Harlem Renaissance authors could count as black female authors who had enjoyed any type of national audience. After the 1970s, it was indeed possible to say that Toni Morrison, Alice Walker, Toni Cade Bambara, Gloria Naylor, and others were among America's best-known authors, and also most honored. The phenomenal success of *The Color Purple* in 1983 heralded unprecedented interest in writing by black women—yet this, too, came at a price. Many black male authors were out-raged by the depictions of sexism in black family life that the novel offered, and still more poignantly, a great deal of the interest generated in the book seemed to accrue because of its lesbian theme, a theme with which radical white feminists could most easily identify. Thus *The Color Purple*, while benefiting from mass marketing, also again left an analyst with the same sensation of postmodern malaise that we have articulated here with respect to other areas. It is not at all clear how much of the success of the novel was related to a kind of appropriation of its themes by persons for whom, pre-sumably, it was never intended. Furthermore, unfortunately, it is not clear how much of its success was attached to a rather spurious conviction on the part of many white feminists that black women finally "got" the mes-sage that patriarchy was limiting. One could surmise that many of them had gotten that message all along. So an argument might well be made that the success of the work said a great deal more about the power of white feminists than it did about the work of black women.

Nevertheless, it is important to examine other phenomena involving black women that may speak, at least obliquely, to the notion of black female success on the literary scene. It has long been the case that black males have been seen as so threatening in America that it has opened a space, socially, for black women. This particular locus is still evident and available, and much of what we know about black education today, both in the higher and lower levels, signals that black girls and their behavior are regarded as being more acceptable than black boys and their behavior. The education researchers Gwendolyn Cartledge, Veronica Adedapo, and Carolyn Talbert Johnson, for example, report that, in a study they created, "It may be for these low-income, inner-city parents, high levels of aggressive behaviors for boys are not only compatible with being socially skilled but are desired."[42] That education researchers would report such a conclusion not only signals that it is known to social scientists, but, as they implicitly assert, it seems to be a generally held belief throughout the culture. Because of these beliefs, black females, in general, do better in school (a finding also reported by the authors), and in many social situations calling for interaction with the general culture.

The success of black women, then, literary or otherwise, seems to be a phenomenon deeply rooted in American history and in social attitudes that go back hundreds of years. Thus the prominence of black women authors is but one part of this trend; not only have such authors achieved mass market appeal, but they also have affected theory, as has been indicated. Still another related development—and one that is crucial for developing an understanding of black feminist epistemics—is the strong appeal, again theoretical and otherwise, of the work and thinking of black lesbian theorists. Audre Lorde's work, for example, has become a staple not only of black literature courses, but of women's studies courses and other cultural studies arenas. Here the notion seems to be again that the historical strength of black women translates into a stance that, in the case of the black lesbian, is instructive to all concerned. Lorde's status—and that of work by black lesbians in general—is ably articulated by her editor in the introduction to *Sister Outsider*, the best-selling collection of her thoughts and essays:

> Audre Lorde informed me, as we were working one afternoon, that she doesn't write theory. "I am a poet," she said.
>
> Lorde's stature as a poet is undeniable. And yet there can be no doubt that *Sister Outsider*, a collection of essays and speeches drawn from the past eight years of this Black lesbian feminist's nonfiction prose, makes absolutely clear to many what some already knew: Audre Lorde's voice is central to the development of contemporary feminist theory. She is at the cutting edge of consciousness.[43]

We can hypothesize here, with little fear of contradiction, that what gives Lorde such stature is the implicit assumption that the black woman in America has always had to "go it alone." An "out" lesbian black woman is simply assuming a stance that many women have had to assume because of necessity, the stance of being cut off from the world of male assistance and endeavor. Thus the popularity of the voice, and thus the insistence that the voice has something to offer a wide variety of readers.

The comparatively new, mass-market appeal of cultural products created by and/or for black women speaks to a number of issues, then: to the continued strength of black women versus black men in a profoundly racist culture, to the simple commodity-driven nature of much of American life, and also to the notion that, at least for some, it is easier to "read" a problematic if it is cast in such a way that the women's lives discussed or exposed fail to resemble one's own life in some significant way. All of the above may account for another contemporary site of cultural exchange: the spate of popular items, intended for mass consumption, that now include black women or images of black women. One thinks, for example, of the success of Terry McMillan's work: not merely the financial success of *Waiting to Exhale*, the novel, but of the film, of the *Exhale* parties it started, of the crossover appeal of the novel—which, at least superficially, has little to do with issues involving white women or nonblack women—and so forth.[44]

Thus much of what black women do today is being marketed to the population of American women at large, regardless of ethnic identity. Again, this fact seems to be linked to those that we have already analyzed: the cultural strength of black women and the need for women, especially feminist-identified women, to be able to focus on difficulties in a way that slightly distances them from the actual problem. The education researchers Cartledge et al. also note that there is a well-known saying in the black community about perceived differences in the home with respect to the rearing of boys and girls: "One well-known gender-based adage about the child-rearing practices of African American mothers is that they 'raise their daughters and love their sons.' "[45] The juxtaposition of the black woman's historic role within the culture and within American culture in general has been a heady one—as we have seen, it has inculcated a certain strength, which in turn has given her an image that has resonated throughout the culture.

Perhaps one of the greatest testimonies to the contemporary position of black women in the United States has come from a fairly unlikely source: the noted Marxist theoretician C. L. R. James rarely dealt with women's issues, but because he covered such a wide range of topics in his writing, these issues did indeed come up. The Trinidad-born black theorist more standardly wrote on the role of the black population versus Marx's classical proletariat. In an essay titled "Three Black Women Writers," however, he makes the following observations, which do a great deal to sum up some of what we have written here:

> They [Toni Morrison, Alice Walker, and Ntozake Shange] are first-class writers.... There is another reason, also, that I was particularly interested in these: they represent a social movement in the United States. Women all over the world seem to realize that they have been exploited by men.... These three women have begun to write about Black women's daily lives.[46]

Although James is interested in making the tie-in to Marxist theory, he is on the right track—black women's writing has come, at least in the United States, to speak for the exploitation of women in general. That this is so may, as we have indicated here, represent a sort of commodification of victimization. But, in any case, it has brought black women's issues to the forefront in a way that would not have been possible before. No longer are black women in any sense invisible.

A Womanist/Feminist Response

As feminist theory and black women's theory have begun to merge, several black women theorists have either employed new terminology, new categories, or both. Black feminism is, in some circles, being referred to as "womanism"; some place the origin of this phrase with Alice Walker. The theorist bell hooks is at the forefront of black feminist/womanist theory, according to some, because she has made a steadfast effort to incorporate strands of cultural studies, standard black studies and social theory responses into her work. hooks is particularly concerned that cultural studies and other sorts of academic endeavors that focus on the "Other" not get shuffled to the point of reconstituting the Other, rather than getting students to see what their notion of "Otherness" really amounts to. In other words, part of the task of such courses should be to get students to examine themselves and their roles (including, of course, sex/gender roles) in light of whatever insights they may have found about the Other. Thus hooks is trenchant at pointing out the weak spots in the uses of feminism/womanism made by the academy. In a conversation with Cornel West reprinted in *The Cornel West Reader*, she says:

[It has been] exciting because of the eagerness of students of all ethnicities to engage in what Foucault has called "the insurrection of subjugated knowledges." To teach a course on Black women writers and to have hundreds of the students signing up that lets you know that there has been a transformation in the academy.... At a conference sponsored by Men Stopping Violence and the National Organization for Men Against Sexism, I tried to emphasize that all groups of men in the United States can understand masculinity better by understanding Black masculinity.[47]

hooks is making at least two points here: in a sense, work on black women and black women's issues has become "popular." As has been indicated, such work may "stand in" for other sorts of issues that are simply too painful for sustained examination. But at the same time, hooks is noting that one has not really begun to "deal" with these issues, as it is said in the vernacular, until one has realized how these issues are related to one's own life. In this sense, although some have opted for an easy sort of womanism/black feminism, work in this area is not so simple.

At the same time that these terms have caught on theoretically, there is now a push in mainstream white feminist organizations for inclusion of women of color. Although battles over these issues continue to occur—especially given the fact that the history of racism in women's and suffragist organizations in the United States is pronounced and goes back to the nineteenth century—the National Organization for Women, *Ms.* magazine, and other such beacons of standard, mainstream white feminist thought have now made genuine attempts to include women of color. A recent contretemps over remarks made by Los Angeles area offices of NOW in the aftermath of the O. J. Simpson trial (and the subsequent resignation of one NOW officer) is a case in point.

As is the case for many communities of color in the United States, it is probably the case that some of the most exciting work is being done in small groups—some formal, some informal—across the country that deal with community issues. Quite a bit of the newer sociology of the black culture is addressing issues of "gangs": what social scientists refer to as gangs are often, in their own way, self-help groups. Many of these gangs, particularly in large cities, are organizations of young women. As has always been the case, young women are forming these groups as ways to help themselves—and they are very vocal about it. Writing in a recent issue of *Signs*, Sudir Venkatesh notes:

On a park bench in July 1996, Cynthia, Laurie and other officers of the Black
Sisters United (BSU)—Chicago's largest federation of "girl gangs"—reflected
on their efforts to sustain an organization that could represent and act on
behalf of young African-American women in the city. "We was so close!,"
Cynthia said with deep anguish.[48]

Venkatesh is at pains to point out that, although BSU trafficked in illegal
substances, much of the time and effort of members was spent helping each
other with everything from food to diapers.[49] As the members noted, they
had to do this for each other, because the men were of no help.

This type of social structuring, which has been a feature of black life in
the New World, has, as we have seen, historical and cultural antecedents
that preexisted slavery, many of which were perhaps strengthened or
altered in unaccountable ways by slavery and, in the United States, Jim
Crow laws. But in many cases black groups are either women's groups to
begin with—as is the case with Black Sisters United—or they are groups
in which women exert a disproportionate part of the strength and energy of
the membership. "Womanism," then, has come to describe this historical
strength which, because of the indignities heaped on black men, does not
attack their "power" (they have little), but instead builds on the patterns of
self-help and organization already present. Another such local organization, reported in a recent issue of a mainstream feminist organization, is
the Brooklyn-organized Parents United to Rally for Gun Elimination
(PURGE). The small piece in the serial notes, "After her teenage son was
fatally shot in their Brooklyn, New York, neighborhood in 1993, Freddie
Hamilton took on the gun makers."[50] There are many Freddie Hamiltons
across the United States.

Because of the historical problems with racism in the women's movement, many black women's organizations have little to do with white
women's organizations at all, or are in other ways distanced from them. To
recapitulate—and it is important to be accurate, as the older issues affect
contemporary issues—suffragist organizations in the United States, especially during the nineteenth century, were frequently also abolitionist organizations, and there were originally integrated societies to rally for both
causes.[51] After the end of the Civil War, however, and particularly after the
end of Reconstruction (which receives various dates from various historians, but certainly ended in the late 1870s) racism began to affect these organizations in powerful ways. The freeing of the black population, particularly
in the South, meant that many white small-store owners and craftspersons
had genuine competition. The best blacksmith in a given area, in many

cases, would have been a black man, and any given geographical region can support only so many persons in such a trade. It was at this point that outright racism began to permeate a number of organizations that had formerly been integrated and that had originally tried to fight for black rights and women's rights simultaneously. As Giddings writes, by 1890 the National American Women's Suffrage Association was promoting "purity and reverence for white women."[52]

Since this history carried over into the twentieth century, what it has meant in practice is that most feminist organizations had few members of color until comparatively recently—and, even more important, the black women's movement has constructed itself entirely separately and has, in general, not had much interest in the type of feminism that is aimed at white women. Although this has now changed to some extent, it may very well be true that, in the United States, the most effective feminist/womanist work is being done by small groups in any case, especially since larger, more visible organizations frequently come in for so much media criticism. Although in large cities some of these groups may indeed be women of color (black and brown women, for example) in many cases they are still women's groups devoted to women of one community. Because of the history of the United States, this is an accurate description of most black women's groups.

Fannie Lou Hamer is reported to have said that she had a "black man with a size 13 shoe from whom she did not want to be liberated." However apocryphal this statement, it speaks to something profound—the black woman's construal of womanism/feminism in America has always been built on a foundation that included slavery and a complete degradation of the black man as an individual. Institutions that are taken for granted by white women, and hence readily subject to criticism and even contempt, cannot be so seen by many black women because they were never allowed to be part of black history. Here it is relevant to consider what the historian of slave religion Albert Raboteau says on slave marriages:

> The most frequent method of marrying two slaves was the custom of jumping the broomstick. One of several variations of the ritual was described by William Davis: "Dey lays de brooms on de floor and de woman put her broom front de man and he put he broom front de woman."[53]

These "marriage ceremonies" created by scornful whites are but one example of the reconstitution of patriarchal ritual that would have been necessary for slave families at the end of the war. Given what Giddings and other historians have told us about the desire of many black families to try to create something that had been denied, it is scarcely difficult to understand how black women may have come to feel that white or mainstream feminist movements had little to say to them. Given a society in which feeling "real" has a great deal to do with participating in the privileges of the dominant group, the surprise, in a sense, is that black feminism/womanism exists at all. But exist it does.

Black Women's Rebuilding of Knowledge

As Patricia Hill Collins has indicated, black women's knowledge traditions encompass a variety of moves, many of which, because of their West African origins, can be categorized as part of larger takes on feminist constructions of knowledge, such as the standpoint epistemologies or versions of feminist naturalized epistemology. In the same passage in her work in which she cites the words of a traveler in the South who had seen "forty of the largest and strongest women I ever saw together," Angela Davis quotes Marx on the importance of labor and its force in shaping consciousness:

> While it is hardly likely these women were expressing pride in the work they performed under the ever-present threat of the whip, they must have been aware nonetheless of their enormous power—their ability to produce and create. For, as Marx put it, "labor is the living, shaping fire; it represents the impermanence of things, their temporality." ... [P]erhaps these women had learned to extract from the oppressive circumstances of their lives the strength they needed to resist the daily dehumanization of slavery.[54]

Feminist standpoint epistemology has frequently cited its debt to Marx and Marxist theory—part of the idea has been that labor and the division of labor help create the epistemic standpoint of oppressed groups, and women in particular. Nancy Hartsock, in a recent paper delivered at an academic conference, phrased the point simply when she wrote that what characterizes standpoint theories is that they make use of the "importance of specific material conditions."[55] The mainstream interpretation of standpoint theory has always emphasized the extent to which women, globally, have been enmeshed in matters of the body and the senses, and have not been allowed to lead the lives of privileged and detached speculation that have resulted, as we have seen, in a somewhat noticeable similarity of ontology and metaphysics in male-dominated societies cross-culturally. If women then, in general, have been excluded from the speculative ratiocination characteristic not only of Athens, some of seventeenth-century Europe, and much of the history of Sanskrit-associated India, it is also true that the particularities of women's circumstances cross-culturally can be elicited by standpoint theory. Thus, as Davis has noted, a black feminist rebuilding of knowledge would rely not only on such key components as oral tradition, the comparative egalitarianism of women in West African societies, and the family-sundering aspects of slavery, but would also rely on the specific kinds of labor performed by black women in the New World. And here we have indeed food for thought, for, as we have seen, black women's "immersion" in the material world has manifested itself not only in traditional women's labor but in traditional men's (physical) labor. This means that standpoint epistemologies here would have to see the black woman as a double worker in Marx's sense, and the meaning of a phrase such as "double oppression" becomes more epistemically apparent. If special knowledges come from immersion in the realm of the senses and the natural, then black women do indeed have a strong and very material knowledge path, one in which there has been very little of the tradition of privileged and distanced speculation that is so central to patriarchal knowledge construction.

Further issues with respect to black feminist epistemics present themselves in ways that cannot be ignored. On the one hand, our project has enabled us to understand that postcolonial and poststructuralist responses to global challenges about knowledge acquisition are valuable and worth response. On the other hand, we have noted that to fail to engage the issues is to fail to make the political statements necessary for coming to grips with alterations of power and status. We can claim, if we so choose, that it is simply too hegemonic to make inquiries into knowledge patterns of non-white or non–First World women; we can assuage ourselves with the assumption that to do nothing assures us that we have not allowed ourselves to take the "superior" stance.

More so perhaps than any of the communities examined here, black American women, insofar as we may employ that rubric, push us, in their capacity as knowers and engenderers of knowledge, to examine our motives and our theoretical stances. Because black women of the New World, especially those within the United States or its territories/possessions, employ cultural constructs with which most of us are familiar, we may feel more secure in attempting to engage in a project of elucidating black feminist epistemologies. But precisely because the oppression visited upon the black population is one of the most extensive—certainly, in its simultaneous duration and viciousness, a matter of centuries and of legalized slavery—of modern times, the hegemonic stance seems to be foregrounded here in ways that we cannot evade. Thus it is perhaps too easy to write of an inter-section between feminist naturalized epistemologies and black feminist epistemics; perhaps we ought to exert more care.

Naomi Scheman, in an essay titled "Who Wants to Know? The Episte-mological Value of Values," grapples with much of this material.[56] Her remarks on our desires to be able to employ theory to structure phenomena in ways with which are antecedently familiar are especially pertinent:

> Classification can be illuminating, but we need to attend to our own agency in constructing any classificatory scheme, whether it be of elementary particles or of people, and not to mistake it for how the world divides itself up.... [Such theorizing] serve[s] to blur the complexities that the real world has a nasty habit of multiplying. Thus, much recent feminist theory has attempted to repudiate unified models of gender oppression, emphasizing instead the irreducible ... differences among people.[57]

Scheman's caveat is well taken, and if it seems too easy to attempt areas of commonality with respect to women's knowledge constructions in dif-ferent cultures, we might be tempted to cease and desist, resting easy in suspecting that we are on the right track by resisting the larger temptation to mistake our classificatory scheme for "how the world divides itself up." But ultimately, after careful examination of this problem, the essay in ques-tion ends with words that may signal a move forward for projects that attempt to find at least minimal rough-and-ready analogues, or at least delineate small portions of the web of intersection. Naomi Scheman also reminds us that "conceptual tools are not neutral, but neither are they untransformable in the hands of those who never were meant to touch them."[58] Her point is that any tool can provide a starting point for liberat-ing critique; whether it does depends at least in part on the aim.

The great difficulties attendant upon employing theory that was origi-nally written by and aimed largely at white feminist academics for purposes of discussing the knowledge production of black women in the New World then appear to be not insurmountable. There is no question that hegemony is involved; but to avoid a state of denial about such hegemony is already to take a step in the right direction. More important, in alembicating the African-derived patterns of knowledge growth and transmission in black American cultures, we draw attention to areas that previously were com-paratively unexamined. As has been indicated here, constructs having to do with oral tradition, West African female categorization, and the social con-structions stemming from slavery and its aftermath are constructs that, until recently, would scarcely have come under scrutiny by the academy. Thus such a project draws attention to that which was previously hidden and, in so drawing attention, serves as a signal to others.

The black women theorists who have engaged in such projects themselves have had to engage the same sorts of questions and develop their own responses. Thus Patricia Hill Collins and Angela Davis both are careful to state, at every step of the way, how the categories provided for analysis by white and/or nonblack feminist theorists may be useful in some ways and not at all useful in others. To some extent, the black woman of the nineteenth century in the United States was virtually not a "woman"—as Davis has indicated, she was an "anomaly."[59] But in examining her life and the lives of many other women—almost irrespective of the categories employed—we may perhaps be examining our own, and those of other human beings.

The African Diaspora in the New World

In their struggles to present the West African–derived cultural views to white and other critics, black commentators have frequently endeavored to indicate how awareness of these cultural patterns has suffused commentary (from whatever source) since the beginning of the printed word on the American continent. Thus contemporary thinkers such as Henry Louis Gates and Cornel West have made points with respect to the black American cultures very similar to those made by Frederick Douglass and Ida B. Wells; the cultures draw not only on oral tradition but on African metaphysics/ontology, the strength of women in the West African traditions, the importance of trickster figures, and so forth. Each of these features, as we have seen, is related to the functioning of women within the cultures, and each serves as a mirror to help us understand modes of knowing and of knowledge production.

As might be important from a symbolic standpoint, it turns out that the first novel written by a black American female author, *Our Nig*, by Harriet Wilson, was "lost" for more than one hundred years. Due to the investigative efforts of Gates and others, the novel was recovered and is now available in paperback form. In recounting his struggles to find and publish the original manuscript, Gates, in his introduction to the contemporary edition, writes:

> It is curious to trace the disappearance and reappearance of Harriet Wilson and her novel, *Our Nig*. It would be easier to imagine her presence in the tradition if we could identify some nineteenth-century reference to her,

even an obscure reference, which was then overlooked or doubted; but we have found none.[60]

Like much else done by black women, Wilson's initial efforts apparently sank without a trace. But the novel is itself about a young mulatto woman who tries to fight, as Wilson says in her frontispiece, against "slavery's shadows" that fall even in the North.[61]

If it has been difficult, historically, to come to a place where it is even possible to try to delineate a black feminist epistemics, this is scarcely more difficult than the battles fought by the culture as a whole, a point that is made, of course, by most commentators, male and female. Cornel West notes that there is really only one brief period in American history prior to the 1960s in which any attempt was made to achieve a kind of egalitarianism in black/white relations, and, unfortunately, that period was short-lived. He says that, during the twelve years of Reconstruction (roughly 1865–1877), "For the first time, American notions of citizenship are defined in the Fourteenth Amendment. Because the question is, what to do with these newly freed black men and women? ... Yet, come 1877, the military troops are withdrawn and the white supremacist forces come into power."[62] The up-and-down quality of this period is one, that unfortunately, reflects much of the history of the black population in the United States.

Because slavery forced upon the population conditions of work that, in a sense, also became conditions of cultural definition, little choice in the realms of working/knowing/coming to know was offered persons of African ancestry. It is altogether more remarkable, therefore, that the culture retained signal elements of strength and that, insofar as sheer numbers are concerned, the population grew. While the indigenous cultures of the North American region shrank dramatically, for example, and outside of Canada and Mexico number only, at best, two million to three million, black Americans are now some twenty-five million or more of the American population, and their input into the culture has been phenomenal, especially in the arts and areas of entertainment. Thus it may well be that the story that we have told here, of labor shaping (in particular) the modes of response of black women, is generally applicable to the culture, and reflects the role that a mixing of retention of original ontologies with beliefs forged by physical labor can provide. In any case, the striking qualities of the oral tradition were evident even to pre–Civil War commentators, and by the time the Union troops reached some southern areas, many white commentators were very much affected by what they saw and heard.[63]

If labor is, as Marx wrote, the "living fire," then physical strength and proximity to the material conditions of life shape their own ways of seeing. This vision is captured in almost all black literature, and remains a similar vision over a lengthy period of time. From Gayl Jones's *Corregidora* to Louise Meriwether's *Daddy Was a Number Runner*, black women authors have struggled to present the ways in which interactions with the world, by black women and men both, give birth to a vision of the world.[64] Although this endeavor has its analogues in the work produced by some other groups in the United States—notably the Chicana/o cultures—the difference is that the black American culture is, in a very great sense, more fully a product of American circumstances and fortunes. Thus, in comparison to much of what we have examined, black American culture is fundamentally American and is born of American oppression. In addition, most black Americans have had virtually no contact whatsoever with anything that might resemble a "home" culture; few have had the luxury of visiting African nations, and although many black Americans have roots in the West Indies and may have some ties to those areas, the lack of geographical proximity prohibits those ties from being developed.

The feminist epistemologies that we have examined, then, are born of completely different sets of circumstances, a fact that needs to be kept in mind in making an evaluation. Although the Asian nations that we have examined, with the exception of Nepal, have been victimized by colonialism (and even in the case of Nepal, colonialism in South Asia did have some effect), the New World cultures that we have encountered have been affected by a different sort of "colonial" mentality. Mexico and Guatemala have been independent nations long enough that the collective memory of colonialism is rather vague, and in the case of the Chicana/o cultures and the black American culture, the "colonialism" is more of an internalization. Only the black American culture has suffered to such a great extent this internalization—the effects of slavery, a truncation from the original cultures, and an enormous geographical distancing that makes retrieval of the original cultures difficult.

Cornel West has written that the greatest strength of the black American overview is its tradition of prophetic religion, combined with an intense development in the musical arts.[65] Slave preachers took the religion that was forced upon them and developed a new way of seeing—they were able to take that part of the religious view that spoke to them of redemption, and, in general, to reject the heedings of their masters to be "good" slaves. Although most preachers were male, a few were women, and women were, of course, very active in the development of the black church in almost every role that was available to them in the nineteenth century.[66] But for the black woman, this prophetic tradition became more than a way of speaking or relating to others in the community —it became a way of knowing. Manual labor, servitude, immersion in the needs of many bodies, and a strong belief in ultimate deliverance became a mode of functioning for black women and a source of strength for all. If women in every community have had to be the ones who, so to speak, made possible the speculative life of male intellectuals, black women have had to make it possible for plain existence to take place. Since so few in the community have had the luxury of speculation, it does not take the place vis-à-vis the black American community that it does with so many, but what this has meant for women is a redoubling of the problematic involved in the sustenance of everyday life.

Francie, the protagonist of *Daddy Was a Number Runner*, sees at an early age the lack of alternatives and the unrealistic bent of those who do not make an effort to deal with reality as it is.[67] At an early point in the novel, the young adolescent Francie is confronted by one of the ubiquitous speakers on a Harlem streetcorner. He exhorts the crowd to find a country of its own—"Black people should not be encouraged to remain in the white man's land," he says.[68] But Francie, ever the realist, has a different take on things. She knows that some ideas probably will not pan out. As she says to herself as she moves away from the speaker, "Who wanted to go back to Africa? Didn't we have enough trouble right here?"[69] The novel ends with the word "Shit." An older, more mature Francie sees that the struggles that she has to endure will be never-ending, and that the courage to get through those struggles is something that she will have to find on her own. It is this awareness of everyday reality, and the strength to move through it, that has been the hallmark of the black woman's experience in America.[70]

Part 4

Endings

Chapter 10

Retrievals/Outcomes

From the outset, we have admitted that attempting to delineate modes of knowing for women that might in some sense constitute feminist epistemics or gynocentric styles of knowledge construction was a dangerous project. In the introductory chapter, we examined various critiques, both poststructuralist and postcolonial, with an eye to how these lines of criticism might inform our view, admitting that some, perhaps, would claim that no such project could or should be undertaken.

But after having taken a fairly close examination of a number of societies and cultures in which women's knowledge projects have emerged, both for local and international investigators, we are in a position to draw some broad conclusions. Once again, the rough-strokes nature of our conclusions implies that attempting to find areas of commonality may be pushing in the wrong direction. Wittgensteinian family resemblances are best, one would suppose, although on some large issues—such as the differences between cultures originally possessing written languages and those that do not—some common areas may emerge. In addition, our efforts have yielded other fruit, as not all of the questions that one might want to ask about women in a culture involve knowledge or knowledge-related categories. Questions of rights, investigations involving sexualities, abuses both physical and mental all pose themselves almost immediately as areas of endeavor for those interested in women on a global basis.[1] At a later point we will investigate some of these issues, but the scope of our project demands that we make some attempt to characterize those family resemblances or lack of them, so that we can proceed.

Some very broad resemblances, although at best yielding only penultimate constructs, revolve around fundamental androcentric tendencies in many or most cultures, manifesting themselves in a variety of ways. Although a poststructuralist might find it naive to think in these terms, poststructuralism itself has, of course, been used by many feminists to make similar techniques. In cultures without written languages, androcentrism—weaker in some regions, stronger in others—has tended to manifest itself both in kinship structures, property-owning codifications, and systems of worship. Here we must tread especially carefully, for it is evident, merely on the basis of our examination, that many cultures, such as the West African groups that gave rise to the New World African-derived cultures, and some indigenous groups in North America, possess kinships that are more matrilineal and matrifocal. These kinship structures do, of course, affect the ownership of property and its transmission, and are crucial to the notion of rights (itself, of course, a Western notion) within a culture. Likewise, worship, insofar as an account of it may be ascertained that is at least minimally divorced from Eurocentric categorizing, is related to these other cultural constructs.

Again we find that much of what has been done in postmodern attempts to form a critique of theorizing about women is helpful, but only in measured doses. The difficulty, as previously articulated, is that without some attempts at finding family resemblances, much of the political project of feminism fails, and it is also the case that the notion that there is such a thing as a "gender construct" (to which we will return) becomes vitiated. Although our attempts may have a bit of a grosgrain quality, they are valuable nonetheless, both for what they tell us about Eurocentric thinking and for what they tell us about the impact of such thinking on other cultures. Micaela di Leonardo, for example, takes up the ongoing critique of oversimplification and essentialism in anthropology in her own work, and notes the extent to which "archaeologists nowadays more rarely 'map' assumed (often sexist) sex-role behavior onto constructions of prehistoric social life."[2] Nevertheless, it is a constant battle in anthropology, as well as in other social sciences, to avoid the tendency to place the gender constructs of the observers on those observed. Di Leonardo also writes:

> A crosscultural and historical perspective that stresses divisions among women on the basis of class, color, era and culture is the best corrective to this ubiquitous tendency to assume one homogeneous form of female agency and, *a priori*, of female moral superiority.[3]

In a sense, then, what we have done here meets at least minimal standards for Di Leonardo's "corrective." Through the lens of Western feminist scholarship and views, gender roles become much more fluid when examined among the Nyeshangte, as we did in our work on Nepal, or among the

West African groups who are the predominant forebears of black New World cultures. But by the same token, there are indeed some family resemblances and areas of commonality, and one does not have to stretch unduly to find them. Because of the importance of childbearing and taboos regarding sexuality and reproduction in almost all human cultures, stratifications within the cultures involving gender roles frequently employ similar or analogous concepts. To fail to recognize this is, in a sense, to do the situation an injustice, since the implication would be that societies are so grossly different that the birth and rearing of children simply is not important in some societies.

Female agency, then, changes from culture to culture, and it is important to try to recognize the ramifications of this fact. A notion such as *shakti* might simply be glossed as "female power," given a naive view of such a notion, but, as we have seen, this concept is considerably more complex, and rests not only on preceding ontological assumptions (which are seldom set out by observers), but also on concepts having to do with purification attained through ritual, and so forth. This particular construct then becomes one that, although it is not unrecognizable or incomprehensible (after some intellectual effort) illustrates the difficulties involved in easy assumptions and the importance of underlying metaphysical systems in any given culture, particularly insofar as they may relate to gender terms themselves.

If it is the case that essentialist tensions are unavoidable, the very fact of their existence tells us a great deal about the phenomena under examination. We cannot have such tensions unless there do indeed appear to be some constructs that are more-or-less cross-cultural, and unless it is also the case that, in postcolonial vein, we feel somewhat guilty or awkward, as theoreticians, in attempting to push these concepts where they will not or should not go. The latter phrase is revelatory: it is not clear whether they "should not go" because it actually is the case that there is little intellectual fit, or whether we feel, on some inarticulate or semiarticulate level, that they should not go for politicized reasons. Theorists trained in the Eurocentric tradition—and almost every theorist is, to some extent—may feel the dictates of hegemony all too keenly, and may be loath to use concepts even to the minimal extent that they are usable.

A project in feminist epistemics or feminist epistemologies demands that we investigate, insofar as we are able, how knowledge categories are used in other cultures. It is inevitable that when we make this investigation, our yardstick for comparison is the application of similar or analogous conceptualizations in our own cultures. This caveat having been repeated many times, we can either proceed with the project or refrain from proceeding with the project. The project in and of itself would seem to be a valuable one. International statistics indicate the extent to which the vast majority of the world's most severely poor and illiterate people are women and girls.[4] Initiatives, scholarly and otherwise, indicating the extent to which women are either developing new knowledge-related categories or altering preexisting ones would seem to be of great value.

Redefining Essentialisms

Some attempts at employing the category "woman" across cultures have foundered because of what many have deemed to be very real and perhaps misguided attempts to use Western rubrics in a variety of ways. Even within American society, feminist critics have taken to task a number of thinkers for what they appear to believe are gross generalizations about "women."[5] An example of the type of categorization that has proved to be problematic for some is Nancy Chodorow's psychoanalytic construction of the notion of gender reproduction:

> The care and socialization of girls by women ensures the production of feminine personalities founded on relation and connection, with flexible rather than rigid ego boundaries, and with a comparatively secure sense of gender identity.[6]

The assumption by some that Chodorow meant these theses to hold on a "universal" basis (which certainly seems unlikely) has led many to question the applicability of some labels taken from Western feminist theory to other cultures. But there is another, less naive, way of viewing the project of asking questions about women (particularly knowledge-related questions) cross-culturally. Most human cultures will have concepts and categories that have to do with knowledge and knowledge acquisition: human survival demands it. The point of departure then becomes how it is that women function within their societies given the existence of culturally defined norms and constructs. Although some postmodernists may find even this approach too naive, it is one that has been employed, with useful results, in the past.

The danger, of course, is—as has been repeatedly reiterated—in the too easy assumption of areas of commonality or analogy. There simply is no clear way around this conceptual conundrum. We cannot engage in the project of feminist theorizing in the global sense without some kind of a conceptual apparatus with which to begin: inevitably, a penumbra of the thoughts and value systems of those who begin the work hangs over, and to some extent clouds, the endeavors. Perhaps the best tonic for this ailment is a raised consciousness: we need to be aware of our tendencies to project ourselves into other cultures, realizing full well that, even with the greatest care taken, there will be episodes of misunderstanding and chauvinism. Perhaps an aid here would be a brief look at endeavors that did not, originally, have a "raised consciousness." Said's work on Orientalism has achieved the impact that it has precisely because Said was writing about a naive overview that lacked self-consciousness and was unaware of its own assumption of superiority and importance. With respect to some of the late-nineteenth- and early-twentieth-century work on Islamic and Muslim cultures, Said writes:

> Beneath the idioms there was a layer of doctrine about the Orient; this doctrine was fashioned out of the experiences of many Europeans, all of them converging upon such essential aspects of the Orient as the Oriental character, Oriental despotism, Oriental sensuality, and the like. For any European during the nineteenth century—and I think one can say this almost without qualification—Orientalism was such a system of truths.[7]

In other words, there is a difference, and it would appear to be an important one, between articulating a set of "truths" about a culture's "sensuality" or "despotism" and attempting to delineate some areas that might, with varying degrees of strength and weakness, be susceptible to Western categorization or cross-pollination. But in a sense Said is quite right when, at the end of his work, he warns against the "seductive degradation" of knowledge.[8] We must be ever vigilant and ever on guard.

This said, we can recapitulate briefly two related modes of inquiry into knowledge-associated modes of production for women that we have examined here. The first has to do with the importance of female-identified knowledge categories in the given culture: these may be accepted, discarded, or examined to a greater or lesser degree by women within the culture, the capacity to choose varying particularly by the level of formal education received. The second is even more important: that general conceptual schemes having to do with knowledge acquisition within the culture, given the development of most human cultures, are almost always male-identified. Yet women will, as we have seen, reappropriate or internalize these schemes in a variety of ways, and the ways in which they do so are informative—vastly so—for our project.

Although these two notions are not necessarily mutually exclusive, they tend to be exclusionary in the sense that the rejection of one (the female identified, in many cases) signals the reappropriation of the other, or may signal the reconfiguration of the first after a "meeting" with the second, more male-identified, construct. Thus cross-cultural work on feminist epistemics looks not only for knowledge construction and knowledge-related categories, but for the ways in which these categories are defined within a society, and then—most interestingly—for the ways in which the categories are actually employed, especially with respect to gender divisions. Part of the difficulty with this task, as we have seen, is that there may be no ready demarcators of gender divisions, or, if there are such demarcators, they may not be made along lines that are susceptible of analysis in Eurocentric terms. Nevertheless, the human facts of childbirth, menstruation, lactation and other such body-oriented gender divisions indicate, in most societies, at least some differences that are more gender related than not. Taking this broad delineation as a point of departure enables us to be on the lookout for the kinds of truncations and divisions in which we are theoretically interested.

Thus essentialism, especially with regard to gender, women, knowledge and all of the areas that might be implicated in global feminist epistemologies, takes on new meaning. Clearly, it is indeed too naive to construct a category "woman" and then attempt to fit the two billion-plus females on the planet into the category. But the combination of family resemblances, analogies, similarities and parallelisms—although kaleidoscopic in its array—points us in a direction that is helpful and that, perhaps most important, ultimately furthers the goals of empowerment and enfranchisement that almost all of the factual material we have on the status of females indicates are worthy and necessary goals.

Many of those who have become disenchanted with "postmodern" theorizing have complained that the spurious liberatory moves of such thinking do little to alter the plain facts of everyday misery and oppression for most of the human beings on Earth. Moves against "hegemony," particularly those moves that are confined almost entirely to academic circles, most likely do little to feed, clothe, or make literate any number of persons. But some movements, already grounded (whether consciously or not) in a plain appraisal of localized feminist epistemologies, such as those in Bangladesh, are indeed making some small headway against the tide of indifference, corruption, and institutionalized misogyny that works against the vast majority of the world's women. Now we can see how it is that the project of attempting to discern a variety of gynocentric modes of knowing is a valuable one: it not only tells us about ourselves, but it has the incomparably greater value of at least making some small amelioration of suffering possible.

Essentialism, then, may very well be a misplaced concern. It has become a term used by many to attempt to dissuade theorists from searching for the very resemblances and intersections discussed here. But in so far as thinkers are dissuaded, the "antiessentialist" rhetoric may indeed be very wrongheaded. Such rhetoric is enormously disempowering. The struggle to begin to find places for growth, movement, and change cross-culturally and globally can scarcely begin if we do not investigate or attempt to find out anything about other cultures and the positions of women within those cultures.[9]

With Broad Strokes and Grosgrain

In the preceding chapters we have examined eight cultures with an eye toward those aspects of the cultures that are knowledge related and their reappropriation (or, in some cases, their initial appropriation) by women. Although each culture has defining features, and although, again, some might feel it remiss to try to find family resemblances, one piece of information stands out immediately: there seems to be an easy delineation between those cultures that originally possessed written languages and those that did not. For the purposes we have employed here, only four of the social organizations to which we have given close examination originally possessed written cultures in the sense that the writing predates contact with Europeans and is an intrinsic part of the lives of the groups under examination—and even here there will still be some debate. For our purposes, the Sanskrit-derived languages of Northern India, the Dravidian languages of Southern India (particularly Tamil), the Islamic Bengali culture of Bangladesh, and the larger culture of Mexico have written forms and structures. To push the portrayal in the other direction, the mountain cultures of Nepal, although they have in many cases been exposed to written Tibetan (or its variants), rely more on oral tradition, as do the indigenous cultures of Guatemala, although, as we have seen, the *ladino* portion of Guatemalan society is similar in its social structure to much of Mexico. Although Chicana/o cultures exist, of course, in a Spanish medium, oral tradition is very important here, because so many immigrants have had, in the past, little literacy, or little opportunity to use the literacy they possessed. Finally, we understand that importance of oral tradition for much of the New World black culture, since the West African societies from which it predominantly originated did not, in general, have written languages.

These kinds of distinctions, dear to anthropologists and linguists, are crucial for our project because, in general, it is the speculative and caste-dominated tradition of cultures with written languages that most clearly exemplifies androcentric theorizing.[10] In other words, much of what is ratiocinative, unavailable to the senses, and most clearly grand speculative metaphysics (even if it is not labeled as such) in the traditions of various cultures is written and inscribed (literally), not intended for women or unlearned persons, and contains the hierarchic doctrine of the group. As we have seen, these "high" or grand themes of the culture frequently degrade women, posit knowledge categories for which women are deemed incapable or unworthy, and often speak in overarching terms of an inner, yet-to-be-revealed truth. It is clear that with respect to various views of dominant groups in Northern India, Southern India, Bangladesh, and Mexico, the existence of written tradition is crucial.[11]

Oral tradition, even if accompanied in some cases by some cultural artifacts in written form accessible only to the elite, may already indicate cultural views that, because they are presumably older and may precede forms of early settled agriculture, are less intensely androcentric. Thus some West African societies, some indigenous North American groups, and many aspects of animist-oriented Nepalese mountain cultures do not seem to possess, in as great a measure, the static fixedness of intense masculinism that is found in other cultures.

If it is the case, as we are arguing here, that elements of the oral tradition seem tied to elements of originally more matrilineal and quite possibly more gynocentric cultures, one of the conceptualizations that is called into question by such theorizing is indeed ethnicity itself. For if it seems a hallmark of many more technologically sophisticated cultures that the culture defines itself as the expense of women, what it means for a people to form an identifiable ethnic group may itself be called into question. Cynthia Enloe makes a similar point when she claims that "an ethnic group must have reality in the minds of its members, not just in the eye of the beholder."[12] All of the societies and groups examined here may make some minimal claims to cohesion, whether in their own eyes or in the eyes of others, but it is intriguing to note that at least some of that social identity and group structure—in the case of Mexico, for example, or in many of the Northern Indian cultures, such as those of Bengal or Maratha—comes because of the ways in which women are defined in the culture.

Thus the speculative tradition that has been associated with a certain sort of airy philosophizing and the development of a rich metaphysics is, as we have seen, frequently connected to the rise of patriarchy and the development of less gynocentric societies. Although remnants of women's communal modes of knowledge acquisition, goddess obeisance, and other gynocentric forms may still exist within such cultures, they appear to be somewhat stronger in groups such as those of West Africa, indigenous societies of Central America, or mountain societies of Nepal, where there is no strong written tradition and a much sparser written metaphysics.

The existence of women's modes of knowing and reappropriation by women of other forms of knowing may also be related to contemporary industrial strength of cultures. Yet there is no easy answer or facile formula here—as we have seen, some groups can scarcely be said to have begun any process of industrialization, yet due to the ubiquitous movement of Western goods and services (not to mention such comparatively new phenomena as the Internet) a sort of postmodern view has taken hold in many quarters, which may either obviate or even increase gynocentricity. Thus, as we have seen, among the Nyeshangte exposure to Western culture seems to break down, somewhat, the more matrifocal elements of the culture (and even increase spousal abuse), whereas contemporary Chicana work, whether theoretical or lived, seems to reflect the booming and robust postmodern mix that is the American Southwest, with its rampant consumerism, display of commodity labels, and so forth.

In short, there is no one way of conceptualizing the rise in patriarchal thought patterns, either in European cultures or in the cultures that we have examined here, but it is clear that there are some striking parallels. The Eurocentricity of much of the commentary on the "philosophy of India," for example is quite comprehensible, given the ready fit of many European/Western philosophical categories into the thought patterns of the Sanskrit-related languages. Here, whatever the outcome, it is obvious that European theorists did not have to reach to employ such metaphysical terms as "cosmology" and "levels of ontology."

However unhappy the fruits of a Eurocentric analysis may be—and however hegemonic it seems to persist with Eurocentric patterns of categorization—the fruit of such analysis is undeniable, for the conceptualization patterns of many cultures already, because of the structure of many written languages and because of the ways in which written thought tends to proceed, bear the templates that we can use for philosophical exploration. Thus feminist epistemics, while weaving a web in its back-and-forth articulation between a variety of cultures, will in some cases be easier work, in some cases more difficult work, depending, as has already been stated, on the relationships of the cultures in question to Indo-European language groups and categories of thought.

New work in education circles around the globe is making all of us more aware of the divergences in human ontologies and the ways in which the taken-for-grantedness of ontologies within given cultures helps to construct the culture. Educators in Australia, for example, are in the process of coming to grips with the worldviews of the persons referred to as "aboriginals." In doing such work, they are finding that some ways of carving up experience seem to have little, if any, ready intersection with, for example (broadly construed) European ways. But this is particularly what our project is about—although we have examined only a small number of cultures, we can already see the intersections, lack of evident intersections, parallels, rough-and-ready analogues, and, in some cases, no apparent analogues in the cultures in question. It benefits feminist work all over the world for thoughtful feminists to be aware of the enormous variety in human conceptual apparatuses.

Knowledge, Knowing, and Working

If, as Cynthia Enloe writes, contemporary modes of communication can "raise ethnic self-consciousness among persons who hold similar values,"[13] it is also true that modes of labor, forces of agricultural production, ready availability of food and climate all give rise to their own knowledge-related conceptualization patterns and categories. As we saw in an earlier chapter, Wiredu was concerned to make it clear that many West African worldviews are rampantly empirical because he knew that societies that rely on early-settled agriculture modes of production for food cannot afford to look at such production in purely speculative terms.

All over the world, women do an enormous portion of the daily work that is accomplished, and in many cases in closest proximity not only to small children, ill family members and those in need, but in close proximity to the earth and animals. Because of the seasonal nature of plowing and crop growth, men in most developing nations have periods of time that are comparatively free from such work, but women, on the whole, do not. If there are moments free from searching for water or food preparation, then they are probably taken up by the care of small children, aged relatives, or animals that may be in the near vicinity of the home. The unending variety of such tasks, in most cultures, precludes women's having the leisure to spend time in speculation, and, as we have seen, in many or most cultures this has precluded their entering the realms of "higher knowledge," that is, knowledge divorced from the senses.

One might be tempted to be naive about how important this categorization is for knowledge in most cultures until one remembers the history of science, philosophy, and knowledge in general as it is usually presented to Westerners. For once, the Western bias is not terribly important here—as we have seen, in cultures with written languages there tends to be a hierarchical tradition of things "known" and "knowable," and this tradition, at its upper end, is generally thought to be not within the reach of women, laborers, or those who lack whatever it is that the tradition deems to be an intellectual orientation. Jonathan Barnes, in his *Early Greek Philosophy*, describes the origins of science and philosophy insofar as the Eurocentric tradition is concerned:

> First, and most simply, the Presocratics invented the very idea of science and philosophy. They hit upon that special way of looking at the world which is the scientific or rational way. They saw the world as something ordered and intelligible, its history following an explicable course and its different parts arranged in some comprehensible system. The world was not a random collection of bits, its history was not an arbitrary series of events.[14]

The last sentence may indeed be the key here; one wants to say that, indeed, if the world were a "random collection of bits," it would be virtually impossible to determine this, given a set predisposition to interpret the data in a certain way.

But this is precisely what "knowledge," in most traditions, presupposes. To be sure, as we have seen, cultures that proceed by oral tradition generally do not conceptualize in such a rigid fashion—but then again that is why so many such cultures were initially viewed as "primitive" and "savage" by visiting Europeans. The point, then, is that the accumulation of information taken from the senses—especially the type of information gathered through physical labor, the tending of infants, children, the elderly and animals, or through tasks of cleaning and caring—does not, in many or most traditions, count as knowledge. Unless codified, stored, generalized over, and viewed under some hierarchical rubric, such information is usually viewed as myth, fabrication, or, at best, "folk wisdom"—that is to say, no wisdom at all.

Our task with respect to global feminist epistemologies, then, has been to try to articulate what tropes, categories, and concepts women historically have used in a given society, how they are being used today, and, if possible, to determine how women have come to reappropriate (if indeed they have come to reappropriate) categories that have been historically male. Within the Western cultures, it is comparatively easy to trace the path of women epistemically since the Enlightenment, for example. It is a path fraught with obstacles, but one in which women increasingly carved their own way, men increasingly came to be swayed by women's arguments (at least with respect to such specifics as education), and, more recently, women came to reappropriate a wide variety of male conceptual schemes, especially with regard to the sciences, medicine, and the law.

But tracing the path with other cultures has proved to be difficult work. Oral tradition cultures are no longer, in the twentieth century, purely oral tradition cultures. In almost all cases, they have suffered significant contamination at the hands of developed nations, and the contamination itself almost invariably leads to altered views of the status of women—indeed, as we have seen with the Nyeshangte and similar groups, it may lead to views that are to the detriment of women. An additional sort of contamination occurs that frequently renders artifacts of the culture in question valuable commodities from the standpoint of Westerners. With respect to the societies of West Africa, for example, many have been at pains to point out that what is now considered "art" from these societies almost always originally had a function, either sacred or mundane. Then the commentary on such work, again by Westerners or by persons trained in the Western tradition, inevitably distorts the work to some extent as Eurocentric categories are employed to discuss non-Eurocentric phenomena. (Robert Farris Thompson, for example, encounters this problem writ large when he attempts to discuss artifacts from West African cultures. They cannot be discussed or made intelligible for Western readers without some employment of non-African categories.)[15]

Nevertheless, as we have maintained all the way along, we cannot discuss the status of women across the globe in terms of the pressing issues that international organizations strive to bring to our attention without employment of some concepts and terms that are already familiar to us. And it may well be the case—at least our preliminary investigations into some cultures seem to indicate that it is—that the postmodern pastiche that is rapidly taking place over much of the planet has its own susceptibility for feminist growth and development.

Knowledge categories, like cultures, are fluid, and what was once inaccessible to women, the illiterate, or simply those deemed unworthy may become accessible, particularly given the influence of technological change. By the same token, categories that were more traditionally open to women may also change—they may gain or lose status, males may participate, and so forth.[16] "High" knowledge may come to be seen as archaic, and its propounders out of touch with reality, even as, inevitably, some from the disparaged groups will become attracted to the possibility of such knowledge.

Knowing and information acquired from the senses may gain in status when it appears to become marketable, or when it is noticed by visitors who suddenly "appreciate" its worth.

Even in oral tradition cultures, there has almost always been a type of knowledge or activity that is not open to women. Traditionally, it has usually encompassed that which has been believed to be most important, most sacred, most valuable to a people. But as cultures continue to gain contact with each other, it is no longer possible to maintain such rigid boundaries. Just as Enloe reminds us that the notion of an ethnic group is one of shared *"clusters* of beliefs and values" (her emphasis), gender roles have usually been defined in such ways.[17] But definitions of both groups and their ways of knowing are fluid. Changing conditions yield changing definitions and archetypes, and attempting to trace possible future trajectories is contingent upon watching and noticing the altering conceptual schemes. Knowledge and women have, categorically, often been at odds, particularly where knowledge has the highest status. But much that we have seen indicates that this particular opposition is changing at a rapid pace.

Sexualities and Categories

Much of the work that we have done has assumed an implicit sort of heterosexuality, or has left the notion of sexualities unexamined, while pursuing the relationship of knowledge-related concepts to the social structure. But it would be an oversight not to at least examine minimally the relationship between sexualities and knowledge, or the ways in which this social construction influences much of what transpires in human societies.

That androcentric forms of thought have the power they do is more properly related to a take on sexuality that permeates, at an obvious level, much human functioning cross-culturally and globally. Enforced heterosexuality helps to affirm the dominance not only of male power generally, but of privileged male modes of thought. The pristine quality of high-level androcentric theorizing—the type of theorizing that we have just examined with respect to speculation and the establishment of an overview—operates because of the presumed less-than-pristine quality of anything gynocentric. It is, of course, as we have mentioned, the relationship between the gynocentric and birth, lactation, menstruation, and the performance of daily tasks related to the messiness of life in general that drives both the derogation of the gynocentric and the privileging of the androcentric.

Because of this, there is an interesting twist tied to social constructions of differing sorts of sexualities both cross-culturally, and, of course, in the general Western sense. Divergent sexualities have frequently been associated with specialized knowledge—from the berdache of a number of Native American cultures to the eunuch castes of northern India, any deviation from the presumed heterosexual norm has frequently resulted in the assumption that other types of knowledge are at work. Although we cannot investigate those types of knowledge here, what can be said is that this sort of thinking can be used as a counter, as it were, to our main line of argument: the association of homoerotic relationships of both sexes, changes in gender status due to differing dress, or any other type of perceived deviance from heterosexual norms with categories of wisdom or knowing merely recapitulates the enforced hierarchical status of the androcentric, male-associated privileged modes and their "normality." They derive their epistemic force from their opposition to gynocentricity, and any other form of sexuality that moves away from the heterosexual construction appears to undermine the dominance of the androcentric/gynocentric opposition.

When Bette Denich writes, with respect to sexuality among the Montenegrin, "Why should women's sexuality be such an extreme focus for the exertion of male control? Why should the reactions against women's sexual freedom be so severe?," she is categorizing anthropologically and asking questions about the structural import of various kinds of marriages in the societies under examination.[18] But these questions, asked rhetorically, signal the presence of a deeper divide, one of epistemic import.

When women are not under heterosexual control and dominance, they presumably will establish different strategies of knowledge gathering and acquisition, and this will in turn engender, as the current usage goes, different forms of knowledge. Although it may well be too simplistic to suggests that the redoubled force of gynocentrism in lesbian relationships will generally signal differing forms of cognition, it is not beyond the mark to suggest that this is the case. Gloria Anzaldúa, again, suggests that one manifestation of such a move is the tendency to resist the separations, bifurcations, markers, and divisions that normally drive most conceptualizing under androcentric dominance. She provides a small hint of this in an essay in Trujillo's *Living Chicana Theory* anthology when she writes:

> Often I am asked, "What is your primary identity, being lesbian or working-class or Chicana?" . . . I am asked to bracket each, to make boundaries around each, so as to articulate one particular facet of identity only.[19]

Clearly, Anzaldúa feels that the need to label and categorize, in whatever form, is one that is a holdover from androcentric domination and Complete

Accountism. Although this may be somewhat simplistic, the strong effect of gynocentrism that is separated (insofar as that is possible) from male domination and mandatory heterosexuality may be one of breaking down boundaries of all kinds.

Thus Denich's rhetorical question, "Why should women's sexuality be such an extreme focus for the exertion of male control?" is answered partially by the rejoinder that uncontrolled female sexuality breaks down knowledge structures and boundaries. One does not need to be some kind of structuralist to see that this is the case, nor is there a particular need for Continental theory here, although it might in some circumstances be relevant. It is obvious, as feminist theorists have long maintained, that the conceptual apparatuses of most societies (indeed, in this instance one is tempted to say all) are strongly tied to male dominance, and it certainly seems to be the case with those societies possessing written languages, as we have seen.

The dangers posed by changing sexualities, even for developed or First World nations, are not merely social, but cognitive dangers. The contemporary black author Hilton Als is able to write in his recent work *The Women* that the gay black Manhattanite Owen Dodson was his first "woman" because his analysis of the category "Negress" reveals it to be socially defined.[20] The "Negress" avoids self-revelation, but she does so because of the dominance of the black male and his need for affirmation. Als's work, which has left an impression on East Coast literary circles, reminds us of the cognitive dangers involved in sexual identity transgression and the new vistas which may be opened up by such transgression. In many societies, of course, such new vistas cannot be opened up—at least not with ease—without great danger to the openers. It is precisely this type of opening that male cognitive dominance and conceptualization patterns are dedicated to avoiding.

Changing sexualities mark, as has been said by many, the decline in domination not only of patriarchal structures but of any kind of space with clear demarcations and borders. It is probably for this reason that the "borders" metaphor has become such a popular one, and has made its way into many areas of cultural studies. The desire to control the sexuality of women is but one way of controlling knowledge categories, conceptualization schemes, and worldviews, and these ways are all susceptible to derangement once the changes in sexuality that we see currently in many societies are under way.

Lesbian theorists have frequently written of "naming," and the problem of naming is, of course, but one more example of the general problem of

attribution of concepts. The non-male-identified woman was frequently
seen in many previous cultures as a danger; such women were frequently
vulnerable to attack, and in the sixteenth and seventeenth centuries in
Europe were often victimized by the *Malleus Maleficorum* and the search
for witches.[21] Gynocentric knowledge patterns, escape from male dominance, desire for independence, and different ways of seeing were all implicated in this original Renaissance attack on women, and parallel social
structures may be seen in a variety of contexts today. Whether or not sexuality becomes an issue in any given social structure is not important; what
is important is that the issue of sexuality lies at the heart of many of the
controversies, including controversies alluded to here, that surface in culture after culture and society after society. In an androcentrically structured
world in which it is important to keep boundaries impermeable, few phenomena seem to require social control more than the sexualities of women.
A woman who escapes male dominance is a dangerous woman indeed.

Conclusions, Wished-for and Actual

Our project of delineating knowledge categories and worlds of knowing
across several different cultures and societies has helped us point out areas
of commonality and areas of difference across these social structures. If, as
has been said here many times, it seems too naive to hope for many areas of
commonality, it would also be naive to insist that there are no such intersections. As indicated previously, cultures with written languages seem to
possess at least some demonstrable areas of intersection with respect to
gender-related issues simply because of the ways in which the acquisition of
writing in a culture affects conceptualization.

Many of the NGOs and CBOs whose work we have examined in the various groups under perusal here have dealt with similar issues at length.
Specificities with respect to areas of intersection and realms of difference
have manifested themselves in UN conferences on the status of women and
in the work of international rights organizations, such as Amnesty International.[22] There is no easy solution with regard to the continuing problem
of women within various cultures supporting aspects of their culture that
appear, to Western or First World women, to be denigrating to women in
general or to be so wildly sexist and abusive as to not be bearable. But part
of the project of establishing a dialogue between women from various
nations and societies, presumably, would involve demarcating the various
intersections to which we have alluded.

Many of those who have become concerned about the plight of women on an international basis have tried to theorize with respect to transcultural norms on the basis of some value that does indeed seem to be transcultural, such as health. In other words, it might be deemed offensive for a practice to be called into question simply because it violates a norm that is obviously Western or Eurocentric, such as "rights"; on the other hand, an appeal to health matters—since all societies presumably need healthy individuals in order to function—might be more acceptable. Arnold Eiser, for example, has written that appeals based simply on health might be of assistance in reducing the incidence of Female Genital Mutilation:

> I submit that health is a transcultural value that can meet the standard of universality. The universal longing for well-being constitutes the lingua franca of health.... Although cultural differences abound in the population I serve, there is a near unanimity about what patients desire from health services.[23]

But intriguing as Eiser's point is, it leaves comparatively unexamined the sort of claim we are making here: we cannot adequately assess the value of health (or any other good alleged or purported to be transcultural) within a culture without finding out more about epistemic categories within that society. Insofar as a concept of health might be applicable to women—particularly if it is to bear upon any of the number of areas traditionally associated with things female, such as menstruation, lactation, and childbirth—we need more information about how women in such societies have traditionally conceptualized their own relation to their bodies, other members of their societies and the world around them, and we cannot adequately obtain this without a grasp of the relevant epistemological data.

Gynocentric construals of knowing or knowledge-related concepts have always been available for perusal; it simply is the case that, unfortunately, they have in general not been examined (either cross-culturally, or, to some extent, within a given society) until recently. But just as manifestations of the classically masculinist modes of knowing within each cultural group frequently tell us something about the sacred or the transcendental, the ways in which women have historically functioned within a society are helpful in seeing what it is that constitutes "other" forms of knowing—even if they are not labeled as knowledge—within a given group. This derided, obscured, or elided knowledge is often the province of women, and it frequently is the type of knowledge that has a great deal to do with the living of everyday life, as opposed to speculation about it. Insofar as androcentric categorization supersedes or passes over the everyday, it is often of little assistance in the performance of the types of daily tasks that are required for members of a society to obtain food, shelter, or to remain healthy and functional.

Although we might wish for there to be more recognition of the gyno-centric patterns functioning within given groups, experience tells us that such recognition will often be slow in coming, or that when it does arrive, it will often be tied to a masculinist project of reclamation of the gynocentric mode for male-driven purposes. Nevertheless, as we move into the twenty-first century, the well-being of the world depends upon such reclamation.

In his work tieing Mary Shelley and her literary efforts to the path of science in general, Theodore Roszak has written, with respect to the Western formulations of rationality and objectivity:

> If anything, the commitment to demonstrable truth on which scientists have set their hearts may help them to see reality more readily than those whose beliefs have no respect for evidence of any kind. But by the same token, the great pitfall for scientists is to believe they have a method that uniquely and automatically guarantees they will transcend prejudice and preconception.[24]

As Roszak is pointing out, there is no such thing as a method that "uniquely and automatically" guarantees a lock on the actual, and it is a combination of this sort of belief with colonial attitudes and other forms of bigotry that has prevented our making inquiries into the knowledge modes of "others" for such a long time. But the changing structure of the world (not to mention the changing structure of global markets, so important, as we have seen here, to knowledge categorization) demands that we now acknowledge multiple efforts at conceptualization, and the encouraging news is that such acknowledgment appears to be forthcoming, if sometimes only in minimal ways. The Bengali thinker Roksana Nazneen is able to work on the problem of violence in Bangladeshi marriages at least partly because she has been influenced by the work of Western feminists and Western domestic violence groups, even if not all of their work is relevant to the specific Bangladeshi situation.[25]

Not only global change, but movement and variation within Western communities and within more standard sorts of theorizing, signal that the time has come to recognize different sorts of epistemics and the profound implications that their valorization might have for many. Current efforts to resuscitate female thinkers in the Western tradition frequently allude either to the previously little recognized qualities of their thought, or the fact that their work has been overshadowed by the work of male companions, despite whatever original merits the work might have possessed.[26]

Persons who want to learn to think globally about issues involving women—and human beings in general—should take heart from the multiple advertences throughout our culture to new forms of communication and their empowering qualities. In the developed nations even small children are now being encouraged to use the Internet to correspond with others, and the general great change in the availability of travel signals new levels of awareness of international women's and human rights issues. These forms of awareness also come with their own drawbacks, however; there is probably not much that can substitute for living and working in a region if high levels of awareness are to be achieved. The many spurious uses of cyberspace, for example, show that it is both foolish and arrogant to think that technological advances always or even usually have beneficial results. But the good news is that work, both intellectual and otherwise, that had previously been hidden can now be brought to the fore, and many more of us have access to tools and modes of travel that can make other cultures real for us.

Finally, although it might seem unncessary to say so, reading and study can be valuable simply from the standpoint of ordinary consciousness raising. Because so little work was done on global feminist issues until recently, many comparatively well-educated European, American, Canadian, and Australasian feminists knew little about women's issues in other cultures. The advent of new lines of scholarship, however (many of which we have alluded to here) brings to the fore cultural and political foci that have a reverberative effect on one's own cultural constructs and one's life.

The thought patterns of the some six billion individuals on our planet themselves form realms of knowing, as we learn more about cognition, neuroscience, and the influence that environment, heredity, culture, and individual developmental parameters have on adult capacities for thought and reflection. But within each society groups have been marginalized, and there are few, if any, human societies in which marginalization by gender does not play an important role. As we examine, on a global basis, the worlds of knowing of the women whose lives constitute the statistical majority of those lived on our earth, we enrich our own lives. And, if our own lives become sufficiently enriched, they in turn can deepen and transform the lives of many of our fellow human beings.

Notes

Chapter 1: Knowledges/Foci

1. See, for example, Sandra Harding, *Is Science Multicultural?* (Bloomington: Indiana University Press, 1997).
2. For a useful discussion of this issue, see Marianne Janack, "Standpoint Epistemology without the 'Standpoint'?: an Examination of Epistemic Privilege and Epistemic Authority," *Hypatia* 12 (1997): 125–139.
3. Lawrence Cahoone, introduction to *From Modernism to Postmodernism: An Anthology*, ed. Lawrence Cahoone (Malden, MA: Blackwell Publishers, 1996), 2.
4. The Cahoone anthology is an excellent source for material that has come to define the movement(s).
5. *Ibid.*, 2.
6. One such volume is *"Femininity," "Masculinity," and "Androgyny": A Modern Philosophical Discussion*, ed. Mary Vetterling-Braggin (Totowa, NJ: Rowman and Littlefield, 1991).
7. Victoria Barker, "Definition and the Question of 'Woman,' " *Hypatia* 12 (1997): 185–215.
8. Ananda Coomaraswamy, unnumbered footnote in Heinrich Zimmer, *Myths and Symbols in Indian Art and Civilization* (New York: Harper & Row, 1962), 142.
9. Fredric Jameson, "The Cultural Logic of Late Capitalism," in Cahoone, *From Modernism to Postmodernism*, 556–72. This citation p. 561.
10. Moira Ferguson, *Where the Land Meets the Body: Jamaica Kincaid* (Charlottesville: University of Virginia Press, 1994).
11. See, for example, Oyeronke Oyewumi, *The Invention of Women* (Minneapolis: University of Minnesota Press, 1997), for a powerful analysis of the status of the female in Yoruba culture.
12. Chandra Mohanty, "On Race and Voice: Challenges for Liberal Education in the 1990s," in *Between Borders: Pedagogy and the Politics of Cultural Studies*, ed. Henry Giroux and Peter McLaren (New York: Routledge, 1994), 145–66. This citation 145–46).
13. See Robin Lakoff, *Talking Power* (New York: Basic Books, 1990), for a wonderful examination of differences between oral and written traditions.
14. Sara Mills, "Postcolonial Feminist Theory," in *Contemporary Feminist Theories*, ed. Stevi Jackson and Jackie Jones (New York: New York University Press, 1998), 98–112. This citation 102.

15. See fn. 8.
16. Tsenay Serequeberhan, *The Hermeneutics of African Philosophy* (New York: Routledge, 1995), *passim*.
17. Mills, "Postcolonial Feminist Theory," 98.
18. *Ibid*.
19. See Stacy B. Schaeffer and Peter T. Furst, eds., *People of the Peyote* (Albuquerque: University of New Mexico Press, 1996).
20. Oyewumi, *Invention of Women, passim*.
21. Patricia Hill Collins, *Black Feminist Thought* (New York: Routledge, 1991).
22. Carol P. Christ, *The Rebirth of the Goddess* (New York: Addison-Wesley Publishing, 1997), 109.
23. The body of theorizing surrounding twentieth-century science, particularly positivism or logical empiricism, might be thought to be an example of this.
24. Jane Roland Martin, *Changing the Educational* Landscape (New York: Routledge, 1994).
25. This no doubt explains why many feminists have been so ardent in greeting the antianalytic turn in recent American philosophy, as articulated by Joseph Margolis, Richard Rorty, and others.
26. Sandra Harding's original work in this area continues to be one of the best sources. See T*he Science Question in Feminism* (Ithaca, NY: Cornell University Press, 1978).
27. Elizabeth Bumiller, *May You Be the Mother of a Hundred Sons* (New York: Fawcett Columbine, 1990).
28. See Maggie Humm, *Modern Feminisms* (New York: Columbia University Press, 1992), for an excellent comparison of these two strands of feminist theory.
29. The tie-ins to the kinds of self-help projects initiated by Oxfam, for example, are obvious.
30. The cover story for Oxfam America's *Viewpoint* for fall 1998 is titled "A Unique School for Women and Children in Mali, West Africa." Inside, Alhemia Strayouey says, "Before coming here I had no education and no skills.... Now I can teach other women skills that I have acquired" (8–9).
31. See the chapter in Bumiller, *A Hundred Sons*, titled "The Women's Movement."
32. See in particular ch. 5 in *Philosophies of Science/Feminist Theories* (Boulder, CO: Westview Press, 1998).
33. Teresa Jordan, *Cowgirls* (Lincoln: University of Nebraska Press, 1992), xxix–xxx.

Chapter 2: Northern India and Its Culture

1. See, again, Oyewumi for commentary on the extent to which the category "woman" is a construct borrowed from Eurocentric categorization and forced on some West African cultures.
2. Ananda Coomaraswamy, for example, is cited in Heinrich Zimmer's well-known *Myths and Symbols in Indian Art and Civilization* (New York: Harper & Row, 1972), as comparing a certain construal of Brahman taken from the Bhagavad Gita to work in Plato. (Unnumbered footnote, p. 142.)

3. Gavin Flood, *An Introduction to Hinduism* (Cambridge: Cambridge University Press, 1996), 81–82.

4. *Ibid.*, 85. Flood notes: "This impersonalist monism is central to the earlier Upanishads." Zimmer writes: "The chief motivation of Vedic philosophy ... has been, without change, the search for a basic unity underlying the manifold of the universe." (Heinrich Zimmer, *Philosophies of India* [Princeton, NJ: Princeton University Press, 1967], 338).

5. Flood, *Hinduism*, 20.

6. Zimmer, *Philosophies*, 333–334.

7. Flood, *Hinduism*, 20.

8. See Evelyn Fox Keller, *Reflections on Gender and Science* (New Haven: Yale University Press, 1985), and Sandra Harding, *The Science Question in Feminism* (Ithaca, NY: Cornell University Press, 1986), for some of the standard articulations of this point of view.

9. Keller, *Reflections, passim.*

10. Hermann Kulke and Dietmar Rothermund, *A History of India* (New York: Routledge, 1990), 139.

11. Julia Annas, "Plato's Republic and Feminism," in *Feminism and Ancient Philosophy*, ed. Julie Ward (New York: Routledge, 1996), 3.

12. Zimmer, *Philosophies*, 334–335.

13. A. K. Rai, "Paksata in Navya-Nyaya," in *Journal of Indian Philosophy* 23 (1995): 1–9.

14. *Ibid.*, 1.

15. Kulke and Rothermund, *History of India*, 143.

16. Flood, *Hinduism*, 174–175.

17. Jane Roland Martin, *Changing the Educational Landscape* (New York: Routledge, 1994), 234.

18. Flood, *Hinduism*, 185.

19. *Ibid.*, 191.

20. *Ibid.*

21. *Ibid.*, 193–194.

22. *Ibid.*, 174.

23. *Ibid.*, 194.

24. Sara Mitter, *Dharma's Daughters* (New Brunswick, NJ: Rutgers University Press, 1991).

25. *Ibid.*, 71.

26. Francis Watson, *India: a Concise History* (New York: Thames and Hudson, 1979), 26.

27. *Ibid.*, 31.

28. *Ibid.*

29. Mitter, *Dharma's Daughters*, 80.

30. Uma Narayan, *Dislocating Cultures* (New York: Routledge, 1997), 52.

31. Flood, *Hinduism*, 252.

32. Mitter, *Dharma's Daughters*, 168.

33. Kulke and Rothermund, *History of India*, 252.

34. Elizabeth Bumiller, *May You Be the Mother of a Hundred Sons* (New York: Fawcett Columbine, 1990), 206.

35. Mitter, *Dharma's Daughters*, 134–135.

36. *Ibid.*, 142.
37. This is a theme throughout Narayan, *Dislocating Cultures.*
38. Akhil Gupta, *Postcolonial Developments* (Durham, NC: Duke University Press, 1998).
39. *Ibid.*, 139.
40. An account of this intriguing incident takes place on 97–101 of Gupta, *Postcolonial Developments,* under the subhead of "The Place of Patriarchy."
41. *Ibid.*, 99.
42. Mitter, *Dharma's Daughters*, 47.
43. Bumiller, for example, specifically addresses the issue of child care on 234–235 of *A Hundred Sons.*
44. This is a site of lengthy comment by Narayan in *Dislocating Cultures*, especially in the first chapter.
45. Narayan's chap. 2, "Restoring History and Politics to Third-World Traditions," is devoted almost entirely to an extensive discussion of *sati* and to counterargument against the work of some Western feminists. (See 41–80.)
46. See Narayan, *Dislocating Cultures*, especially 72–75.
47. *Ibid.*, 75.
48. Bumiller, *A Hundred Sons*, 114.
49. Ch. 3 of Narayan, *Dislocating Cultures*, for example, contains an extensive analysis of the comparative frequency of "dowry burnings" versus domestic battery leading to death in the United States. The conclusion of her analysis is that, adjusted grossly for populations, the two phenomena occur at roughly the same rate.
50. Bumiller, *A Hundred Sons*, 115.
51. Mitter, *Dharma's Daughters*, 128–145.
52. *Ibid.*, 143.
53. Bumiller, *A Hundred Sons*, 133.
54. *Ibid.*
55. *Ibid.*
56. Flood has extensive commentary on these life stages. See, particularly, his ch. 4, "Yoga and Renunciation," 75–102.
57. Flood, *Hinduism*, 76.
58. Bumiller, *A Hundred Sons*, 136.
59. Flood does give a name for the female renouncer; according to him, she is called *sadhvi* rather than *sadhu*. Flood, *Hinduism*, 92.
60. The phrase taken from Narayan is used by her throughout *Dislocating Cultures.*
61. Mitter, *Dharma's Daughters*, 85.
62. Vandana Shiva, *Ecology.*
63. Flood, *Hinduism*, 236.
64. Zimmer's account also underlines the monism inherent in orthoprax Hinduism. See Zimmer, *Philosophies*, 230 note.
65. Gayatri Chakravorty Spivak, *In Other Worlds* (New York: Routledge, 1988), 199.
66. Chandra Talpante Mohanty, "Under Western Eyes: Feminist Scholarship and

Colonial Discourses," in *Feminisms*, ed. Sandra Kemp and Judith Squires (Oxford: Oxford University Press, 1997), 93.

67. *Ibid.*, 94.
68. Maria Mies and Vandana Shiva, "Ecofeminism," in Kemp and Squires, *Feminisms*, 498.
69. See fn. 5.
70. *Bhagavad Gita*, trans. Juan Mascaró (Harmondsworth, UK: Penguin, 1975), 9–10.
71. For a comparison of some ideas surrounding gender in the Yoruba culture, see Oyeronke Oyewumi, *The Invention of Women* (Minneapolis: University of Minnesota Press, 1997).
72. Shiva.
73. Mascaró, *Gita*, 14.

Chapter 3: Dravidian India and Its Culture

1. The first translation of the Bhagavad Gita into English, interestingly enough, was done as early as 1785.
2. Benjamin Rowland, for years the foremost authority on the art and architecture of India, makes a clear distinction when speaking of Dravidian art. (Rowland, *The Art and Architecture of India* [Baltimore: Penguin, 1967].)
3. Zimmer, *Philosophies*, 106n.
4. Zimmer actually goes so far as to call this a "simple ... clean-cut ... pessimistic dualism" (Zimmer, *Philosophies*, 219).
5. Zimmer, *Philosophies*, 378–379.
6. Flood, *Hinduism*, 23.
7. Kulke and Rothermund, *History of India*, 99.
8. *Ibid.*, 103.
9. Sandra Harding, "Is There a Feminist Method?," in Kemp and Squires, *Feminisms*, 161.
10. Vasumathi K. Duvvury, *Play, Symbolism, and Ritual: A Study of Brahmin Women's Rites of Passage* (New York: Peter Lang, 1991), 8.
11. *Ibid.*, 9–10.
12. *Ibid.*, 19.
13. The issue of *Chronicle of Higher Education* dated March 25, 1999, contains a lengthy article on this debate, with special reference to the work of Wendy Doniger of the University of Chicago. She is best known, of course, for her work on the Hindu tradition and religions of India. (*Chronicle*, March 25, 1999, pp. A19–20.)
14. *Ibid.*, A19.
15. Flood, *Hinduism*, 196.
16. *Ibid.*, 194–195.
17. Margaret Egnor, "On the Meaning of Sakti to the Women of Tamil Nadu," in *The Powers of Tamil Women*, ed. Susan S. Wadley (Syracuse, NY: Foreign and Comparative Studies Series, Syracuse University, 1980).
18. Egnor is especially explicit about this relationship on 22–24 of her essay.
19. *Ibid.*, 26.
20. Duvvury, *Play*, 20.

21. Renee Lorraine, "A Gynecentric Aesthetic," in *Aesthetics in Feminist Perspective*, ed. Hilde Hein and Carolyn Korsmeyer (Bloomington: Indiana University Press, 1993), 36–52.

22. *Ibid.*, 38–39.

23. Susan S. Wadley, "The Paradoxical Powers of Tamil Women," in Wadley, *Powers of Tamil Women*, 154.

24. Duvvury, *Play*, 77.

25. *Ibid.*, 81.

26. Kumari Jayawardena, *The White Woman's Other Burden* (New York: Routledge, 1995), 1.

27. *Ibid.*, 4–5.

28. A. L. Basham, *The Wonder That Was India* (New York: Hawthorn Books, 1963), 310–311.

29. Duvvury, *Play*, 26–27.

30. Sheryl Daniel, "Women in Tamil Culture: The Problem of Conflicting 'Models,' " in Wadley, *Powers of Tamil Women*, 61–91. This citation is from 61.

31. Jayawardena, *White Woman*, 88, 39–40.

32. Sandhya Venkateswaran, *Environment, Technology, and the Gender Gap* (New Delhi: Sage Publications, 1995), 165–166.

33. K. C. Zachariah and S. Irudaya Rajan, *Kerala's Demographic Transition: Determinants and Consequences* (New Delhi: Sage Publications, 1997), 17.

34. As this is written the national government led by the BJP coalition is having to re-form because of movements by the Dravidian political groups.

35. Bumiller, *A Hundred Sons*, 35.

36. *Ibid.*, 108.

37. Robert L. Hardgrave Jr., *The Dravidian Movement* (Bombay: Popular Prakashan, 1965), 13.

38. Cheryl Johnson-Odim and Margaret Strobel, eds., *Expanding the Boundaries of Women's History* (Bloomington: Indiana University Press, 1992), p. 35. The quotation is from a Mrs. Mitchell. Janaki Nair also notes that the "Marimakkathayam or matrilineal tradition of the Nairs ... revealed an empowering of women which had disrupted tidy notions of patriarchal power to which England had beome accustomed."

39. Mitter, *Dharma's Daughters*, 98.

40. Egnor, "Meaning of Sakti," in Wadley, *Powers of Tamil Women*, 11.

41. During the week beginning April 12, 1999, the *New York Times* frequently reported on Indian political alliances. It was announced at one point that Sonia Gandhi had been seeking out Jayalalitha, presumably to attempt an alliance with the Congress Party.

42. An excellent compendium of material taken from *Manushi* has been published in the United Kingdom and is available in the United States. *In Search of Answers: Indian Women's Voices from Manushi*, ed. Madhu Kishwar and Ruth Vanita (London: Zed Books, 1984), is an anthology of material from the periodical's first five years.

43. Narayan is quick to note the paradoxicality of the problematic with regard to the "Western import" of feminism and India. See *Dislocating Cultures*, *passim*.

44. Kishwar and Vanita, *In Search of Answers*, 1.
45. *Ibid.*, 299.
46. India has more than one Communist Party, dating back to the Cold War split between the Soviet Union and China. The more active of the two is usually known by the initials "ML," standing for Marxist-Leninist. Its activists are often referred to as "Naxalites."
47. Kishwar and Vanita, *In Search of Answers*, p. 202.
48. Vijay Agnew, "The West in Indian Feminist Discourse and Practice," *Women's Studies International Forum* 20 (1997): 3–19. This citation 18.
49. Kishwar and Vanita, *In Search of Answers*, 181.
50. Agnew, in "Indian Feminist Discourse," 4.
51. As of this writing, the DMK and other such Dravidian parties hold the balance of power in creating coalitions for the formation of a new government after the demise of the BJP in a recent parliamentary vote-of-confidence maneuver.
52. Leslie J. Calman, *Toward Empowerment: Women and Movement Politics in India* (Boulder, CO: Westview Press, 1992), 176.
53. *Ibid.*
54. Basham, *Wonder*, 478.
55. Ananda Coomaraswamy, *The Dance of the Shiva* (New York: Noonday Press, 1970), 69–70.
56. See, for example, the discussion of the rival schools, particularly the older ones, in Basham, *Wonder*, 324–331.
57. *Ibid.*, 327.
58. Kishwar and Vanita, *In Search of Answers*, 34.
59. Egnor, "Meaning of Shakti," in Wadley, *Powers of Tamil Women*, 17, 16.
60. *Ibid.*, 15–16.
61. Zimmer, *Philosophies*, 207–208.
62. These phrases are taken directly from the titles of their respective books.
63. See Oyewumi, *Invention of Women, passim*.
64. Basham has a particularly strong section on the Tamil written tradition toward the end of his chapter on languages and literature, 488–580.
65. Again, see any one of a number of regional episodes recounted in Kishwar and Vanita, *In Search of Answers*.
66. As of this writing, Jayalalitha, the most prominent among Dravidian spokespersons, holds the key to the formation of national coalitions for the constitution of a new Lok Sabha (lower house) and government.
67. The author visited this community in 1971, when it had 200–300 members.
68. See Wadley, *Powers of Tamil Women, passim*.
69. Wadley, introduction to *Powers of Tamil Women*, ix–x.
70. Zimmer is particularly strong in this regard.
71. See Kishwar and Vanita, *In Search of Answers, passim*.

Chapter 4: Bangladesh and Islam

1. Akbar S. Ahmed, *Jinnah, Pakistan, and Islamic Identity* (New York: Routledge, 1997), 238.
2. The existence of such rural programs and the impact that they have had on

lives has even been on *60 Minutes*. Another outstanding source of commentary is Martha Nussbaum, *Sex and Social Justice* (New York: Oxford University Press, 1999).

3. Ahmed, *Jinnah*, 216–217.

4. *Ibid.*, 217.

5. This point is made several times in Ahmed, *Jinnah*, *passim*.

6. *Ibid.*, 238.

7. Craig Baxter, *Bangladesh: From a Nation to a State* (Boulder, CO: Westview Press, 1997), 6.

8. *Ibid.*, 7.

9. *Ibid.*, 5.

10. Kenneth Cragg and Marston Speight, *Islam from Within* (Belmont, CA: Wadsworth Publishing Co., 1980), 112–114. Cragg and Speight is an excellent source for information on Islam making specific reference to Islamic scripture.

11. Jane Duran, "Al-Andalus: Islamic Form and Visual Expression," *Iyyun* 12 (1995): 13–19.

12. Cragg and Speight, *Islam from Within*, 1.

13. An excellent overview is provided by Martha Alter Chen, *A Quiet Revolution: Women in Transition in Rural Bangladesh* (Cambridge, MA: Schenkman Publishing, 1983). Among NGOs frequently cited, the Grameen Bank and its microcredit programs probably ranks first. In this chapter I will largely be concerned with the BRAC.

14. Chen, *Quiet Revolution*, 57–58.

15. *Ibid.*, 58.

16. Baxter, *Bangladesh*, 6. In the past few years, there has begun to be a fundamentalist movement, and it has had definite effects, particularly with respect to controversies involving freedom of the press. See Elora Shehabuddin, "Contesting the Illicit: Gender and the Politics of Fatwas in Bangldesh," *Signs* 24 (1999): 1011–1044.

17. Cragg and Speight, *Islam from Within*, 112.

18. *Ibid.*

19. Chen, *Quiet Revolution*, 57.

20. Patricia Hill Collins, *Black Feminist Thought* (New York: Routledge, 1990).

21. Chen, *Quiet Revolution*, 67.

22. *Ibid.*, 73.

23. Elizabeth Ann Dobie, "Interweaving Feminist Frameworks," in *Feminism and Tradition in Aesthetics*, ed. Peggy Zeglin Brand and Carolyn Korsmeyer (University Park: Pennsylvania State University Press, 1995), 215–234. This citation 220.

24. Chen, *Quiet Revolution*, 204.

25. Jayawardena, *White Woman*, 192.

26. *Ibid.*

27. Baxter, *Bangladesh*, 22.

28. Wiebke Walther, *Women in Islam* (New York: Markus Wiener Publishing, 1993), 94.

29. Baxter, *Bangladesh*, 8.

30. Chen, *Quiet Revolution*, 166.

31. Walther, *Women in Islam*, 69.
32. Chen, *Quiet Revolution*, 204.
33. Baxter, *Bangladesh*, 6.
34. Chen, *Quiet Revolution*, x.
35. Catherine H. Lovell, *Breaking the Cycle of Poverty: The BRAC Strategy* (West Hartford, CT: Kumarian Press, 1992), 1.
36. *Ibid.*, 15.
37. Particularly helpful in this respect is the chapter in Chen titled "Three Women Speak," 195–218.
38. Amartya Sen, *Resources, Values and Development* (Oxford: Basil Blackwell, 1984). Sen notes, with respect to famine and starvation in 1974 Bangladesh: "It appears that the destitutes were almost entirely from rural areas.... [I]f we look at the relative *intensity* of destitution, it would appear that rural labourers as a group had a much higher level of destitution than the farmers." (472).
39. *Ibid.*, 28, fn. 89.
40. Cragg and Speight, *Islam from Within*, 112.
41. Lovell, *Breaking the Cycle*, 41.
42. Both Lovell and Chen have extensive lists of such groups. Many of the NGO's, such as BRAC, are large enough that they are divided into subgroups focusing on particular areas of endeavor, such as women's health or literacy.
43. Lovell writes, with respect to the small, local village groups: "In a recent small example, an elderly mullah publicly slapped the face of one of the BRAC NFPE teachers when she was on the village street and berated her for her public activities." Lovell, *Breaking the Cycle*, 42.
44. One such theorist, for example, is Lynn Hankinson Nelson, *Who Knows: From Quine to a Feminist Empiricism* (Philadelphia, PA: Temple University Press, 1991).
45. Chen is careful to note that these sorts of changes may be thought to be among the most important taking place. See Chen, *Quiet Revolution*, 165–193.
46. *Ibid.*, 166.
47. *Ibid.*, 176.
48. Of the formation of tradition in early Islam, Wiebke Walther writes: "However, the misogynistic elements among the pious of the first few centuries, whose numbers evidently increased after contact with Christian asceticism in particular, circulated a tradition [with respect to women] that was frequently quoted in later years" (Walther, *Women in Islam*, 51).
49. Chen, *Quiet Revolution*, 172. The relevant section is to be found on 172–175.
50. *Ibid.*, 174.
51. Cragg and Speight, *Islam from Within*, 38.
52. Walther, *Women in Islam*, 51.
53. Baxter, *Bangladesh*, 6.
54. Most commentators agree that the variations between these two traditions have little genuine bearing on, for example, the conduct of women or the regulation of households.
55. Walther, *Women in Islam*, 48.
56. Such remarks are to be found throughout Chen, *Quiet Revolution*.

57. Peter van der Veer, *Religious Nationalism* (Berkeley: University of California Press, 1994). What Van der Veer says in this context is fascinating, because it seems to speak to the heart of our endeavor. He notes that "These Sufis 'converted' large parts of the population to a form of Islam. Especially in the Punjab and in East Bengal Sufi centers were eminently successful" (35).

58. It will be recalled that the Al-Hilli commentary, for example, enjoins a wife to "be most careful in taking care of my possessions" (Cragg and Speight, *Islam from Within*, 112).

59. Chen, *Quiet Revolution*, 189.

60. Many of the women cited in Chen employ moving metaphors to speak of their experiences in groups formed through BRAC. Some say "We have become wise," or "We were blind, although we had eyes" (Chen, *Quiet Revolution*, 190).

61. Walther, *Women in Islam*, 70.

62. Partha Chatterjee, *Texts of Power: Emerging Disciplines in Colonial Bengal* (Minneapolis: University of Minnesota Press, 1994), 22.

63. Cragg and Speight, *Islam from Within*, 112.

64. Chen, *Quiet Revolution*, ix. This is also the origin of the group on which we have focused in this chapter, the BRAC, or Bangladesh Rural Advancement Committee.

65. As Chen indicates, "Other villagers will not issue invitations to households that are ostracized, nor will they attend the ceremonies in those households. Marriage proposals from such households are not considered" (Chen, *Quiet Revolution*, 174).

66. *Ibid.*, 204.

67. Cragg and Speight have an excellent chapter on Sufism and mysticism (Cragg and Speight, *Islam from Within*, 173–207).

68. Chen has amply documented the effects on "neighborliness." (Chen, *Quiet Revolution*, 166–178).

69. Howard Eilberg-Schwartz and Wendy Doniger, *Off with Her Head!* (Berkeley: University of California Press, 1995).

70. Carol Delaney, "Untangling the Meanings of Hair in Turkish Society," in Eilberg-Schwartz and Doniger, *Off with Her Head!*, 53–74. This citation 54.

71. Walther indicates that the commentary contains a very wide range of views, "some of which are contradictory" (Walther, *Women in Islam*, 48).

72. Van Der Veer, *Nationalism*, 35. It is impossible to close a chapter on women in Bangladesh without mentioning the controversy surrounding the author Taslima Nasrin. She has currently been banned from the nation for her novels and writings depicting Muslim-Hindu communal relations. (See Taslima Nasrin, *Shame* [Amherst, NY: Prometheus Books, 1997].) A fine short piece on the general situation is in Hagar Scher, "A Writer Banished," *Ms.* 9, 1999, 89–92.

Chapter 5: Nepal and the Himalayan Societies

1. Leo E. Rose and John T. Scholz, *Nepal: Profile of a Himalayan Kingdom* (Boulder, CO: Westview Press, 1980), 71.

2. *Ibid.*

3. Until as recently as twenty or thirty years ago, the young girl selected led a cloistered life away from others for many years.

4. Some of this entrepreneurial spirit informs the lives of the Nyeshangte women, investigated by Joanne Watkins in her fascinating book *Spirited Women: Gender, Religion, and Cultural Identity in the Nepal Himalaya* (New York: Columbia University Press, 1996).

5. Watkins, *Spirited Women*, 11.

6. Frederick Gaige, *Regionalism and National Unity in Nepal* (Berkeley: University of California Press, 1975), 12.

7. *Ibid.*, 13.

8. Watkins, *Spirited Women*, 195.

9. *Ibid.*, 195.

10. Watkins's first chapter, "Kathmandu Connections," 4–30, contains a marvelous compendium of anecdotes about Nepalese teenagers who are regularly mistaken for Americans at various embassies and official stop points.

11. *Ibid.*, 195–196.

12. *Ibid.*, 196.

13. *Ibid.*, 191.

14. Kathryn Blackstone, *Women in the Footsteps of the Buddha: Struggle for Liberation in the Therigatha* (Richmond, UK: Curzon Press, 1998), 10.

15. Blackstone uses this term to describe the Buddha's historic position with respect to women (Blackstone, *Footsteps*, 118).

16. Watkins, *Spirited Women*, 227.

17. Blackstone, *Footsteps*, 1.

18. *Ibid.*, 117.

19. Watkins's analysis of the Nyeshangte culture includes an entire chapter on women's particpation in rituals, "With Only the Body of a Woman," 215–258.

20. *Ibid.*, 223.

21. Diana Y. Paul, *Women in Buddhism: Images of the Feminine in Mahayana Tradition* (Berkeley, CA: Asian Humanities Press, 1979), 287.

22. Broughton Coburn, *Nepali Aama: Portrait of a Nepalese Hill Woman* (Santa Barbara, CA: Ross-Erikson, 1982), 25–26.

23. See, for example, Ellen Handler Spitz, "Mothers and Daughters: Ancient and Modern Myths," in Brand and Korsmeyer, *Feminism and Tradition*, 354–370.

24. Gaige, *Regionalism*, 24.

25. Watkins, *Spirited Women*, 112–113.

26. *Ibid.*, 113.

27. *Ibid.*, 50–51.

28. *Ibid.*, 49.

29. *Ibid.*, 45.

30. *Ibid.*, 55–56.

31. Coburn, *Nepali Aama*, 69.

32. Rex L. Jones and Shirley Kurz Jones, *The Himalayan Woman: A Study of Limbu Women in Marriage and Divorce* (Palo Alto, CA: Mayfield Publishing, 1976).

33. Steven Parish, *Moral Knowing in a Hindu Sacred City: An Exploration of Mind, Emotion and Self* (New York: Columbia University Press, 1994).

34. Watkins, *Spirited Women*, 11.
35. *Ibid.*, 10.
36. Paul, *Women in Buddhism*, 107.
37. Watkins, *Spirited Women*, 13–14.
38. *Ibid.*, 104–105.
39. Jones and Jones, *Himalayan*, 121.
40. *Ibid.*, 124.
41. Watkins, *Spirited Women*, 10.
42. I was unable to find direct evidence of such groups, but as we saw in chapters 3 and 4 in the cases of both north and south India, educated women—particularly those who have lived abroad—frequently form such groups upon their return. A more important question then becomes what we can find to be feminist among movements taking place in the areas less frequented by wealthy, Westernized women.
43. Watkins, *Spirited Women*, 49.
44. See Rose and Scholz, *Nepal, passim,* and Gaige, *Regionalism, passim.*
45. Watkins, *Spirited Women*, 158–159.
46. *The Human Rights Watch Global Report on Women's Human Rights* (New York: Human Rights Watch, 1995), 230.
47. *Ibid.*, 257.
48. *Ibid.*, 230.
49. Barbara J. Scot, *The Violet Shyness of Their Eyes* (Corvallis, OR: Calyx Books, 1993).
50. Paul, *Women in Buddhism*, 3–59.
51. Benedict de Spinoza, *On the Improvement of the Understanding*, trans. R. H. M. Elwes (New York: Dover Publications, 1955). In one passage, Spinoza notes that "confused ideas" are "often formed against our will" (40). By this he presumably means that the world of the senses forces itself on us, a forcing that Buddhism also would like us to try to obviate.
52. Paul, *Women in Buddhism*, 216.
53. *Ibid.*, 219. Of the many passages in her work that discuss this difficulty, this particular comment is one of the clearest.
54. *Ibid.*, 107.
55. Elizabeth D. Harvey and Kathleen Okruhlik, *Women and Reason* (Ann Arbor: University of Michigan Press, 1992), 64.
56. Watkins, *Spirited Women*, 193.
57. The chapters are titled "The Bodhisattvas with Sexual Transformation," 166–216, and "The Bodhisattvas without Sexual Transformation," 217–244.
58. Going beyond the notion of the Bodhisattva and dealing directly with the notion of the Buddha nature, Paul addresses this question on 281ff.
59. Watkins, *Spirited Women*, 49.
60. *Ibid.*, 14–20.
61. Blackstone, for example, refers to the *Therigatha* as "the only canonical text in the world's relgiions" written by a female and about female experiences (Blackstone, *Footsteps*, 1).
62. Gaige, *Regionalism*, 24–26.
63. Jones and Jones, *Himalyan*, 133.

64. The last chapter of Paul's book is titled "A Female Buddha?" (Paul, *Women in Buddhism*, 281–302.)
65. Paul, *Women in Buddhism*, 281–282.
66. Gaige makes this point throughout his work (Gaige, *Regionalism*, *passim*).
67. Watkins, *Spirited Women*, 44. Since this chapter has been written, further work has been done on how the mountaineering/trekking industries are changing life in Nepal. See Sherry B. Ortner, *Life and Death on Mt. Everest: Sherpas and Himalayan Mountaineering* (Princeton, NJ: Princeton University Press, 1999). An interesting review of this book appeared in *Lingua Franca*, November 1999, B40–B41.
68. Jones and Jones, *Himalayan*, *passim*.
69. Zimmer, *Philosophies*, 498.
70. Jones and Jones make specific comparisons in *Himalayan*, 130–132.

Chapter 6: Mexico and the *Mestizaje*

1. Robert Ryan Miller, *Mexico: A History* (Norman: University of Oklahoma Press, 1985), 40–65.
2. *Ibid.*, 64–65.
3. *Ibid.*, 102.
4. *Ibid.*, 100.
5. Howard F. Cline, *The United States and Mexico* (New York: Atheneum, 1963), 29.
6. *Ibid.*, 30.
7. Enrique Krauze, *Mexico: Biography of Power* (New York: HarperCollins, 1997), 4–5.
8. *Ibid.*, 12.
9. A useful edition of Vasconcelos's major work is José Vasconcelos, *La Raza Cósmica*, trans. Didier Jaen (Los Angeles: Centro de Publicaciones CSULA, 1979).
10. *Ibid.*, 21–22, 31.
11. Krauze, *Mexico: Biography*, 55.
12. Augustine, *Confessions* (New York: Liveright Publishing Co., 1943), 154–55.
13. Robert McMahon, *Augustine's Prayerful Ascent* (Athens: University of Georgia Press, 1989).
14. C. A. Burland, *The Gods of Mexico* (New York: G.P. Putnam's Sons, 1967), 47–59. This chapter, specifically on the Aztecs, is well worth perusal.
15. Miller, *Mexico: A History*, 291.
16. *Ibid.*, 292.
17. Burland, *Gods*, ix–xi.
18. There are indeed other female deities mentioned by Burland in the text at other points, but not on this list, as for example Mayauel, the "pulque goddess."
19. Miller, *Mexico: A History*, 145.
20. Lourdes Arizpe, "Peasant Women and Silence," in *Women's Writing in Latin America*, ed. Sara Castro-Klarén, Sylvia Molloy, and Beatriz Sarlo (Boulder, CO: Westview Press, 1991), 334, 338.
21. The critic Daniel Balderston has done interesting work on the notion of

macho and its relation to the Revolution. He writes: "[F]ighting words, written by one group of Mexican intellectuals against another in 1934, define the ways in which the cultural nationalism of the Mexican Revolution was marked as masculinist and heterosexist." (Daniel Balderston, "Poetry, Revolution, Homophobia: Polemics from the Mexican Revolution," in *Hispanisms and Homosexualities*, ed. Sylvia Molloy and Robert McKee Irwin [Durham, NC: Duke University Press, 1998].)

22. Kathleen Lennon and Margaret Whitford, introduction to *Knowing the Difference: Feminist Perspectives in Epistemology*, ed. Kathleen Lennon and Margaret Whitford (New York: Routledge, 1994).

23. Even a general historian such as Miller is struck by this feature of her work. (Miller, *Mexico: A History*, 155.)

24. *Ibid.*

25. Janna Thompson, "Moral Difference and Moral Epistemology," in Lennon and Whitford, *Knowing*, 217–229. This citation 217.

26. Miller, *Mexico: A History*, 5, 6.

27. According to Miller, when Cortes landed he found two Spaniards who had been castaway from previous voyages. "One of the rescued men ... [was delighted] to join [him]. ... The other castaway ... refused to join the Spaniards because he had 'gone native' ... and he had an Indian wife and three children, the first known *mestizos*" (Miller, *Mexico: A History*, 75).

28. *Ibid.*, 76.

29. "Children of the one who was violated," to employ a somewhat euphemistic translation.

30. Miller, *Mexico: A History*, 140.

31. *Ibid.*, 155.

32. Sor Juana had started her epistolary or literary endeavors by writing a document that praised the somewhat heretical opinions of another cleric, Antonio de Vieyra. When the bishop of Puebla found out about it, he composed a reply under the fictitious name of "Sor Filotea de la Cruz." Thus Sor Juana's defense—explaining her quest for intellectual freedom, which she does not try to divorce from her desire to lead a convent life—is titled *The Reply to Sor Filotea* (Gerard Flynn, *Sor Juana Ines de la Cruz* [New York: Twayne Publishers, 1971, 11–25]). Among the most important contemporary works on Sor Juana is Octavio Paz's massive *Sor Juana, or the Traps of Faith*, trans. Margaret Sayers Peden (Cambridge, MA: Belknap of Harvard University Press, 1988). Because of my reliance on Paz for other matters, I will not cite this work here.

33. Quoted in Flynn, *Sor Juana*, 20–21.

34. Arizpe, "Peasant Women," in Castro-Klarén et al., *Women's Writing*, 333.

35. Miller notes that many Indian women served in convents (Miller, *Mexico: A History*, 149).

36. Octavio Paz, *The Labyrinth of Solitude* (New York: Grove Press, 1961), 86–87.

37. Paz even goes so far as to compare the psychology of the Mexican mestizo, aware of his origins, to that of "slaves, servants, and submerged races" (Paz, *Labyrinth*, 70).

38. Elena Poniatowska, "Voices from Tlatelolco," in Castro-Klarén et al., *Women's Writing*, 308–314. This citation 310.
39. Miller, *Mexico: A History*, 335.
40. Margo Glantz, "Genealogies," in in Castro-Klarén et al., *Women's Writing*, 197–200. This citation 197.
41. Miller, *Mexico: A History*, 367.
42. One commentator has defined *machismo* as the attitude by which "Mexican men demonstrate their manhood through fathering of numerous offspring" (Miller, *Mexico: A History*, 356).
43. *Ibid.*, 354–355.
44. Krauze, *Mexico: Biography*, 786–787.
45. Sue Ellen M. Charlton, *Women in Third World Development* (Boulder, CO: Westview Press, 1984), 130.
46. *Ibid.*, 133.
47. Carola García Calderón, *Revistas Femeninas: la mujer como objeto de consumo* (Mexico, DF: Ediciones Caballito, 1980), 126–127.
48. Translation by this author.
49. Eyewitness Jorge Avila R., cited in Poniatowska, "Voices from Tlatelolco," in Castro-Klarén et al. *Women's Writing*, 312.
50. An exhibit in a Los Angeles museum devoted to Latino culture recently chronicled the use of such calendars and their development. The exhibit took place from July 2, 1999 to August 31, 1999 at the Latino Museum of History, Art and Culture in downtown Los Angeles, and was titled "La Patria Portátil: 100 Years of Mexican Chromo Art Calendars."
51. Unfortunately, a great deal of the work chronicling feminism in Mexico has not been translated and is available only in Spanish. Another body of such work tends to chronicle the women's movement in Latin America as a whole, and often focuses on nations other than Mexico. One of the best available works in English is *Compañeras: Voices from the Latin American Women's Movement*, ed. Gaby Kuppers (London: Latin American Bureau, Ltd., 1994).
52. Elizabeth Maier, "Debating the Social Movement," in Kuppers, *Compañeras*, 41–42.
53. *Ibid.*, 42.
54. *Ibid.*, 40.
55. JoAnn Martin, "Antagonisms of Gender and Class in Morelos," in *Women of the Mexican Countryside, 1850–1990*, ed. Heather Fowler-Salamini and Mary Kay Vaughan (Tucson: University of Arizona Press, 1994), 225–242. This citation 226.
56. *Ibid.*, 232.
57. Marta Lamas, "Debate Feminista: a bridge between academia and activism," in Kuppers, *Compañeras*, 160–162. This citation 161.
58. Claudia Colimoro, "A prostitute's election campaign," in Kuppers, *Compañeras*, 92–96. This citation 93.
59. *Ibid.*
60. See, for example, *Hypatia* 8 (1994) with its special cluster on Latin American feminism. Two of the four articles are by Mexican women, including Graciela Hierro and Griselda Gutiérrez Castañeda.
61. For an intriguing account of such an effort, see Marie Cort Daniels, "Teaching

Mexican Culture in Mexico from a Women's Studies Perspective," in *Women's Studies International Forum* 14 (1991): 311–320.

62. Griselda Gutiérrez Castañeda, in *Hypatia* 8 (1994): 186–187.
63. Flynn, *Sor Juana*, 17–19.
64. *Ibid.*, 22–24.
65. Augustine, *Confessions*, 139.
66. Robert McMahon, *Augustine's Prayerful Ascent* (Athens: University of Georgia Press, 1989), 95.
67. Sor Juana Ines de la Cruz, quoted in Flynn, *Sor Juana*, 22.
68. Work that is relevant is Nelson, *Who Knows*, and essays in *A Mind of One's Own*, ed. Louise Antony and Charlotte Witt (Boulder, CO: Westview Press, 1993).
69. Arizpe has still other works not currently available in translation, such as Lourdes Arizpe, *La Mujer en el Desarollo de México y de America Latina* (Cuernavaca, Morelos: Centro Regional de Investigaciones Multidisciplinarias, 1989).
70. Arizpe, "Peasant Women," in Castro-Klarén et al., *Women's Writing*, 335.
71. The notion of a community is alluded to at several points in Arizpe's essay. One of the most crucial points is on 336, where she writes of "the deliberate resistance of the peasants." Another crucial work in Mexican feminism, although in a somewhat different vein, is Graciela Hierro, *Etica y Feminismo* (UNAM: México, D.F. 1985).
72. In "The Scope and Language of Science," for example, Quine writes: "Let us suppose that one of the early words acquired by a child is 'red.' How does he learn it? He is treated to utterances of the word simultaneously with red presentations." (W. V. O. Quine, "The Scope and Language of Science," in *Ways of Paradox* [New York: Random House, 1966, 218].)
73. Nelson, *Who Knows*, 14.
74. See Marija Gimbutas, *The Living Goddesses* (Berkeley: University of California Press, 1998), for an excellent overview of matrilineality and matrifocality in preceding cultures. Although it is difficult to generalize, the focus on violent worship in the ancient Mexican cultures is one indicator of significant differences.
75. Martin, "Antagonisms," in Fowler-Salamini and Vaughan, *Women of Mexican Countryside*, 232.
76. Krauze specifically mentions cuisine, vocabulary, customs with respect to the dead, and so forth, as areas of Mexican culture in which remnants of the indigenous worldviews are overwhelmingly strong (Krauze, *Mexico: Biography*, 57–58).
77. Elena Poniatowska, "Prólogo," in Irene Matthews, *Nellie Campobello: la centaura del norte* (Mexico, DF: Los Libros de la Condesa, 1997), I. (The precise quote in Spanish is: "es parte de una generación que lleva las imágenes de la Revolución archivada en su memoria donde otros guardan canciones infantiles.")
78. Antonia Darder, "The Politics of Biculturalism: Power and Difference in the Formation of *Warriors for Gringostroika* and The New Mestizas," in *The Latino Studies Reader*, ed. Antonia Darder and Rodolfo D. Torres (Malden, MA: Blackwell Publishers, 1998).

Chapter 7: Guatemala and the Indigenous

1. Rigoberta Menchú, *I, Rigoberta Menchú: An Indian Woman in Guatemala*, ed. Elizabeth Burgos-Debray (London: Verso, 1984).
2. W. George Lovell, *Conquest and Survival in Colonial Guatemala* (Montreal: McGill-Queen's University Press, 1992), xvii–xix.
3. See, for example, Irene Matthews, "Torture as Text," in *The Women and War Reader*, ed. Irene Matthews (New York: NYU Press, 1996), 184–191.
4. *Ibid.*, 188.
5. Lovell, *Conquest*, 37.
6. Peter Calvert, *Guatemala: A Nation in Turmoil* (Boulder, CO: Westview Press, 1985), 20.
7. *Ibid.*, 22.
8. Although all the indigenous groups in Guatemala are related to Mayan language groups, strictly speaking not all such groups can be labeled "Quiché." For purposes here, however, I use the terms interchangeably (Calvert, *Guatemala*, 14–15).
9. James D. Sexton, *Ignacio: The Diary of a Mayan Indian of Guatemala* (Philadelphia: University of Pennsylvania Press, 1992).
10. *Ibid.*, 14.
11. *Ibid.*, 3.
12. According to Calvert, the United States State Department says that the situation exhibits "a capacity for gratuitous massacre that is difficult to credit" (Calvert, *Guatemala*, 113).
13. *Ibid.*, 24–25.
14. *Ibid.*, 23.
15. *Ibid.*, 103.
16. *Ibid.*, 36.
17. Sexton, *Ignacio*, 12.
18. Calvert, *Guatemala*, 24.
19. *Ibid.*
20. Matthews, "Torture," in *Women and War*, 190.
21. Miller, *Mexico: A History*, 19.
22. Krauze, *Mexico: Biography*, 221–222.
23. Lovell, *Conquest*, 34.
24. Gimbutas, *Living Goddesses, passim*.
25. Calvert, *Guatemala*, 22–23.
26. Nancy Black, "Anthropology and the Study of Quiché Maya Women in the Western Highlands of Guatemala," in *Lucha: the Struggles of Latin American Women*, ed. Connie Weil (Minneapolis, MN: The Prisma Institute, 1988), 75–111. This citation 90, 96.
27. Black also alludes to the systematic violence. She notes: "The Organization of American States has identified the Republic of Guatemala as one of the worst violators of human rights in the Western Hemisphere. Over 100,000 Guatemalans have been killed by security forces since 1954" (Black, "Anthropology," in Weil, *Lucha*, 100).
28. Matthews, "Torture," in *Women and War*, 190.
29. *Ibid.*

30. Tracy Bachrach Ehlers, *Silent Looms: Women and Production in a Guatemalan Town* (Boulder, CO: Westview Press, 1990), 6.
31. *Ibid.*
32. Lovell, *Conquest*, 58–59.
33. *Ibid.*, 60.
34. Ehlers, *Looms*, 41–42.
35. *Ibid.*, 160.
36. Lovell, *Conquest*, 126.
37. Grant D. Jones, *The Conquest of the Last Maya Kingdom* (Stanford, CA: Stanford University Press, 1998), xxi–xxiii.
38. One of the best brief summarizations available of the situation in Guatemala was done by Peter Canby in the *New York Review of Books* in response to the publication of David Stoll's book attacking Rigoberta Menchú. Canby aptly condenses the information on the four-pronged umbrella group that signed a treaty with the government after international urging. (Peter Canby, "The Truth About Rigoberta Menchú," in *NYRB*, Vol. LXVI, No. 6, April 8, 1999, 28–33.)
39. Ehlers, *Looms*, 58–60.
40. See Rosalina Tuyuc, "Human Rights and Women's Rights," in Kuppers, *Compañeras*, 111–116. Tuyuc is a coworker of Menchú's, and is cited in her most recent book, *Crossing Borders*, trans. Ann Wright (London: Verso, 1998), 8–9.
41. Canby cites a Ladina as noting that "little by little the Maya are beginning to become integrated" (Canby, "Truth," in *NYRB*, 28).
42. Ehlers, *Looms*, 58.
43. Black, in "Anthropology," in Weil, *Lucha*, 91.
44. *Ibid.*, 93.
45. *Ibid.*, 92.
46. *Ibid.*, 80.
47. Sexton, *Ignacio*, 110.
48. *Ibid.*, 112.
49. *Ibid.*, 112–113.
50. Menchú, *Borders*, 9.
51. Margaret Randall, *Our Voices/Our Lives* (Monroe, ME: Common Courage Press, 1995), 36.
52. Adrianne Aron, Shawn Corne, Anthea Fursland, and Barbara Zelwer, "The Gender-Specific Terror of El Salvador and Guatemala: Post-Traumatic Stress Disorder in Central American Refugee Women," in *Women's Studies International Forum* 14 (1991): 37–47.
53. Aron et al. note that GAM organizes public demonstrations "to demand the return of the disappeared," *ibid.*, 41.
54. Randall, *Our Lives*, 41–42; Menchú, *Borders*, 3–4.
55. *Ibid.*, 42.
56. Margaret Hooks, *Guatemalan Women Speak* (London: Catholic Institute for International Relations, 1991).
57. As one of Hooks's informants movingly said, "This struggle has given us women friendship and support.... There's none of this 'I prefer her, or her.' We are very close" (Hooks, *Guatemalan Women*, 32).

58. *Ibid.*, 30–31.
59. *Ibid.*, 117.
60. This informant reports that she has gone from her former life, which consisted largely (partially because of the number of her children) of cooking, cleaning, and indoor work, to looking after animals, taking them to pasture, and a great deal of time spent outdoors. But now she can sell what she grows and raises in the market (Hooks, *Guatemalan Women*, 41–42).
61. Matthews, "Torture," 189.
62. One complete interview with such a *ladina* woman is under the title "Faith in the Far Right," in Hooks, *Guatemalan Women*, 114–118.
63. Margaret Ramirez, "The Sacred Book of the Maya Re-creates a Tradition," in the *Los Angeles Times*, Metro Section, B2–B3, Saturday, September 25, 1999.
64. Gimbutas, *Living Goddesses, passim.*
65. Lovell succinctly adumbrates this controversy by noting, "In the words of the Dominican chronicler Francisco Ximénez, the parish priest of Santo Tomás Chichicastenango who in the early eighteenth century was shown or first found the Popol Vuh: 'they [the Indians] changed their way of writing their histories into our way of writing'" (Lovell, *Conquest*, 47).
66. Sandra Harding, "Conclusion: Epistemological Questions," in *Feminism and Methodology*, ed. Sandra Harding (Bloomington: Indiana University Press, 1988), 181–190. This citation 185.
67. Jones, *Last Maya Kingdom*, 12.
68. Caroline Whitbeck, "A Different Reality: Feminist Ontology," in *Women, Knowledge, and Reality: Explorations in Feminist Philosophy*, ed. Ann Garry and Marilyn Pearsall (Winchester, MA: Unwin Hyman, 1989), 51–76. This citation 51.
69. A detailed account of Violeta's funeral-related *tienda* is given in Ehlers, *Looms*, 58–60.
70. Ramirez, in *Times*, B2.
71. Miller, *Mexico: A History*, 14.
72. G. S. Kirk and J. E. Raven, *The Presocratic Philosophers: A Critical History with a Selection of Texts* (London: Cambridge University Press, 1971).
73. *Ibid.*, 98.
74. Again, the work of Evelyn Fox Keller is central here, particularly the essay "Love and Sex in Plato's Epistemology," in Keller, *Reflections*, 1985.
75. See fn. 38.
76. Hooks, *Guatemalan Women*, 116.
77. Whitbeck, "Different Reality," 68.

Chapter 8: Chicana/os

1. The original work is by Gloria Anzaldúa, *Borderlands/La Frontera* (Trumansburg, NY: Crossing Press, 1989).
2. The explosive growth of literature on this topic is nothing short of phenomenal. One new anthology, *Living Chicana Theory*, ed. Carla Trujillo (Berkeley, CA: Third Woman Press, 1998), lists more than a dozen such works in its "Books Available" section.
3. The effect on the Chicana/o movement of presence in American universities

is examined by Teresa Córdova in an essay in *Living Chicana Theory* titled "Power and Knowledge: Colonialism in the Academy" (Trujillo, *Living Chicana*, 17–45).

4. Many of the missions predate 1776, with the "newer" missions being no more recent than the first decade of the nineteenth century.

5. José Antonio Burciaga, *Drink Cultura: Chicanismo* (Santa Barbara, CA: Joshua Odell Editions, 1993), 6–7.

6. The cover of Burciaga's book shows a stylized Coca-Cola bottle along with the title *Drink Cultura*.

7. At an earlier point I alluded to the recent (1999) exhibit of such work in downtown Los Angeles. Many of the photographs in the exhibit showed the common usage of the calendars as decorative items in Chicano homes.

8. Aida Hurtado, "The Politics of Sexuality in the Gender Subordination of Chicanos," in Trujillo, *Living Chicana*, 383–428. Hurtado notes that she is borrowing heavily from Yolanda Broyles, *El Teatro Campesino: Theater in the Chicano Movement* (Austin: University of Texas Press, 1994).

9. Hurtado, "Politics," in Trujillo, *Living Chicana*, 385.

10. *Ibid.*

11. *Ibid.*, 387.

12. *Ibid.*, 386.

13. Julian Samora and Patricia Vandel Simon, *A History of the Mexican-American People* (Notre Dame, IN: University of Notre Dame Press, 1993). See especially ch. 21, 223–234.

14. Samora notes, for example, that "French Oblate priests resisted their new assignment to Brownsville, characterizing the Mexicans as 'greasers' and 'uncivilized' " (231).

15. *Ibid.*, ch. 21.

16. Personal testimony from many Mexicano/Chicano families indicates that the use of railroad boxcars as homes was common throughout the Southwest during the 1930s and '40s.

17. John O. West, *Mexican-American Folklore* (Little Rock, AR: August House, 1988), 75.

18. The catalog of the exhibit "La Patria Portátil" indicates that the chromo calendars were so important that the hanging of the calendar often literally established the place in question as a "home."

19. See *Ruben Salazar: Border Correspondent*, ed. and with an introduction by Mario T. Garcia (Berkeley: University of California Press, 1998). Many of the collected pieces from Salazar's years in California in Section II of this work are articles taken from the *Los Angeles Times* about the extremely impoverished living conditions of migrating Chicano and Mexican-American immigrant workers.

20. West, *Mexican-American Folklore*, 143.

21. *Ibid.*, 144.

22. Samora, *History of Mexican-American People*, 229.

23. Lara Medina, "*Los Espiritus Siguen Hablando*: Chicana Spiritualities," in Trujillo, *Living Chicano*, 189–213.

24. *Ibid.*, 189.

25. Catalog of "La Patria Portátil," 98.

26. See, especially, 97–98 of the catalog.

27. Carey McWilliams, *North from Mexico* (New York: Greenwood Press, 1968). The first edition of this work was published in 1948.

28. McWilliams's very straightforward recounting of this series of events, including its overtones of Red-baiting, is ch. 12, 227–243, of his work.

29. *La Raza: The Forgotten Americans,* ed. Julian Samora (Notre Dame, IN: University of Notre Dame Press, 1966). The chapter in question was written by the Rev. William E. Scholes and constitutes 63–94 of the text.

31. Paul M. Sheldon's piece "Community Participation and the Emerging Middle Class" comprises ch. 6 of Samora's *La Raza,* and is 125–157 in the text.

32. Sheldon, "Community," in Samora, *La Raza,* 142.

33. *Ibid.,* 145.

34. See fn. 28.

35. McWilliams, *North from Mexico,* 243.

36. Scholes, "The Migrant Worker," in Samora, *La Raza,* 87.

37. Vicki L. Ruiz, *From out of the Shadows: Mexican Women in Twentieth-Century America* (Oxford: Oxford University Press, 1988), 79.

38. *Ibid.,* 74.

39. *Ibid.,* 137.

40. *Ibid.*

41. Carl Gutiérrez-Jones, *Rethinking the Borderlands* (Berkeley: University of California Press, 1995), 118–119.

42. *Ibid.*

43. Ruiz, *Shadows,* 106–107.

44. The recent chromo exhibit at the Latino Museum of History, Art, and Culture in Los Angeles is a case in point. The cash registers and sales desks were being worked by local young Chicanas who obviously, although apparently still in high school or the early years of college, had been influenced by and were completely comfortable with the various twists on the images involved.

45. Ruiz, *Shadows,* 103.

46. *Ibid.,* 53.

47. *Ibid.,* 121.

48. Mary S. Pardo, *Mexican American Women Activists: Identity and Resistance in Two Los Angeles Communities* (Philadelphia, PA: Temple Univesity Press, 1998).

49. *Ibid.,* 1.

50. As is customary, the term "Latino" is used to designate those who are of some other (non-Mexican) Latin American ancestry or identification.

51. United Neighborhood Organizations (UNO) is a Catholic group in Los Angeles that also has ties to Alinsky-style radicalism (Pardo, *Activists,* 34).

52. *Ibid.,* 37.

53. Pardo, *Activists,* 66.

54. *Ibid.,* 68.

55. Ruiz, *Shadows,* 144–145.

56. *Ibid.,* 145.

57. *Ibid.*

58. *Ibid.,* 146.

59. Vrinda Dalmiya and Linda Alcoff, "Are 'Old Wives' Tales' Justified?" in *Feminist Epistemologies,* ed. Linda Alcoff and Elizabeth Potter (New York: Routledge, 1993), 217–244. As Dalmiya and Alcoff write, "[N]evertheless, it remains the case that they [folk beliefs] are considered to be *mere tales* or unscientific hearsay and fail to get accorded the honorific status of *knowledge"* (217).

60. Bat-Ami Bar On, "Marginality and Epistemic Privilege," in Alcoff and Potter, *Epistemologies,* 83–100.

61. *Ibid.,* 88–89.

62. At the very end of her essay, Bar On says: "Although the claim to epistemic privilege as a tool may seem to be a claim of the oppressed, due to some of its history, it nevertheless reveals itself also as a master's tool" (97).

63. It is interesting to note that a version of the Virgin trope, called by its authors the "Maria paradox," or "marianismo," has become the crux of a self-help book authored by Latinas and specifically aimed at Latinas (although not, specifically, at Chicanas). See Rosa Maria Gil and Carmen Inoa Vasquez, *The Maria Paradox* (New York: Berkley Publishing Group, 1996).

64. See contents in Trujillo, *Living Chicana.*

65. Gutiérrez-Jones, *Rethinking the Borderlands,* 19.

66. Much of this is not included in the catalog, although at least one such reproduction is found on 102–103.

67. Gutiérrez-Jones, *Rethinking the Borderlands,* 22.

68. This film, by the Macarthur-winning Anders, has been criticized in some quarters but nevertheless was made with the help of some of the East Los Angeles community.

69. Lynn Hankinson Nelson, "Epistemological Communities," in Alcoff and Potter, *Epistemologies,* 121–59. This citation 150.

70. Writing in Samora, *La Raza,* John R. Martinez notes: "[Mexican-American civil rights organizations] were successful in winning various city council posts for Mexican Americans where members of this group had never even been admitted to city swimming pools" ("Leadership and Politics," *La Raza,* 47–62. This citation 55). The state is Arizona, although Martinez does not specify cities.

Chapter 9: The African Diaspora in the United States

1. W. E. B. Du Bois, *Black Reconstruction* (New York: Simon and Schuster, 1995).

2. Two novels that rely on extended discussions of slavery and the slave cultures are Gloria Naylor's *Mama Day* (New York: Vintage Books, 1993), and Gayl Jones's *Corregidora* (Boston: Beacon, 1986). *Mama Day,* in particular, ties together contemporary black folklore of the South and its African roots.

3. Robert Farris Thompson, *Flash of the Spirit* (New York: Vintage Books, 1984), 16.

4. The debate ignited by Paulin Hountondji notwithstanding, many theorists, such as Thompson, feel that the notion that the West African cultures possess "philosophies" is incontrovertible.

5. Kwasi Wiredu, "African Philosophical Tradition: A Case Study of the Akan," in *Philosophical Forum* 24 (1992–93): 35–62. This citation 50.

6. For a superb account of these matters insofar as they affect the development of African-derived New World cultures, see Sterling Stuckey, *Slave Culture* (New York: Oxford University Press, 1987). On 6 he notes, with respect to the ubiquitous notion of "spirit," that an appropriate punishment in West African cultures for those who had committed heinous crimes was "an endless journey of spiritual unrest, a punishment markedly African."

7. Oyeronke Oyewumi, *The Invention of Women* (Minneapolis: University of Minnesota Press, 1997).

8. Thompson, *Flash*, 103–116.

9. Paula Giddings, *When and Where I Enter* (New York: Morrow, 1984), 62–63.

10. Thompson, *Flash*, 104. Thompson goes on to remark that "Kongo civilization and art were not obliterated in the New World."

11. *Ibid.*, 106–107.

12. *Ibid.*, 105.

13. Giddings, *When and Where*, 60.

14. With respect to commodification of slave women, Jones has a character in Corregidora note, "That's why they burned all the papers, so there wouldn't be no evidence to hold up against them" (Jones, *Corregidora*, 14).

15. Giddings says it most explicitly when she notes: "Following the Civil War, men attempted to vindicate their manhood largely through asserting their authority over women" (61).

16. Gimbutas, *Goddess*, is an excellent source of these beliefs on an international scale.

17. John Blassingame, *Slave Testimony* (Baton Rouge: Louisiana State University Press, 1977), 601ff.

18. Wiredu, "African Philosophical," 41.

19. Giddings, *When and Where*, 60.

20. Oyewumi, *Invention of Women*, passim.

21. Thompson, *Flash*, 18.

22. Thompson describes Nana Bukuu as a "superlative warrior, utterly fearless, who razed the mythic city of Teju-ade" (Thompson, *Flash*, 68).

23. Thompson, *Flash*, 18.

24. Angela Y. Davis, *Women, Race, and Class* (New York: Vintage Books, 1983).

25. Davis, *Women, Race*, 11. (The interior quotation is from Frederick Law Olmsted, *A Journey in the Back Country* [New York: 1860, 14–15].)

26. Patricia Hill Collins, *Black Feminist Thought* (New York: Routledge, 1991), 73.

27. Giddings, *When and Where*, 101. See also Collins, *Black Feminist Thought*, 60–63.

28. Giddings, *When and Where*, 277. (Emphasis in original.)

29. Joy James, "Black Feminisms: Liberation Limbos and Existence in Gray," in *Existence in Black*, ed. Lewis R. Gordon (New York: Routledge, 1997), 215–224. This citation 217.

30. In a passage near the one we have cited earlier, Angela Davis writes: "Women were not too 'feminine' to work in coal mines, in iron foundries or to be lumberjacks and ditch diggers" (Davis, *Women, Race*, 10).

31. The philosopher Naomi Zack has observed that "the scientific and popular attitudes regarding interracial sex ranged over a *tectonic* of interlocking

beliefs." (Naomi Zack, *Race and Mixed Race* [Philadelphia: Temple University Press, 1993], 116. Emphasis hers.)

32. Zack, *Mixed Race*, 117–118.
33. Charlotte Forten Grimke, *Journals* (New York: Oxford University Press, 1991).
34. For a detailed examination of the differences between white and black women's roles, see Davis, *Women, Race*, 3–29.
35. Grimke, *Journals*, 60.
36. *Ibid.*, 63.
37. Ida Wells, quoted in Giddings, *When and Where*, 29.
38. Giddings, *When and Where*, 85–93.
39. *Ibid.*, 81.
40. Davis, *Women, Race*, 149–171.
41. Ida B. Wells-Barnett, *Selected Works of Ida B. Wells-Barnett* (New York: Oxford University Press, 1991), 77.
42. Gwendolyn Cartledge, Veronica Adedapo, and Carolyn Talbert Johnson, "Teacher and Parent Assessments of the Social Competence of Inner-City Children: Issues of Gender Within Race," in *Journal of Negro Education* 67 (1988): 122.
43. Nancy K. Bereano, introduction to Audre Lorde, *Sister Outsider* (Freedom, CA: Crossing Press, 1984), 7.
44. At the time of the publication of the book (1995), national publications such as the *New York Times* devoted extensive commentary to its "surprising" popularity.
45. Cartledge et al., "Teacher and Parent," 123.
46. C. L. R. James, *The C.L.R. James Reader*, ed. Anna Grimshaw (Malden, MA: Blackwell Publishers, 1992), 411.
47. bell hooks, "Conversation with bell hooks," in *The Cornel West Reader* (New York: Basic Books, 1999), 541–542.
48. Sudhir Allahadi Venkatesh, "Gender and Outlaw Capitalism: A Historical Account of the Black Sisters United 'Girl Gang'," in *Signs* 23 (1998), 683–709. This citation 683.
49. *Ibid.*, 684.
50. "Women to Watch," in *Ms.* 9, no. 5 (1999).
51. Particularly effective writing on this topic is found in Davis's *Women, Race*: it is ch. 2, "The Anti-Slavery Movement and the Birth of Women's Rights," 30–45.
52. Giddings, *When and Where*, 82.
53. Albert J. Raboteau, *Slave Religion* (New York: Oxford University Press, 1978), 228.
54. Davis, *Women, Race*, 11.
55. Nancy Hartsock, invited manuscript delivered at the conference of the American Philosophical Association, Seattle, WA, March 1996.
56. Naomi Scheman, "Who Wants to Know? The Epistemological Value of Values," in *(En)Gendering Knowledge*, ed. Joan E. Hartman and Ellen Messer-Davidow (Knoxville: University of Tennessee Press, 1991), 179–200.
57. *Ibid.*, 190.

58. *Ibid.*, 197.
59. Davis, *Women, Race,* 5.
60. Henry Louis Gates Jr., introduction to Harriet Wilson, *Our Nig* (New York: Vintage Books, 1983), p. xxxi.
61. *Ibid.,* reproduced frontispiece of facsimile edition of text.
62. Cornel West, in *Jews & Blacks,* Michael Lerner and Cornel West (New York: Plume, 1996), 47.
63. Raboteau, *Slave Religion,* 235.
64. Gayl Jones, *Corregidora* (Boston: Beacon Press, 1996). Louise Meriwether, *Daddy Was a Number Runner* (New York: Feminist Press of the CUNY, 1986).
65. Cornel West, *Prophesy Deliverance!* (Philadelphia, PA: Westminster Press, 1982).
66. Raboteau, *Slave Religion, passim.*
67. See fn. 64.
68. *Ibid.,* 77.
69. *Ibid.*
70. *Ibid.,* 208.

Chapter 10: Retrievals/Outcomes

1. A recent excellent compendium of some of the new work on women's rights globally is *Violence against Women,* ed. Stanley G. French, Wanda Teays, and Laura M. Purdy (Ithaca, NY: Cornell University Press, 1998).
2. Micaela di Leonardo, "Contingencies of Value in Feminist Anthropology," in *(En)Gendering,* ed. Hartman and Messer-Davidow, 140–158. This citation 144.
3. *Ibid.,* 147.
4. As indicated earlier, Amnesty International has a separate subgroup category for "Women's Rights." ("Membership Information" packet, Amnesty International.)
5. See, for example, Elizabeth Spelman, *Inessential Woman* (Boston: Beacon Press, 1989).
6. Nancy Chodorow, "Family Structure and Feminine Personality," in *Woman, Culture, and Society,* ed. Michelle Zimbalist Rosaldo and Louise Lamphere (Stanford, CA: Stanford University Press, 1974), 43–66. This citation 58.
7. Edward Said, *Orientalism* (New York: Vintage Books, 1979), 203–204.
8. *Ibid.,* 328.
9. Although the anthology is now somewhat dated, many of the essays in *Woman, Culture, and Society,* ed. Rosaldo and Lamphere, were early efforts in this very direction.
10. See, for example, the comments of the linguist Robin Lakoff on the distinction between written and spoken language in *Talking Power,* 48ff.
11. Indeed, in many of these traditions the "mystical" aspect of the tradition is that which attempts to go beyond text and get to the inner core of the doctrine (see Said, *Orientalism,* 268–270).

12. Cynthia Enloe, *Ethnic Conflict and Political Development* (Boston: Little, Brown, 1973), 16.
13. *Ibid.*
14. Jonathan Barnes, *Early Greek Philosophy* (New York: Penguin Books, 1987), 16.
15. Thompson, *Flash, passim.* For example, Thompson, who goes about his tasks with care, writes, "Much Yoruba art is informed by *itutu.*" (Thompson, *Flash,* 12.)
16. In their examination of the Huichol society, Schaefer and Furst note, "Shamans are generally male, but the vocation is open to both genders, and there are also some women shaman-singers" (Schaefer and Furst, *Peyote,* 11). One wonders if this has always been the case, or is a recent development.
17. Enloe, *Conflict,* 17.
18. Bette S. Denich, "Sex and Power in the Balkans," in Rosaldo and Lamphere, *Woman, Culture,* 243–262. This citation 254.
19. Gloria Anzaldúa, "To(o) Queer the Writer—Loca, escritora y Chicana," in *Living Chicana,* 263–276. This citation 267.
20. Hilton Als, *The Women* (New York: Farrar, Straus & Giroux), 1999.
21. See the essays in the excellent anthology edited by Renate Bridenthal, *Becoming Visible* (New York: Macmillan, 1997).
22. See fn. 4.
23. Arnold R. Eiser, "Violence and Transcultural Values," in *Violence,* ed. French, Teays, and Purdy, 161–167. This citation 166.
24. Theodore Roszak, *The Gendered Atom* (Berkeley, CA: Conari Press, 1999), 20–21.
25. Roksana Nazneen, "Violence in Bangladesh," in *Violence,* 77–91. It is noteworthy that Nazneen writes: "Established notions that husbands and fathers have authority over women and children are found in the Judeo-Christian traditions and among other world religions such as Islam, Buddhism, Confucianism and Hinduism" (90).
26. See Linda Lopez McAlister, *Hypatia's Daughters* (Bloomington: Indiana University Press, 1996), for a compendium of work on women philosophers and other thinkers whose writings have only recently achieved full recognition. A recent issue of *Hypatia* 14 (1999) is devoted, for example, to "The Philosophy of Simone de Beauvoir" (ed. Margaret A. Simons) as awareness increases that some women thinkers were much more independent and full-blooded theoreticians than had previously been believed.

Index